The CAR Book

2014

DISCARD

by
Jack Gillis

with
Amy Curran
Peter Kitchen
Brennan Gillis
Eli Greenspan

Foreword by
Clarence Ditlow
Center for Auto Safety

A Center for Auto Safety Publication

ACKNOWLEDGMENTS

Once again, for edition 34, Peter Kitchen ably managed and organized this extraordinary effort. There are literally thousands of data points that go into compiling *The Car Book* and Peter managed them all. For 23 years, Amy Curran has been expertly preparing all the graphics necessary to clearly present the data, managing the logistics necessary to get a printed book in the hands of the public, and keeping the project on track. This year Eli Greenspan jumped in at the last minute for some serious research and data analysis. Also crunching the numbers and organizing data was Brennan Gillis, who has followed his three siblings as *Car Book* co-authors. Thanks to Amy, Peter, Eli, and Brennan, consumers have the information they need to make a smart, sensible new car choice.

As has been the case for 33 years, this year's edition would not have been possible without the essential contributions from Clarence Ditlow and the staff of the Center for Auto Safety, including Michael Brooks and Jon Robinson.

As always, the most important factor in being able to bring this information to the American car buyer for 34 years is the encouragement, support, and love from my brilliant and beautiful wife, Marilyn Mohrman-Gillis. For her and four terrific children–Katie, John, Brian and Brennan–I am eternally grateful.

—*J.G.*

As Always,

for Marilyn &
Katie, John, Brian, and Brennan

CLARENCE DITLOW

Is the safety glass half-full or half-empty. On the one hand driver distraction threatens to become a worse vehicle safety problem than drunk driving while advanced vehicle electronics such as Crash Immiment Braking, Lane Departure Controls, Blind Spot Detection and Backup Cameras can significantly reduce vehicle crashes, deaths and injuries. Which technology controls will determine whether vehicle deaths continue to go down or go back up.

The effect of this explosive growth is readily observable by simply going to a new-car showroom, where virtually every new vehicle—whether it be a car, truck, or SUV—is equipped with hardware and software that enables occupants to connect their iPhones and iPods to the vehicle's audio-control system.

Vehicle electronics are estimated to reach 40% of the production cost for vehicles by 2015. This growth is generated by advances in vehicle safety technology, fuel economy, and consumer demand for communications, navigation aids, and entertainment. The average vehicle on the road already possesses more computing power than the Apollo guidance system that first took man to the moon.

Consumer demand for vehicle integrated communication and entertainment has exploded in the past ten years and shows no signs of slowing, providing vehicle manufacturers with a slew of new selling points, while ushering an entirely new series of distractions into the cockpit for drivers. Multiple companies now provide aftermarket entertainment systems that can be integrated with a vehicle's existing telematics.

Consumer demand for safety electronics is not nearly as great as it is for telematics in large part because industry profits more from telematics than safety. Once a consumer buys a new vehicle with a child safe backup camera, there is no annual subscription to generate more revenues for auto makers and communications companies.

The media recently focused on the fatal crashes involving Jacqueline Mars, the Mars candy heiress, whose 2004 Porsche Cayennne crossed the centerline and hit another vehicle; and Paul Walker, star of Fast and Furious, who was killed in a 2005 Porsche Carrera that veered off the road in a high speed crash. Yet the media did not ask why Mars and Walker, who could have afforded any vehicle, did not pick a newer Porsche or another performance sports car with electronic stability control or lane departure control that might have prevented their tragic, fatal crashes.

Most celebrities in America have agents to help them negotiate their contracts, run their finances and advance their careers. Yet how many have an agent to select a safe car which will insure their career or life will not be cut short by a tragic car crash such as were Grace Kelley, Steve Allen, and James Dean.

The 2014 *Car Book* is the average consumer's answer to finding a new car that has the advanced safety features like lane departure, radar braking and adaptive cruise control, active pre-crash safety and automatic crash notification that will be options only on some models. Use *The Car Book* and its new comprehensive crash safety rating to buy a car that's going to protect you in a crash. Use *The Car Book's* Safety Chapter to find out all the optional safety features and which models have them when you buy a new vehicle. Your buying decision not only may save your life but also sends a message to automakers not to withhold vital safety features.

By using *The Car Book* to buy a safer car, you have taken an important first step toward your personal vehicle safety and helping CAS reach our Vision of Zero Traffic Deaths by 2050. The next step is to support the Center for Auto Safety which works every day on your behalf to ensure that all Americans ride in safe and reliable vehicles. Go to our Website www.auto-safety.org and find out how you can support the Center and have CAS be your safety and lemon insurance.

—CMD

JACK GILLIS

As dashboards look more like iPads and smart phones, the electronic sophistication of the 2014 models is nothing short of amazing. While these innovations may lead to more distracted driving, they're becoming standard even in the lower priced models. These new electronics definitely offer some benefits, but they do require a bit more 'fingers-on' testing while you're in the showroom.

While some of us may long for the simple knobs of the past, new electronics are also responsible for some great new safety features such as automatic braking, better performing airbags, self-parking and a child safety 'must have,' rear cameras. While tragically, the U.S. Department of Transportation has failed to implement the requirement that all vehicles be equipped with child saving rear camera technology, it's becoming more and more available as an option.

Another piece of good news, there are some car dealers across the nation that are following the lead of Washington DC area dealer Jack Fitzgerald and offering 'no-haggle' pricing. This is removing one of the most distasteful aspects of car buying, trying to match wits with a seasoned negotiator and get the best price for your new car.

So with lots of new electronics, improved safety features, and some improvement in the buying experience, *The Car Book* is ready to guide you to a great new 2014 vehicle!

Working closely with the Center for Auto Safety's Clarence Ditlow and his staff, as we have for 34 years, my goal is to sift through the myriad of government and industry data on cars and present the information so you can actually use it. Thirty-three years ago, *The Car Book* was the first publication to give consumers the ability to make an informed choice on one of the most important and complex items that they will ever purchase. Today, thanks in large part to the efforts of the Center for Auto Safety in Washington, DC, our mission has never wavered.

In setting out to change the way people buy their cars, *The Car Book* was able to change the way car companies made them.

In keeping with *The Car Book*'s philosophy of making it as easy as possible to identify the truly good performers in the government crash tests, we provide a unique *Car Book* Combined Crash Test Rating which combines all of the complex government testing into a simple, straightforward number. In addition, we take the step of comparing the vehicles on a relative basis to each other so you can easily tell the best performers from the worst.

Unfortunately, not all of the 2014 vehicles have been crash tested. While we (and you!) look forward to the day when all of your choices have been tested, our safety ratings will provide a good indication of which cars can be expected to best protect you.

Before *The Car Book*, consumers had no idea which warranties were better, what you could expect to pay for typical repairs, which cars cost the most and least to insure, or how they stacked up in government complaints. Now you have this information all in one place.

Our exclusive car-by-car ratings at the end of the book provide an overview of all the criteria you need to make a good choice. Here, you'll be able to quickly assess key features and see how the car you're interested in stacks up against its competition so you can make sure your selection is the best car for you.

Even though the choices get better each year and safety is improved, it's still a challenge to separate the lemons from the peaches. There are notable differences in how cars protect you in a crash, how much they cost to maintain, the benefits of their warranties, and how far they'll go on a gallon of expensive gasoline. Nevertheless, if you use the information in *The Car Book*, there is no reason why your next car should not last *at least* 150,000 miles.

Our "Showroom Strategies" section will give you the keys to getting the best deal. In spite of all the new car technology and the Internet, the fundamentals of buying a good, safe, reliable car remain the same: do your homework; shop around; and remember that car dealers need you more than you need them!

The information in *The Car Book* is based on data collected and developed by our staff, the U.S. Department of Transportation, and the Center for Auto Safety. With all of this information in hand, you'll find some great choices for 2014.

—*Jack*

USING THE BUYING GUIDE

The "Buying Guide" provides a quick comparison of the 2014 cars in terms of their safety, warranty, fuel economy, complaint rating, and price range—arranged by size class. To fully understand the information in the charts, it is important to read the related section in the book.

Overall Rating: This shows how well this car stacks up on a scale of 1 to 10 when compared to all others on the market. Because safety is the most important component of our ratings, cars with no crash test results at printing are not given an overall rating.

Combined Crash Test Rating: This indicates how well the car performed in the government's frontal and side crash test programs compared to this year's vehicles tested to date. See page 18 for details.

Warranty Rating: This is an overall comparative assessment of the car's warranty.

Fuel Economy: This is the EPA city/highway mpg for, what is expected to be, the most popular version of each model.

Complaint Rating: This is based on complaints received by the U.S. Department of Transportation. If not rated, the vehicle is too new to have a complaint rating.

Price Range: This will give you a general idea of the "sticker," or suggested retail price.

Indicates a *Car Book* Best Bet. See page 13.

ABOUT THE CAR BOOK BEST BETS

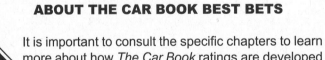

It is important to consult the specific chapters to learn more about how *The Car Book* ratings are developed and to look on the car pages, beginning on page 81, for more details on these vehicles. In order to be considered as a "Best Bet" the vehicle must have a crash test rating as safety is a critical factor in gaining that recognition. <u>Vehicles with "Poor" (3 or 4) or "Very Poor" (1 or 2) in Combined Crash Tests, or Front or Side Crash Test Ratings, or an additional injury warning were not considered a "Best Bet."</u> Because most people are considering vehicles in the same size category, the "Best Bets" are by size—indicating how these vehicles compared against others in the same size class.

Vehicle	Page #	Overall Rating	Combined Crash Test Rating	Warranty Rating	Fuel Economy	Complaint Rating	Price Range
Subcompact							
Chevrolet Sonic	116	10	Very Good	Good	26/35	Average	$15-$21,000
Chevrolet Spark	117	6	Poor	Good	30/39		$13-$27,000
Fiat 500	132	4	Very Poor	Poor	27/34	Poor	$16-$26,000
Ford Fiesta	140			Poor	29/39	Very Poor	$14-$21,000
Hyundai Accent	155	6	Poor	Very Good	27/37	Average	$14-$17,000
Hyundai Veloster	163			Very Good	26/35	Very Poor	$17-$23,000
Kia Rio	180	6	Very Poor	Very Good	27/37	Good	$14-$17,000
Kia Soul	182	7	Very Good	Very Good	24/30		$14-$20,000
Mazda Mazda2	198			Very Poor	28/34	Very Good	$14-$17,000
Mazda MX-5 Miata	202			Very Poor	21/28	Very Good	$23-$30,000
Mini Cooper	210			Good	28/36		$19-$35,000
Mini Countryman	211			Good	25/30	Average	$22-$34,000
Mitsubishi Mirage	213			Very Good	34/42		$12-$15,000
Nissan Versa	228	2	Very Poor	Very Poor	26/35	Good	$12-$16,000
Scion xB	234			Very Poor	22/28	Good	$16-$20,000
Scion xD	235			Very Poor	27/33	Very Good	$15-$16,000
Smart ForTwo	236			Very Poor	34/38	Poor	$12-$17,000
Toyota Prius C	251	5	Very Poor	Very Poor	53/46	Very Good	$19-$23,000
Toyota Yaris	259	6	Poor	Very Poor	30/36	Very Good	$14-$17,000
Volkswagen Beetle	260	3	Poor	Average	22/29	Poor	$19-$31,000
Compact							
Acura ILX	81	6	Average	Average	24/35	Good	$26-$31,000
Acura TSX	86			Average	22/31	Very Good	$30-$39,000
Audi A4	87	6	Average	Good	20/29	Good	$33-$45,000
BMW 3 Series	92	10	Good	Very Good	23/35	Poor	$32-$49,000
BMW 4 Series	93			Very Good	23/35		$40-$48,000
Buick Verano	104	10	Very Good	Average	21/32	Good	$23-$29,000
Cadillac ATS	105	9	Very Good	Very Good	22/33	Very Poor	$33-$48,000
Chevrolet Cruze	111	9	Good	Good	22/35	Average	$18-$23,000
Chevrolet Volt	121	9	Poor	Good	35/40	Very Poor	$34-$34,000
Dodge Dart	128	9	Good	Good	25/36		$15-$22,000
Fiat 500L	133			Poor	25/33		$19-$24,000

Vehicle	Page #	Overall Rating	Combined Crash Test Rating	Warranty Rating	Fuel Economy	Complaint Rating	Price Range
Compact (cont.)							
Ford C-MAX	134	4	Poor	Poor	43/43	Very Poor	$25-$32,000
Ford Focus	142	5	Average	Poor	27/37	Very Poor	$16-$39,000
Honda Civic	148	6	Average	Very Poor	31/41	Good	$18-$27,000
Honda Insight	151			Very Poor	41/44	Good	$18-$23,000
Hyundai Elantra	157	6	Average	Very Good	28/38	Average	$17-$21,000
Kia Forte	178	4	Very Poor	Very Good	24/36		$17-$19,000
Lexus CT	187			Average	43/40	Poor	$32-$33,000
Lexus IS	191	7	Average	Average	21/30		$35-$41,000
Mazda Mazda3	199			Very Poor	30/41		$17-$25,000
Mercedes-Benz C-Class	203	4	Average	Very Poor	20/29	Good	$35-$62,000
Mercedes-Benz CLA-Class	204			Very Poor	26/38		$29-$31,000
Mitsubishi Lancer	212	5	Poor	Very Good	26/34	Average	$18-$40,000
Nissan Leaf	220	4	Very Poor	Very Poor	126/101	Very Poor	$28-$34,000
Nissan Sentra	226	3	Poor	Very Poor	30/39	Poor	$17-$19,000
Scion FR-S	232			Very Poor	22/30	Very Poor	$24-$28,000
Scion tC	233	6	Average	Very Poor	23/31	Very Good	$19-$22,000
Subaru BRZ	237			Very Poor	22/30	Very Poor	$25-$28,000
Subaru Impreza	239			Very Poor	27/36	Good	$18-$37,000
Subaru XV Crosstrek	243			Very Poor	25/33		$21-$26,000
Toyota Corolla	247	7	Good	Very Poor	27/36		$16-$20,000
Toyota Prius	250	5	Poor	Very Poor	51/48	Very Poor	$23-$39,000
Toyota Prius V	252	7	Good	Very Poor	44/40		$26-$30,000
Volkswagen Golf	262			Average	23/30	Poor	$19-$27,000
Volkswagen Jetta	263	6	Very Good	Average	23/29	Average	$15-$31,000
Intermediate							
Acura TL	85	3	Very Poor	Average	20/29	Good	$36-$45,000
Audi A5	88			Good	20/29	Very Good	$39-$56,000
Audi A6	89			Good	18/27	Good	$43-$60,000
BMW 5 Series	94	9	Very Good	Very Good	20/30	Very Poor	$49-$63,000
BMW 6 Series	95			Very Good	22/32	Very Good	$74-$93,000
Buick Regal	103	7	Average	Average	19/31	Good	$29-$39,000
Cadillac CTS	106			Very Good	18/27		$45-$64,000
Chevrolet Camaro	109	8	Very Good	Good	19/30	Average	$23-$54,000
Chevrolet Corvette	110			Good	16/28		$51-$58,000
Chevrolet Malibu	114			Good	25/36	Average	$22-$29,000
Chrysler 200	122	2	Very Poor	Good	20/31	Poor	$21-$33,000
Dodge Avenger	125	3	Very Poor	Good	21/30	Poor	$19-$25,000
Ford Fusion	143	5	Average	Poor	22/34	Poor	$21-$40,000

Vehicle	Page #	Overall Rating	Combined Crash Test Rating	Warranty Rating	Fuel Economy	Complaint Rating	Price Range
Intermediate (cont.)							
Ford Mustang	144	2	Poor	Poor	19/29	Poor	$22-$54,000
Honda Accord	147	7	Good	Very Poor	27/36	Very Poor	$22-$39,000
Hyundai Azera	156			Very Good	19/29	Very Poor	$32-$32,000
Hyundai Genesis	158			Very Good	18/27	Very Poor	$25-$46,000
Hyundai Sonata	161	7	Good	Very Good	24/35	Very Poor	$21-$30,000
Infiniti Q50	164	6	Average	Good	19/27		$36-$48,000
Infiniti Q60	165			Good	19/27	Very Good	$40-54,000
Infiniti Q70	166	4	Average	Good	18/26	Very Poor	$48-55,000
Kia Optima	179	5	Average	Very Good	24/34	Poor	$21-$36,000
Lexus ES	188	6	Average	Average	21/31	Very Good	$36-$38,000
Lexus GS	189			Average	19/29	Poor	$47-$59,000
Lincoln MKZ	195	4	Average	Poor	19/28	Good	$35-$37,000
Mazda Mazda6	201			Very Poor	28/40		$20-$29,000
Mercedes-Benz E-Class	205	4	Poor	Very Poor	21/31	Very Good	$51-$102,000
Nissan Altima	216	6	Good	Very Poor	27/38	Very Poor	$22-$30,000
Nissan Maxima	221	2	Very Poor	Very Poor	19/26	Good	$31-$34,000
Subaru Legacy	240	5	Good	Very Poor	24/32	Average	$21-$28,000
Subaru Outback	241	6	Very Good	Very Poor	24/30	Poor	$24-$32,000
Toyota Camry	246	6	Average	Very Poor	25/35	Good	$22-$30,000
Volkswagen CC	261			Average	22/31	Poor	$31-$41,000
Volkswagen Passat	264	6	Good	Average	22/31	Average	$20-$33,000
Volvo S60	267	10	Very Good	Good	20/29	Average	$32-$42,000
Large							
Acura RLX	84			Average	20/31		$48-$60,000
BMW 7 Series	96			Very Good	17/25	Average	$74-$141,000
Buick LaCrosse	102	8	Very Good	Average	18/28	Average	$33-$39,000
Cadillac XTS	108	10	Very Good	Very Good	18/28	Very Good	$44-$69,000
Chevrolet Impala	113	8	Average	Good	19/29		$26-$35,000
Chrysler 300	123	4	Average	Good	15/25	Average	$30-$48,000
Dodge Challenger	126	5	Good	Good	18/27	Poor	$26-$44,000
Dodge Charger	127	6	Average	Good	18/27	Poor	$26-$42,000
Ford Taurus	145	4	Good	Poor	19/29	Average	$26-$39,000
Jaguar XF	171			Poor	17/28	Very Poor	$46-$99,000
Kia Cadenza	177			Very Good	19/28		$35-$35,000
Lexus LS	192			Average	16/24	Very Good	$72-$120,000
Lincoln MKS	194	3	Good	Poor	19/28	Poor	$40-$47,000
Mercedes-Benz S-Class	209			Very Poor	17/26		$93-$212,000
Toyota Avalon	245	7	Good	Very Poor	21/31	Very Poor	$31-$41,000

Vehicle	Page #	Overall Rating	Combined Crash Test Rating	Warranty Rating	Fuel Economy	Complaint Rating	Price Range
Large (cont.)							
Volvo S80	268			Good	20/29	Average	$39-$43,000
Minivan							
Chrysler Town and Country	124			Good	17/25	Poor	$30-$41,000
Dodge Grand Caravan	130	6	Poor	Good	17/25	Poor	$19-$29,000
Honda Odyssey	152			Very Poor	19/28	Average	$28-$44,000
Mazda Mazda5	200			Very Poor	22/28	Poor	$19-$24,000
Nissan Quest	224			Very Poor	19/25	Very Poor	$25-$42,000
Toyota Sienna	255	2	Average	Very Poor	18/25	Poor	$26-$40,000
Small SUV							
Acura RDX	83	7	Very Good	Average	19/27	Average	$34-$39,000
Audi Q5	90			Good	20/28	Very Good	$37-$54,000
BMW X1	97			Very Good	22/33	Good	$30-$38,000
Buick Encore	101	9	Good	Average	23/30	Very Good	$24-$30,000
Cadillac SRX	107	8	Good	Very Good	17/24	Average	$37-$50,000
Ford Escape	136	5	Average	Poor	22/31	Very Poor	$22-$30,000
Honda Crosstour	149			Very Poor	22/31		$27-$37,000
Honda CR-V	150	6	Average	Very Poor	22/30	Good	$22-$30,000
Hyundai Tucson	162	4	Poor	Very Good	21/28	Average	$20-$27,000
Infiniti QX50	167			Good	17/24	Very Good	$34-$38,500
Jeep Cherokee	172			Good	21/28		$22-$29,000
Jeep Compass	173	5	Very Poor	Good	21/28	Poor	$18-$27,000
Jeep Patriot	175	3	Very Poor	Good	21/27	Poor	$15-$25,000
Jeep Wrangler	176			Good	17/21	Very Poor	$22-$34,000
Kia Sportage	183	6	Average	Very Good	21/28	Good	$19-$28,000
Mazda CX-5	196	6	Very Good	Very Poor	26/35	Very Poor	$22-$28,000
Mercedes-Benz GLK-Class	207			Very Poor	19/24	Very Good	$37-$39,000
Mitsubishi Outlander Sport	215	6	Poor	Very Good	24/31	Very Good	$20-$23,000
Nissan Juke	219	4	Very Poor	Very Poor	25/30	Very Good	$18-$25,000
Subaru Forester	238	4	Good	Very Poor	24/32		$22-$32,000
Toyota RAV4	253	5	Poor	Very Poor	22/29	Average	$23-$28,000
Volkswagen Tiguan	265	2	Very Poor	Average	21/26	Very Poor	$25-$38,000
Mid-Size SUV							
Acura MDX	82	8	Good	Average	18/27		$42-$56,000
Audi Q7	91			Good	16/22	Very Good	$47-$64,000
BMW X3	98			Very Good	19/26	Average	$39-$44,000
BMW X5	99			Very Good	18/27		$52-$68,000
Chevrolet Equinox	112	3	Poor	Good	22/32	Poor	$24-$33,000
Dodge Journey	131			Good	17/25	Very Poor	$19-$30,000

Vehicle	Page #	Overall Rating	Combined Crash Test Rating	Warranty Rating	Fuel Economy	Complaint Rating	Price Range
Mid-Size SUV (cont.)							
Ford Edge	135	1	Very Poor	Poor	19/27	Average	$27-$39,000
Ford Explorer	138	4	Good	Poor	17/23	Very Poor	$29-$40,000
Honda Pilot	153	2	Very Poor	Very Poor	17/24	Average	$29-$41,000
Hyundai Santa Fe	159			Very Good	18/25	Very Poor	$24-$34,000
Hyundai Santa Fe Sport	160	8	Good	Very Good	20/27		$24-$29,000
Infiniti QX60	168	3	Average	Good	19/25	Very Poor	$41-$42,000
Jeep Grand Cherokee	174	7	Average	Good	17/25	Average	$30-$63,000
Kia Sorento	181	5	Good	Very Good	18/25	Very Poor	$24-$40,000
Land Rver Rnge Rver Evoque	185			Poor	21/30	Poor	$41-$51,000
Lexus RX	193	5	Very Poor	Average	18/25	Very Good	$39-$47,000
Mazda CX-9	197	1	Very Poor	Very Poor	16/22	Average	$29-$36,000
Mercedes-Benz M-Class	208	5	Very Good	Very Poor	17/22	Very Good	$47-$97,000
Mitsubishi Outlander	214			Very Good	24/29		$22-$27,000
Nissan Murano	222	3	Very Poor	Very Poor	18/23	Very Good	$28-$39,000
Nissan Rogue	225			Very Poor	25/32		$22-$29,000
Nissan Pathfinder	223	3	Average	Very Poor	19/25	Very Poor	$28-$41,000
Nissan Xterra	229			Very Poor	15/20	Poor	$23-$31,000
Porsche Cayenne	230			Average	17/23	Very Good	$48-$108,000
Subaru Tribeca	242			Very Poor	16/21	Good	$34-$38,000
Toyota FJ Cruiser	248			Very Poor	17/20	Very Poor	$27-$28,000
Toyota Venza	258	4	Average	Very Poor	20/26	Good	$27-$39,000
Volkswagen Touareg	266			Average	17/23	Very Poor	$43-$64,000
Volvo XC60	269	10	Very Good	Good	18/25	Good	$34-$45,000
Volvo XC90	270			Good	16/25	Poor	$39-$44,000
Large SUV							
Buick Enclave	100	7	Very Good	Average	17/24	Average	$38-$48,000
Chevrolet Suburban	118	6	Very Good	Good	15/21	Good	$45-$59,000
Chevrolet Tahoe	119	7	Very Good	Good	15/21	Good	$41-$57,000
Chevrolet Traverse	120	9	Very Good	Good	17/24	Good	$30-$43,000
Dodge Durango	129	7	Average	Good	17/24	Poor	$29-$43,000
Ford Expedition	137	2	Poor	Poor	13/18	Average	$38-$54,000
Ford Flex	141			Poor	18/25	Poor	$31-$44,000
Infiniti QX70	169			Good	16/22	Very Good	$44-$61,000
Infiniti QX80	170			Good	14/20	Very Good	$61-$64,000
Land Rover Range Rover	184			Poor	13/19	Good	$83-$135,000
Land Rover Range Rover Sport	186			Poor	14/19		$63-$93,000
Lexus GX	190			Average	15/20	Good	$49-$60,000
Mercedes-Benz GL-Class	206			Very Poor	14/19	Good	$63-$118,000

Vehicle	Page #	Overall Rating	Combined Crash Test Rating	Warranty Rating	Fuel Economy	Complaint Rating	Price Range
Large SUV (cont.)							
Nissan Armada	217			Very Poor	13/19	Poor	$36-$52,000
Toyota 4Runner	244			Very Poor	17/21	Very Good	$32-43,400
Toyota Highlander	249			Very Poor	18/24		$28-$46,000
Toyota Sequoia	254			Very Poor	13/17	Good	$43-$63,000
Compact Pickup							
Nissan Frontier	218			Very Poor	15/21	Average	$20-$33,000
Toyota Tacoma	256	1	Very Poor	Very Poor	16/21	Good	$17-$27,000
Standard Pickup							
Chevrolet Silverado	115	8	Very Good	Good	16/22		$27-$43,000
Ford F-150	139	1	Poor	Poor	15/21	Average	$23-$52,000
GMC Sierra	146	9	Very Good	Average	16/22	Very Good	$24-$43,000
Honda Ridgeline	154			Very Poor	15/21	Very Good	$29-$37,000
Nissan Titan	227			Very Poor	12/17	Poor	$29-$43,000
Ram 1500	231	5	Average	Good	13/19	Average	$24-$49,000
Toyota Tundra	257			Very Poor	13/17	Very Good	$25-$47,000

T he following is our list of the highest rated vehicles in each size category. The ratings are based on expected performance in nine important categories–Combined Crash Rating, Safety Features, Rollover, Preventive Maintenance, Repair Costs, Warranty, Fuel Economy, Complaints, and Insurance Costs–with the heaviest emphasis placed on safety. (See box on previous page.)

CHEVROLET SONIC — SUBCOMPACT

Combo Crash Tests	9	Warranty	8
Safety Features	8	Fuel Economy	8
Rollover	6	Complaints	5
PM	9	Insurance	1
Repair Costs	10	**OVERALL RATING**	**10**

Page 116

KIA SOUL — SUBCOMPACT

Combo Crash Tests	9	Warranty	9
Safety Features	4	Fuel Economy	7
Rollover	5	Complaints	–
PM	4	Insurance	1
Repair Costs	8	**OVERALL RATING**	**7**

Page 182

BMW 3 SERIES — COMPACT

Combo Crash Tests	7	Warranty	9
Safety Features	8	Fuel Economy	7
Rollover	9	Complaints	3
PM	10	Insurance	8
Repair Costs	3	**OVERALL RATING**	**10**

Page 92

BUICK VERANO — COMPACT

Combo Crash Tests	10	Warranty	6
Safety Features	9	Fuel Economy	6
Rollover	7	Complaints	8
PM	7	Insurance	5
Repair Costs	7	**OVERALL RATING**	**10**

Page 104

CADILLAC ATS — COMPACT

Combo Crash Tests	9	Warranty	9
Safety Features	7	Fuel Economy	6
Rollover	9	Complaints	1
PM	10	Insurance	5
Repair Costs	3	**OVERALL RATING**	**9**

Page 105

CHEVROLET CRUZE

COMPACT

Combo Crash Tests	8	Warranty	8
Safety Features	8	Fuel Economy	7
Rollover	8	Complaints	5
PM	5	Insurance	1
Repair Costs	9	**OVERALL RATING...**	**9**

Page 111

DODGE DART

COMPACT

Combo Crash Tests	8	Warranty	8
Safety Features	4	Fuel Economy	8
Rollover	8	Complaints	–
PM	6	Insurance	3
Repair Costs	9	**OVERALL RATING...**	**9**

Page 128

TOYOTA COROLLA

COMPACT

Combo Crash Tests	8	Warranty	2
Safety Features	2	Fuel Economy	9
Rollover	7	Complaints	–
PM	10	Insurance	1
Repair Costs	8	**OVERALL RATING...**	**7**

Page 247

TOYOTA PRIUS V

COMPACT

Combo Crash Tests	7	Warranty	2
Safety Features	4	Fuel Economy	10
Rollover	5	Complaints	–
PM	10	Insurance	5
Repair Costs	5	**OVERALL RATING...**	**7**

Page 252

BMW 5 SERIES

INTERMEDIATE

Combo Crash Tests	9	Warranty	9
Safety Features	8	Fuel Economy	5
Rollover	10	Complaints	2
PM	10	Insurance	5
Repair Costs	2	**OVERALL RATING...**	**9**

Page 94

BUICK REGAL
INTERMEDIATE

Combo Crash Tests 6
Safety Features 6
Rollover 8
PM 5
Repair Costs. 6
Warranty. 6
Fuel Economy. 5
Complaints 8
Insurance 3
OVERALL RATING. . . 7

Page 103

CHEVROLET CAMARO
INTERMEDIATE

Combo Crash Tests 10
Safety Features 4
Rollover 10
PM 5
Repair Costs. 7
Warranty. 8
Fuel Economy. 4
Complaints 6
Insurance 1
OVERALL RATING. . . 8

Page 109

HONDA ACCORD
INTERMEDIATE

Combo Crash Tests 7
Safety Features 4
Rollover 9
PM 4
Repair Costs. 9
Warranty. 1
Fuel Economy. 9
Complaints 2
Insurance 8
OVERALL RATING. . . 7

Page 161

HYUNDAI SONATA
INTERMEDIATE

Combo Crash Tests 7
Safety Features 3
Rollover 9
PM 5
Repair Costs. 9
Warranty. 10
Fuel Economy. 8
Complaints 2
Insurance 1
OVERALL RATING. . . 7

Page 161

VOLVO S60
INTERMEDIATE

Combo Crash Tests 9
Safety Features 8
Rollover 9
PM 9
Repair Costs. 7
Warranty. 8
Fuel Economy. 5
Complaints 6
Insurance 5
OVERALL RATING. . 10

Page 267

BUICK LACROSSE — LARGE

Page 102

Combo Crash Tests 9	Warranty 6
Safety Features 8	Fuel Economy 4
Rollover 7	Complaints 5
PM 5	Insurance 5
Repair Costs 3	**OVERALL RATING. . . 8**

CADILLAC XTS — LARGE

Page 108

Combo Crash Tests 10	Warranty 9
Safety Features 8	Fuel Economy 4
Rollover 7	Complaints 9
PM 10	Insurance 8
Repair Costs 3	**OVERALL RATING. . 10**

TOYOTA AVALON — LARGE

Page 245

Combo Crash Tests 7	Warranty 2
Safety Features 7	Fuel Economy 5
Rollover 8	Complaints 2
PM 10	Insurance 8
Repair Costs 3	**OVERALL RATING. . . 7**

ACURA RDX — SMALL SUV

Page 83

Combo Crash Tests 9	Warranty 5
Safety Features 2	Fuel Economy 4
Rollover 4	Complaints 6
PM 6	Insurance 10
Repair Costs 6	**OVERALL RATING. . . 7**

BUICK ENCORE — SMALL SUV

Page 101

Combo Crash Tests 8	Warranty 6
Safety Features 9	Fuel Economy 6
Rollover 2	Complaints 10
PM . . . .–	Insurance 8
Repair Costs . . . .–	**OVERALL RATING. . . 9**

CADILLAC SRX

SMALL SUV

Page 107

Combo Crash Tests	7	Warranty	9
Safety Features	8	Fuel Economy	2
Rollover	3	Complaints	6
PM	10	Insurance	8
Repair Costs	5	**OVERALL RATING. . .**	**8**

ACURA MDX

MID-SIZE SUV

Page 82

Combo Crash Tests	8	Warranty	5
Safety Features	9	Fuel Economy	3
Rollover	4	Complaints	–
PM	6	Insurance	10
Repair Costs	5	**OVERALL RATING. . .**	**8**

HYUNDAI SANTE FE SPORT

MID-SIZE SUV

Page 160

Combo Crash Tests	7	Warranty	10
Safety Features	4	Fuel Economy	4
Rollover	5	Complaints	–
PM	4	Insurance	8
Repair Costs	8	**OVERALL RATING. . .**	**8**

VOLVO XC60

MID-SIZE SUV

Page 269

Combo Crash Tests	9	Warranty	8
Safety Features	8	Fuel Economy	3
Rollover	3	Complaints	7
PM	9	Insurance	10
Repair Costs	6	**OVERALL RATING. .**	**10**

BUICK ENCLAVE

LARGE SUV

Page 100

Combo Crash Tests	9	Warranty	6
Safety Features	6	Fuel Economy	2
Rollover	4	Complaints	6
PM	6	Insurance	10
Repair Costs	2	**OVERALL RATING. . .**	**7**

CHEVROLET TAHOE

LARGE SUV

Combo Crash Tests	9	Warranty	8
Safety Features	5	Fuel Economy	1
Rollover	1	Complaints	8
PM	5	Insurance	10
Repair Costs	5	**OVERALL RATING...**	**7**

Page 119

CHEVROLET TRAVERSE

LARGE SUV

Combo Crash Tests	9	Warranty	8
Safety Features	6	Fuel Economy	2
Rollover	4	Complaints	8
PM	6	Insurance	10
Repair Costs	4	**OVERALL RATING...**	**9**

Page 120

CHEVROLET SILVERADO

STANDARD PICKUP

Combo Crash Tests	10	Warranty	8
Safety Features	5	Fuel Economy	2
Rollover	3	Complaints	–
PM	5	Insurance	10
Repair Costs	6	**OVERALL RATING...**	**8**

Page 115

GMC SIERRA

STANDARD PICKUP

Combo Crash Tests	10	Warranty	6
Safety Features	5	Fuel Economy	2
Rollover	3	Complaints	10
PM	5	Insurance	10
Repair Costs	5	**OVERALL RATING...**	**9**

Page 146

CRASH TESTS

Safety is likely the most important factor that most of us consider when choosing a new car. In the past, evaluating safety was difficult. Now, thanks to the information in *The Car Book*, it's much easier to pick a safe vehicle. The bottom line: For the greatest protection, you'll want the maximum number of safety features (See Safety Checklist, pages 78-79) and good crash test results (the following tables).

A key factor in occupant protection is how well the car protects you in a crash. This depends on its ability to absorb the force of the impact rather than transfer it to the occupant. In 2011, the government began a new crash test program with more sophisticated dummies, additional test measurements, and a small female dummy.

In the frontal test, the vehicle impacts a solid barrier at 35 mph. In the side test, a moving barrier is crashed into the side of the vehicle at 38.5 mph. A second side test, new in 2011, simulates hitting a tree or roadside pole by smashing a vertical pole into the driver side door at 20 mph. The only occupant in this side pole test is a small female dummy in the driver seat.

The new dummies measure impact on a different scale from previous tests, and the new test measures neck injuries and chest deflexion which were not included in the previous tests. In addition, these new test results cannot be compared with older results.

Not all 2014 vehicles have undergone the new tests. The good news is that by carrying forward previous tests from cars that haven't changed, we have results for 109 2014 models. The bad news is that there are 81 models for which we don't have crash test results.

How the Cars are Rated: The combined crash test ratings are based on the <u>relative</u> performance of the vehicles tested to date using the new test. This is a big difference from the government's "star" program. Rather than large groups of undifferentiated vehicles, *The Car Book* rates them from best to worst. This means that those manufacturers really working on safety, each year, will rise to the top.

The first column provides *The Car Book's* Combined Crash Test Rating. The cars are rated from 10 Best to 1 Worst. The front is weighted 60%, the side 36%, and the pole test 4% with results compared among all new 2014 crash tests to date.

Next are the individual front and side tests. Again, relative to all other 2014 vehicles tested, we indicate if the vehicle was Very Good, Good, Average, Poor or Very Poor. For side tests, the cars are rated separately from the trucks. Because of their construction the dynamics of a side test are different in cars and trucks.

The next five columns indicate the likelihood of the occupant sustaining a life-threatening injury. The percent likelihood is listed for the driver and front passenger in the front test, the driver and rear passenger in the side test, and the driver in the side pole test. Lower percentages mean a lower likelihood of being seriously injured. This information is taken directly from the government's analysis of the crash test results.

USING CRASH TEST DATA

One of the most important results of our being the first to publish crash test data, and later develop our relative comparative ratings, is that it has put enormous pressure on the manufacturers to improve. Whereas years ago, competition was based on moon-roofs and color-keyed interiors, today the manufacturers are feverously competing on safety features. While the most important factors in evaluating the safety of today's vehicles are crash test performance and advanced safety features, size and weight do play a role. It is important to compare vehicles in the size classes that follow. For example, in a frontal collision between a subcompact and SUV rated 'Very Good," you'll be better off in the SUV. Nevertheless, selecting the best performers in whatever size class you are buying, is fundamental to protecting yourself. And remember, these tests are conducted with fully belted dummies, if you are not wearing your safety belt, then test results do not really apply.

CRASH TESTS

Crash Test Performance (10=Best, 1=Worst)	Combined Car Book Crash Test Rating	Test Type	Car Book Crash Test Rating - Index (Lower numbers are better)	Likelihood of Life Threatening Injury				
				Front Fixed Barrier		Side Moving Barrier		Side Pole
				Front Driver	Front Pass.	Side Driver	Side Pass.	Pole Driver
Subcompact								
Chevrolet Sonic	9	Front	Very Good-166	8.7%	8.7%			
		Side	Good-113			7.0%	4.6%	7.1%
Chevrolet Spark	3	Front	Poor-228	13.6%	10.7%			
		Side	Poor-147			9.2%	6.8%	5.6%
Fiat 500	2	Front	Very Poor-256	11.4%	16.0%			
		Side	Poor-148			5.3%	8.0%	15.8%
Hyundai Accent[1]	3	Front	Average-209	9.2%	12.8%			
		Side	Very Poor-234			8.6%	17.0%	4.3%
Kia Rio[2]	3	Front	Poor-230	10.8%	13.7%			
		Side	Very Poor-177			13.5%	7.0%	3.5%
Kia Soul	9	Front	Good-180	7.6%	11.2%			
		Side	Very Good-81			4.7%	4.0%	2.6%
Nissan Versa	1	Front	Very Poor-295	12.2%	19.7%			
		Side	Very Poor-256			16.4%	13.5%	4.7%
Toyota Prius C[3]	2	Front	Poor-215	12.2%	10.5%			
		Side	Very Poor-239			14.8%	12.0%	8.1%
Toyota Yaris	4	Front	Poor-217	9.9%	13.1%			
		Side	Poor-159			7.3%	8.7%	10.1%
Volkswagen Beetle	5	Front	Poor-216	9.6%	13.2%			
		Side	Average-125			7.3%	6.0%	5.3%
Compact								
Acura ILX	5	Front	Average-193	9.3%	11.0%			
		Side	Poor-139			8.0%	5.2%	13.9%
Audi A4	6	Front	Good-178	9.5%	9.1%			
		Side	Poor-152			12.8%	4.8%	3.8%
BMW 3 Series	7	Front	Average-194	11.6%	8.9%			
		Side	Good-108			7.9%	4.3%	2.3%
Buick Verano	10	Front	Very Good-155	7.5%	8.7%			
		Side	Very Good-75			6.1%	1.9%	4.3%

[1,2,3] Additional Injury Potential: Due to the intrusion of the left rear door during the side impact test, the interior door panel struck the torso of the rear passenger dummy, causing a high lower spine acceleration. High lower spine accelerations, in excess of 82 g's, indicate a higher likelihood of thoracic injury.

CRASH TESTS

Crash Test Performance (10=Best, 1=Worst)	Combined Car Book Crash Test Rating	Test Type	Car Book Crash Test Rating - Index (Lower numbers are better)	Likelihood of Life Threatening Injury				
				Front Fixed Barrier		Side Moving Barrier		Side Pole
				Front Driver	Front Pass.	Side Driver	Side Pass.	Pole Driver
Compact (cont.)								
Cadillac ATS	9	Front	Very Good-162	8.2%	8.7%			
		Side	Good-111			4.7%	6.6%	5.2%
Chevrolet Cruze	8	Front	Good-176	8.2%	10.2%			
		Side	Good-114			7.1%	4.8%	6.7%
Chevrolet Volt	5	Front	Average-205	8.8%	12.9%			
		Side	Poor-141			7.9%	7.9%	2.0%
Dodge Dart	8	Front	Good-188	9.2%	10.6%			
		Side	Very Good-78			4.1%	4.1%	2.4%
Ford C-MAX	5	Front	Poor-224	10.9%	12.9%			
		Side	Average-119			6.2%	5.7%	8.1%
Ford Focus	6	Front	Average-192	8.1%	12.1%			
		Side	Average-116			10.3%	3.0%	3.4%
Honda Civic	5	Front	Average-209	11.1%	11.0%			
		Side	Average-118			5.6%	6.5%	5.7%
Hyundai Elantra	5	Front	Average-199	9.7%	11.3%			
		Side	Poor-146			12%	3.9%	7.8%
Kia Forte	1	Front	Very Poor-296	8.8%	22.8%			
		Side	Very Poor-171			14.4%	5.0%	6.1%
Lexus IS	6	Front	Poor-226	10.8%	13.2%			
		Side	Very Good-85			5.4%	3.2%	5.9%
Mercedes-Benz C-Class	5	Front	Poor-239	10.6%	14.9%			
		Side	Good-102			2.6%	6.6%	8.7%
Mitsubishi Lancer	4	Front	Poor-214	9.4%	13.3%			
		Side	Very Poor-199			4.0%	16.4%	5.6%
Nissan Leaf	2	Front	Poor-229	9.2%	15.1%			
		Side	Very Poor-215			5.6%	17.0%	5.0%
Nissan Sentra	3	Front	Very Poor-263	10.4%	17.7%			
		Side	Average-118			6.6%	6.6%	1.7%
Scion tC	6	Front	Average-201	9.1%	12.1%			
		Side	Good-89			2.7%	6.1%	4.0%

CRASH TESTS

Crash Test Performance (10=Best, 1=Worst)	Combined Car Book Crash Test Rating	Test Type	Car Book Crash Test Rating - Index (Lower numbers are better)	Likelihood of Life Threatening Injury				
				Front Fixed Barrier		Side Moving Barrier		Side Pole
				Front Driver	Front Pass.	Side Driver	Side Pass.	Pole Driver
Compact (cont.)								
Toyota Corolla	8	Front	Good-187	8.1%	11.6%			
		Side	Very Good-87			3.1%	5.1%	6.6%
Toyota Prius	4	Front	Poor-227	11.4%	12.8%			
		Side	Good-114			5.1%	5.7%	10.0%
Toyota Prius V	7	Front	Average-211	10.3%	12.0%			
		Side	Very Good-70			4.3%	1.5%	10.5%
Volkswagen Jetta	8	Front	Average-200	10.0%	11.1%			
		Side	Very Good-78			4.2%	3.9%	3.8%
Intermediate								
Acura TL	1	Front	Very Poor-258	12.0%	15.7%			
		Side	Very Poor-233			16.0%	11.3%	3.4%
BMW 5 Series	9	Front	Very Good-165	8.5%	8.8%			
		Side	Good-113			7.0%	4.6%	7.0%
Buick Regal	6	Front	Average-199	9.9%	11.1%			
		Side	Average-116			4.1%	7.8%	4.3%
Chevrolet Camaro	10	Front	Very Good-171	9.6%	8.3%			
		Side	Very Good-66			5.7%	1.5%	3.2%
Chrysler 200	1	Front	Very Poor-245	10.5%	15.7%			
		Side	Very Poor-280			8.8%	10.3%	63.7%
Dodge Avenger	2	Front	Poor-240	10.0%	15.5%			
		Side	Very Poor-246			16.6%	8.8%	20.1%
Ford Fusion	5	Front	Good-176	7.5%	10.9%			
		Side	Very Poor-195			18.4%	5.0%	2.8%
Ford Mustang	3	Front	Average-210	12.5%	9.8%			
		Side	Very Poor-261			7.8%	18.7%	14.7%
Honda Accord	7	Front	Average-201	11.0%	10.2%			
		Side	Very Good-60			3.4%	2.9%	2.6%
Hyundai Sonata	7	Front	Average-197	8.9%	11.9%			
		Side	Good-103			7.6%	2.6%	9.2%

CRASH TESTS

Crash Test Performance (10=Best, 1=Worst)	Combined Car Book Crash Test Rating	Test Type	Car Book Crash Test Rating - Index (Lower numbers are better)	Likelihood of Life Threatening Injury				
				Front Fixed Barrier		Side Moving Barrier		Side Pole
				Front Driver	Front Pass.	Side Driver	Side Pass.	Pole Driver
Intermediate (cont.)								
Infiniti Q50	5	Front	Very Poor-246	10.7%	15.6%			
		Side	Very Good-68			6.5%	1.2%	2.6%
Infiniti Q70	5	Front	Poor-227	9.8%	14.3%			
		Side	Good-107			8.4%	3.9%	1.8%
Kia Optima	5	Front	Good-174	8.6%	9.6%			
		Side	Very Poor-167			16.8%	2.0%	7.9%
Lexus ES	6	Front	Good-187	9.7%	9.9%			
		Side	Average-134			11.7%	2.9%	6.9%
Lincoln MKZ	5	Front	Good-176	7.5%	10.9%			
		Side	Very Poor-195			18.4%	5.0%	2.8%
Mercedes-Benz E-Class	4	Front	Very Poor-265	13.7%	14.8%			
		Side	Average-116			2.2%	6.7%	17.8%
Nissan Altima	8	Front	Very Good-165	7.2%	10.0%			
		Side	Average-134			12.2%	3.3%	3.6%
Nissan Maxima	1	Front	Very Poor-297	11.1%	20.9%			
		Side	Very Poor-168			15.6%	4.0%	4.3%
Subaru Legacy	7	Front	Very Good-163	8.6%	8.5%			
		Side	Poor-159			5.2%	9.3%	15.8%
Subaru Outback	10	Front	Very Good-163	8.6%	8.5%			
		Side	Very Good-78			2.7%	3.1%	13.7%
Toyota Camry	5	Front	Average-202	9.0%	12.2%			
		Side	Average-122			7.4%	5.3%	6.8%
Volkswagen Passat	8	Front	Very Good-155	7.7%	8.5%			
		Side	Average-137			13.1%	2.7%	3.9%
Volvo S60	9	Front	Very Good-158	8.3%	8.2%			
		Side	Average-119			9.8%	3.7%	3.2%
Large								
Buick LaCrosse	9	Front	Very Good-169	7.9%	9.8%			
		Side	Good-112			5.7%	4.9%	10.5%
Cadillac XTS	10	Front	Very Good-160	7.6%	9.1%			
		Side	Good-88			4.2%	4.3%	6.7%

CRASH TESTS

Crash Test Performance (10=Best, 1=Worst)	Combined Car Book Crash Test Rating	Test Type	Car Book Crash Test Rating - Index (Lower numbers are better)	Likelihood of Life Threatening Injury				
				Front Fixed Barrier		Side Moving Barrier		Side Pole
				Front Driver	Front Pass.	Side Driver	Side Pass.	Pole Driver
Large (cont.)								
Chevrolet Impala	7	Front	Good-173	7.5%	10.6%			
		Side	Poor-142			10.1%	6.1%	2.9%
Chrysler 300	5	Front	Good-186	9.4%	10.2%			
		Side	Poor-152			16.1%	0.8%	8.4%
Dodge Challenger[4]	6	Front	Good-172	9.1%	8.9%			
		Side	Poor-154			11.9%	0.7%	26.3%
Dodge Charger	7	Front	Good-190	9.7%	10.3%			
		Side	Average-128			13.5%	0.7%	7.0%
Ford Taurus	7	Front	Very Good-164	8.4%	8.7%			
		Side	Poor-154			8.3%	8.3%	5.8%
Lincoln MKS	7	Front	Very Good-164	8.4%	8.7%			
		Side	Poor-154			8.3%	8.3%	5.8%
Toyota Avalon	7	Front	Average-193	10.4%	9.9%			
		Side	Good-91			6.2%	2.3%	10.2%
Minivan								
Dodge Grand Caravan	4	Front	Average-206	11.2%	10.6%			
		Side	Very Poor-153			7.5%	8.8%	5.5%
Toyota Sienna	5	Front	Poor-234	8.4%	16.4%			
		Side	Good-59			3.3%	2.7%	3.6%
Small SUV								
Acura RDX	9	Front	Very Good-149	7.0%	8.5%			
		Side	Average-76			3.5%	3.0%	9.6%
Buick Encore	8	Front	Very Good-165	8.3%	9.0%			
		Side	Average-84			4.9%	4.3%	2.2%
Cadillac SRX	7	Front	Good-191	8.6%	11.4%			
		Side	Good-67			2.7%	1.7%	14.8%
Ford Escape	5	Front	Poor-230	10.9%	13.5%			
		Side	Good-60			2.0%	3.5%	5.0%
Honda CR-V	6	Front	Good-189	10.3%	9.6%			
		Side	Average-85			4.1%	3.9%	7.5%

[4] During the side impact test, the driver door unlatched and opened. A door opening during a side impact crash increases the likelihood of occupant ejection.

CRASH TESTS

Crash Test Performance (10=Best, 1=Worst)	Combined Car Book Crash Test Rating	Test Type	Car Book Crash Test Rating - Index (Lower numbers are better)	Likelihood of Life Threatening Injury				
				Front Fixed Barrier		Side Moving Barrier		Side Pole
				Front Driver	Front Pass.	Side Driver	Side Pass.	Pole Driver
Small SUV (cont.)								
Hyundai Tucson	3	Front	Poor-230	11.4%	13.1%			
		Side	Poor-104			8.6%	2.3%	7.5%
Jeep Compass	1	Front	Very Poor-314	17.4%	17.0%			
		Side	Poor-106			9.3%	2.4%	4.8%
Jeep Patriot	1	Front	Very Poor-296	18.6%	13.5%			
		Side	Poor-108			6.4%	4.5%	7.3%
Kia Sportage	6	Front	Good-185	8.9%	10.5%			
		Side	Poor-101			7.7%	3.5%	3.3%
Mazda CX-5	9	Front	Very Good-155	7.6%	8.6%			
		Side	Good-64			2.3%	3.3%	7.1%
Mitsubishi Outlander Sport	3	Front	Average-203	10.0%	11.4%			
		Side	Very Poor-200			6.6%	13.7%	9.9%
Nissan Juke	1	Front	Very Poor-289	12.5%	18.7%			
		Side	Very Poor-185			11.7%	9.1%	4.8%
Subaru Forester	7	Front	Average-205	9.0%	12.7%			
		Side	Very Good-56			3.1%	2.6%	2.9%
Toyota RAV4	4	Front	Very Poor-245	11.2%	15.0%			
		Side	Good-63			2.6%	1.6%	13.7%
Mid-Size SUV								
Volkswagen Tiguan	2	Front	Very Poor-287	13.2%	17.9%			
		Side	Poor-86			3.3%	4.2%	10.0%
Acura MDX	8	Front	Very Good-168	8.3%	9.2%			
		Side	Average-68			2.5%	4.2%	3.6%
Chevrolet Equinox	3	Front	Poor-216	9.5%	13.4%			
		Side	Poor-120			11.7%	2.0%	4.5%
Ford Edge	2	Front	Very Poor-313	16.1%	18.1%			
		Side	Average-81			5.3%	2.3%	8.3%
Ford Explorer	8	Front	Very Good-183	10.4%	8.8%			
		Side	Good-63			4.2%	1.6%	7.1%
Honda Pilot	2	Front	Poor-221	9.4%	14.1%			
		Side	Very Poor-185			6.4%	12.3%	9.8%

CRASH TESTS

Crash Test Performance (10=Best, 1=Worst)	Combined Car Book Crash Test Rating	Test Type	Car Book Crash Test Rating - Index (Lower numbers are better)	Likelihood of Life Threatening Injury				
				Front Fixed Barrier		Side Moving Barrier		Side Pole
				Front Driver	Front Pass.	Side Driver	Side Pass.	Pole Driver
Mid-Size SUV (cont.)								
Hyundai Santa Fe Sport	7	Front	Good-184	9.2%	10.1%			
		Side	Average-71			3.6%	3.2%	6.3%
Infiniti QX60	6	Front	Average-196	11.2%	9.5%			
		Side	Good-64			4.9%	1.8%	4.2%
Jeep Grand Cherokee	6	Front	Good-178	9.4%	9.3%			
		Side	Poor-93			8.3%	2.3%	2.4%
Kia Sorento	8	Front	Very Good-154	8.2%	7.9%			
		Side	Average-80			4.3%	3.0%	8.9%
Lexus RX	2	Front	Poor-234	11.5%	13.4%			
		Side	Very Poor-148			3.2%	10.8%	9.9%
Mazda CX-9	1	Front	Very Poor-302	16.7%	16.2%			
		Side	Very Poor-126			6.1%	4.5%	18.3%
Mercedes-Benz M-Class	10	Front	Very Good-168	8.1%	9.5%			
		Side	Very Good-41			3.3%	1.1%	2.3%
Nissan Murano	2	Front	Very Poor-270	13.3%	15.8%			
		Side	Very Poor-165			4.4%	11.5%	10.7%
Nissan Pathfinder	6	Front	Average-196	11.2%	9.5%			
		Side	Good-48			4.9%	1.8%	4.2%
Toyota Venza	6	Front	Average-196	9.4%	11.2%			
		Side	Good-65			3.9%	1.7%	9.0%
Volvo XC60	9	Front	Very Good-165	8.2%	9.0%			
		Side	Good-60			4.0%	2.1%	4.0%
Large SUV								
Buick Enclave	9	Front	Good-181	9.6%	9.3%			
		Side	Very Good-57			2.1%	3.4%	3.8%
Chevrolet Suburban	9	Front	Good-180	9.1%	9.9%			
		Side	Very Good-32			2.1%	0.3%	6.3%
Chevrolet Tahoe	9	Front	Good-185	9.3%	10.1%			
		Side	Very Good-53			4.7%	0.3%	6.5%
Chevrolet Traverse	9	Front	Good-181	9.6%	9.3%			
		Side	Very Good-57			2.1%	3.4%	3.8%

CRASH TESTS

Crash Test Performance (10=Best, 1=Worst)	Combined Car Book Crash Test Rating	Test Type	Car Book Crash Test Rating - Index (Lower numbers are better)	Likelihood of Life Threatening Injury				
				Front Fixed Barrier		Side Moving Barrier		Side Pole
				Front Driver	Front Pass.	Side Driver	Side Pass.	Pole Driver
Large SUV (cont.)								
Dodge Durango	5	Front	Poor-226	14.1%	9.9%			
		Side	Good-63			6.4%	0.6%	2.9%
Ford Expedition	4	Front	Poor-248	15.6%	10.9%			
		Side	Average-74			2.7%	1.2%	20.7%
Compact Pickup								
Toyota Tacoma	1	Front	Very Poor-284	15.0%	15.7%			
		Side	Very Poor-134			11.4%	1.9%	12.9%
Regular Pickup								
Chevrolet Silverado Crew Cab	10	Front	Very Good-172	9.4%	8.7%			
		Side	Very Good-54			2.4%	1.6%	9.8%
Regular Cab		Front	Very Good-156	8.1%	8.1%			
		Side	No Index-			2.7%		11.7%
Ext Cab	8	Front	Very Good-156	8.1%	8.1%			
		Side	Average-80			2.7%	3.7%	11.7%
Ford F-150 Supercab	4	Front	Very Poor-276	12.4%	17.3%			
		Side	Very Good-59			2.2%	1.4%	14.0%
Regular Cab		Front	Very Poor-276	12.4%	17.3%			
		Side	No Index			2.2%		14.0%
GMC Sierra Crew Cab	10	Front	Very Good-172	9.4%	8.7%			
		Side	Very Good-54			2.4%	1.6%	9.8%
Regular Cab		Front	Very Good-156	8.1%	8.1%			
		Side	No Index			2.7%		11.7%
Ext. Cab	8	Front	Very Good-156	8.1%	8.1%			
		Side	Average-80			2.7%	3.7%	11.7%
Ram 1500 Quad Cab	6	Front	Poor-214	10.8%	11.9%			
		Side	Very Good-59			5.2%	0.3%	7.3%
Regular Cab		Front	Average-214	10.8%	11.9%			
		Side	No Index			5.2%		7.3%
Crew Cab	3	Front	Poor-228	12.6%	11.7%			
		Side	Average-85			7.2%	0.6%	0.7%

AUTOMATIC SAFETY PROTECTION

The concept of automatic safety protection is not new. Automatic fire sprinklers in public buildings, oxygen masks in airplanes, purification of drinking water, and pasteurization of milk are all commonly accepted forms of automatic safety protection. Airbags provide automatic crash protection in cars.

Automatic crash protection protects people from what is called the "second collision," when the occupant collides with the interior of the vehicle. Because the "second collision" occurs within milliseconds, providing automatic rather than manual protection dramatically improves the chances of escaping injury.

Automatic crash protection comes in two basic forms, airbags and automatic control of safety features.

Since airbags were introduced over 30 years ago, they have been so successful in saving lives that car makers now include a variety of types which deploy from 4 to 10 different points.

The automatic control of safety features was first introduced with anti-lock brakes. Today, Electronic Stability Control (ESC) and other automatic functions such as Collision Avoidance Braking and Lane Departure are improving the safety of new cars.

Electronic Stability Control (ESC) takes advantage of anti-lock brake technology and helps minimize the loss of control. Each car maker will have its own name for this feature, but they all work in a similar fashion.

For ESC, anti-lock brakes work by using speed sensors on each wheel to determine if one or more of the wheels is locking up or skidding. ESC then uses these speed sensors and a unit that determines the steering angle to monitor what's happening with the vehicle. A special control device measures the steering and rotation of the tires in order to detect when a vehicle is about to go in a direction different from the one indicated by the steering wheel–or out of control! This will typically occur during a hard turn or on slippery surfaces. The control unit will sense whether the car is over-steering (turning sharper than you intended resulting in the back wheels slipping sideways) or under-steering (continuing to move forward despite your intended turn). When either of these events occur, the control unit will automatically apply the brakes to the appropriate wheels to correct the situation and, in some cases, automatically slow down the engine.

ESC will not keep the vehicle under control in severely out of control situations nor does it work as well on curvey roads as on straight roads. Nevertheless, according to the IIHS, ESC can reduce the chance of a single vehicle crash by over 50%. Its benefit is that it will prevent more typical losses of control from escalating into a crash.

TELEMATICS

Telematic systems are subscription-based services ($100-$300 per year) that use a combination of cellular technology and global positioning systems to provide a variety of safety and convenience features. The main safety feature is automatic crash notification (ACN) which connects the vehicle's occupants to a private call center that directs emergency medical teams to the car. This system can be activated by pressing a button on the dash or rear view mirror or it is automatically activated if the airbag deploys. Once the system is activated, the call center receives the exact location of your vehicle and notifies the local emergency response team. This can potentially reduce the time it takes for an emergency team to reach your vehicle. Other safety features can include roadside assistance, remote door unlocking, stolen vehicle tracking, and driving directions.

Caution! Some manufacturers are adding cell phone capability to the ACN system which increases the risk of a crash 4-fold when talking on the ACN cell phone. This is about the same effect as drinking and driving. Don't drink and drive or phone and drive!

CHILD SAFETY

Seat Belts for Kids: How long should children use car seats? For school-age children, a car seat is twice as effective in preventing injury as an adult lap and shoulder harness—use a booster as long as possible. Most children can start using seat belts at 4'9" and when tall enough for the shoulder belt to cross the chest, not the neck. The lap section of the belt should be snug and as low on the hips as possible. If the shoulder belt does cross the face or neck, use a booster seat.

Never:

☒ Use the same belt on two children.

☒ Move a shoulder belt behind a child's back or under an arm.

☒ Buckle in a pet or any large toys with the child.

☒ Recline a seat with a belted child.

☒ Use a twisted seat belt. The belt must be straight and flat.

☒ Use pillows or cushions to boost your child.

☒ Place a belt around you with a child in your lap. In an accident or sudden stop, your child would absorb most of the crash force.

Incorrect Installation: Surveys show up to 85 percent of parents do not install their child seats properly. Incorrect installation of a child safety seat can deny the child lifesaving protection and may even contribute to further injuring the child. Read the installation instructions carefully. If you have any questions about the correct installation in your particular car, contact the National Highway Traffic Safety Administration's website at www.nhtsa.gov. They can direct you to the nearest child seat inspection station that will check to see if you have installed your child seat correctly and instruct you on the proper way to install the seat if you have any questions. There is no charge for this service.

Following are some common mistakes parents make when installing a child safety seat.

☒ Infant is in safety seat facing forward, rather than to the rear.

☒ Child safety seat in front with an airbag.

☒ Child is not secured by safety seat harness and is sitting loose in safety seat.

☒ Booster seat used without a shield or a shoulder belt.

☒ Safety belt is fastened to or around wrong part of safety seat.

☒ Tether strap is not used, missing, or at wrong angle of attachment, when required.

☒ Use of incompatible safety belts.

☒ Safety belt is not used to secure safety seat in vehicle. The safety seat is loose on vehicle seat.

☒ Harness strap adjustment slides are not securely locked, permitting straps to release in a crash.

Warning: After an accident, rescue experts suggest that the entire seat be removed from the car, rather than unbuckling the child first.

CHILD SAFETY SEAT RECALLS

Manufacturers are required to put address cards in child seat packages. Mail the registration card as soon as you open the box! This is the only way you will receive notification of a seat recall. Keep a copy of the manufacturer's address and contact the manufacturer if you move. To find out if the seat you are using has ever been recalled go to www-odi.nhtsa.dot.gov/owners/SearchChildSeats. You can also contact the Auto Safety Hotline at 800-424-9393.

ROLLOVER

The risk of rollover is a significant safety issue, especially with sport utility vehicles. Because of their relatively high center of gravity, they don't hug the road like smaller, lower automobiles and trucks. As a result, they are more likely to turn over on sharp turns or when tripped by a curb. Not only does a rollover increase the likelihood of injuries, but it also increases the risk of the occupant being thrown from the vehicle. In fact, the danger of rollover with sport utilities is so severe that manufacturers are required to place a sticker where it can be seen by the driver every time the vehicle is used. Each year, approximately 10,000 people die in rollover-related accidents.

To understand the concept behind these vehicles' propensity to roll over, consider this: place a section of 2x4 lumber on its 2-inch side. It is easily tipped over by a force pushing against the side. But if you place it on its 4-inch side, the same force will cause it to slide rather than tip over. Similarly, in a moving vehicle, the forces generated by a turn can cause a narrow, tall vehicle to roll over. This is why SUVs are more susceptible to rolling over.

In the safety checklist we include a feature called roll-sensing side airbags. Roll-sensing side airbags are a special side airbag system which keeps the side airbags inflated longer in the event of a rollover. This feature is found in many SUVs and can reduce the likelihood of injury when a vehicle flips. See the car pages (81-270) for which 2014 models have this feature.

Congress required the U.S. Department of Transportation to develop a dynamic (moving) rating system to accompany the static (stationary) rating system. To date, this complex test has resulted in a simple "tip" or "no-tip" rating. Consumers are never told the speed of the tip and certain vehicles are not tested, just listed as "no tip."

Following are rollover ratings for many 2014 vehicles. We published these ratings for years before the National Highway Traffic Safety Administration adopted this rating system.

The rollover rating is based on the Static Stability Factor (SSF) and consists of a formula that uses the track width of the vehicle (tire to tire) and height to determine which vehicles are more or less likely to roll over when compared to each other. You can't use this information to exactly predict rollovers. However, all things being equal, if two vehicles are in the same situation where a rollover could occur, the one with a high SSF is less likely to roll over than one with a lower SSF. Because this formula doesn't consider such things as driver behavior and the weight of the vehicle, among other factors, some experts do not believe it tells the whole story. We agree, and urged the government to provide an even better rollover rating system.

In the meantime, knowing how the vehicles rate using the SSF can be a key consideration in your evaluation of the vehicle.

! ROOF CRUSH !

The government standard for roof crush (the ability of the roof to keep from collapsing in a rollover) is woefully inadequate. Roofs often crush in rollover accidents and seriously injure seat-belted occupants. Rollovers and roof crush break windshields and windows creating portals for occupants to be ejected from the vehicle. See page 31 for details.

! GOVERNMENT WARNING !

To alert consumers to rollover, the following warning is required on certain vehicles:

This is a multipurpose passenger vehicle which will handle and maneuver differently from an ordinary passenger car, in driving conditions which may occur on streets and highways and off road. As with other vehicles of this type, if you make sharp turns or abrupt manuevers, the vehicle may roll over or may go out of control and crash. You should read driving guielines and instructions in the Owner's Manual, and wear your seat belt at all times.

ROOF CRUSH

Since 1970, the auto industry has fought efforts by the National Highway Traffic Safety Administration to issue a dynamic roof crush standard to protect occupants in rollover crashes. From 1971 to 2005 when NHTSA finally proposed to upgrade the 1971 standard, the number of deaths to occupants in rollover crashes climbed from 1,400 to 10,870 while annual occupant fatalities declined from 43,000 to 31,549. NHTSA stuck with the outdated, static roof crush standard issued in 1971 even though it was to have been phased out by 1977 for a dynamic standard. Yet NHTSA issued effective dynamic front and side crash test standards that have significantly reduced death and serious injury.

The 1971 standard called for roofs to withstand 1.5 times the weight of the vehicle, applied to one side of the roof, for vehicles up to 6,000 pounds. Vehicles weighing more need not meet any standard. The new standard will be phased in for 2013 to 2016 models which will double the roof strength requirement for vehicles weighing up to 6,000 pounds. Both the driver and passenger sides of the roof will have to withstand a force equal to three times the weight of the vehicle. Vehicles over 6,000 pounds have until 2017 to meet a two sided standard at 1.5 times the weight of the vehicle. While a significant improvement, the new standard falls short of requiring a dynamic crash test that better replicates what happens in real world crashes.

Today, some vehicles have strong roofs but all too many have weak roofs. In a rollover crash, the first side of a vehicle that hits the ground generally does not crush but the second, or trailing side, that hits the ground often does crush.

This failure will either break the windows and allow the occupants to eject or crush the occupants that stay in the vehicle. To identify vehicles which have strong roofs, the Center for Auto Safety (CAS) had the Center for Injury Research (CfIR) conduct dynamic rollover roof crush tests using the Jordan Rollover System (JRS). Funded by the Santos Family Foundation, the CAS testing played a major role in NHTSA going to two-sided testing in its new standard.

The table below shows the results of the CAS testing. The cumulative crush is how much the roof will crush inward after two full rolls. More than 5 inches of roof crush is unacceptable because an occupant's head is likely to be hit. The Strength to Weight Ratio (SWR) is how much weight the roof on one side will support before crushing inward 5 inches when tested in a static fashion as the government does.

The dynamic rollover test shows that good roof design can result in a vehicle with a lower static SWR outperforming a vehicle with a higher static SWR in limiting roof intrusion in a roll-over, demonstrating the problem with the static government test. CAS has developed a comparative rating for the roof strength that ranges from Very Good to Very Poor.

Dynamic tests, such as the JRS, show how vehicle geometry effects safety. Vehicles with the very square roofs such as the Ridgeline are more vulnerable to roof crush. A vehicle with a more rounded roof, such as the XC90, will roll more like a barrel with less force on the corners of the roof.

The design of the roof in unison with the body of the vehicle is critical to its ability to protect occupants. If any of the critical roof structural elements buckles the roof will collapse and injure belted occupants who are seated underneath.

Good design will also keep windows in place to prevent occupants from being ejected in rollovers. Only a dynamic test can demonstrate whether seat belts, pre-tensioners and side curtains function together to protect occupants from ejection and injury in rollovers.

Center for Auto Safety Roof Crush Test Results

Vehicle*	Cumulative Crush (in.)	Dynamic SWR	Static SWR	Rating
Kia Soul 2010-12	1.6	5.2	4.3	Very Good
Volvo XC90 2005-09	1.8	5.2	4.6	Very Good
Toyota Highlander Hybrid 2008-12	2.3	4.9	4.7	Very Good
VW Tiguan 2009-11	2.4	4.9	4.4	Very Good
VW Jetta 2007-09	3.4	4.4	5.1	Good
Honda CR-V 2007-10	3.6	4.3	2.6	Good
Toyota Camry Hybrid 2007-10	4.3	4.2	3.9	Good
Toyota Prius 2010	3.8	4.2	4.2	Good
Toyota Camry 2007-09	4.3	4	4.3	Good
Nissan Versa 2009-10	4.4	4	3.7	Good
Subaru Forester 2003-08	4.6	3.9	4.3	Moderate
Hyundai Sonata 2006-09	4.6	3.9	3.2	Moderate
Chevrolet Malibu 2009-10	5	3.7	4.4	Moderate
Pontiac G6 2006-09	7	2.8	2.3	Poor
Ford F-150 Supercab 2010-12	7.2	2.7	4.7	Poor
Chrysler 300 2006-09	7.4	2.6	2.5	Poor
Jeep Gr. Cherokee 2007-10	9.1	1.8	2.2	Very Poor
Scion xB 2008-10	10.4	1.2	6.8	Very Poor
Chevy Tahoe 2007-09	10.9	1	2.1	Very Poor
Honda Ridgeline 2006-09	10.9	1	2.4	Very Poor

*Year tested is first model year listed with later models having similar roof strength and design.

This work was funded by the Santos Family Foundation on sixteen vehicles donated by the State Farm Insurance Company.

STATIC STABILITY FACTOR

Vehicle	SSF (High=Better)/ Chance of Rollover		Vehicle	SSF (High=Better)/ Chance of Rollover		Vehicle	SSF (High=Better)/ Chance of Rollover	
Acura ILX	1.42	Low	GMC Sierra	1.22	High	Mini Countryman	1.31*	Moderate
Acura MDX	1.26	High	Honda Accord	1.46	Very Low	Mitsubishi Lancer	1.36	Moderate
Acura RDX	1.26	High	Honda Civic	1.37	Low	Mitsubishi Mirage	1.26*	High
Acura RLX	1.48*	Very Low	Honda Crosstour	1.37*	Low	Mitsubishi Outlander	1.19*	High
Acura TL	1.49	Very Low	Honda CR-V	1.22	High	Mitsu. Outlander Sport	1.19	High
Acura TSX	1.46*	Very Low	Honda Insight	1.38*	Low	Nissan Altima	1.44	Low
Audi A4	1.46	Very Low	Honda Odyssey	1.29*	Moderate	Nissan Armada	1.14*	Very High
Audi A5	1.54*	Very Low	Honda Pilot	1.24	High	Nissan Frontier	1.15*	Very High
Audi A6	1.47*	Very Low	Honda Ridgeline	1.24*	High	Nissan Juke	1.27	Moderate
Audi Q5	1.27*	High	Hyundai Accent	1.35	Moderate	Nissan Leaf	1.41	Low
Audi Q7	1.24*	High	Hyundai Azera	1.46*	Very Low	Nissan Maxima	1.45	Very Low
BMW 3 Series	1.48	Very Low	Hyundai Elantra	1.41	Low	Nissan Murano	1.2	High
BMW 4 Series	1.54*	Very Low	Hyundai Genesis	1.45*	Very Low	Nissan Pathfinder	1.23*	High
BMW 5 Series	1.49	Very Low	Hyundai Santa Fe	1.26*	High	Nissan Quest	1.24*	High
BMW 6 Series	1.59*	Very Low	Hyundai Santa Fe Sport	1.27	Moderate	Nissan Rogue	1.21*	High
BMW 7 Series	1.48*	Very Low	Hyundai Sonata	1.47	Very Low	Nissan Sentra	1.37	Low
BMW X1	1.27*	Moderate	Hyundai Tucson	1.21	High	Nissan Titan	1.16*	Very High
BMW X3	1.25*	High	Hyundai Veloster	1.49*	Very Low	Nissan Versa	1.29	Moderate
BMW X5	1.21*	High	Infiniti Q50	1.47	Very Low	Nissan Xterra	1.07*	Very High
Buick Enclave	1.23	High	Infiniti Q60	1.43	Low	Porsche Cayenne	1.27*	High
Buick Encore	1.18	Very High	Infiniti Q70	1.39	Low	Ram 1500	1.15	Very High
Buick LaCrosse	1.37	Low	Infiniti QX50	1.32*	Moderate	Scion FR-S	1.59*	Very Low
Buick Regal	1.41	Low	Infiniti QX60	1.23	High	Scion tC	1.41	Low
Buick Verano	1.39	Low	Infiniti QX70	1.27*	High	Scion xB	1.23*	High
Cadillac ATS	1.45	Very Low	Infiniti QX80	1.16*	Very High	Scion xD	1.3*	Moderate
Cadillac CTS	1.43*	Low	Jaguar XF	1.44*	Low	Smart ForTwo	1.15*	Very High
Cadillac SRX	1.21	High	Jeep Cherokee	1.22*	High	Subaru BRZ	1.59*	Very Low
Cadillac XTS	1.37	Low	Jeep Compass	1.2	High	Subaru Forester	1.23	High
Chevrolet Camaro	1.53	Very Low	Jeep Grand Cherokee	1.17	Very High	Subaru Impreza	1.37*	Low
Chevrolet Corvette	1.71*	Very Low	Jeep Patriot	1.15	Very High	Subaru Legacy	1.45	Very Low
Chevrolet Cruze	1.41	Low	Jeep Wrangler	1.13*	Very High	Subaru Outback	1.22	High
Chevrolet Equinox	1.19	High	Kia Cadenza	1.45*	Low	Subaru Tribeca	1.22*	High
Chevrolet Impala	1.36	Moderate	Kia Forte	1.44	Low	Subaru XV Crosstrek	1.26*	High
Chevrolet Malibu	1.44*	Low	Kia Optima	1.48	Very Low	Toyota 4Runner	1.12	Very High
Chevrolet Silverado	1.22	High	Kia Rio	1.38	Low	Toyota Avalon	1.42	Low
Chevrolet Sonic	1.34	Moderate	Kia Sorento	1.24	High	Toyota Camry	1.43*	Low
Chevrolet Spark	1.22*	High	Kia Soul	1.27	Moderate	Toyota Corolla	1.37	Low
Chevrolet Suburban	1.13	Very High	Kia Sportage	1.22	High	Toyota FJ Cruiser	1.14*	Very High
Chevrolet Tahoe	1.14	Very High	Land Rover Range Rover	1.19*	High	Toyota Highlander	1.23*	High
Chevrolet Traverse	1.23	High	Lnd Rvr Rng Rvr Evoque	1.29*	Moderate	Toyota Prius	1.36	Moderate
Chevrolet Volt	1.49	Very Low	Lnd Rvr Rng Rover Sport	1.23*	High	Toyota Prius C	1.37	Low
Chrysler 200	1.4	Low	Lexus CT	1.41*	Low	Toyota Prius V	1.31	Moderate
Chrysler 300	1.39	Low	Lexus ES	1.4	Low	Toyota RAV4	1.23	High
Chrys. Town and Country	1.24*	High	Lexus GS	1.45*	Low	Toyota Sequoia	1.19*	High
Dodge Avenger	1.37	Low	Lexus GX	1.09*	Very High	Toyota Sienna	1.3	Moderate
Dodge Challenger	1.4	Low	Lexus IS	1.48	Very Low	Toyota Tacoma	1.19	High
Dodge Charger	1.45	Very Low	Lexus LS	1.47*	Very Low	Toyota Tundra	1.18	Very High
Dodge Dart	1.42	Low	Lexus RX	1.25*	High	Toyota Venza	1.26	High
Dodge Durango	1.16	Very High	Lincoln MKS	1.39	Low	Toyota Yaris	1.31	Moderate
Dodge Grand Caravan	1.24	High	Lincoln MKZ	1.41	Low	Volkswagen Beetle	1.43	Low
Dodge Journey	1.21*	High	Mazda CX-5	1.22	High	Volkswagen CC	1.46*	Very Low
Fiat 500	1.29	Moderate	Mazda CX-9	1.29	Moderate	Volkswagen Golf	1.38*	Low
Fiat 500L	1.16*	Very High	Mazda Mazda2	1.33*	Moderate	Volkswagen Jetta	1.4*	Low
Ford C-MAX	1.29	Moderate	Mazda Mazda3	1.43*	Low	Volkswagen Passat	1.42	Low
Ford Edge	1.25	High	Mazda Mazda5	1.23*	High	Volkswagen Tiguan	1.2	High
Ford Escape	1.19	High	Mazda Mazda6	1.45*	Very Low	Volkswagen Touareg	1.24*	High
Ford Expedition	1.18*	Very High	Mazda MX-5 Miata	1.6*	Very Low	Volvo S60	1.45	Very Low
Ford Explorer	1.22	High	Merc.-Benz C-Class	1.43	Low	Volvo S80	1.41*	Low
Ford F-150	1.14	Very High	Merc.-Benz CLA-Class	1.43*	Low	Volvo XC60	1.22	High
Ford Fiesta	1.32*	Moderate	Merc.-Benz E-Class	1.46	Very Low	Volvo XC90	1.19*	Very High
Ford Flex	1.23*	High	Merc.-Benz GL-Class	1.13*	Very High			
Ford Focus	1.38	Low	Merc.-Benz GLK-Class	1.19*	Very High			
Ford Fusion	1.41	Low	Merc.-Benz M-Class	1.21	High			
Ford Mustang	1.53	Very Low	Merc.-Benz S-Class	1.46*	Very Low			
Ford Taurus	1.39	Low	Mini Cooper	1.41*	Low	*Calculated		

As gas prices bounce up and down, regular driving still takes a big bite out of our pocketbooks. The good news is that higher fuel efficiency standards are forcing car companies to provide more fuel efficient vehicles. Buying right and practicing more fuel efficient driving will make a huge difference in your vehicle's operating costs.

Using the EPA ratings is the best way to incorporate fuel efficiency in selecting a new car. By comparing these ratings, even among cars of the same size, you'll find that fuel efficiency varies greatly. One compact car might get 36 miles per gallon (mpg) while another compact gets only 22 mpg. If you drive 15,000 miles a year and you pay $3.43 per gallon for fuel, the 36 mpg car will save you $909 *a year* over the "gas guzzler."

In 2008, the EPA changed the way it estimates miles per gallon to better represent today's driving conditions. Their new method adjusts for aggressive driving (high speeds and faster acceleration), air conditioning use, and cold temperature operation.

Octane Ratings: Once you've purchased your car, you'll be faced with choosing the right gasoline. Oil companies spend millions of dollars trying to get you to buy so-called higher performance or high octane fuels. Using high octane fuel can add considerably to your gas bill, and the vast majority of vehicles do not need it. Check your owner's manual and only use what's recommended, which is usually 87. Very few vehicles require "premium" gasoline.

The octane rating of a gasoline is not a measure of power or quality. It is simply a measure of the gas' resistance to engine knock, which is the pinging sound you hear when the air and fuel mixture in your engine ignites prematurely during acceleration.

Your engine may knock when accelerating a heavily loaded car uphill or when the humidity is low. This is normal and does not call for a higher-octane gasoline.

FIVE FACTORS AFFECTING FUEL ECONOMY

1. Engine Size: The smaller the engine the better your fuel efficiency. A 10% increase in the size of your engine can increase your fuel consumption rate by 6%. Smaller engines can be cheaper to maintain as well.

2. Transmission: If used properly, manual transmissions are generally more fuel-efficient than automatics. In fact, a 5-speed manual can add up to 6.5 mpg over a 4-speed automatic transmission. Getting an automatic with an overdrive gear can improve your fuel economy by up to 9 percent.

3. Cruise Control: Using cruise control can save fuel because driving at a constant speed uses less fuel than changing speeds frequently.

4. Trim Packages and Power Options: Upgrading a car's trim level and adding options such as navigation systems or a sunroof can increase the weight of your car. Every 200 pounds of weight shaves off about 1 mile per gallon off your mileage. The weight of the average car in 1981 was 3,202 pounds, today it's around 4,000 pounds.

5. Hybrids: Most manufacturers offer hybrid vehicles that have both gasoline and electric engines. Hybrids can offer 30% better fuel economy and lower emissions.

TWELVE WAYS TO SAVE MONEY AT THE PUMP

Here are a few simple things you can do that will save you a lot of money. Note: Savings are based on gas at $3.43.

1. Make Sure Your Tires are Inflated Properly: 27% of vehicles have tires that are under-inflated. Properly inflated tires can improve mileage by 3%, which is like getting 10 cents off a gallon of gas. Check the label on your door or glove box to find out what the pressure range should be for your tires. Don't use the "max pressure" written on your tire. Electronic gauges are fast, easy to use and accurate. Don't rely on the numbers on the air pump.

2. Check Your Air Filter: A dirty air filter by itself can rob a car by as much as 10% percent of its mileage. If an engine doesn't get enough air, it will burn too much gasoline. Replacing a dirty filter can knock 34 cents off a gallon of gas.

3. Get Your Alignment Checked: Not only does poor alignment cause your tires to wear out faster and cause poor handling, but it can cause your engine to work harder and reduce your fuel efficiency by 10%.

4. Don't Use High Octane Gasoline: Check your owner's manual. Very, very few cars actually need high-octane gas. Using 87-octane gas will save you over 10 cents per gallon over mid-grade and 20 cents over premium.

5. Get a Tune Up: A properly tuned engine is a fuel saver. Have a trusted mechanic tune your engine to exact factory specifications and you could save up to 13 cents a gallon.

6. Check Your Gas Cap: It is estimated that nearly 15 % of the cars on the road have broken or missing gasoline caps. This hurts your mileage and can harm the environment by allowing your gasoline to evaporate. Many Ford products have a capless gas filler, which is a great convenience.

7. Don't Speed: A car moving at 55 mph gets better fuel economy than the same car at 65 mph. For every 5 mph you reduce your highway speed, you can reduce fuel consumption by 7%, which is like getting 24 cents off a gallon of gas.

8. Avoid Excess Idling: An idling car gets 0 mpg. Cars with larger engines typically waste more gas at idle than cars with smaller engines.

9. Drive Smoother: The smoother your accelerations and decelerations, the better your mileage. A smooth foot can save 57 cents a gallon.

10. Combine Trips: Short trips can be expensive because they usually involve a "cold" vehicle. For the first mile or two before the engine gets warmed up, a cold vehicle only gets 30 to 40% of the mileage it gets at full efficiency.

11. Empty your Roof Rack and Trunk: 50% of engine power, traveling at highway speed, is used in overcoming aerodynamic drag or wind resistance. Any protrusion on a vehicle's roof can reduce gas mileage, typical roof racks reduce fuel economy by about 6 mpg. 100 lbs. of extra weight will reduce your mileage by .5 mpg.

12. Choose Your Gas Miser: If you own more than one vehicle, choosing to drive the one with better gas mileage will save you money. If you drive 15,000 miles per year, half in a vehicle with 20 mpg and half with a 30 mpg vehicle and switch to driving 75% of your trips in the 30 mpg vehicle, you will save $214 annually with gas at $3.43.

TIP

FUEL ECONOMY

Get up-to-date information about fuel economy at www.fueleconomy.gov, a joint website created by the U.S. Department of Energy and the EPA. There you'll find the EPA's Fuel Economy Guide, allowing you to compare fuel economy estimates for 2014 models back to 1985 models. You'll also find out about the latest technological advances pertaining to fuel efficiency. The site is extremely useful and easy to navigate. We've added fuel economy ratings and a Fuel Factor section to the At-a-glance box on our car rating pages.

FUEL ECONOMY MISERS AND GUZZLERS

Because the success of the EPA program depends on consumers' ability to compare the fuel economy ratings easily, we have included key mileage figures on our ratings pages. Listed below are the best and worst of this year's ratings according to annual fuel cost. The complete EPA fuel economy guide is available at www.fueleconomy.gov.

Vehicle	Specifications	MPG (city/hwy)	Annual Fuel Cost
FUEL ECONOMY MISERS AND GUZZLERS			
THE BEST			
Plug In Hybrid Electric Vehicles (PHEVs)*			
Chevrolet Volt	1.4L, 4 cyl., Continuously Variable, FWD	35/40	$900
Toyota Prius Plug-in Hybrid	1.8L, 4 cyl., Continuously Variable, FWD	51/49	$950
Honda Accord Plug-in Hybrid	2L, 4 cyl., Continuously Variable, FWD	47/46	$950
Ford Fusion Energi Plug-in Hybrid	2L, 4 cyl., Continuously Variable, FWD	44/41	$950
Gas			
Toyota Prius	1.8L, 4 cyl., Continuously Variable, FWD	51/48	$1,036
Honda Accord	2L, 4 cyl., Continuously Variable, FWD	50/45	$1,077
Ford Fusion Hybrid FWD	2L, 4 cyl., Continuously Variable, FWD	47/47	$1,095
Lincoln MKZ Hybrid FWD	2L, 4 cyl., Continuously Variable, FWD	45/45	$1,143
Honda Insight	1.3L, 4 cyl., Continuously Variable, FWD	41/44	$1,215
Toyota Prius V	1.8L, 4 cyl., Continuously Variable, FWD	44/40	$1,219
Lexus CT 200h	1.8L, 4 cyl., Continuously Variable, FWD	43/40	$1,235
Toyota Camry Hybrid LE	2.5L, 4 cyl., Continuously Variable, FWD	43/39	$1,249
Volkswagen Jetta Hybrid	1.4L, 4 cyl., 7-sp. Automated Manual, FWD	42/48	$1,252#
Mitsubishi Mirage	1.2L, 3 cyl., Continuously Variable, FWD	37/44	$1,281
Lexus ES 300h	2.5L, 4 cyl., Selectable Continuously Variable, FWD	40/39	$1,301
Toyota Avalon Hybrid	2.5L, 4 cyl., Selectable Continuously Variable, FWD	40/39	$1,301
Toyota Camry Hybrid XLE/SE	2.5L, 4 cyl., Continuously Variable, FWD	40/38	$1,335
Ford Fiesta SFE FWD	1L, 3 cyl., 5 sp. Manual, FWD	32/45	$1,359
Mitsubishi Mirage	1.2L, 3 cyl., 5 sp. Manual, FWD	34/42	$1,368
Honda CR-Z	1.5L, 4 cyl., Selectable Continuously Variable, FWD	36/39	$1,378
Scion iQ	1.3L, 4 cyl., Continuously Variable, FWD	36/37	$1,412
BMW 328d xDrive	2L, 4 cyl., 8 sp. Automatic, AWD	31/43	$1,413
Acura ILX	1.5L, 4 cyl., Selectable Continuously Variable, FWD	39/38	$1,431#
Toyota Corolla LE ECO	1.8L, 4 cyl., Continuously Variable, FWD	30/42	$1,453
Nissan Versa	1.6L, 4 cyl., Continuously Variable, FWD	31/40	$1,468
BMW 328d	2L, 4 cyl., 8 sp. Automatic, RWD	32/45	$1,478^
Chevrolet Spark	1.2L, 4 cyl., Continuously Variable, FWD	30/39	$1,511
Volkswagen Passat	2L, 4 cyl., 6 sp. Manual, FWD	31/43	$1,537
Mercedes-Benz Smart Fortwo	1L, 3 cyl., 5 sp. Automated Manual, RWD	34/38	$1,563#
THE WORST**			
Mercedes-Benz G 63 AMG	5.5L, 8 cyl., 7 sp. Automatic, 4WD	12/14	$4,337#
Mercedes-Benz G 550	5.5L, 8 cyl., 7 sp. Automatic, RWD	12/15	$4,191#
Ford F150 Raptor Pickup 4WD	6.2L, 8 cyl., 6 sp. Semi-Automatic, 4WD	11/16	$3,883
Audi R8 Spyder	5.2L, 10 cyl., 6 sp. Manual, AWD	12/18	$3,806#
Chevrolet Camaro	6.2L, 8 cyl., 6 sp. Semi-Automatic, RWD	12/18	$3,806#
Cadillac CTS/CTS V/CTS Wagon	6.2L, 8 cyl., 6 sp. Semi-Automatic, RWD	12/18	$3,806#
Mercedes-Benz CL 65 AMG	6L, 12 cyl., 5 sp. Automatic, RWD	12/18	$3,806#
Mercedes-Benz CL 600	5.5L, 12 cyl., 5 sp. Automatic, RWD	12/18	$3,806#
BMW X6 M	4.4L, 8 cyl., 6 sp. Semi-Automatic, AWD	13/17	$3,780#
Ford F150 Pickup 4WD	6.2L, 8 cyl., 6 sp. Semi-Automatic, 4WD	12/16	$3,728
Audi R8	4.2L, 8 cyl., 6 sp. Manual, AWD	11/20	$3,718#
Audi R8	5.2L, 10 cyl., 6 sp. Manual, AWD	12/19	$3,693#
Nissan Titan 4WD	5.6L, 8 cyl., 5 sp. Automatic, 4WD	12/17	$3,611
Audi R8 Spyder	4.2L, 8 cyl., 6 sp. Manual, AWD	11/20	$3,587#
Land Rover Range Rover	5.0L, 8 cyl., 8 sp. Semi-Automatic, 4WD	13/19	$3,564#
Nissan Armada 4WD	5.6L, 8 cyl., 5 sp. Automatic, 4WD	12/18	$3,500
Toyota Sequoia 4WD	5.7L, 6 cly., 8 sp. Semi-Automatic, 4WD	13/17	$3,476
BMW 760Li	6L, 12 cyl., 8 sp. Semi-Automatic, RWD	13/20	$3,464#
Cadillac Escalade AWD	6.2L, 8 cyl., 6 sp. Automatic, AWD	13/18	$3,374
Ford Expedition 4WD FFV	5.4, 8 cyl., 6 sp. Automatic, 4WD	13/18	$3,374
Ford F150 Pickup 2WD	6.2L, 8 cyl., 6 sp. Semi-Automatic, RWD	13/18	$3,374
GMC K10 Yukon Denali AWD	6.2L, 8 cyl., 6 sp. Automatic, AWD	13/18	$3,374
Lincoln Navigator	5.4L, 8 cyl., 8-sp. Automatic, 4WD	13/18	$3,374
Jeep Grand Cherokee SRT8	6.4L, 8 cyl., 8-sp. Automatic, 4WD	13/19	$3,277

Note: 2014 annual fuel cost based on driving 15,000 miles and a projected regular gas price of $3.43; #=Premium Required; ^=Diesel Required; *=Fuel Economy rating based on hybrid function only; annual cost based on epa estimate for gas and electric use; **=Low volume exotic vehicles (over $120,000) and cargo vans were excluded.

COMPARING WARRANTIES

After buying your car, maintenance will be a significant portion of your operating costs. The strength of your warranty and the cost of repairs after the warranty expires will determine these costs. Comparing warranties and repair costs, before you buy, can save you thousands of dollars down the road.

Along with your new car comes a warranty which is a promise from the manufacturer that the car will perform as it should. Most of us never read the warranty until it is too late. In fact, because warranties are often difficult to read and understand, most of us don't really know what our warranty offers.

To keep your warranty in effect, you must operate and maintain your car according to the instructions in your owner's manual. It is important to keep a record of all maintenance performed on your car.

Be careful not to confuse a warranty with a service contract. A service contract must be purchased separately while a warranty is yours at no extra cost when you buy the car.

Warranties are difficult to compare because they contain fine print and confusing language. The following table will help you compare this year's new car warranties. Because the table does not contain all the details about each warranty, review the actual warranty to understand its fine points. You have the right to inspect a warranty before you buy—it's the law.

The table provides information on five critical items in a warranty:

The **Basic Warranty** covers most parts against manufacturer's defects. Tires, batteries, and items you add to the car are covered under separate warranties. The table describes coverage in terms of months and miles. For example, 48/50 means the warranty is good for 48 months or 50,000 miles, whichever comes first. This is the most important part of your warranty.

The **Power Train Warranty** often lasts longer than the basic warranty. Because each manufacturer's definition of the power train is different, it is important to find out exactly what your warranty will cover. Power train coverage should include the engine, transmission, and drive train. Some luxury cars will cover additional systems such as steering, suspension, and electrical systems.

The **Corrosion Warranty** usually applies only to actual holes due to rust. Read this section carefully because many corrosion warranties do not apply to what the manufacturer may describe as cosmetic rust or bad paint.

The **Roadside Assistance** column indicates whether or not the manufacturer offers a program for helping with breakdowns, lockouts, jump starts, flat tires, running out of gas, and towing. Some have special limitations or added features. Because each one is different, check yours carefully.

The **Scheduled Maint. (Free)** column indicates whether or not free scheduled maintenance is included and for how long. This can be a money saver as well as encourage you to follow the manufacturer's recommended maintenance schedule. These programs cover parts scheduled to be replaced such as filters. If there is an asterisk next to the coverage, that means the manufacturer also covers the cost of any parts that need to be replaced because of wear. Covering the cost of "wear" parts is a terrific feature and offered by very few manufacturers.

The last column, the **Warranty Rating Index**, provides an overall assessment of this year's warranties. **The higher the Index number, the better the warranty.** The Index number incorporates the important features of each warranty. We give the most weight to the basic and power train components of the warranties. Roadside assistance was weighted somewhat less, and corrosion resistance received the least weight.

Finally, we also considered special features such as extra coverage on batteries or wheel alignment. These benefits added to the overall ratings, whereas certain limitations (shortened transferability) took away.

The best ratings are in **BOLD**.

WARRANTY COMPARISON

Manufacturer	Basic Warranty	Power Train Warranty	Corrosion Warranty	Roadside Assistance	Scheduled Maint. (Free)	Index	Warranty Rating
Acura	48/50	72/70	60/Unlimited	48/50		1130	Average
Audi	48/50	48/50	144/Unlimited	48/Unlimited	12/5	1293	Good
BMW	**48/50**	**48/50**	**144/Unlimited**	**48/Unlimited**	**48/50***	**1427**	**Very Good**
Buick	48/50	72/70	72/100	72/70	24/24	1239	Average
Cadillac	**48/50**	**72/70**	**72/Unlimited[1]**	**72/70**	**48/50**	**1499**	**Very Good**
Chevrolet	36/36	60/100	72/100[2]	60/100	24/24	1360	Good
Chrysler	36/36	60/100	60/100[3]	60/100		1366	Good
Dodge	36/36	60/100	60/100[4]	60/100		1366	Good
Fiat	48/50	48/50	60/100	48/Unlimited		1044	Poor
Ford	36/36	60/60	60/Unlimited	60/60		993	Poor
GMC	36/36	60/100	72/100	60/100	24/24	1216	Average
Honda	36/36	60/60	60/Unlimited	Optional		813	Very Poor
Hyundai	**60/60**	**120/100**	**84/Unlimited**	**60/Unlimited**		**1618**	**Very Good**
Infiniti	48/60	72/70	84/Unlimited	48/Unlimited		1287	Good
Jaguar	48/50	48/50	72/Unlimited	48/50	12/10	1048	Poor
Jeep	36/36	60/100	60/100[5]	60/100		1366	Good
Kia	**60/60**	**120/100[6]**	**60/100**	**60/60**		**1420**	**Very Good**
Land Rover	48/50	48/50	72/Unlimited	48/50	12/10	1048	Poor
Lexus[7]	48/50	72/70	72/Unlimited	48/Unlimited		1222	Average
Lincoln	36/36	60/60	60/Unlimited	60/60		993	Poor
Mazda	36/36	60/60	60/Unlimited	36/36		921	Very Poor
Mercedes-Benz[8]	48/50	48/50	48/50	Lifetime[9]		938	Very Poor
Mini	48/50	48/50	144/Unlimited	48/Unlimited	36/36*	1388	Good
Mitsubishi	**60/60**	**120/100**	**84/100**	**60/Unlimited**		**1572**	**Very Good**
Nissan	36/36	60/60	60/Unlimited	36/36		921	Very Poor
Porsche	48/50	48/50	144/Unlimited	48/50		1229	Average
Ram	36/36	60/100	60/100[10]	60/100		1366	Good
Scion	36/36	60/60	60/Unlimited	24/Unlimited	24/25	949	Very Poor
Smart[11]	48/50	48/50	0/0	48/50		839	Very Poor
Subaru[12]	36/36	60/60	60/Unlimited	36/36		957	Very Poor
Toyota	36/36	60/60	60/Unlimited	24/25	24/25	923	Very Poor
Volkswagen	36/36	60/60	144/Unlimited	36/36	24/24	1188	Average
Volvo	48/50	48/50	144/Unlimited	48/Unlimited	36/36	1334	Good

*Includes needed parts
[1] All Corrosion 48/50
[2] All Corrosion 36/36
[3] All Corrosion 36/Unlimited
[4] All Corrosion 36/Unlimited
[5] All Corrosion 36/Unlimited
[6] Only transferable up to 60,000 miles

[7] Wheel alignment and balancing 12/20
[8] Wheel alignment and balancing 12/12
[9] Only if serviced at Mercedes Benz dealerships
[10] All Corrosion 36/Unlimited
[11] Wheel alignment and balancing 12/12
[12] Wear items 36/36

SECRET WARRANTIES

If dealers report a number of complaints about a certain part and the manufacturer determines that the problem is due to faulty design or assembly, the manufacturer may permit dealers to repair the problem at no charge to the customer even though the warranty is expired. In the past, this practice was often reserved for customers who made a big fuss. The availability of the free repair was never publicized, which is why we call these "secret warranties."

Manufacturers deny the existence of secret warranties. They call these free repairs "policy adjustments" or "goodwill service." Whatever they are called, most consumers never hear about them.

Many secret warranties are disclosed in service bulletins that the manufacturers send to dealers. These bulletins outline free repair or reimbursement programs, as well as other problems and their possible causes and solutions.

Service bulletins from many manufacturers may be on file at the National Highway Traffic Safety Administration. You can visit www.nhtsa.gov to access NHTSA's Service Bulletin database.

If you find that a secret warranty is in effect and repairs are being made at no charge after the warranty has expired, contact the Center for Auto Safety, 1825 Connecticut Ave. NW, #330, Washington, DC 20009. They will publish the information so others can benefit.

Disclosure Laws: Spurred by the proliferation of secret warranties and the failure of the FTC to take action, California, Connecticut, Virginia, Wisconsin, and Maryland have passed legislation that requires consumers to be notified of secret warranties on their cars. Several other states have introduced similar warranty bills.

Typically, the laws require the following: direct notice to consumers within a specified time after the adoption of a warranty adjustment policy; notice of the disclosure law to new car buyers; reimbursement within a number of years after payment to owners who paid for covered repairs before they learned of the extended warranty service; and dealers must inform consumers who complain about a covered defect that it is eligible for repair under warranty.

If you live in a state with a secret warranty law already in effect, write your state attorney general's office (in care of your state capital) for information. To encourage passage of such a bill, contact your state representative (in care of your state capital).

Some state lemon laws require dealers and manufacturers to give you copies of Technical Service Bulletins on problems affecting your vehicle. These bulletins may alert you to a secret warranty on your vehicle or help you make the case for a free repair if there isn't a secret warranty. See page 59 for an overview of your state's lemon law. If you would like to see the complete law, go to www.autosafety.org to view your state's lemon laws.

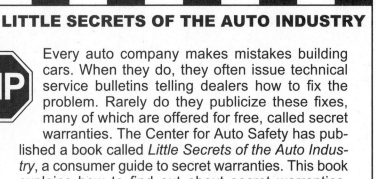

LITTLE SECRETS OF THE AUTO INDUSTRY

TIP

Every auto company makes mistakes building cars. When they do, they often issue technical service bulletins telling dealers how to fix the problem. Rarely do they publicize these fixes, many of which are offered for free, called secret warranties. The Center for Auto Safety has published a book called *Little Secrets of the Auto Industry*, a consumer guide to secret warranties. This book explains how to find out about secret warranties, offers tips for going to small claims court and getting federal and state assistance, and lists information on state secret warranty laws. To order a copy, send $17.50 to: Center for Auto Safety, Pub. Dept. CB, 1825 Connecticut Ave. NW, Suite 330, Washington, DC 20009.

KEEPING IT GOING

Comparing maintenance costs before you buy can help decide which car to purchase. These costs include preventive maintenance servicing—such as changing the oil and filters—as well as the cost of repairs after your warranty expires. Below we enable you to compare the costs of preventive maintenance and nine likely repairs for the 2014 models.

Preventive Maintenance: The first column in the table is the periodic servicing, specified by the manufacturer, that keeps your car running properly. For example, regularly changing the oil and oil filter. Every owner's manual specifies a schedule of recommended servicing for at least the first 60,000 miles and many now go to 100,000 miles. The tables on the following pages estimate the labor cost of following this preventive maintenance schedule for 60,000 miles, the length of a typical warranty. Service parts are not included in this total.

Repairs Costs: The tables also list the costs for nine repairs that typically occur during the first 100,000 miles. There is no precise way to predict exactly when a repair will be needed. But if you keep a car for 75,000 to 100,000 miles, it is likely that you will experience most of these repairs at least once. The last column provides a relative indication of how expensive these nine repairs are for many cars. Repair cost is rated as Very Good if the total for nine repairs is in the lowest fifth of all the cars rated, and Very Poor if the total is in the highest fifth.

Most repair shops use "flat-rate manuals" to estimate repair costs. These manuals list the approximate time required for repairing many items. Each automobile manufacturer publishes its own manual and there are several independent manuals as well. For many repairs, the time varies from one manual to another. Some repair shops even use different manuals for different repairs. To determine a repair bill, a shop multiplies the time listed in its manual by its hourly labor rate and then adds the cost of parts.

Some dealers and repair shops create their own maintenance schedules which call for more frequent (and thus more expensive) servicing than the manufacturer's recommendations. If the service recommended by your dealer or repair shop doesn't match what the manufacturer recommends, make sure you understand and agree to the extra items. Our cost estimates are based on published repair times multiplied by a nationwide average labor rate of $90 per hour and include the cost of replaced parts and related adjustments.

Prices in the following tables may not predict the exact costs of these repairs. For example, labor rates for your area may be more or less than the national average. However, the prices will provide you with a relative comparison of costs for various automobiles.

SAVE YOUR RECEIPTS

Keeping it going means taking advantage of your warranty and, if you've purchased a service agreement, getting what's coming to you. Because warranties and service agreements are protected against consumer abuse, sometimes the repair shop may try to blame the mechanical problem on your failure to properly maintain the vehicle. Unscrupulous service providers do this in order to keep from having to reimburse you for the repair. According to the Center for Auto Safety, a common claim is to blame the problem on your failure to regularly change the oil. To insure that you get the warranty coverage you have a right to, or the service contract coverage you paid for, religiously keep your receipts. That's the best way to prove that you're not the one at fault.

	PM Costs to 60,000 Miles	REPAIR COSTS								
		Front Brake Pads	Starter	Fuel Injector	Fuel Pump	Struts/ Shocks	Timing Belt/Chain	Water Pump	Muffler	Headlamps	Relative Repair Cost*
Subcompact											
Chevrolet Sonic	675	216	389	132	394	148	309	266	495	766	Vry. Gd.
Chevrolet Spark	747	234	331	165	407	265	1222	279	622	766	Average
Fiat 500	459	172	303	401	469	124	319	418	208	820	Vry. Gd.
Ford Fiesta	1089	148	440	95	482	135	373	236	316	354	Vry. Gd.
Hyundai Accent	792	136	354	167	413	197	419	272	357	467	Vry. Gd.
Hyundai Veloster	882	163	354	149	426	308	523	326	414	702	Vry. Gd.
Kia Rio	774	147	380	198	347	339	414	282	409	737	Vry. Gd.
Kia Soul	954	147	371	208	364	427	418	385	417	1142	Good
Mazda Mazda2	855	149	396	193	363	295	586	406	283	758	Vry. Gd.
Mazda MX-5 Miata	864	191	291	229	368	409	474	261	671	1369	Good
Mini Cooper	576	205	504	193	505	340	928	425	508	1502	Average
Mini Countryman	684	219	462	198	419	337	1032	410	632	851	Average
Mitsubishi Mirage											
Nissan Versa	594	167	376	304	475	167	433	245	323	304	Vry. Gd.
Scion xB	702	163	465	273	428	237	783	360	263	800	Good
Scion xD	297	147	478	246	430	289	1251	277	292	497	Good
Smart ForTwo	1017	175	463	198	438	557	1436	470	971	766	Poor
Toyota Prius C	468	138	0	377	482	183	1053	646	254	863	Good
Toyota Yaris	333	147	388	237	451	209	553	242	261	686	Vry. Gd.
Volkswagen Beetle	657	171	494	299	392	407	962	468	867	1174	Poor
Compact											
Acura ILX	1008	159	564	225	488	441	503	293	222	1520	Average
Acura TSX	846	146	606	145	476	297	459	245	734	1520	Average
Audi A4	855	272	748	605	494	830	590	706	569	507	Poor
BMW 3 Series	180	209	505	310	388	634	1301	631	593	1236	Poor
BMW 4 Series	180	207	633	215	393	721	932	720	794	1294	Poor
Buick Verano	666	243	351	342	454	341	607	598	311	914	Good
Cadillac ATS	252	249	330	345	664	357	754	413	1229	1163	Poor
Chevrolet Cruze	864	216	371	135	522	224	435	334	583	578	Vry. Gd.
Chevrolet Volt	738	174	0	119	452	141	1250	451	536	885	Good
Dodge Dart	765	195	224	105	404	256	517	223	597	1050	Vry. Gd.
Fiat 500L											
Ford C-MAX	1089	152	301	297	495	189	579	245	325	737	Vry. Gd.
Ford Focus	819	152	301	297	495	189	579	245	325	737	Vry. Gd.
Honda Civic	702	146	571	272	438	307	543	263	205	747	Vry. Gd.
Honda Insight	918	151	796	272	394	370	507	316	573	980	Average
Hyundai Elantra	1013	145	352	162	230	321	526	290	362	741	Vry. Gd.
Kia Forte	585	161	290	192	323	364	513	294	405	517	Vry. Gd.
Lexus CT	486	147	0	440	462	275	1620	566	591	1908	Poor
Lexus IS	684	160	897	663	439	698	2403	592	821	1349	Vry. Pr.
Mazda Mazda3	909	168	242	411	420	260	396	339	595	669	Vry. Gd.
Mercedes-Benz C-Class	1791	193	1025	375	579	669	1199	699	973	1212	Vry. Pr.
Mercedes-Benz CLA-Class	1962	193	1025	375	579	669	1199	699	973	1212	Vry. Pr.
Mitsubishi Lancer	504	187	884	367	614	497	564	511	427	1175	Poor
Nissan Leaf	666	128	0	0	0	314	0	535	0	2009	Vry. Gd.
Nissan Sentra	702	155	364	360	525	297	410	233	383	812	Vry. Gd.
Scion FR-S	1629	190	1322	584	696	373	626	390	618	969	Poor
Scion tC	315	167	658	341	442	258	1378	330	275	969	Average
AVERAGE OF ALL VEHICLES	**$783**	**$193**	**$479**	**$302**	**$509**	**$432**	**$934**	**$470**	**$623**	**$1,096**	

	PM Costs to 60,000 Miles	REPAIR COSTS									Relative Repair Cost*
		Front Brake Pads	Starter	Fuel Injector	Fuel Pump	Struts/ Shocks	Timing Belt/Chain	Water Pump	Muffler	Headlamps	
Subaru BRZ	905	190	1322	584	696	373	626	390	618	824	Poor
Subaru Impreza	1008	154	549	230	453	540	393	452	429	824	Good
Subaru XV Crosstrek	1008	154	549	230	453	540	393	452	429	824	Good
Toyota Corolla	396	143	469	291	421	276	999	254	391	533	Good
Toyota Prius	396	138	0	449	435	241	1598	561	284	861	Average
Toyota Prius V	396	172	0	449	482	241	1620	561	272	864	Average
Volkswagen Golf	657	185	533	316	384	414	597	484	470	606	Good
Volkswagen Jetta	657	206	526	444	504	420	711	654	742	770	Average
Intermediate											
Acura TL	1008	163	479	150	490	271	422	546	877	1761	Poor
Audi A5	855	214	395	354	392	952	608	744	1039	557	Poor
Audi A6	846	182	552	445	670	502	2005	348	705	544	Poor
BMW 5 Series	180	298	650	210	596	510	1247	754	864	1529	Vry. Pr.
BMW 6 Series	180	184	555	442	443	418	1108	750	667	4107	Vry. Pr.
Buick Regal	864	287	347	414	571	252	481	580	465	1158	Average
Cadillac CTS	252	249	330	345	664	357	754	413	1229	1163	Poor
Chevrolet Camaro	891	290	254	291	373	200	596	413	1196	509	Good
Chevrolet Corvette	747	378	650	244	2158	328	888	451	893	2520	Vry. Pr.
Chevrolet Malibu	864	194	351	149	564	240	539	620	677	708	Good
Chrysler 200	801	178	246	105	404	289	517	219	600	1050	Vry. Gd.
Dodge Avenger	765	195	224	105	404	256	517	223	597	1050	Vry. Gd.
Ford Fusion	855	177	287	146	410	214	583	236	447	835	Vry. Gd.
Ford Mustang	1341	148	282	191	417	192	838	303	464	740	Vry. Gd.
Honda Accord	990	146	606	118	412	310	503	236	515	711	Vry. Gd.
Hyundai Azera	972	179	410	312	375	322	849	364	538	2478	Poor
Hyundai Genesis	1044	206	452	285	398	440	1357	346	570	1011	Average
Hyundai Sonata	891	154	317	209	341	201	633	354	651	749	Vry. Gd.
Infiniti Q50	594	177	465	376	471	544	1024	670	596	2035	Vry. Pr.
Infiniti Q60	594	252	465	353	471	544	1024	603	595	2062	Vry. Pr.
Infiniti Q70	702	221	456	344	476	771	1024	646	685	2611	Vry. Pr.
Kia Optima	864	161	362	245	371	385	609	348	1002	824	Average
Lexus ES	963	147	505	381	408	768	1742	866	492	2432	Vry. Pr.
Lexus GS	711	150	536	422	456	684	2218	411	849	2283	Vry. Pr.
Lincoln MKZ	855	178	224	232	395	263	872	1292	1006	1407	Poor
Mazda Mazda6	693	184	232	136	475	207	542	232	357	744	Vry. Gd.
Mercedes-Benz E-Class	1386	197	763	690	532	1283	1242	681	666	1253	Vry. Pr.
Nissan Altima	594	146	430	333	462	247	874	269	506	695	Good
Nissan Maxima	828	146	407	408	462	389	943	407	664	713	Average
Subaru Legacy	1323	163	440	208	417	484	363	410	384	745	Vry. Gd.
Subaru Outback	1323	163	440	208	417	484	288	410	384	889	Good
Toyota Camry	504	138	496	309	433	398	1783	294	384	895	Poor
Volkswagen CC	738	226	684	476	434	453	765	749	459	876	Average
Volkswagen Passat	657	175	537	386	452	409	1626	480	707	680	Poor
Volvo S60	513	192	445	356	909	216	452	461	669	502	Good
Large											
Acura RLX	510	303	1216	195	445	551	413	522	537	2422	Vry. Pr.
BMW 7 Series	180	137	659	314	526	1912	2950	754	710	3257	Vry. Pr.
Buick LaCrosse	864	286	402	377	528	735	961	449	841	1102	Poor
Cadillac XTS	252	249	330	345	664	357	754	413	1229	1163	Poor
AVERAGE OF ALL VEHICLES	**$783**	**$193**	**$479**	**$302**	**$509**	**$432**	**$934**	**$470**	**$623**	**$1,096**	

	PM Costs to 60,000 Miles	Front Brake Pads	Starter	Fuel Injector	Fuel Pump	Struts/ Shocks	Timing Belt/ Chain	Water Pump	Muffler	Headlamps	Relative Repair Cost*
					REPAIR COSTS						
Chevrolet Impala	891	250	389	336	648	357	1006	395	597	646	Average
Chrysler 300	846	163	237	170	358	344	678	259	812	1392	Average
Dodge Challenger	774	273	221	182	358	421	469	195	764	662	Vry. Gd.
Dodge Charger	657	299	221	182	435	205	717	196	825	676	Good
Ford Taurus	909	148	412	218	375	259	1086	1125	715	1078	Poor
Jaguar XF	1395	260	902	897	557	973	2024	360	607	1340	Vry. Pr.
Lexus LS	891	178	1151	705	637	2792	1467	405	609	2795	Vry. Pr.
Lincoln MKS	828	152	412	223	414	248	951	1044	1109	2327	Vry. Pr.
Mercedes-Benz S-Class	1701	208	745	451	509	2850	1132	866	1149	2153	Vry. Pr.
Toyota Avalon	378	138	474	417	453	381	1994	393	348	901	Poor
Volvo S80	513	205	436	343	996	491	640	388	602	539	Average
Minivan											
Chrysler Town and Country	531	253	405	209	543	166	874	292	563	726	Good
Dodge Grand Caravan	558	239	405	209	543	114	564	397	563	726	Good
Honda Odyssey	936	163	512	195	446	299	422	499	644	577	Good
Mazda Mazda5	918	168	242	90	480	170	542	283	460	1311	Good
Nissan Quest	702	155	482	385	490	403	1448	484	521	1036	Poor
Toyota Sienna	738	144	505	368	1035	242	1800	1284	399	1033	Vry. Pr.
Small SUV											
Acura RDX	828	163	520	127	476	198	497	307	480	1817	Average
Audi Q5	855	213	758	378	702	363	632	672	586	1132	Poor
BMW X1	180	207	681	319	521	946	1018	795	1161	1147	Vry. Pr.
Cadillac SRX	252	211	362	381	510	334	772	440	883	1051	Average
Ford Escape	774	152	406	117	392	189	514	218	416	484	Vry. Gd.
Honda Crosstour	990	146	573	123	456	417	381	394	823	729	Good
Honda CR-V	864	156	589	150	393	406	548	236	398	797	Vry. Gd.
Hyundai Tucson	972	145	343	200	513	320	532	372	568	687	Good
Infiniti QX50	594	190	456	358	478	477	647	812	637	966	Average
Jeep Cherokee											
Jeep Compass	450	209	286	114	295	242	503	243	455	1012	Vry. Gd.
Jeep Patriot	450	173	286	105	295	219	503	243	577	377	Vry. Gd.
Jeep Wrangler	477	234	190	268	453	174	608	427	348	362	Vry. Gd.
Kia Sportage	927	161	227	218	336	486	618	348	323	766	Vry. Gd.
Mazda CX-5	792	185	278	102	373	338	540	226	655	1376	Good
Mercedes-Benz GLK-Class	1647	191	980	424	427	598	1541	677	1215	1265	Vry. Pr.
Mitsubishi Outlander Sport	504	277	906	360	780	439	623	529	468	1477	Poor
Nissan Juke	594	137	523	387	445	285	1040	330	362	522	Good
Subaru Forester	1008	154	549	239	417	461	666	456	357	840	Good
Toyota RAV4	387	160	478	300	688	203	1927	285	712	690	Poor
Volkswagen Tiguan	738	185	535	476	377	407	876	726	456	934	Average
Mid-Size SUV											
Acura MDX	828	163	535	267	453	213	390	501	639	1823	Average
Audi Q7	1017	260	878	603	529	2256	2459	411	1399	372	Vry. Pr.
BMW X3	180	207	681	319	521	946	1018	795	1161	1147	Vry. Pr.
BMW X5	180	241	623	394	523	1055	941	783	1340	3645	Vry. Pr.
Chevrolet Equinox	891	299	357	396	808	190	512	571	725	1007	Average
Dodge Journey	846	234	405	200	707	389	973	293	908	796	Average
Ford Edge	756	170	407	209	436	284	1104	1198	540	933	Poor
Ford Explorer	909	157	358	173	520	287	914	1027	918	769	Average
Honda Pilot	918	163	529	204	499	267	399	526	643	846	Good
Hyundai Santa Fe	972	174	299	141	444	247	527	321	583	1100	Good
AVERAGE OF ALL VEHICLES	**$783**	**$193**	**$479**	**$302**	**$509**	**$432**	**$934**	**$470**	**$623**	**$1,096**	

42

	PM Costs to 60,000 Miles	Front Brake Pads	Starter	Fuel Injector	Fuel Pump	Struts/ Shocks	Timing Belt/ Chain	Water Pump	Muffler	Headlamps	Relative Repair Cost*
						REPAIR COSTS					
Hyundai Santa Fe Sport	972	174	290	141	444	247	527	321	583	1100	Good
Infiniti QX60	702	155	419	390	458	625	1661	686	678	3638	Vry. Pr.
Jeep Grand Cherokee	657	244	446	191	737	263	820	212	815	812	Average
Kia Sorento	936	152	253	281	429	217	1291	394	674	448	Good
Land Rover Range Rover Evoque	333	282	592	375	582	640	533	249	641	532	Average
Lexus RX	729	148	772	418	470	181	1859	870	605	1159	Vry. Pr.
Mazda CX-9	774	177	282	227	568	311	1097	1168	514	1120	Poor
Mercedes-Benz M-Class	1728	280	871	758	645	1597	1593	668	859	1449	Vry. Pr.
Mitsubishi Outlander	981	187	317	266	759	213	623	524	413	783	Good
Nissan Murano	702	184	451	385	516	425	1628	466	513	972	Poor
Nissan Pathfinder	1080	155	392	343	573	156	854	347	522	426	Good
Nissan Rogue	702	155	342	363	402	223	1141	313	596	831	Average
Nissan Xterra	1080	155	401	363	490	212	854	348	522	698	Good
Porsche Cayenne	1080	379	719	393	342	1034	1315	504	1768	1011	Vry. Pr.
Subaru Tribeca	1368	168	422	190	402	491	418	557	377	889	Good
Toyota FJ Cruiser	513	172	495	327	532	205	1931	402	360	659	Average
Toyota Venza	765	144	487	300	483	520	1760	303	586	931	Poor
Volkswagen Touareg	648	323	616	792	450	782	1784	722	920	1328	Vry. Pr.
Volvo XC60	513	241	441	309	804	555	464	422	620	524	Average
Volvo XC90	594	242	450	335	740	290	644	388	816	554	Average
Large SUV											
Buick Enclave	819	275	371	359	558	292	1073	449	1055	2144	Vry. Pr.
Chevrolet Suburban	891	270	315	187	674	166	866	510	1043	2124	Vry. Pr.
Chevrolet Tahoe	891	270	315	228	665	261	866	510	1080	630	Average
Chevrolet Traverse	819	275	371	312	594	182	1289	449	669	1167	Poor
Dodge Durango	657	222	315	223	508	145	935	265	635	305	Vry. Gd.
Ford Expedition	972	181	375	190	550	291	963	291	613	607	Good
Ford Flex	801	152	412	245	423	248	1004	1032	763	1017	Poor
Infiniti QX70	702	185	428	360	475	599	1150	655	683	3638	Vry. Pr.
Infiniti QX80	1080	169	523	349	531	509	796	328	382	1669	Poor
Land Rover Range Rover	927	429	758	1039	493	749	1408	381	816	3141	Vry. Pr.
Land Rover Range Rover Sport	927	242	820	418	394	1419	1408	381	339	2265	Vry. Pr.
Lexus GX	711	151	1235	431	599	198	1251	529	690	1172	Vry. Pr.
Mercedes-Benz GL-Class	1782	269	704	276	555	814	988	732	740	1044	Vry. Pr.
Nissan Armada	1080	164	528	300	548	351	1717	341	626	917	Poor
Toyota 4Runner	513	151	549	354	590	190	2075	523	513	838	Poor
Toyota Highlander	531	144	528	397	1049	512	1917	582	712	681	Vry. Pr.
Toyota Sequoia	576	168	943	372	679	299	1292	526	417	835	Poor
Compact Pickup											
Nissan Frontier	1080	155	432	363	579	214	854	348	407	725	Good
Toyota Tacoma	486	173	490	359	809	143	1355	421	483	762	Average
Standard Pickup											
Chevrolet Silverado	891	284	315	187	567	301	866	497	828	721	Average
Ford F-150	1278	181	369	166	579	159	1210	297	564	585	Good
GMC Sierra	891	270	315	263	590	375	857	497	874	887	Average
Honda Ridgeline	900	163	516	186	503	328	422	517	423	597	Vry. Gd.
Nissan Titan	1080	164	564	300	548	268	1717	341	597	887	Poor
Ram 1500	576	149	270	111	510	141	907	354	403	308	Vry. Gd.
Toyota Tundra	576	168	898	309	679	185	1116	409	569	835	Poor
AVERAGE OF ALL VEHICLES	$783	$193	$479	$302	$509	$432	$934	$470	$623	$1,096	

SERVICE CONTRACTS

Service contracts are one of the most expensive options you can buy. In fact, service contracts are a major profit source for many dealers.

A service contract is not a warranty. It is more like an insurance plan that, in theory, covers repairs that are not covered by your warranty or that occur after the warranty runs out. They are often inaccurately referred to as "extended warranties."

Service contracts are generally a poor value. The companies who sell contracts are very sure that, on average, your repairs will cost considerably less than what you pay for the contract—if not, they wouldn't be in business.

Here are some important questions to ask before buying a service contract:

How reputable is the company responsible for the contract? If the company offering the contract goes out of business, you will be out of luck. The company may be required to be insured, but find out if they actually are and by whom. Check with your Better Business Bureau or office of consumer affairs if you are not sure of a company's reputation. Service contracts from car and insurance companies are more likely to remain in effect than those from independent companies.

Exactly what does the contract cover and for how long? Service contracts vary considerably—different items are covered and different time limits are offered. This is true even among service contracts offered by the same company. For example, one company has plans that range from 4 years/36,000 miles maximum coverage to 6 years/100,000 miles maximum coverage, with other options for only power train coverage. Make sure you know what components are covered because if a breakdown occurs on a part that is not covered, you are responsible for the repairs.

If you plan to resell your car in a few years, you won't want to purchase a long-running service contract. Some service contracts automatically cancel when you resell the car, while others require a hefty transfer fee before extending privileges to the new owner.

Some automakers offer a "menu" format, which lets you pick the items you want covered in your service contract. Find out if the contract pays for preventive maintenance, towing, and rental car expenses. If not written into the contract, assume they are not covered.

Make sure the contract clearly specifies how you can reach the company. Knowing this before you purchase a service contract can save you time and aggravation in the future.

How will the repair bills be paid? It is best to have the service contractor pay bills directly. Some contracts require you to pay the repair bill, and reimburse you later.

Where can the car be serviced? Can you take the car to any mechanic if you have trouble on the road? What if you move?

What other costs can be expected? Most service contracts will have a deductible expense. Compare deductibles on various plans. Also, some companies charge the deductible for each individual repair while other companies pay per visit, regardless of the number of repairs being made.

What are your responsibilities? Make sure you know what you have to do to uphold the contract. For example if you have to follow the manufacturer's recommended maintenance, keep detailed records or the contract could be voided. You will find your specific responsibilities in the contact. Be sure to have the seller point them out.

SERVICE CONTRACTS VS. SAVINGS ACCOUNT

One alternative to buying a service contract is to deposit the cost of the contract into a savings account. If the car needs a major repair not covered by your warranty, the money in your account will cover the cost. Most likely, you'll be building up a down payment for your next car!

TIPS FOR DEALING WITH A MECHANIC

Call around. Don't choose a shop simply because it's nearby. Calling a few shops may turn up estimates cheaper by half.

Don't necessarily go for the lowest price. A good rule is to eliminate the highest and lowest estimates; the mechanic with the highest estimate is probably charging too much, and the lowest may be cutting too many corners.

Check the shop's reputation. Call your local consumer affairs agency and the Better Business Bureau. They don't have records on every shop, but unfavorable reports on a shop should disqualify it.

Look for certification. Mechanics can be certified by the National Institute for Automotive Service Excellence, an industry-wide yardstick for competence. Certification is offered in eight areas of repair and shops with certified mechanics are allowed to advertise this fact. However, make sure the mechanic working on your car is certified for the repair you need.

Take a look around. A well-kept shop reflects pride in workmanship. A skilled and efficient mechanic would probably not work in a messy shop.

Don't sign a blank check. The service order you sign should have specific instructions or describe your vehicle's symptoms. Avoid signing a vague work order. Be sure you are called for final approval before the shop does extra work. Many states require a written estimate signed by you and require that the shop get your permission for repairs that exceed the estimate by 10%.

Show interest. Ask about the repair. But don't act like an expert if you don't really understand what's wrong. Express your satisfaction. If you're happy with the work, compliment the mechanic and ask for him or her the next time you come in. You will get to know each other and the mechanic will get to know your vehicle.

Take a test-drive. Before you pay for a major repair, you should take the car for a test-drive. The few extra minutes you spend checking out the repair could save you a trip back to the mechanic. If you find that the problem still exists, there will be no question that the repair wasn't properly completed.

REPAIR PROTECTION BY CREDIT CARD

Paying your auto repair bills by credit card can provide a much needed recourse if you are having problems with an auto mechanic. According to federal law, you have the right to withhold payment for sloppy or incorrect repairs. Of course, you may withhold no more than the amount of the repair in dispute.

In order to use this right, you must first try to work out the problem with the mechanic. Also, unless the credit card company owns the repair shop (this might be the case with gasoline credit cards used at gas stations), two other conditions must be met. First, the repair shop must be in your home state (or within 100 miles of your current address), and second, the cost of repairs must be over $50. Until the problem is settled or resolved in court, the credit card company cannot charge you interest or penalties on the amount in dispute.

If you decide to take action, send a letter to the credit card company and a copy to the repair shop, explaining the details of the problem and what you want as settlement. Send the letter by certified mail with a return receipt requested.

Sometimes the credit card company or repair shop will attempt to put a "bad mark" on your credit record if you use this tactic. Legally, you can't be reported as delinquent if you've given the credit card company notice of your dispute, but a creditor can report that you are disputing your bill, which goes in your record. However, you have the right to challenge any incorrect information and add your side of the story to your file.

For more information, write to the Federal Trade Commission, Credit Practices Division, 601 Pennsylvania Avenue, NW, Washington, DC 20580.

TIRES

TIRE RATINGS

Buying tires has become an infrequent task because today's radial tires last much longer than the tires of the past. Surprisingly, a tire has to perform more functions simultaneously than any other part of the car (steering, bearing the load, cushioning the ride, and stopping).

Because comparing tires is difficult, many consumers mistakenly use price and brand name to determine quality. Because there are hundreds of tire lines to choose from, and only a few tire manufacturers, the difference in many tires may only be the brand name.

But there is help. The U.S. government requires tires to be rated according to their safety and expected mileage.

Treadwear, traction, and heat resistance grades are printed on the sidewall and are attached to the tire on a paper label. Ask the dealer for the grades of the tires they sell. Using this rating system, a sampling of top rated tires follows on page 48.

Treadwear: The treadwear grade gives you an idea of the mileage you can expect from a tire. It is shown in numbers–720, 700, 680, 660, and so forth. Higher numbers mean longer tire life. A tire with a grade of 600 should give you twice as much mileage as one rated 300. Use the treadwear grade as a relative basis of comparison.

Traction: Traction grades of AA, A, B, and C describe the tire's ability to stop on wet surfaces. Tires graded AA will stop on a wet road in a shorter distance than tires graded B or C. Tires rated C have poor traction.

Heat Resistance: Heat resistance is graded A, B, and C. An A rating means the tire will run cooler than one rated B or C and be less likely to fail if driven over long distances at highway speeds. Tires that run cooler tend to be more fuel-efficient. Hot-running tires can result in blow-outs or tread separation.

TIRE CARE

Pump 'em Up: An estimated one-third of us are driving on underinflated tires. Because even good tires lose air, it is important to check your tire pressure monthly. Underinflated tires can be dangerous, use more fuel and cause premature tire failure. When checking your tires, be sure to use an accurate gauge and inflate to the pressure indicated in your owner's manual, not the maximum pressure printed on your tire.

When to Replace: If any part of Lincoln's head is visible when you insert the top of a penny into a tread groove, it's time to replace the tire. While this old rule of thumb is still valid, today's tires also have a built-in wear indicator. A series of horizontal bars appear across the surface when the tread depth reaches the danger zone.

GETTING THE BEST PRICE

The price of the same tire can vary depending on where you shop so shopping around is vital to finding a good buy. Most tire ads appear in the sports section of your Wednesday and Saturday daily newspaper. You are most likely to find the best prices at independent tire dealers who carry a variety of tire brands.

The price of a tire is based on its size, and tires come in as many as nine sizes. For example, the list price of the same tire can range from $74.20 to $134.35, depending on its size.

To get the best buy:

1. Check to see which manufacturer makes the least expensive "off brand." Only a few manufacturers produce the over 1,800 types of tires sold in the U.S.

2. Don't forget to compare balancing and mounting costs. These extra charges can add up to more than $25 or be offered at no cost.

3. Never pay list price for a tire. A good rule of thumb is to pay at least 30-40 percent off the suggested list price.

4. Use the treadwear grade the same way you would the "unit price" in a supermarket. The tire with the lowest cost per grade point is the best value. For example, if tire A costs $100 and has a treadwear grade of 600, and tire B costs $80 and has a treadwear grade of 300, tire A is the better buy, even though its initial cost is more.

Tire A: $100÷600=$0.17 per point
Tire B: $80÷300=$0.27 per point

Where you live is a key factor in how long your tires will last. In addition to construction and design, tire wear is affected by the level of abrasive material in the road surface. Generally, the road surfaces of the West Coast, Great Lakes region, and northern New England are easiest on tires. The Appalachian and Rocky Mountain areas are usually hardest on tires.

HOW TO READ A TIRE

Tire Type and Size: The most important information on a tire are the letters and the numbers indicating its type and size.

1. Tire Type: The P at the beginning of the tire size indicates that the tire is a passenger vehicle tire. LT indicates light truck tire, and T indicates a temporary or spare tire.

2. Tire Width is the first part of the number and is measured in millimeters, from sidewall to sidewall.

3. Tire Height is the next number and tells you the height of the tire from the bead to the tread. This is described as a percentage of the tire width. In our example, the tire's height is 65 percent of its width. The smaller the aspect ratio, the wider the tire in relation to its height.

4. Tire Construction designates how the tire was made. R indicates radial construction which is the most common type. Older tires were made using diagonal bias D or bias belted B construction, but these tire types are no longer used on passenger vehicles.

5. Wheel Diameter identifies the wheel rim diameter (in inches-15) needed for this tire.

6. Load Index: The load rating indicates the maximum load for that tire. A higher number indicates a higher load capacity. The rating 95, for example, corresponds to a load capacity of 1521 pounds. Larger vehicles, SUVs and pickups need tires with a higher load capacity.

Labels around tire diagram:
1. Tire Type
2. Width
3. Height
4. Construction
5. Wheel Diameter
6. Load Index
7. Speed Rating
9. U.S. DOT Tire Identification Number
10. Tire ply composition and material
11. Treadwear, traction, and temperature grades
12. Max. Load
13. Max. Pressure

P215/65R15 95H
TIRE NAME
MANUFACTURER
TREADWEAR 220 TRACTION A TEMPERATURE A

7. Speed Rating indicates the maximum speed that the tire can sustain a ten minute endurance test without being in danger. All passenger car tires are rated at least S and pass the test at speeds up to 112 mph. Other ratings are as follows: T up to 118 mph, H up to 130 mph, V up to 149 mph and Z 150 mph or higher. Other types of tires, temporary spares and snow tires are lower on the rating scale.

8. Severe Conditions: M+S indicates the tire meets the Rubber Manu. Association's definition of a mud and snow tire. There are no performance tests for this standard. If the tire has an M+S and a "mountain and snowflake" symbol then the traction is at least 10% better than the regular version of the tire. These symbols are not in the above example.

9. Tire Identification Number
Example: DOT NJ HR 2AF 5212
The letters DOT certify compliance with all applicable safety standards established by the U.S. Department of Transportation. The next four characters is a code where the first two characters indicate the manufacturer and the second two characters indicate the plant where the tire was made.

Next you may see an optional string of three to four characters. Most manufacturers use these to record company specific information they use to identify their products or that can be used to identify tires in the market for recall purposes.

The last four digits determine the week and year the tire was made. The digits 5212 would signify that the tire was made during the 52nd week of 2012. Don't buy tires more than two years old. Tires naturally degrade with age, so you want the newest possible tires for the longest life (and safe operation.)

10. Tire Ply Composition and Material indicates the type of cord (polyester or steel) and number of plies in the tire, 4-ply, 6-ply, 8-ply, for both the tread and the sidewall.

11. Treadwear, Traction and Temperature Grades are three performance grades assigned to the tire and are the best way to truly evaluate the tires expected performance in these three critical areas. See page 46 for more information.

12. Max Load Limit tells you the cold inflation load limit in lbs. (pounds) and in kg (kilograms). The number corresponds to the load index.

13. Max Pressure is the maximum recommended pressure in psi (pounds per square inch) and in kPa (kilopascals). However, this is not the tire pressure for your car. You must check your owner's manual for the proper tire pressure for the tires on your car.

A Sampling of Top Rated Tires

Brand Name	Model	Description	Traction	Heat	Treadwear
Michelin	Hydroedge	ALL	A	B	760
Goodyear	Assurance Tripletred	ALL	A	B	740
Vogue	Wide Trac Touring LI	S-Rated	A	B	720
Cooper	Lifeliner STE	ALL	A	B	700
Cordovan	Grand Spirit Touring LS	ALL	A	B	700
Mastercraft	Touring LX	ALL	A	B	700
Toyo	800 Ultra	ALL	A	B	700
Michelin	X One With Durablack	ALL	A	B	700
Michelin	Cross Terrain Suv S-SP Rated	ALL	A	B	700
Big O	Legacy Tour Plus	P185,195,205 & 215/70R14 T	A	B	700
Big O	Legacy Tour Plus	P205,215/65R15 T	A	B	700
Big O	Legacy Tour Plus	P205,215,225 & 235/70R15 T	A	B	700
Big O	Legacy Tour Plus	P255 & 215/60R16 T	A	B	700
Big O	Legacy Tour Plus	P215/65R16 T	A	B	700
Big O	Legacy Tour Plus	P195/65R14 T	A	B	700
Big O	Legacy Tour Plus	P195/65R15 T	A	B	700
Mentor	Vantage Touring LE	ALL	A	B	700
Co-op	Goldenmark Luxury Touring (T)	ALL	A	B	700
Multi-Mile	Excel	ALL	A	B	700
Cordovan	Century	ALL	A	B	700
Bridgestone	Turanza LS "T"	ALL	A	B	700
Monarch	Ultra Tour LS	ALL	A	B	700
Lee	Ultra Tour LS	ALL	A	B	700
Kelly	Navigator Platinum TE	ALL Except	A	B	700
Republic	Ultra Tour LS	ALL	A	B	700
National	Ovation	P235/75R15	A	B	700
Delta	Esteem XLE	P235/75R15	A	B	700
Laramie	Grandeur Touring GT 60/65/70 Series	14-16	A	B	700
Jetzon	Grandeur Touring GT 60/65/70 Series	14-16	A	B	700
Telstar	Grandeur Touring GT 60/65/70 Series	14-16	A	B	700
Neutral	Touring LST	ALL Others	A	B	700
Goodyear	Assurance Comfortred	ALL	A	B	700
Bridgestone	Dueler HL Alenza T-Rated	ALL	A	B	700
Michelin	X Radial	ALL	A	B	680
National	Ovation	ALL 15 Except	A	B	680
Delta	Esteem XLE 70 & 75 Series	ALL 15 Except	A	B	680
Michelin	Harmony	ALL	A	B	680
Michelin	Destiny	ALL	A	B	680
Michelin	Agility	ALL	A	B	680
Big O	Legacy Tour Plus 60/65/70 Series	14-16	A	B	660
Riken	Raptor Touring Edition 70/75 Series	P205+	A	B	660
American	Gold Tour Plus 70/75 Series	P205+	A	B	660
Cavalier	Primera 70/75 Series	P205+	A	B	660
Trivant	Primera 70/75 Series	P205+	A	B	660
Co-op	Goldenmark Luxury Touring (S)	ALL	A	B	660
National	Ovation 70 & 75 Series	ALL 14	A	B	660
Delta	Esteem XLE 70 & 75 Series	ALL 14	A	B	660
Neutral	Touring LST 75 Series	ALL	A	B	660
Mastercraft	Touring LX	13 Only	A	B	640
Goodyear	Aquatred 3	ALL Others	AA	B	640
BFGoodrich	The Advantage Plus 70/75 Series	ALL	A	B	640
Hallmark	Ultra Touring GT	ALL	A	B	640
Lee	Ultra Touring GT	ALL	A	B	640
Riken	Raptor Touring Edition 70/75 Series	Thru P195	A	B	640
Cooper	Lifeliner STE	13	A	B	640
Sigma	Supreme Touring S-Series	ALL Others	A	B	640

For a complete listing of all the tires on the market, you can call the Auto Safety Hot Line toll free, at 888-327-4236 or 800-424-9153(TTY). Or, go to www.safercar.gov

WARNING

As tires age, they naturally dry out and can become potentially dangerous. Some experts recommend getting rid of a six-year-old tire no matter what condition it is in. Recently, a national news organization went undercover and found 12 year old tires for sale, so be sure to check your tire date before purchasing. Ask for tires that are less than one year old.

Insurance is a big part of ownership expenses, yet it's often forgotten in the show-room. As you shop, remember that the car's design and accident history may affect your insurance rates. Some cars cost less to insure because experience has shown that they are damaged less, less expensive to fix after a collision, or stolen less.

Shop Around: You can save hundreds of dollars by shopping around for insurance.

There are a number of factors that determine what coverage will cost you. A car's design can affect both the chances and severity of an accident. For example, a well-designed bumper may escape damage in a low-speed crash. Some cars are easier to repair than others or may have less expensive parts. Cars with four doors tend to be damaged less than cars with two doors.

Other factors that effect your insurance costs include:

Your Annual Mileage: The more you drive, the more your vehicle will be "exposed" to a potential accident. Driving less than 7,500 miles per year often gets a discount. Ask your insurer if they offer this option.

Where You Drive: If you regularly drive and park in the city, you will most likely pay more than if you drive in rural areas.

Youthful Drivers: Usually the highest premiums are paid by male drivers under the age of 25. Whether or not the under-25-year-old male is married also affects insurance rates. (Married males pay less.) As the driver gets older, rates are lowered.

Insurance discounts and surcharges depend upon the way a vehicle is traditionally driven. Sports cars, for example, are usually surcharged due, in part, to the typical driving habits of their owners. Four-door sedans and station wagons generally merit discounts.

Not all companies offer discounts or surcharges, and many cars receive neither. Some companies offer a discount or impose a surcharge on collision premiums only. Others apply discounts and surcharges on both collision and comprehensive coverage. Discounts and surcharges usually range from 10–30 percent. Remember that one company may offer a discount on a particular car while another may not.

TYPES OF COVERAGE

Collision Insurance: This pays for the damage to your car after an accident.

Comprehensive Physical Damage Insurance: This pays for damages when your car is stolen or damaged by fire, flood, or other perils.

Property Damage Liability: This pays claims and defense costs if your car damages someone else's property.

Medical Payments Insurance: This pays for your car's occupants' medical expenses resulting from an accident.

Bodily Injury Liability: This provides money to pay claims against you and to pay for the cost of your legal defense if your car injures or kills someone.

Uninsured Motorists Protection: This pays for injuries caused by an uninsured or a hit-and-run driver.

REDUCING INSURANCE COSTS

Get Your Discounts: After you have shopped around and found the best deal by comparing the costs of different coverages, be sure you get all the discounts you are entitled to.

Most insurance companies offer discounts of 5-30 percent on various parts of your insurance bill. Ask your insurance company for a complete list of the discounts that it offers. These can vary by company and from state to state.

Here are some of the most common insurance discounts:

Driver Education/Defensive Driving Courses: Discounts for completing a state-approved driver education course can mean a $40 reduction in the cost of coverage. Discounts of 5–15 percent are available in some states to those who complete a defensive driving course.

Good Student Discounts of up to 25 percent for full-time high school or college students who are in the upper 20 percent of their class, on the dean's list, or have a B or better grade point average.

Good Driver Discounts are available to drivers with an accident and violation-free record, (or no incidents in 3 years).

Mature Driver Credit: Drivers ages 50 and older may qualify for up to a 10 percent discount or a lower price bracket.

Sole Female Driver: Some companies offer discounts of 10 percent for females, ages 30 to 64, who are the only driver in a household.

Non-Drinkers and Non-Smokers: A limited number of companies offer incentives ranging from 10–25 percent to those who abstain.

Farmer Discounts: Many companies offer farmers either a discount of 10–30 percent or a lower price bracket.

! DON'T SPEED !

Besides endangering the lives of your passengers and other drivers, speeding tickets will increase your insurance premium. It only takes one speeding ticket to lose your "preferred" or "good driver" discount, which requires a clean driving record. Two or more speeding tickets or accidents can increase your premium by 40% to 200%. Some insurers may simply drop your coverage. According to the Insurance Institute for Highway Safety (IIHS), you are 17% more likely to be in an accident if you have just one speeding ticket. Insurance companies know this and will charge you for it.

YOUNG DRIVERS

Each year, teenagers account for about 15 percent of highway deaths. According to the Insurance Institute for Highway Safety (IIHS), the highest driver death rate per 100,000 people is among 18-year-olds. Parents need to make sure their children are fully prepared to be competent, safe drivers before letting them out on the road. All states issue learner's permits. However, only 35 states and the District of Columbia require permits before getting a driver's license. It isn't difficult for teenagers to get a license and only 14 states prohibit teenagers from driving during night and early morning. Call your state's MVA for young driver laws.

Car Pooling: Commuters sharing driving may qualify for discounts of 5–25 percent or a lower price bracket.

Children away at school don't drive the family car very often, so if they're on your policy and they're at school, let your company know. If you insure them separately, discounts of 10–40 percent or a lower price bracket are available.

Desirable Cars: Premiums are usually much higher for cars with high collision rates or that are the favorite target of thieves.

Anti-Theft Device Credits: Discounts of 5-15 percent are offered in some states for cars equipped with a hood lock and an alarm or a disabling device (active or passive) that prevents the car from being started.

Multipolicy and Multicar Policy Discount: Some companies offer discounts of up to 10–20 percent for insuring your home and auto with the same company, or more than one car.

First Accident Allowance: Some insurers offer a "first accident allowance," which guarantees that if a customer achieves five accident-free years, his or her rates won't go up after the first at-fault accident.

Deductibles: Opting for the largest reasonable deductible is the obvious first step in reducing premiums. Increasing your deductible to $500 from $200 could cut your collision premium about 20 percent. Raising the deductible to $1,000 from

$200 could lower your premium about 45 percent. The discounts may vary by company.

Collision Coverage: The older the car, the less the need for collision insurance. Consider dropping collision insurance entirely on an older car. Regardless of how much coverage you carry, the insurance company will only pay up to the car's "book value." For example, if your car requires $1,000 in

repairs, but its "book value" is only $500, the insurance company is required to pay only $500.

Organizations: If you are a member of AARP, AAA, the military, a union, a professional group, an alumni association, or similar organization, you may be able to get a discount. Often insurance companies will enter joint ventures with organizations.

AUTO THEFT

The Highway Loss Data Institute (HLDI) regularly compiles statistics on motor vehicle thefts. Using the frequency of theft claims per 1,000 insured vehicles, the HLDI lists the following as the most and least stolen vehicles among the 2008-2010 models.

Most Stolen	Claim Frequency*
Ford F-250 crew 4WD	7.0
Chevrolet Silverado 1500 crew	6.7
Chevrolet Avalanche 1500	6.1
GMC Sierra 1500 crew	6.0
Ford F-350 crew 4WD	5.6
Cadillac Escalade 4WD	5.5
Chevrolet Suburban 1500	5.4
GMC Sierra 1500 extended cab	4.7
GMC Yukon	4.5
Chevrolet Tahoe	4.4

Least Stolen	Claim Frequency*
Dodge Journey 4WD	0.4
Volkswagen Tiguan 4WD	0.4
Audi A4 4-door	0.4
Acura RDX	0.4
Toyota Matrix	0.4
Lexus HS 250 hybrid 4-door	0.4
Honda CR-V	0.4
Hyundai Tucson 4WD	0.4
Toyota Sienna 4WD	0.5
Jeep Compass 4WD	0.5
Average All Passenger Vehicles	**1.2**

*Claim Frequency means the number of vehicles stolen per 1000 insured vehicles, for example about 7 Ford F-250s are stolen or broken into for every 1,000 insured. Source: Highway Loss Data Institute (www.iihs.org)

BUMPERS

The main purpose of the bumper is to protect your car in low-speed collisions. Despite this intention, many of us have been victims of a $500-$3500 repair bill resulting from a seemingly minor impact. The federal government used to require that automakers equip cars with bumpers capable of withstanding up to 5 mph crashes with no damage. Unfortunately, in the early eighties, under pressure from car companies, the government rolled back this requirement. Now, the federal law only requires car companies to build bumpers that protect cars in 2.5 mph collisions-about the speed at which we walk. This rollback enables the car companies to sell lots of expensive parts, and has cost consumers millions of dollars in increased insurance premiums and repair costs.

The state of California requires that companies disclose which bumpers meet the old 5 mph standard. Unfortunately, few, if any, California cars contain this disclosure.

In order to see how well bumpers actually protect our vehicles, the Insurance Institute for Highway Safety conducts a variety of bumper tests. In their low speed (6 mph) tests, it's shocking how poorly bumpers protect vehicles. In these tests, it can easily cost $2-$3,700 after a low speed fender bender.

Unfortunately, we can't simply look at a bumper and determine how good it will be at doing its job-protecting a car from inevitable bumps. The solution to this problem is quite simple—require carmakers to tell the consumer the highest speed at which their car could be crashed with no damage.

Federal standards *do* require that car bumpers be designed to match up to each other in a collision. This is an attempt to enable the bumpers to hit each other and absorb the energy of the crash rather than other parts of the car. Unfortunately there is a big hole in this federal requirement because SUVs, pickups, and minivans don't have to meet the same bumper height rules as cars. With such a high percentage of SUVs, pickups and minivans on the road, huge bumper mismatches in crashes are quite common. Mismatching between cars and SUVs results in excessive damage and pricey repairs.

In order to see how well bumpers actually function in car and SUV collisions, the Insurance Institute for Highway Safety conducted two types of tests at 10 mph; one with an SUV hitting the rear of a car and one with a car traveling at 10 mph and crashing into the rear of an SUV. For more results, visit the Insurance Institute for Highway Safety at www.iihs.org. The table below shows how much this bumper mismatch problem can cost you.

DAMAGE REPAIR COSTS IN 10 MPH FRONT-INTO-

Source: Insurance Institute for Highway Safety

REAR CRASH TESTS

SUV INTO CAR	SUV Damage	Car Damage	Total Damage
Honda CR-V into Honda Civic	$1,721	$1,274	$2,995
Toyota RAV4 into Toyota Corolla	$1,434	$2,327	$3,761
Hyundai Tucson into Kia Forte	$850	$3,223	$4,073
Volkswagen Tiguan into Volkswagen Golf	$2,329	$2,058	$4,387
Jeep Patriot into Dodge Caliber	$1,415	$3,095	$4,510
Ford Escape into Ford Focus	$1,470	$3,386	$4,856
Nissan Rogue into Nissan Sentra	$2,884	$4,560	$7,444

CAR INTO SUV	Car Damage	SUV Damage	Total Damage
Kia Forte into Hyundai Tucson	$1,510	$2,091	$3,601
Dodge Caliber into Jeep Patriot	$2,559	$1,338	$3,897
Honda Civic into Honda CR-V	$4,921	$1,053	$5,974
Volkswagen Golf into Volkswagen Tiguan	$4,555	$1,872	$6,427
Nissan Sentra into Nissan Rogue	$5,114	$1,428	$6,542
Ford Focus into Ford Escape	$5,203	$2,208	$7,411
Corolla into Toyota RAV4	$3,852	$6,015	$9,867

See www.IIHS.org

COMPLAINTS

Americans spend billions of dollars on vehicle repairs every year. While many of those repairs are satisfactory, there are times when getting your vehicle fixed can be a very difficult process. In fact, vehicle defects and repairs are the number one cause of consumer complaints, according to the Federal Trade Commission. This chapter is designed to help you resolve your complaint, whether it's for a new vehicle still under warranty or for one you've had for years. In addition, we offer a guide to arbitration, the names and addresses of consumer groups, federal agencies, and the manufacturers themselves. Finally, we tell you how to take the important step of registering your complaint with the U.S. Department of Transportation.

No matter what your complaint, keep accurate records. Copies of the following items are indispensable in helping to resolve your problems:

☑ your service invoices

☑ bills you have paid

☑ letters you have written to the manufacturer or the repair facility owner

☑ written repair estimates from your independent mechanic.

☑ notes on discussion with company representatives including names and dates.

RESOLVING COMPLAINTS

Here are some basic steps to help you resolve your problem:

1 First, return your vehicle to the repair facility that did the work. Bring a written list of the problems and make sure that you keep a copy of the list. Give the repair facility a reasonable opportunity to examine your vehicle and attempt to fix it. Speak directly to the service manager (not to the service writer who wrote up your repair order), and ask him or her to test drive the vehicle with you so that you can point out the problem.

2 If that doesn't resolve the problem, take the vehicle to a diagnostic center for an independent examination. This may cost $45 to $60. Get a written statement defining the problem and outlining how it may be fixed. Give your repair shop a copy. If your vehicle is under warranty, do not allow any warranty repair by an independent mechanic; you may not be reimbursed by the manufacturer.

3 If your repair shop does not respond to the independent assessment, present your problem to a mediation panel. These panels hear both sides of the story and try to come to a resolution.

If the problem is with a new vehicle dealer, or if you feel that the manufacturer is responsible, you may be able to use one of the manufacturer's mediation programs.

If the problem is solely with an independent dealer, a local Better Business Bureau (BBB) may be able to mediate your complaint. It may also offer an arbitration hearing. In any case, the BBB should enter your complaint into its files on that establishment.

When contacting any mediation program, determine how long the process takes, who makes the final decision, whether you are bound by that decision, and whether the program handles all problems or only warranty complaints.

4 If there are no mediation programs in your area, contact private consumer groups, local government agencies, or your local "action line" newspaper columnist, newspaper editor, or radio/TV broadcaster. A phone call or letter from them may persuade a repair facility to take action. Send a copy of your letter to the repair shop.

5 One of your last resorts is to bring a lawsuit against the dealer, manufacturer, or repair facility in small claims court. The fee for filing such an action is usually small, and you generally act as your own attorney, saving attorney's fees. There is a monetary limit on the amount you can claim, which varies from state to state. Your local consumer affairs office, state attorney general's office, or the clerk of the court can tell you how to file such a suit.

6 Finally, talk with an attorney. It's best to select an attorney who is familiar with handling automotive problems. Call the lawyer referral service listed in the telephone directory and ask for the names of attorneys who deal with automobile problems. If you can't afford an attorney, contact the Legal Aid Society.

WARRANTY COMPLAINTS
If your vehicle is under warranty or you are having problems with a factory-authorized dealership, here are some special guidelines:

1 Have the warranty available to show the dealer. Make sure you call the problem to the dealer's attention before the end of the warranty period.

2 If you are still dissatisfied after giving the dealer a reasonable opportunity to fix your vehicle, contact the manufacturer's representative (also called the zone representative) in your area. This person can authorize the dealer to make repairs or take other steps to resolve the dispute. Your dealer will have your zone representative's name and telephone number. Explain the problem and ask for a meeting and a personal inspection of your vehicle.

3 If you can't get satisfaction from the zone representative, call or write the manufacturer's owner relations department. Your owner's manual contains this phone number and address. In each case, as you move up the chain, indicate the steps you have already taken and keep careful records of your efforts.

4 Your next option is to present your problem to a complaint handling panel or to the arbitration program in which the manufacturer of your vehicle participates.

If you complain of a problem during the warranty period, you have a right to have the problem fixed even after the war-

ranty runs out. If your warranty has not been honored, you may be able to "revoke acceptance," which means that you return the vehicle to the dealer. If you are successful, you may be entitled to a replacement vehicle or to a full refund of the purchase price and reimbursement of legal fees under the Magnuson-Moss Warranty Act. Or, if you are covered by one of the state lemon laws, you may be able to return the vehicle and receive a refund or replacement from the manufacturer.

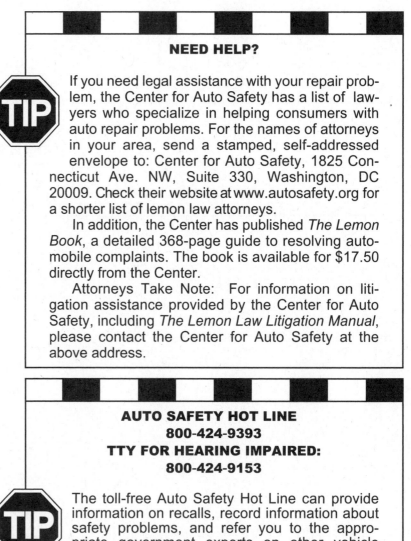

NEED HELP?

If you need legal assistance with your repair problem, the Center for Auto Safety has a list of lawyers who specialize in helping consumers with auto repair problems. For the names of attorneys in your area, send a stamped, self-addressed envelope to: Center for Auto Safety, 1825 Connecticut Ave. NW, Suite 330, Washington, DC 20009. Check their website at www.autosafety.org for a shorter list of lemon law attorneys.

In addition, the Center has published *The Lemon Book*, a detailed 368-page guide to resolving automobile complaints. The book is available for $17.50 directly from the Center.

Attorneys Take Note: For information on litigation assistance provided by the Center for Auto Safety, including *The Lemon Law Litigation Manual*, please contact the Center for Auto Safety at the above address.

AUTO SAFETY HOT LINE
800-424-9393
TTY FOR HEARING IMPAIRED:
800-424-9153

The toll-free Auto Safety Hot Line can provide information on recalls, record information about safety problems, and refer you to the appropriate government experts on other vehicle related problems. You can even have recall information mailed to you within 24 hours of your call at no charge. Most importantly, you can call the hot line to report safety problems which will become part of the National Highway Traffic Safety Administration's complaint database.

COMPLAINT INDEX

Thanks to the efforts of the Center for Auto Safety, we are able to provide you with the vehicle complaints on file with the National Highway Traffic Safety Administration (NHTSA). Each year, thousands of Americans file online or call the government in order to register complaints about their vehicles.

The complaint index is the result of our analysis of these complaints. It is based on a ratio of the number of complaints for each vehicle to the sales of that vehicle. In order to predict the expected complaint performance of the 2014 models, we have examined the complaint history of that car's series. The term series refers to the fact that when a manufacturer introduces a new model, that vehicle remains essentially unchanged, on average, for four to six years. For example, the Cadillac Escalade was redesigned in 2002 and remains essentially the same car for 2014. As such, we have compiled the complaint experience for that series in order to give you some information to use in deciding which car to buy. For vehicles introduced or significantly changed in 2014, we do not yet have enough data to develop a complaint index.

The following table presents the projected best and worst complaint ratings for the 2014 models for which we can develop ratings. Higher index numbers mean the vehicle generated a greater number of complaints. Lower numbers indicate fewer complaints.

2014 PROJECTED COMPLAINT INDEX

THE BEST	INDEX*
Mitsubishi Outlander Sport	0
Infiniti Q60	143
Mazda Mazda2	287
Toyota Yaris	443
Buick Encore	628
Infiniti QX70	628
Lincoln Navigator	686
Cadillac Escalade ESV	735
GMC Sierra	803
BMW 6 Series	804
Mercedes Benz E-Class	876
Scion xD	931
Scion tC	953
Mazda MX-5 Miata	961
Nissan Juke	971
Lexus ES	997
Toyota Prius C	1,119
Lexus RX	1,128
Audi A5	1,150
Cadillac XTS	1,127
Audi Q7	1,229

THE WORST	INDEX*
Nissan Pathfinder	29,527
Infiniti QX60	23,691
Hyundai Santa Fe	23,657
Ford Focus	13,179
Cadillac ATS	11,181
Hyundai Veloster	11,071
Ford C-MAX	10,221
Toyota Prius	9,352
Subaru BRZ	9,304
Jeep Wrangler	9,236
Nissan Altima	9,231
Chevrolet Volt	8,868
Nissan Leaf	8,314
Dodge Journey	8,038
Ford Fiesta	7,343
Kia Sorento	6,645
Hyundai Sonata	6,593
Mazda CX-5	6,419
Ford Escape	5,975
Scion FR-S	5,829

*IMPORTANT NOTE: The numbers represent relative index scores, not the number of complaints received. The complaint index score considers sales volume and years on the road. Lower index numbers are better.

CENTER FOR AUTO SAFETY

Every year automobile manufacturers spend millions of dollars making their voices heard in government decision making. For example, General Motors and Ford have large staffs in Detroit and Washington that work solely to influence government activity. But who looks out for the consumer?

For over 40 years, the nonprofit Center for Auto Safety (CAS) has told the consumer's story to government agencies, to Congress, and to the courts. Along with countless recalls, CAS got airbags in every car and lemon laws in every state.

CAS was established in 1970 by Ralph Nader and Consumers Union. As consumer concerns about auto safety issues expanded, so did the work of CAS. CAS' activities include:

Initiating Safety Recalls: CAS analyzes over 20,000 consumer complaints each year. CAS requests government investigations and recalls of defective vehicles. CAS was responsible for the Ford Pinto faulty gas tank recall, the Firestone 500 steel-belted radial tire recall, the record recall of over three million Evenflo One Step child seats, and Jeep Grand Cherokees with Pinto like fuel systems. Other CAS influenced recalls include Fords with transmissions that jump out of park, Toyota unintended acceleration, exploding Honda airbags, Ford cruise control switch fires and many others.

Representing the Consumer in Washington: CAS follows the activities of federal agencies and Congress to ensure that they carry out their responsibilities to the American taxpayer. CAS brings a consumer's point of view to vehicle safety policies and rule-making. Since 1970, CAS has submitted more than 500 petitions and comments on federal safety standards.

One major effort on safety standards has been the successful fight to get airbags in every car. After opposing airbags for decades, the auto industry now can't get enough lifesaving airbags in cars with some models having ten airbags. With airbags to protect consumers in front and side crashes, CAS worked to strengthen weak roofs that crush in rollovers. Beginning in 2013, vehicles will have roofs more than twice as strong as before. Between stronger roofs and Electronic Stability Control deaths and serious injuries in rollovers have already decreased by more than 30% from 27,000 in 2005.

In the 1990's, CAS uncovered a fire defect that dwarfed the highly publicized flammability of the Ford Pinto. Side saddle gas tanks on full size 1973–87 GM pickups and 1988–90 crew cabs can explode on impact. Over 2,000 people have been killed in fire crashes involving these trucks. After mounting a national campaign to warn consumers to steer clear of these GM fire hazards, the Department of Transportation granted CAS' petition and conducted one of its biggest defect investigations in history. The result—GM was asked to recall its pickups. GM, sadly, denied this request and was left off with a $50 million slap on the wrist.

Exposing Secret Warranties: CAS played a prominent role in the disclosure of secret warranties, "policy adjustments," as they are called by manufacturers. These occur when an automaker agrees to pay for repair of certain defects beyond the warranty period but refuses to notify consumers. Thanks to years of CAS prodding, DOT will soon be publishing every auto company Service Bulletin on its website with a index to guide consumes to secret warranties.

Lemon Laws: CAS' work on Lemon Laws aided in the enactment of state laws which make it easier to return a defective new automobile and get money back.

Tire Ratings: Consumers have reliable treadwear ratings to help them get the most miles for their dollar thanks to a CAS' lawsuit overturning DOT's revocation of this valuable tire information program.

Legal Action: When CAS has exhausted other means of obtaining relief for consumer problems, it initiates legal action. For example, in 1978 when the Department of Energy attempted to raise the price of unleaded gasoline four cents per gallon without notice or comment, CAS succeeded in stopping this illegal move through a lawsuit, thus

CENTER FOR AUTO SAFETY ONLINE

TIP The Center for Auto Safety has a website at www.autosafety.org to provide information to consumers and to organize consumer campaigns against auto companies on safety defects. Detailed information and advice on defects in specific makes and models are on CAS' website. Consumers with lemons can file online complaints with CAS and get referred to lemon lawyers.

www.autosafety.org

saving consumers $2 billion over 3-years.

A 1985 Center for Auto Safety lawsuit against the Environmental Protection Agency (EPA) forced the EPA to recall polluting cars, rather than let companies promise to make cleaner cars in the future. As part of the settlement, GM (which was responsible for the polluting cars) funded a $7 million methanol bus demonstration program in New York City.

In 2003, a CAS lawsuit forced the Department of Transportation to require auto companies to use more accurate tire pressure monitors on the vehicle dash that identified which tire had low pressure versus an indirect system that only told consumers they had low tire pressure on some tire.

CAS also challenges class actions settlements that don't deliver for consumers. We have knocked off coupon settlement after coupon settlement in which consumers got useless coupons to buy a new car while trial lawyers got cold cash. In 2010 we challenged a Honda Civic Hybrid gas mileage settlement that gave consumers a DVD on how to drive better. In 2009, we challenged a Ford Explorer rollover settlement that gave consumers a restricted $300-500 coupon toward a new $30,000 Ford that only 148 out of 1,000,000 class members redeemed while attorneys got $25 million in fees and costs.

CAS is your safety and lemon insurance. CAS depends on public support to do all its good work. Annual membership is $25. All contributions are tax-deductible. To contribute by credit card, go to the CAS website at: www.auto-safety.org/make-donation-cas.

To contribute by mail, send a check to: Center for Auto Safety, 1825 Connecticut Ave., NW #330, Washington, DC 20009-5708.

Consumer Groups and Government

Below are the names of additional consumer groups you may find helpful:

Advocates for Highway and Auto Safety
750 First St., NE, Suite 901
Washington, DC 20002
(202) 408-1711/408-1699 fax
www.saferoads.org
An alliance of consumer, health and safety groups and insurance companies.

Consumer Action
221 Main St., Suite 480
San Francisco, CA 94105
(415) 777-9635
www.consumer-action.org
Complaint handling and advocacy related to consumer rights.

Consumers for Auto Reliability and Safety
1303 J St., Suite 270
Sacramento, CA 95814
(530) 759-9440/www.carconsumers.org
Auto safety, airbags, and lemon laws.

KIDS AND CARS
10 Righters Ferry Rd.
Bala Cynwyd, PA 19004
(484) 278-4641
www.kidsandcars.org
Safety and advocacy related to protecting children in and around motor vehicles.

**Public Health Advocacy Institute
Motor Vehicle Hazard Archives Project**
www.AutoHazardInfo.org
mvhap_phai@yahoo.com
The Project's mission is to preserve and broaden access to historical and current information about motor vehicle hazards and injury control. The website offers free information about vehicle safety and motor vehicle hazard control.

SafetyBelt Safe, U.S.A.
P.O. Box 553
Altadena, CA 91003
(800) 745-SAFE, stombrella@carseat.org
www.carseat.org
Excellent information and training on child safety seats and safety belt usage.

S.A.N.E., Inc.
2470 N. Park Road, #209 South
Hollywood, FL 33021
(954) 989-1251/www.saferautos.org
namrissam@bellsouth.net
Advocates and distributes information for better driving behavior and vehicle safety.

Several federal agencies conduct automobile- related programs. Following is each agency with a description of the type of work it performs and how to contact them.

National Highway Traffic Safety Administration
1200 New Jersey Ave., SE, West Bldg.
Washington, DC 20590
(888) 327-4236/www.nhtsa.gov
www.safercar.gov
NHTSA issues safety and fuel economy standards for new motor vehicles; investigates safety defects and enforces recall of defective vehicles and equipment; conducts research and demonstration programs on vehicle safety, fuel economy, driver safety, and automobile inspection and repair; provides grants for state highway safety programs in areas such as police traffic services, driver education and licensing, emergency medical services, pedestrian safety, and alcohol abuse.

Environmental Protection Agency
1200 Pennsylvania Ave., NW
Washington, DC 20460
(202) 272-0167/www.epa.gov
www.fueleconomy.gov
EPA's responsibilities include setting and enforcing air and noise emission standards for motor vehicles and measuring fuel economy in new vehicles (EPA Fuel Economy Guide).

Federal Trade Commission
600 Pennsylvania Ave., NW
Washington, DC 20580
(202) 326-2222/www.ftc.gov
The FTC regulates advertising, credit practices, marketing abuses, and professional services and ensures that products are properly labeled (as in fuel economy ratings). The commission covers unfair or deceptive trade practices in motor vehicle sales and repairs, as well as non-safety defects.

U.S. Department of Justice
Consumer Protection Branch
950 Pennsylvania Ave., NW
Washington, DC 20503
(202) 514-2000
www.usdoj.gov/civil.feedback@doj.gov
The DOJ enforces federal law that requires manufacturers to label new automobiles and forbids removal or alteration of labels before delivery to consumers. Labels must contain make, model, vehicle identification number, dealer's name, suggested base price, manufacturer option costs, and manufacturer's suggested retail price.

AUTOMOBILE MANUFACTURERS

Acura (Division of Honda)
Jeff Conrad, Vice President-General Mgr.
See Honda for address
Customer Relations: 800-382-2238

Audi (Division of Volkswagen)
Scott Keogh, President
See Volkswagen for address
Customer Relations: 877-615-2834

BMW
Ludwig Willisch, President
300 Chestnut Ridge Road
Woodcliff Lake, NJ 07677-7731
Customer Relations: 800-831-1117

Buick (Division of General Motors)
P.O. Box 33136
Detroit, MI 48232-5136
Customer Relations: 800-521-7300

Cadillac (Division of General Motors)
P.O. Box 33169
Detroit, MI 48232-5169
Customer Relations: 800-458-8006

Chevrolet (Division of General Motors)
P.O. Box 33170
Detroit, MI 48232-5170
Customer Relations: 800-222-1020
Fax: 313-556-5108

Chrysler (Chrysler, Dodge, Jeep, Ram)
Sergio Marchionne, CEO
1000 Chrysler Drive
Auburn Hills, MI 48326
Customer Relations: 800-992-1997

Dodge (Division of Chrysler)
P.O. Box 21-8004
Auburn Hills, MI 48321-8007
Customer Relations: 800-423-6343

Fiat (Division of Chrysler)
P.O. Box 21-8004
Auburn Hills, MI 48321
Customer Relations: 888-242-6342

Ford (Ford, Lincoln)
Alan Mulally, President and CEO
P.O. Box 6248, Dearborn, MI 48126
Customer Relations: 800-392-3673

General Motors
(Buick, Cadillac, Chevrolet, GMC)
Daniel Akerson, Chairman and CEO
300 Renaissance Center
Detroit, MI 48265

GMC (Division of General Motors)
P.O. Box 33172
Detroit, MI 48232
Customer Relations: 800-462-8782

Honda (Honda, Acura)
Tetsuo Iwamura, President and CEO
1919 Torrance Blvd.
Torrance, CA 90501
Customer Relations: 800-999-1009

Hyundai
John Krafcik, President and CEO
3200 Park Center Dr
Costa Mesa, CA 92626
Customer Relations: 800-633-5151
E-mail: consumeraffairs@hmausa.com

Infiniti (Division of Nissan)
See Nissan for address and executive
Customer Relations: 800-647-7261

Jaguar, Land Rover
Andy Goss, President
555 MacArthur Blvd.
Mahwah, NJ 07430
Jag Customer Relations: 800-452-4827
Land Rover Cust. Relations: 800-637-6837

Jeep (Division of Chrysler)
P.O. Box 21-8004
Auburn Hills, MI 48321-8004
Customer Relations: 877-426-5337

Kia
Byung Mo Ahn, President and CEO
P.O. Box 52410
Irvine, CA 92619-2410
Customer Relations: 800-333-4542

Land Rover (See Jaguar)
Customer Relations: 800-637-6837
Fax: 201-760-8514

Lexus (Division of Toyota)
Mark Templin, VP and General Mgr.
P.O. Box 2991
Mail Drop L201
Torrance, CA 90509-2991
Customer Relations: 800-255-3987

Lincoln (Division of Ford)
Jim Farley, Executive Vice President
See Ford for address
Customer Relations: 800-521-4140

Mazda
Jim O' Sullivan, President and CEO
P.O. Box 19734
Irvine, CA 92623-9734
Customer Relations: 800-222-5500

Mercedes-Benz
Stephen Cannon, President and CEO
P.O. Box 350
Montvale, NJ 07645
Customer Relations: 800-367-6372

Mini (Division of BMW)
Jim McDowell, Vice President
P.O. Box 1227
Westwood, NJ 07675-1227
Customer Relations: 866-275-6464

Mitsubishi
Yoichi Yokozawa, President and CEO
P.O. Box 6400, Cypress, CA 90630-9998
Customer Relations: 888-648-7820

Nissan
Carlos Ghosn, President and CEO
P.O. Box 685003
Franklin, TN 37068-5003
Customer Relations: 800-647-7261

Porsche
Detlev von Platen, President and CEO
980 Hammond Dr., Suite 1000
Atlanta, GA 30328
Customer Relations: 800-767-7243

Ram (Division of Chrysler)
P.O. Box 21-8007
Auburn Hills, MI 48321-8004
Customer Relations: 866-726-4636

Scion (Division of Toyota)
Jack Hollis, Vice President
P.O. Box 2742
Torrence, CA 90509-2742
Customer Relations: 866-707-2466

Smart (Division of Mercedes-Benz)
Mark Webster, General Manager
See Mercedes-Benz for address
Customer Relations: 800-762-7887

Subaru
Takeshi Tachimori, President and CEO
Subaru Plaza
P.O. Box 6000
Cherry Hill, NJ 08034-6000
Customer Relations: 800-782-2783

Toyota (Toyota, Lexus, Scion)
Jim Lentz, President and CEO
19001 S. Western Ave.
Torrance, CA 90501
Customer Relations: 800-331-4331

Volkswagen
Jonathan Browning, President and CEO
2200 Ferdinand Porsche Dr.
Herndon, VA 20171
Customer Relations: 800-822-8987

Volvo
John Maloney, President and CEO
One Volvo Dr.
PO Box 914
Rockleigh, NJ 07647
Customer Relations: 800-458-1552

LEMON LAWS

Sometimes, despite our best efforts, we buy a vehicle that just doesn't work right. There may be little problem after little problem, or perhaps one big problem that never seems to be fixed. Because of the "sour" taste that such vehicles leave in the mouths of consumers who buy them, these vehicles are known as "lemons."

In the past, it's been difficult to obtain a refund or replacement if a vehicle was a lemon. The burden of proof was left to the consumer. Because it is hard to define exactly what constitutes a lemon, many lemon owners were unable to win a case against a manufacturer. And when they won, consumers had to pay for their attorneys giving them less than if they had traded in their lemon.

Thanks to "Lemon Laws" passed by all states, lemon-aide is available when consumers get stuck with a lemon. Although there are some important state-to-state variations, all of the laws have similarities: They establish a period of coverage, usually two years from delivery or the written warranty period, whichever is shorter; they may require some form of noncourt arbitration; and most importantly they define a lemon. In most states a new car, truck, or van is "presumed" to be a lemon when it has been taken back to the shop 3 to 4 times for the same problem or is out of service for a total of 30 days during the covered period. This time does not mean consecutive days and can be for different problems. 15 states have safety lemon provisions which presume a vehicle is a lemon after only 1 to 2 repairs of a defect likely to cause death or serious injury. Be sure to keep careful records of your repairs since some states now require only one of the repairs to be within the specified time period. Thirty-three states provide for the award of attorney fees with the other 17 relying on the Federal lemon law for fees.

A vehicle may be covered by the lemon law even though it doesn't meet the "presumption."

Specific information about your state's law can be obtained from your state attorney general's office or at the Center for Auto Safety's website. The following table offers a general description of the Lemon Law in your state and what you need to do to set it in motion (Notification/Trigger). We indicate where state-run arbitration programs are available. State-run programs are the best type of arbitration. Be aware, a few state lemon laws are so bad consumers should only rely on the Federal lemon law and state contract law. We have marked these bad laws with a ☒ while the best laws have a ☑.

> ☑ **The Best Lemon Laws**
> ☒ **The Worst Lemon Laws**

Alabama	Qualification: 3 unsuccessful repairs or 30 calendar days within shorter of 24 months or 24,000 miles, provided 1 repair attempt or 1 day out of service is within shorter of 1 year or 12,000 miles. Notice/Trigger: Certified mail to manufacturer + opportunity for final repair attempt within 14 calendar days.
Alaska	Qualification: 3 unsuccessful repairs or 30 business days out of service within shorter of 1 year or warranty. Notice/Trigger: Certified mail to manufacturer + dealer (or repair agent) that problem has not been corrected in reasonable number of attempts + refund or replacement demanded within 60 days. Manufacturer has 30 calendar days for final repair attempt.
Arizona	Qualification: 4 unsuccessful repairs or 30 calendar days out of service within warranty period or shorter of 2 years or 24,000 miles. Notice/Trigger: Written notice + opportunity to repair to manufacturer.
Arkansas ☑ BEST	Qualification: 3 unsuccessful repairs, 5 total repairs of any nonconformity, or 1 unsuccessful repair of problem likely to cause death or serious bodily injury within longer of 24 months or 24,000 miles. Notice/Trigger: Certified or registered mail to manufacturer who has 10 days to notify consumer of repair facility. Facility has 10 days to repair.

L—Law specifically applies to leased vehicles; S-C—State has certified guidelines for arbitration; S-R—State-run arbitration mechanism available

California ☑ BEST	Qualification: 4 repair attempts or 30 calendar days out of service or 2 repair attempts for defect likely to cause death or serious bodily injury within shorter of 18 months or 18,000 miles, or "reasonable" number of attempts during entire express warranty period. Notice/Trigger: Direct written notice to manufacturer at address clearly specified in owner's manual. Covers small businesses with up to 5 vehicles under 10,000 pounds GVWR.
Colorado ☒ WORST	Qualification: 4 unsuccessful repairs or 30 business days out of service within shorter of 1 year or warranty. Notice/Trigger: Prior certified mail notice + opportunity to repair for manufacturer.
Connecticut	Qualification: 4 unsuccessful repairs or 30 calendar days out of service within shorter of 2 years or 24,000 miles, or 2 unsuccessful repairs of problem likely to cause death or serious bodily injury within warranty period or 1 year. Notice/Trigger: Report to manufacturer, agent, or dealer. Written notice to manufacturer only if required in owner's manual or warranty. S-R
Delaware	Qualification: 4 unsuccessful repairs or 30 calendar days out of service within shorter of 1 year or warranty. Notice/Trigger: Written notice + opportunity to repair to manufacturer.
D.C.	Qualification: 4 unsuccessful repairs or 30 calendar days out of service or 1 unsuccessful repair of safety-related defect, within shorter of 2 years or 18,000 miles. Notice/Trigger: Report to manufacturer, agent, or dealer.
Florida	Qualification: 3 unsuccessful repairs or 15 calendar days within 24 months from delivery. Notice/Trigger: Certified or express mail notice to manufacturer who has 10 days to notify consumer of repair facility plus 10 more calendar days for final repair attempt after delivery to designated dealer. S-R
Georgia	Qualification: 1 unsuccessful repair of serious safety defect or 3 unsuccessful repair attempts or 30 calendar days out of service within shorter of 24,000 miles or 24 months. Notification/Trigger: Overnight or certified mail notice return receipt requested. Manufacturer has 7 days to notify consumer of repair facility & consumer has 14 days from manufacturer receipt of original notice to deliver vehicle to repair facility. Facility has 28 calendar days from manufacturer receipt of original notice to repair. State-run arbitration mechanism available. Law specifically applies to leased vehicles.
Hawaii	Qualification: 3 unsuccessful repair attempts, or 1 unsuccessful repair attempt of defect likely to cause death or serious bodily injury, or out of service for total of 30 days within shorter of 2 years or 24,000 miles. Notice/Trigger: Written notice + opportunity to repair to manufacturer. S-R
Idaho	Qualification: 4 repair attempts or 30 business days out of service within shorter of 2 years or 24,000 miles, or 1 repair of complete failure of braking or steering likely to cause death or serious bodily injury. Notice/Trigger: Written notice to manufacturer or dealer + one opportunity to repair to manufacturer. S-R.
Illinois	Qualification: 4 unsuccessful repairs or 30 business days out of service within shorter of 1 year or 12,000 miles. Notice/Trigger: Written notice + opportunity to repair to manufacturer.
Indiana ☒ WORST	Qualification: 4 unsuccessful repairs or 30 business days out of service within shorter of 18 months or 18,000 miles. Notice/Trigger: Written notice to manufacturer only if required in the warranty.

L—Law specifically applies to leased vehicles; S-C—State has certified guidelines for arbitration; S-R—State-run arbitration mechanism available

Iowa	Qualification: 3 unsuccessful repairs, or 1 unsuccessful repair of nonconformity likely to cause death or serious bodily injury, or 30 calendar days out of service within shorter of 2 years or 24,000 miles. Notice/Trigger: Certified registered mail + final opportunity to repair within 10 calendar days of receipt of notice to manufacturer.
Kansas	Qualification: 4 unsuccessful repairs or 30 calendar days out of service or 10 total repairs within shorter of 1 year or warranty. Notice/Trigger: Actual notice to manufacturer.
Kentucky	Qualification: 4 unsuccessful repairs or 30 calendar days out of service within shorter of 1 year or 12,000 miles. Notice/Trigger: Written notice to manufacturer.
Louisiana	Qualification: 4 unsuccessful repairs or 90 calendar days out of service within shorter of 1 year or warranty. Notice/Trigger: Report to manufacturer or dealer.
Maine	Qualification: 3 unsuccessful repairs (or 1 unsuccessful repair of serious failure of brakes or steering) or 15 business days out of service within shorter of warranty or 3 years or 18,000 miles. Applies to vehicles within first 18,000 miles or 3 years regardless of whether claimant is original owner. Notice/Trigger: Written notice to manufacturer or dealer. Manufacturer has 7 business days after receipt for final repair attempt. S-R
Maryland	Qualification: 4 unsuccessful repairs, 30 calendar days out of service or 1 unsuccessful repair of braking or steering system within shorter of 15 months or 15,000 miles. Notice/Trigger: Certified mail return receipt requested + opportunity to repair within 30 calendar days of receipt of notice to manufacturer or factory branch.
Massachusetts	Qualification: 3 unsuccessful repairs or 10 business days out of service within shorter of 1 year or 15,000 miles. Notice/Trigger: Notice to manufacturer or dealer who has 7 business days to attempt final repair. S-R
Michigan	Qualification: 4 unsuccessful repairs within 2 years from date of first unsuccessful repair or 30 calendar days within shorter of 1 year or warranty. Notice/Trigger: Certified mail return receipt requested to manufacturer who has 5 business days to repair after delivery. Consumer may notify manufacturer after third repair attempt.
Minnesota	Qualification: 4 unsuccessful repairs or 30 business days or 1 unsuccessful repair of total braking or steering loss likely to cause death or serious bodily injury within shorter of 2 years or warranty. Notice/Trigger: Written notice + opportunity to repair to manufacturer, agent, or dealer.
Mississippi	Qualification: 3 unsuccessful repairs or 15 business days out of service within shorter of 1 year or warranty. Notice/Trigger: Written notice to manufacturer who has 10 business days to repair after delivery to designated dealer.
Missouri	Qualification: 4 unsuccessful repairs or 30 business days out of service within shorter of 1 year or warranty. Notice/Trigger: Written notice to manufacturer who has 10 calendar days to repair after delivery to designated dealer.
Montana	Qualification: 4 unsuccessful repairs or 30 business days out of service after notice within shorter of 2 years or 18,000 miles. Notice/Trigger: Written notice + opportunity to repair to manufacturer. S-R
Nebraska	Qualification: 4 unsuccessful repairs or 40 calendar days out of service within shorter of 1 year or warranty. Notice/Trigger: Certified mail + opportunity to repair to manufacturer.

L—Law specifically applies to leased vehicles; S-C—State has certified guidelines for arbitration; S-R—State-run arbitration mechanism available

Nevada	Qualification: 4 unsuccessful repairs or 30 calendar days out of service within shorter of 1 year or warranty. Notice/Trigger: Written notice to manufacturer.
New Hampshire	Qualification: 3 unsuccessful repairs by same dealer or 30 business days out of service within warranty. Notice/Trigger: Report to manufacturer, distributor, agent, or dealer (on forms provided by manufacturer) + final opportunity to repair before arbitration. S-R
New Jersey ☑ BEST	Qualification: 3 Unsuccessful repairs or 20 calendar days out of service within shorter of 2 years or 24,000 miles; or 1 unsuccessful repair of a serious safety defect likely to cause death or serious bodily injury. Notice/Trigger: Certified mail notice, return receipt requested to manufacturer who has 10 days to repair. Consumer may notify manufacturer at any time after the second repair attempt, or after the first repair attempt in the case of a serious safety defect.
New Mexico ☒ WORST	Qualification: 4 unsuccessful repairs or 30 business days out of service within shorter of 1 year or warranty. Notice/Trigger: Written notice + opportunity to repair to manufacturer, agent, or dealer.
New York	Qualification: 4 unsuccessful repairs or 30 calendar days out of service within shorter of 2 years or 18,000 miles. Notice/Trigger: Notice to manufacturer, agent, or dealer.
North Carolina	Qualification: 4 unsuccessful repairs within shorter of 24 months, 24,000 miles or warranty or 20 business days out of service during any 12 month period of warranty. Notice/Trigger: Written notice to manufacturer + opportunity to repair within 15 calendar days of receipt only if required in warranty or owner's manual.
North Dakota ☒ WORST	Qualification: 3 unsuccessful repairs or 30 business days out of service within shorter of 1 year or warranty. Notice/Trigger: Direct written notice + opportunity to repair to manufacturer. (Manufacturer's informal arbitration process serves as prerequisite to consumer refund or replacement.)
Ohio ☑ BEST	Qualification: 3 unsuccessful repairs of same nonconformity, 30 calendar days out of service, 8 total repairs of any nonconformity, or 1 unsuccessful repair of problem likely to cause death or serious bodily injury within shorter of 1 year or 18,000 miles. Notice/Trigger: Report to manufacturer, its agent, or dealer.
Oklahoma	Qualification: 4 unsuccessful repairs or 30 calendar days out of service within shorter of 1 year or warranty. Notice/Trigger: Written notice + opportunity to repair to manufacturer.
Oregon	Qualification: 4 unsuccessful repairs or 30 business days within shorter of 1 year or 12,000 miles. Notice/Trigger: Direct written notice + opportunity to repair to manufacturer.
Pennsylvania	Qualification: 3 unsuccessful repairs or 30 calendar days within shorter of 1 year, 12,000 miles, or warranty. Notice/Trigger: Delivery to authorized service + repair facility. If delivery impossible, written notice to manufacturer or its repair facility obligates them to pay for delivery.
Rhode Island	Qualification: 4 unsuccessful repairs or 30 calendar days out of service within shorter of 1 year or 15,000 miles. Notice/Trigger: Report to dealer or manufacturer who has 7 days for final repair opportunity.

L—Law specifically applies to leased vehicles; S-C—State has certified guidelines for arbitration; S-R—State-run arbitration mechanism available

South Carolina	Qualification: 3 unsuccessful repairs or 30 calendar days out of service within shorter of 1 year or 12,000 miles. Notice/Trigger: Certified mail + opportunity to repair (not more than 10 business days) to manufacturer only if manufacturer informed consumer of such at time of sale.
South Dakota	Qualification: 4 unsuccessful repairs, 1 of which occurred during shorter of 1 year or 12,000 miles, or 30 calendar days out of service during shorter of 24 months or 24,000 miles. Notice/Trigger: Certified mail to manufacturer + final opportunity to repair + 7 calendar days to notify consumer of repair facility.
Tennessee	Qualification: 4 unsuccessful repairs or 30 calendar days out of service within shorter of 1 year or warranty. Notice/Trigger: Certified mail notice to manufacturer + final opportunity to repair within 10 calendar days.
Texas	Qualification: 4 unsuccessful repairs when 2 occurred within shorter of 1 year or 12,000 miles, + other 2 occur within shorter of 1 year or 12,000 miles immediately following second repair attempt; or 2 unsuccessful repairs of serious safety defect when 1 occurred within shorter of 1 year or 12,000 miles + other occurred within shorter of 1 year or 12,000 miles immediately following first repair; or 30 calendar days out of service within shorter of 2 years or 24,000 miles + at least 2 attempts were made within shorter of 1 year or 12,000 miles. Notice/Trigger: Written notice to manufacturer. S-R
Utah	Qualification: 4 unsuccessful repairs or 30 business days out of service within shorter of 1 year or warranty. Notice/Trigger: Report to manufacturer, agent, or dealer. S-R
Vermont	Qualification: 3 unsuccessful repairs when at least first repair was within warranty, or 30 calendar days out of service within warranty. Notice/Trigger: Written notice to manufacturer (on provided forms) after third repair attempt, or 30 days. Arbitration must be held within 45 days after notice, during which time manufacturer has 1 final repair. S-R Note: Repairs must been done by same authorized agent or dealer, unless consumer shows good cause for taking vehicle to different agent or dealer.
Virginia	Qualification: 3 unsuccessful repairs, or 1 repair attempt of serious safety defect, or 30 calendar days out of service within 18 months. Notice/Trigger: Written notice to manufacturer. If 3 unsuccessful repairs or 30 days already exhausted before notice, manufacturer has 1 more repair attempt not to exceed 15 days.
Washington	Qualification: 4 unsuccessful repairs, 30 calendar days out of service (15 during warranty period), or 2 repairs of serious safety defect, first reported within shorter of warranty or 24 months or 24,000 miles. One repair attempt + 15 of 30 days must fall within manufacturer's express warranty of at least 1 year of 12,000 miles. Notice/Trigger: Written notice to manufacturer. S-R Note: Consumer should receive replacement or refund within 40 calendar days of request.
West Virginia ☑ BEST	Qualification: 3 unsuccessful repairs or 30 calendar days out of service or 1 unsuccessful repair of problem likely to cause death or serious bodily injury within shorter of 1 year or warranty. Notice/Trigger: Written notice + opportunity to repair to manufacturer.
Wisconsin	Qualification: 4 unsuccessful repairs or 30 calendar days out of service within shorter of 1 year or warranty. Notice/Trigger: Report to manufacturer or dealer. Note: Consumer should receive replacement or refund within 30 calendar days after offer to return title.
Wyoming	Qualification: 3 unsuccessful repairs or 30 business days out of service within 1 year. Notice/Trigger: Direct written notice + opportunity to repair to manufacturer. S-R

L—Law specifically applies to leased vehicles; S-C—State has certified guidelines for arbitration; S-R—State-run arbitration mechanism available

5 BASIC STEPS TO CAR BUYING

B uying a car means matching wits with a seasoned professional. But if you know what to expect, you'll have a much better chance of getting a really good deal!

There's no question that buying a car can be an intimidating experience. But it doesn't have to be. First of all, you have in your hands all of the information you need to make an informed choice. Secondly, if you approach the purchase logically, you'll always maintain control of the decision. Start with the following basic steps:

1 Narrow your choice down to a particular class of car— sports, station wagon, minivan, sedan, large luxury, SUV, truck, or economy car. These are general classifications and some cars may fit into more than one category. In most cases, *The Car Book* presents the vehicles by size class.

2 Determine what features are really important to you. Most buyers consider safety on the top of their list, which is why the "Safety" chapter is right up front in *The Car Book*. Airbags, power options, ABS, and the number of passengers, as well as "hidden" elements such as maintenance and insurance costs, should be considered at this stage in your selection process.

3 Find three or four cars that meet the needs you outlined above and your pocketbook. It's important not to narrow your choice down to one car because then you lose all your bargaining power in the showroom. (Why? Because you might lose the psychological ability to walk away from a bad deal!) In fact, because cars today are more similar than dissimilar, it's not hard to keep three or four choices in mind. In the car rating pages in the back of the book, we suggest some competitive choices for your consideration. For example, if you are interested in the Honda Accord, you should also consider the Toyota Camry and Ford Fusion.

4 Make sure you take a good, long test drive. The biggest car buying mistake most of us make is to overlook those nagging problems that seem to surface only after we've brought the car home. Spend at least an hour driving the car without a salesperson preferably. If a dealership won't allow you to testdrive a car without a salesperson, go somewhere else. The test-drive should include time on the highway, parking, taking the car in and out of your driveway or garage, sitting in the back seat, and using the trunk or storage area.

TIP: Whatever you do, don't talk price until you're ready to buy!

5 This is the stage most of us dread—negotiating the price. While price negotiation is a car buying tradition, a few carmakers and dealers are trying to break tradition by offering so-called "no-haggle pricing." Since they're still in the minority and because it's very hard for an individual to establish true competition between dealers, we offer a great means to avoid negotiating altogether by using the non-profit CarBargains pricing service described on page 68.

THE 180-DEGREE TURN

TIP

When buying a car, remember that you have the most important weapon in the bargaining process: the 180-degree turn. Be prepared to walk away from a deal, even at the risk of losing the "very best deal" your salesperson has ever offered, and you will be in the best position to get a real "best deal." Remember: Dealerships need you, the buyer, to survive.

IN THE SHOWROOM

Being prepared is the best way to turn a potentially intimidating showroom experience into a profitable one. Here's some advice on handling what you'll find in the showroom.

Beware of silence. Silence is often used to intimidate, so be prepared for long periods of time when the salesperson is "talking with the manager." This tactic is designed to make you want to "just get the negotiation over with." Instead of becoming a victim, do something that indicates you are serious about looking elsewhere. Bring the classified section of the newspaper and begin circling other cars or review brochures from other manufacturers. By sending the message that you have other options, you increase your bargaining power and speed up the process.

Don't fall in love with a car. Never look too interested in any particular car. Advise family members who go with you against being too enthusiastic about any one car. Tip: Beat the dealers at their own game—bring along a friend who tells you that the price is "too much compared to the other deal."

Keep your wallet in your pocket. Don't leave a deposit, even if it's refundable. You'll feel pressure to rush your shopping, and you'll have to return and face the salesperson again before you are ready.

Shop at the end of the month. Salespeople anxious to meet sales goals are more willing to negotiate a lower price at this time.

Buy last year's model. The majority of new cars are the same as the previous year, with minor cosmetic changes. You can save considerably by buying in early fall when dealers are clearing space for "new" models. The important trade-off you make using this technique is that the carmaker may have added a new safety feature to an otherwise unchanged vehicle.

Buying from stock. You can often get a better deal on a car that the dealer has on the lot. However, these cars often have expensive options you may not want or need. Do not hesitate to ask the dealer to remove an option (and its accompanying charge) or sell you the car without charging for the option. The longer the car sits there, the more interest the dealer pays on the car, which increases the dealer's incentive to sell.

Ordering a car. Cars can be ordered from the manufacturer with exactly the options you want. Simply offering a fixed amount over invoice may be attractive because it's a sure sale and the dealership has not invested in the car. All the salesperson has to do is take your order.

If you do order a car, make sure when it arrives that it includes only the options you requested. Don't fall for the trick where the dealer offers you unordered options at a "special price," because it was their mistake. If you didn't order an option, don't pay for it.

BEWARE OF MANDATORY ARBITRATION AGREEMENTS

More and more dealers are adding mandatory binding arbitration agreements, which they often call "dispute resolution mechanisms," to your purchase contract. What this means is that you waive the right to sue or appeal any problem you have with the vehicle. Before you start negotiating the price, ask if the dealer requires Mandatory Binding Arbitration. If so, and they won't remove that requirement, you should buy elsewhere. Many dealers do not have this requirement.

GETTING THE BEST PRICE

One of the most difficult aspects of buying a new car is getting the best price. Most of us are at a disadvantage negotiating because we don't know how much the car actually cost the dealer. The difference between what the dealer paid and the sticker price represents the negotiable amount.

Beware, now that most savvy consumers know to check the so-called "dealer invoice," the industry has camouflaged this number. Special incentives, rebates, and kickbacks can account for $500 to $2,000 worth of extra profit to a dealer selling a car at "dealer invoice." The non-profit Center for the Study of Services recently discovered that in 37 percent of cases when dealers are forced to bid against each other for the sale, they offered the buyer a price below the "dealer invoice"—an unlikely event if the dealer was actually losing money. The bottom line is that "dealer invoice" doesn't really mean dealer cost.

You can't really negotiate with only one dealer, you need to get two or three bidding against each other. Introducing competition is the best way to get the lowest price on a new car. To do this you have to convince two or three dealers that you are, in fact, prepared to buy a car; that you have decided on the make, model, and features; and that your decision now rests solely on which dealer will give you the best price. You can try to do this by phone, but often dealers will not give you the best price, or will quote you a price over the phone that they will not honor later. Instead, you should try to do this in person. As anyone knows who

has ventured into an auto showroom simply to get the best price, the process can be lengthy as well as terribly arduous. Nevertheless, if you can convince the dealer that you are serious and are willing to take the time to go to a number of dealers, it will pay off. Other-wise, we suggest you use the CarBargains service described on page 68.

Here are some other showroom strategies:

Shop away from home. If you find a big savings at a dealership far from your home or on the Internet, call a local dealer with the price. They may very well match it. If not, pick up the car from the distant dealer, knowing your trip has saved you hundreds of dollars. You can still bring it to your local dealer for warranty work and repairs.

Beware of misleading advertising. New car ads are meant to get you into the showroom. They usually promise low prices, big rebates, high trade-in, and spotless integrity—don't be deceived. Advertised prices are rarely the true selling price. They usually exclude transportation charges, service fees, or document fees. And always look out for the asterisk, both in advertisements and on invoices. It can be a signal that the advertiser has something to hide.

Don't talk price until you're ready to buy. On your first few trips to the showroom, simply look over the cars, decide what options you want, and do your test-driving.

Shop the corporate twins. Page 75 contains a list of corporate twins—nearly identical cars that carry different name plates. Check the price and options of the twins of the car you like. A higher-priced twin may have more options, so it may be a better deal than the lower-priced car without the options you want.

Watch out for dealer preparation overcharges. Before paying the dealer to clean your car, make sure that preparation is not included in the basic price. The price sticker will state: "Manufacturer's suggested retail price of this model includes dealer preparation."

If you must negotiate . . . negotiate up from the "invoice" price rather than down from the sticker price. Simply make an offer close to or at the "invoice" price. If the salesperson says that your offer is too low to make a profit, ask to see the factory invoice.

Don't trade in. Although it is more work, you can usually do better by selling your old car yourself than by trading it in. To determine what you'll gain by selling the car yourself, check the NADA Official Used Car Guide at your credit union or library. On the web, the Kelly Blue Book website at kbb.com is a good source for invoice pricing. The difference between the trade-in price (what the dealer will give you) and the retail price (what you typically can sell it for) is your extra payment for selling the car yourself.

If you do decide to trade your car in at the dealership, keep the buying and selling separate. First, negotiate the best price for your new car, then find out how much the dealer will give you for your old car. Keeping the two deals separate ensures that you know what you're paying for your new car and simplifies the entire transaction.

Question everything the dealer writes down. Nothing is etched in stone. Because things are written down, we tend not to question them. This is wrong— always assume that anything written down is negotiable.

BUYING FOR SAFETY

So how do you buy for safety? Many consumers mistakenly believe that handling and performance are the key elements in the safety of a car. While an extremely unresponsive car could cause an accident, most new cars meet basic handling requirements. In fact, many people actually feel uncomfortable driving high performance cars because the highly responsive steering, acceleration, and suspension systems can be difficult to get used to. But the main reason handling is overrated as a safety measure is that automobile collisions are, by nature, accidents. Once they've begun, they are beyond human capacity to prevent, no matter how well your car handles. So the key to protecting yourself is to purchase a car that offers a high degree of crash protection.

AVOIDING LEMONS

One way to avoid the sour taste of a lemon after you've bought your car is to protect yourself before you sign on the dotted line. These tips will help you avoid problems down the road.

1 Avoid new models. Any new car in its very first year of production often turns out to have a lot of defects. Sometimes the manufacturer isn't able to remedy the defects until the second, third, or even fourth year of production. If the manufacturer has not worked out problems by the third model year, the car will likely be a lemon forever.

2 Avoid the first cars off the line. Most companies close down their assembly lines every year to make annual changes. In addition to adding hundreds of dollars to the price of a new car, these changes can introduce new defects. It can take a few months to iron out these bugs. Ask the dealer when the vehicle you are interested in was manufactured, or look on the metal tag found on the inside of the driver-side door frame to find the date of manufacture.

3 Avoid delicate options. Delicate options have the highest frequency-of-repair records. Power seats, power windows, and special roofs are nice conveniences—until they break down. Of all the items on the vehicles, they tend to be the most expensive to repair.

4 Inspect the dealer's checklist. Request a copy of the dealer's pre-delivery service and adjustment checklist (also called a "make-ready list") at the time your new vehicle is delivered. Write the request directly on the new vehicle order. This request informs the dealer that you are aware of the dealer's responsibility to check your new car for defects.

5 Examine the car on delivery. Most of us are very excited to take the vehicle home. A few minutes of careful inspection can save hours of misery later. Look over the body for any damage; check for the spare tire and jack equipment; make sure all electrical items work, and all the hubcaps and body molding are on. You may want to take a short test-drive. Finally, make sure you have the owner's manual, warranty forms, and all the legal documents.

CarBargains' Best Price Service

Even with the information that we provide you in this chapter of *The Car Book*, many of us still will not be comfortable negotiating for a fair price. In fact, as we indicated on the previous page, we believe it's really very difficult to negotiate the best price with a single dealer. The key to getting the best price is to get dealers to compete with each other.

CarBargains is a service of the non-profit Consumers' CHECK-BOOK, a consumer group that provides comparative price and quality information for many products and services.

CarBargains will "shop" the dealerships in your area and obtain at least five price quotes for the make and model of the car that you want to buy. The dealers who submit quotes know that they are competing with other area dealerships and have agreed to honor the prices that they submit. It is important to note that CarBargains is not an auto broker or "car buying" service; they have no affiliation with dealers.

Here's how the service works:

1. You provide CarBargains with the make, model, and style of car you wish to buy (Toyota Camry XLE, for example) by phone or mail.

2. Within two weeks, CarBargains will send you dealer quote sheets from at least five local dealers who have bid against one another to sell you that car. Each dealer's offer is actually a commitment to a dollar amount above (or below) "factory invoice cost" for that model. You get the name and phone number of the manager responsible for handling the quote.

You will also receive a print-out that enables you to figure the exact cost for each available option you might want on the vehicle.

3. Determine which dealer offers the best price using the dealer quote sheets. Add up the cost including the specific options you want. Contact the sales manager of that dealership and arrange to purchase the car.

If a car with the options you want is not available on the dealer's lot, you can, in many cases, have the dealer order the car from the factory or from another dealer at the agreed price.

When you receive your quotes, you will also get some suggestions on low-cost sources of financing and a valuation of your used car (trade-in).

The price for this service ($200) may seem expensive, but when you consider the savings that will result by having dealers bid against each other, as well as the time and effort of trying to get these bids yourself, we believe it's a great value. The dealers know they have a bona fide buyer (you've paid for the service); they know they are bidding against five to seven of their competitors; and, you have Car-Bargains' experts on your side.

To obtain CarBargains' competitive price quotes, call them at 800-475-7283 or visit their website at www.carbargains.org. Or, you can send a check for $200 to CarBargains, 1625 K St., NW, 8th Floor, Washington, DC 20006. Be sure to include your complete mailing address, phone number, and e-mail address (in case of questions), and the exact make, model, style, and year of the car you want to buy. You should receive your report within two weeks.

! AUTO BROKERS !

While CarBargains is a non-profit organization created to help you find the best price for the car you want to purchase, auto brokers are typically in the business to make money. As such, the price you end up paying for the car will include additional profit for the broker. There have been cases where the auto broker makes certain promises, takes your money, and you never hear from him again. While many brokers are legitimately trying to get their customers the best price, others have developed special relationships with certain dealers and may not do much shopping for you. As a consumer, it is difficult to tell which are which. This is why we recommend CarBargains. If CarBargains is not for you, then we suggest you consider using a buying service associated with your credit union or auto club. They can arrange for the purchase of a car at some fixed price over "dealer invoice."

FINANCING

You've done your test-drive, researched prices, studied crash tests, determined the options you want, and haggled to get the best price. Now you have to decide how to pay for the car.

If you have the cash, pay for the car right away. You avoid finance charges, you won't have a large debt haunting you, and the full value of the car is yours. You can then make the monthly payments to yourself to save up for your next car.

However, most of us cannot afford to pay cash for a car, which leaves two options: financing or leasing. While leasing may seem more affordable, financing will actually cost you less. When you finance a car, you own it after you finish your payments. At the end of a lease, you have nothing. We don't recommend leasing, but if you want more information, see page 71.

Shop around for interest rates. Most banks and credit unions will knock off at least a quarter of a percent for their customers. Have these quotes handy when you talk financing with the dealer.

The higher your down payment, the less you'll have to finance. This will not only reduce your overall interest charges, but often qualifies you for a lower interest rate.

Avoid long car loans. The monthly payments are lower, but you'll pay far more in overall interest charges. For example, a two-year, $20,000 loan at 7 percent will cost you $1,491 in interest; the same amount at five years will cost you $3,761—over twice as much!

Beware of manufacturer promotional rates—the 0 to 1 percent rates you see advertised. These low rates are usually only valid on two or three-year loans and only for the most credit-worthy customers.

Read everything you are asked to sign and ask questions about anything you don't fully understand.

Make sure that an extended warranty has not been added to the purchase price. Dealers will sometimes do this without telling you. Extended warranties are generally a bad value. See the "Warranties" chapter for more information.

Credit Unions vs. Banks: Credit unions generally charge fewer and lower fees and offer better rates than banks. In addition, credit unions offer counseling services where consumers can find pricing information on cars or compare monthly payments for financing. You can join a credit union either through your employer, an organization or club, or if you have a relative who is part of a credit union.

DON'T BE TONGUE-TIED

TIP

Beware of high-pressure phrases like "I've talked to the manager and this is really the best we can do. As it is, we're losing money on this deal." Rarely is this true. Dealers are in the business to make money and most do very well. Don't tolerate a take-it-or-leave-it attitude. Simply repeat that you will only buy when you see the deal you want and that you don't appreciate the dealer pressuring you. Threaten to leave if the dealer continues to pressure you to buy today.

Don't let the dealer answer your questions with a question. If you ask, "Can I get air conditioning with this car?" and the salesperson answers, "If I get you air conditioning in this car, will you buy today?" this response tries to force you to decide to buy before you are ready. Ask the dealer to just answer your question and say that you'll buy when you're ready. It's the dealer's job to answer questions, not yours.

If you are having a difficult time getting what you want, ask the dealer: "Why won't you let me buy a car today?" Most salespeople will be thrown off by this phrase as they are often too busy trying to use it on you. If they respond in frustration, "OK, what do you want?" then you can make straightforward answers to simple questions.

Get a price; don't settle for: "If you're shopping price, go to the other dealers first and then come back." This technique ensures that they don't have to truly negotiate. Your best response is: "I only plan to come back if your price is the lowest, so that's what I need today, your lowest price."

TYPICAL OPERATING COSTS

Here are the annual operating costs for some popular vehicles. These costs include operating expenses (fuel, oil, maintenance, and tires) and ownership expenses (insurance, financing, taxes, depreciation, and licensing) and are based on keeping the vehicle for 3 years and driving 20,000 miles per year. This information is from Runzheimer International. Runzheimer evaluated thirty 2014 model cars, vans, SUVs, and light trucks and determined the most and least expensive to operate among those vehicles. (Source: Runzheimer International, www.runzheimer.com)

Projected Ownership and Operating Costs for Selected 2014 Cars

Most Expensive

BMW 550I 8-cyl. 4.4L	$23,109
Mercedes E350 6-cyl. 3.5L	$20,565
Cadillac CTS Luxury 6-cyl. 3.6L	$20,245
Chysler 300S 8-cyl. 5.7L	$16,714
Chevrolet Impala 2LZ 6-cyl. 3.6L	$16,263

Least Expensive

Ford Focus Titanium 4-cyl. 2L	$11,559
Nissan Altima S 4-cyl. 2L	$10,867
Chevrolet Sonic LTZ 4-cyl. 1.8L	$10,384
Ford Focus SE 4-cyl. 2L	$10,344
Toyota Corolla LE 4-cyl. 1.8L	$9,390

Projected Ownership and Operating Costs for Selected 2014 Light Trucks, Vans, and SUVs

Most Expensive

Chevrolet Tahoe LS 4WD 8-cyl. 5.3L	$17,855
GMC Sierra 2500 Work 2WD 8 ft.	$16,523
FordEdge SEL AWD 6-cyl. 3.5L	$14,455
Dodge Grand Caravan R/T 6-cyl. 3.6L	$14,440
Jeep Grand Cherokee Laredo 2WD 6-cyl. 3.6L	$13,473

Least Expensive

Chevrolet Equinox 2LT FWD 4-cyl. 2.4L	$12,572
Chevrolet Silverado 1500 2WD 6-cyl. 4.3L	$12,443
Ford Escape SE ECO FWD 4-cyl. 2L	$12,341
Toyota Sienna 6-cyl. 3.5L	$12,320
Toyota Tacoma 2WD 6 ft. 4-cyl. 2.7L	$9,846

Runzheimer International is a management consulting firm that provides workforce mobility solutions relating to business vehicles, relocation, travel management, route logistics, and mobile device management programs. Runzheimer International is providing this information for reference only. Any direct reproduction or publication of this data in its entirety without prior consent from Runzheimer International is strictly forbidden.

(Source: Runzheimer International, www.runzheimer.com)

LEASING VS. BUYING

Because the unpredictibility of the value of a vehicle at the end of a lease, more and more companies are getting out of the leasing business. That's good news because, in general, leasing costs more than buying outright or financing. When you pay cash or finance a car, you own an asset; leasing leaves you with nothing except all the headaches and responsibilities of ownership with none of the benefits. When you lease you pay a monthly fee for a predetermined time in exchange for the use of a car. However, you also pay for maintenance, insurance, and repairs as if you owned the car. Finally, when it comes time to turn in the car, it has to be in top shape—otherwise, you'll have to pay for repairs or body work.

If you are considering a lease, here are some leasing terms you need to know and some tips to get you through the process:

Capitalized Cost is the price of the car on which the lease is based. Negotiate this as if you were buying the car. Capitalized Cost Reduction is your down payment.

Know the make and model of the vehicle you want. Tell the agent exactly how you want the car equipped. You don't have to pay for options you don't request. Decide in advance how long you will keep the car.

Find out the price of the options on which the lease is based. Typically, they will be full retail price. Their cost can be negotiated (albeit with some difficulty) before you settle on the monthly payment.

Make sure options like a sunroof or stereo are added to the Capitalized Cost. When you purchase dealer-added options, be sure they add the full cost of the option to the Capitalized Cost so that you only pay for the depreciated value of the option, not the full cost.

Find out how much you are required to pay at delivery. Most leases require at least the first month's payment. Others have a security deposit, registration fees, or other "hidden costs." When shopping around, make sure price quotes include security deposit and taxes—sales tax, monthly use tax, or gross receipt tax. Ask how the length of the lease affects your monthly cost.

Find out how the lease price was determined. Lease prices are generally based on the manufacturer's suggested retail price, less the predetermined residual value. The best values are cars with a high expected residual value. To protect themselves, leasers tend to underestimate residual value, but you can do little about this estimate.

Find out the annual mileage limit. Don't accept a contract with a lower limit than you need. Most standard contracts allow 15,000 to 18,000 miles per year. If you go under the allowance one year, you can go over it the next. Watch out for Excess Mileage fees. If you go over, you'll get charged per mile.

Avoid "capitalized cost reduction" or "equity leases." Here the leaser offers to lower the monthly payment by asking you for more money up front—in other words, a down payment.

Ask about early termination. Between 30 and 40 percent of two-year leases are terminated early and 40–60 percent of four-year leases terminate early—this means expensive early termination fees. If you terminate the lease before it is up, what are the financial penalties? Typically, they are very high so watch out. Ask the dealer exactly what you would owe at the end of each year if you wanted out of the lease. Remember, if your car is stolen, the lease will typically be terminated. While your insurance should cover the value of

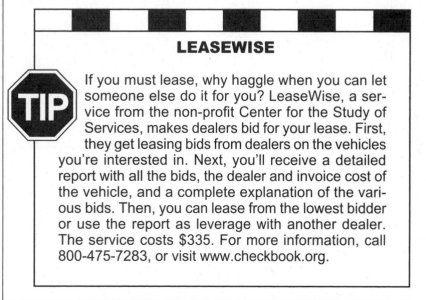

LEASEWISE

TIP

If you must lease, why haggle when you can let someone else do it for you? LeaseWise, a service from the non-profit Center for the Study of Services, makes dealers bid for your lease. First, they get leasing bids from dealers on the vehicles you're interested in. Next, you'll receive a detailed report with all the bids, the dealer and invoice cost of the vehicle, and a complete explanation of the various bids. Then, you can lease from the lowest bidder or use the report as leverage with another dealer. The service costs $335. For more information, call 800-475-7283, or visit www.checkbook.org.

the car, you still may owe additional amounts per your lease contract.

Avoid maintenance contracts. Getting work done privately is cheaper in the long run. And don't forget, this is a new car with a standard warranty.

Arrange for your own insurance. By shopping around, you can generally find less expensive insurance than what's offered by the leaser.

Ask how quickly you can expect delivery. If your agent can't deliver in a reasonable time, maybe he or she can't meet the price quoted.

Retain your option to buy the car at the end of the lease at a predetermined price. The price should equal the residual value; if it is more then the leaser is trying to make an additional profit. Regardless of how the end-of-lease value is determined, if you want the car, make an offer based on the current "Blue Book" value of the car at the end of the lease.

Residual Value is the value of your car at the end of the lease.

Here's what Automotive Lease Guide estimates the residual value after five years will be for a few 2013 vehicles:

Hyundai Elantra	41%
Toyota Prius	40%
Acura MDX	37%
Jeep Patriot	33%
Nissan Titan	26%

LEASING VS. BUYING

The following table compares the costs of leasing vs. buying the same car over three and six years. Your actual costs may vary, but you can use this format to compare the cars you are considering. Our example assumes the residual value to be 68 percent after three years and 43 percent after six years.

3 Years

	Lease	Finance
MSRP	$29,000.00	$29,000.00
Purchase Cost of Car	$26,100.00	$26,100.00
Down Payment	$2,436.00[5]	$2,900.00
Monthly Payment	$273.00[5]	$432.00
Total Payments	$9,828.00	$15,552.00[1]
Amount left on loan		$9,909.00
Value of vehicle at 3 yrs.		$19,720.00
Excess miles & disposition[7]	$825.00	
Overall Cost, first 3 yrs.	$13,089.00	$8,641.00
Savings over Leasing		**$4,448.00**

If you choose to keep the car you financed for six years, the savings over leasing becomes huge!

6 Years

	Lease[2]	Finance[3]
MSRP	$30,450.00	$29,000.00
Cost of Car	$27,405.00	$26,100.00
Down Payment	$2,740.50[5]	$2,900.00
Monthly Payment	$273.00[5]	$432.00
Total Payments	$9,828.00	$25,920.00
Amount Left on Loan		–
Value of vehicle at 6 yrs.[8]		$12,470.00
Excess miles & disposition[7]	$825.00	
Overall Cost, 6 yrs.	$23,742.00[4]	$16,350.00
Savings over Leasing		**$7,392.00**

[1] First 3 years of 5-year loan with 4.5 percent annual percentage rate.
[2] These are the second 3 year lease costs which assume a 5% increase for a similar vehicle.
[3] Five year loan with 4.5 percent annual percentage rate, no monthly payments in sixth year.
[4] Two 3-year leases.
[5] Initial lease and monthly payments based on lease deals for January 2014 offered by major manufacturers on US News and World Report.
[6] 68% based on average actual 36-month residual value for the top 100 selling vehicles for model year 2006, 07 and 08.
[7] Total average excess miles fee of $475 based on 12000 miles limit and 25% of consumers driving over the mile limit unexpectedly for 1500 miles with charges of $0.17/mile, 50% pre-paying for expected mile overages of 1500 miles at $0.12/mile, and 25% not exceeding the mileage limit. Disposition fee based on average of $350.
[8] 43% based on average actual 36-month residual value for the top 100 selling vehicles for model year 2003, 04 and 05.

USING THE INTERNET

The Internet is changing the way car buyers research and shop for cars. But the Internet should be used with caution. Anyone— and we mean *anyone*—can publish a website with no guarantee concerning the accuracy of the information on it. We advise that you only visit websites that have a familiar non-web counterpart. A good example is the Center for Auto Safety's website at www.autosafety.org where you can find information on auto safety, including publications and newsletters which are typically mailed out to subscribers.

Use the Internet as an information resource. Unfortunately, most automaker websites are nothing more than sophisticated ads with little comparative information.

Good information, like pricing and features, *can* be found online. We've listed some useful websites on this page.

There are also several online car shopping services that have launched. We view most of them with skepticism. Many online car shopping services are tied to a limited, often non-competitive, group of dealers. They may claim the lowest price, but you'll most likely have a dealer calling you with a price that is not much better than what you'd get if you went into a dealership to haggle.

Auto insurance and financing sites are sometimes no better. Don't rely solely on these online services; getting quotes from other sources is the only way to make sure you truly have the best deal.

Finally, clicking a mouse is no substitute for going out and test-driving a car. If you are shopping for a used car, you must check out the actual car before signing on the dotted line. Do not rely on online photos. In fact, online classifieds for cars are no more reliable than looking in a newspaper.

If you do use an online car shopping service, be sure to shop around on your own. Visit dealerships, get quotes from several car shopping services, and research the value of your used car (see www.nadaguides.com). Beware that if you give anyone online your phone number, or email address, you are opening yourself up to unwanted email, junk mail, and even sales calls.

ON THE WEB

TIP

autosafety.org
The Center for Auto Safety (CAS) provides consumers with a voice for auto safety and quality in Washington and to help lemon owners fight back across the country.

carfax.com
Used car buyers will want to visit Carfax. Carfax collects information from numerous sources to provide a vehicle history on a specific vehicle, based on the Vehicle Identification Number (VIN). Carfax can help uncover costly and potentially dangerous hidden problems or confirm the clean history of a vehicle.

checkbook.org
The Center for the Study of Services (CSS) is an independent, nonprofit consumer organization and the creator of Consumers' CHECKBOOK. One of the few car buying services worth using, CHECKBOOK's CarBargains service pits dealers against each other, keeping you from haggling, and using the power of competitive bidding to get you a great price.

nhtsa.gov
The National Highway Traffic Safety Administration (NHTSA) website contains useful information on safety standards, crash tests, recalls, technical service bulletins, child seats, and safety advisories.

fueleconomy.gov
This joint effort by the Department of Energy and the Environmental Protection Agency contains EPA fuel economy ratings for passenger cars and trucks from 1985 to the present, gas saving tips, greenhouse gas and air pollution ratings, energy impact scores, a downloadable Fuel Economy Guide, and a variety of other useful information in a very user-friendly format.

DEPRECIATION

Over the past 20 years, new vehicle depreciation costs have steadily increased. A study conducted by Runzheimer International shows that depreciation and interest now account for just over 50 percent of the costs of owning and operating a vehicle. Recently, however, the increasing cost of depreciation has slowed down. This is due to the relatively stable prices of new vehicles and to the slow increase in finance rates. The higher cost of gasoline consumes a larger percentage of the automotive dollar than ever before. Other costs, including insurance, maintenance, and tires, have remained at relatively steady shares of the automotive dollar.

While there is no foolproof method for predicting retained vehicle value, your best bet is to purchase a popular vehicle model. Chances are it will also be a popular used vehicle model, meaning that the retained value may be higher when you go to sell it.

Most new cars are traded in within four years and are then available on the used car market. The priciest used cars may not be the highest quality. Supply and demand, as well as appearance, are important factors in determining used car prices.

The following table indicates which of the top-selling 2010 cars held their value the best and which did not.

2010 VEHICLES WITH THE BEST AND WORST RESALE VALUE

THE BEST				THE WORST			
Model	2010 Price	2013 Price	Retain. Value	Model	2010 Price	2013 Price	Retain. Value
Dodge Ram	$20,610	$20,500	99.5%	Ford Fusion	$27,790	$13,425	48.3%
Mini Cooper	$27,150	$25,150	92.6%	Buick Enclave	$46,000	$22,850	49.7%
Jeep Wrangler	$21,165	$19,225	90.8%	Chevrolet Impala	$23,890	$12,225	51.2%
Toyota 4Runner	$35,700	$30,700	86.0%	Ford Crown Victoria	$26,950	$14,000	51.9%
Dodge Challenger	$22,141	$18,500	83.6%	BMW 5 Series	$45,950	$24,325	52.9%
Toyota Tacoma	$20,105	$16,600	82.6%	Chevrolet Cobalt	$14,990	$8,275	55.2%
Nissan Frontier	$23,340	$18,925	81.1%	Hyundai Sonata	$20,195	$11,200	55.5%
Chevrolet Camaro	$22,680	$17,675	77.9%	Chevrolet Malibu	$21,825	$12,125	55.6%
Toyota Yaris	$13,705	$10,650	77.7%	Chev. Express/G van	$28,515	$15,925	55.8%
Ford Ranger	$20,580	$15,975	77.6%	Buick LaCrosse	$27,085	$15,300	56.5%
Kia Sorento	$22,395	$17,325	77.4%	Chevrolet HHR	$18,720	$10,600	56.6%
Toyota Tundra	$28,405	$21,900	77.1%	Chrysler T&C	$28,425	$16,200	57.0%
Chrysler 300	$27,260	$20,975	76.9%	Cadillac CTS	$35,165	$20,225	57.5%
GMC Sierra	$32,525	$24,950	76.7%	Jeep Grand Cherokee	$32,680	$19,050	58.3%
Honda Fit	$15,700	$11,950	76.1%	Nissan Maxima	$30,460	$18,025	59.2%
Suburu Forester	$23,795	$18,100	76.1%	Dodge Caliber	$16,975	$10,050	59.2%
Hyundai Tucson	$23,195	$17,625	76.0%	Merc.-Benz E Class	$56,300	$33,350	59.2%
Lexus RX	$38,200	$28,925	75.7%	Toyota Sienna	$29,235	$17,350	59.3%
Toyota Corolla	$17,350	$13,075	75.4%	Acura TL	$35,105	$20,900	59.5%
Kia Soul	$16,195	$12,200	75.3%	Dodge Avenger	$20,230	$12,050	59.6%
Honda Civic	$22,255	$16,700	75.0%	BMW 3 Series	$33,150	$19,775	59.7%
Chevrolet Silverado	$33,510	$24,900	74.3%	Ford Taurus	$29,020	$17,350	59.8%
Dodge Grand Caravan	$21,800	$16,100	73.9%	Mazda Mazda6	$20,470	$12,375	60.5%
Ford Mustang	$27,995	$20,625	73.7%	Chrysler 200	$20,120	$12,175	60.5%
GMC Terrain	$26,000	$19,000	73.1%	Ford Flex	$33,120	$20,150	60.8%

CORPORATE TWINS

"Corporate twins" refers to vehicles that have different names but share the same mechanics, drivetrain, and chassis. In most cases the vehicles are identical. Sometimes the difference is in body style, price, or options as with the Chevrolet Tahoe and the Cadillac Escalade. Traditionally, corporate twins have been limited mainly to domestic car companies. However, several Asian and European car companies have started the practice.

CORPORATE TWINS

Chrysler Corp.
Chrysler 200
Dodge Avenger

Chrysler 300
Dodge Charger

Chrysler Town & Country
Dodge Grand Caravan

Ford Motor Co.
Ford Edge
Lincoln MKX

Ford Expedition
Lincoln Navigator

Ford Fusion
Lincoln MKZ

General Motors
Buick Verano
Chevrolet Cruze

General Motors (cont.)
Cadillac Escalade
Chevrolet Tahoe
GMC Yukon

Cadillac Escalade ESV
Chevrolet Suburban
GMC Yukon XL

Chevrolet Equinox
GMC Terrain

Chevrolet Traverse
GMC Acadia

Honda
Acura ILX
Honda Civic

Acura TL
Honda Accord

Hyundai-Kia
Hyundai Accent
Kia Rio

Hyundai Tucson
Kia Sportage

Nissan
Nissan Pathfinder
Infiniti QX60

Toyota
Scion FR-S
Subaru BRZ

Lexus GX
Toyota 4Runner

Volkswagen
Porsche Cayenne
Volkswagen Touareg

Cadillac Escalade

Chevrolet Tahoe

GMC Yukon

his section provides an overview of the most important features of this year's new models. Nearly all the information you'll need to make a smart choice is concisely presented on one page. (The data are collected for the model expected to be the most popular.) Here's what you'll find and how to interpret the data we've provided:

The Ratings

These are the ratings in nine important categories, as well as an overall comparative rating. We have adopted the Olympic rating system with "10" being the best.

Overall Rating: This is the "bottom line." Using a combination of all of the key ratings, this tells how this vehicle stacks up against the others on a scale of 1 to 10. Due to the importance of safety, the combined crash test rating is 20 percent of the overall rating while the other eight ratings are 10 percent each. Vehicles with no front or side crash test results, as of our publication date, cannot be given an overall rating. In other categories, if information is unavailable, an "average" is included in order to develop an overall rating.

Overall Crash Test: This rating represents a combination of the front and side crash test ratings and provides a relative comparison of how this year's models did against each other. We give the best performers a 10 and the worst a 1. Remember to compare crash test results relative to other cars in the same size class. For details, see page 18.

Safety Features: This is an evaluation of how much extra safety is built into the car. We give credit for rear head, torso and pelvis side airbags, roll-sensing side airbags, knee bolster bag, crash imminent braking, daytime running lamps, adjustable upper seat belt anchorages, lane keeping assist, pedestrian crash avoidance, automatic crash notification, lane departure warning, dynamic brake support, and frontal collision warning. We also include dynamic head restraint, backup cameras and blind spot detection among other important safety features. See the "Safety Checklist" box on each page for more details.

Rollover: Many consumers are aware that vehicles with higher centers of gravity could be more likely to roll over. Comparing the tendency of a vehicle to roll over is very difficult, as there is no agreed upon comparative rating system. The U.S. government adopted the rating system that we have been using called the static stability formula (SSF). The government provides the SSF rating for some vehicles. For those vehicles not on the government list, we use the SSF formula to provide a rating. The details behind the SSF appear on page 30.

Preventive Maintenance: Each manufacturer suggests a preventive maintenance schedule designed to keep the car in good shape and to protect your rights under the warranty. Those with the lowest estimated PM costs get a 10 and the highest a 1. See pages 39-43 for the estimated costs and more information.

Repair Costs: It is virtually impossible to predict exactly what any new car will cost you in repairs. As such, we take nine typical repairs that you are likely to experience after your warranty expires and compare those costs among this year's models. Those with the lowest cost get a 10 and the highest a 1. See pages 39-43 for specific part repair cost and more information.

Warranty: This is an overall assessment of the manufacturer's basic, powertrain, corrosion, and roadside assistance warranties compared to all other manufacturer warranties. We also give credit for perks like free scheduled maintenance. We give the highest-rated warranties a 10 and the lowest a 1. For details, see page 36.

Fuel Economy: Here we compare the EPA mileage ratings of each car. The misers get a 10 and the guzzlers get a 1. For the purposes of the overall rating we pick the fuel economy rating of what is expected to be the most popular engine and drive train configuration. See page 33 for more information.

Complaints: This is where you'll find how each vehicle stacks up against hundreds of others on the road, based on the U.S. government complaint data for that vehicle. If the car has not been around long enough to have developed a complaint history, it is given a 5 (average).

The least complained about cars get a 10 and the most problematic a 1. See page 55 for details.

Insurance Costs: Insurance companies rate vehicles to determine how much they plan to charge for insurance. Here, you'll find whether you can expect to pay higher or lower insurance premium for what we expect to be the most popular model. We looked at data from the insurance rating program of the largest insurer in America. Vehicles with a low rating (1 or 3) are more expensive to insure, vehicles with a high rating (8 or 10) are less expensive to insure and those receiving a 5 are typical. This rating will give you a basic idea of the cost to insure the vehicle. Because insurance companies may rate vehicles differently, it's best to compare prices between companies.

At-a-Glance

Status: Here we tell you if a vehicle is all-new, unchanged, or has received appearance change. All-new vehicles (the minority) are brand new from the ground up. Unchanged vehicles are essentially the same, but could have some different color or feature options. Vehicles with an appearance change are those whose internal workings stayed essentially the same, but have updated body panels.

Year Series Started: We generally recommend against buying a car during its first model year of production. Each year the model is made, the production usually improves and as a result there are fewer defects. Therefore, the longer a car has been made, the less likely you are to be plagued with manufacturing and design defects. On the other hand, the newer a car is, the more likely it is to have the latest in features and safety.

Twins: These are cars with different make and model names but share the same mechanics, drive train, and chassis. In some cases the vehicles are identical, in other cases the body style, pricing or options are different.

Body Styles: This is a listing of the various body styles available such as coupe, sedan, wagon, etc. SUVs and mini-vans are only offered in one body style. Data on the page are for the first style listed.

Seating: This is the number of seating positions in the most popular model. When more than one number is listed (for example, 5/6) it means that different seat configurations are available.

Anti-theft Device: This lists the anti-theft devices standard for the vehicle. An immobilizer is an electronic device fitted to an automobile which prevents the engine from running unless the correct key (or other token) is present. This prevents the car from being "hot-wired" and driven away. A car alarm is an electronic device that emits high-volume sound and can sometimes flash the vehicles headlights in an attempt to discourage theft of the vehicle itself, its contents, or both. Passive devices automatically enter an armed state after the ignition is turned off and doors are closed. Active devices require the user to perform some action like pressing a button to arm and disarm the system.

Parking Index Rating: Using the car's length, wheelbase, and turning circle, we have calculated how easy it will be to maneuver this car in tight spots. This rating of "very easy" to "very hard" is an indicator of how much difficulty you may have parking.

Where Made: Here we tell you where the car was assembled. You'll find that traditional domestic companies often build their vehicles in other countries. Also, many foreign companies build their cars in the U.S.

Fuel Factor

MPG Rating (city/hwy): This is the EPA-rated fuel economy for city and highway driving measured in miles per gallon. Most models have a variety of fuel economy ratings because of different engine and transmission options. We've selected the combination expected to be most popular.

Driving Range: Given the car's expected fuel economy and gas tank size, this value gives you an idea of the number of miles you can expect to go on one tank of gas.

Fuel: The type of fuel specified by the manufacturer: regular, premium, E85.

Annual Fuel Cost: This is an estimate based on driving 15,000 miles per year at $3.43/gallon for regular and $3.73/gallon for premium. If the vehicle takes E85 (85% ethanol and 15% gasoline) or gasoline we calculated the annual cost using gasoline.

Gas Guzzler Tax: Auto companies are required to pay a gas guzzler tax on the sale of cars with exceptionally low fuel economy.

This tax does not apply to light trucks.

Greenhouse Gas Emissions: This shows the amount (in tons) of greenhouse gases (carbon dioxide, nitrous oxide, and methane) that a vehicle emits per year along with the CO_2 emitted in producing and distributing the fuel.

Barrels of Oil Used Per Year: This is the number of barrels of petroleum the vehicle will likely use each year. One barrel, once refined, makes about 19.5 gallons of gas.

Competition

Here we tell you how the car stacks up with some of its key competitors. Use this information to broaden your choice of new car possibilities. This list is only a guideline, not an all-inclusive list of every possible alternative.

Price Range

This box contains information on the MSRP. When available, we offer a variety of prices between the base and the most luxurious version of the car. The difference is often substantial. Usually the more expensive versions have fancy trim, larger engines, and lots of automatic equipment. The least expensive versions usually have manual transmissions and few extra features. In addition to the price range, we provide the estimated dealer markup. Be prepared for higher retail prices when you get to the showroom.

Manufacturers like to load their cars with factory options, and dealers like to add their own items such as fabric protection and paint sealant. Remember, prices and dealer costs can change during the year. Use these figures for general reference and comparisons, not as a precise indication of exactly how much the car you are interested in will cost. See page 68 for a buying service designed to ensure that you get the very best price.

Safety Checklist

Crash Tests

Frontal and Side Crash Test Ratings: Here's where we tell you if the front or side crash test index was very good, good, average, poor or very poor when compared to 2014 cars tested to date. To provide this rating we use the crash test for the vehicles with the best available safety equipment among the models when multiple models were tested. In 2011, the government developed a new crash test program. Because only about half

TYPES OF AIRBAGS

Airbags were introduced over 30 years ago and have been so successful in saving lives that car makers now include a variety of types. Here's a rundown of the basic types of airbags available. Manufacturers have varying marketing names for these airbags.

Front: These deploy toward the front occupants and are now standard in all vehicles.
Side: These deploy from the side of the seat or door and protect both the front and rear passengers in a side impact. Bags mounted in seats offer protection in a wider range of seating positions.
Head: These deploy from above the doors and are often called curtain airbags. They can reduce head injuries, shield from spraying glass, and provide protection in rollovers.
Rollover Protection: These head curtain airbags remain inflated for five seconds to protect in a sustained rollover.
Knee Bolster: These fill space between the front occupant's knees and instrument panel protecting the knees and legs.

the vehicles have been tested under the new program, many will not have a rating. For details about the crash test programs, see page 19.

Airbags

All vehicles have dual front airbags and nearly all have head airbags. For the following types of airbags, we point out the differences among the vehicles.

Head Side Airbag: This side airbag protects the head area from impacting the roof, door, and window and can offer extra rollover protection.

Torso Side Airbag: This type of side airbag protects the chest from serious injury in a side impact crash.

Pelvis Side Airbag: Provides extra protection around the pelvis and hip area, as this portion of the body is usually closest to the vehicles interior.

Rollover Sensing Airbags: Some companies offer a special side airbag system which keeps the side airbags inflated longer in the event of a rollover. This can reduce the likelihood of injury when a vehicle flips.

Knee Bolster Airbag: The airbag is inflated to fill space between the knees of the front occupant and the instrument panel.

Crash Avoidance

Crash Avoidance: Great new technology is available that is designed to react faster than you can in the event of a frontal collision. These systems are designed to be most effective in lower speed collisions. There are three basic technologies available and are combined in this safety feature rating: Crash Imminent Braking (CIB), Dynamic Brake Support (DBS), and Frontal Collision Warning (FCW). All of these systems use radar or laser sensors to either alert the driver (FCW) or actively intervene to apply the brakes prior to a crash. Crash Imminent Braking will actually apply the brakes if you are about to experience a frontal crash. Dynamic Brake Support will increase your braking if the sensors determine that you are not applying enough force to stop the car in time. Frontal Collision Warning will merely sound an alarm in the event of an imminent frontal collision. We believe that Crash Imminent Braking and Dynamic Brake Support are more useful than Frontal Collision Warning (and thus rated higher), however Frontal Collision Warning is still a useful safety feature.

Blind Spot Detection: This is a blind spot monitor that uses radar or other technologies to detect objects in the driver's blind spot. When switching lanes a visible and/or audible alert warns if a vehicle has entered your blind spot.

Lane Keeping Assist: Going one step beyond a Lane Departure Warning, cars with this technology will actually apply pressure to the brakes or adjust the steering when it senses that a car is drifting out of its lane. Lane Departure Warning will simply alert the driver. We have combined the two since the technology for Lane Departure Warning is required for Lane Keeping Assist, which we believe to be a better technology.

Backup Camera: This camera placed somewhere on the rear bumper of the car allows the driver to see what is behind them on a screen in the car. It will also alert you to an object that is in the way of your car. This is a critically important safety feature if you have children or drive near or around children.

Pedestrian Crash Avoidance: These systems utilize a variety of technologies (infrared, camera, radar) to detect pedestrians and adjust the car's course to avoid a collision.

General

Automatic Crash Notification: Using cellular technology and global positioning systems, some vehicles have the ability to send a call for help in the event of airbag deployment or accident. Often free initially, you'll have to pay extra for this feature.

Daytime Running Lights: Some cars offer daytime running lights that can reduce your chances of being in a crash by up to 40 percent by increasing the visibility of your vehicle. We indicate whether daytime running lights are standard, optional, or not available.

Safety Belts/Restraints

Dynamic Head Restraints: Many people position their seat and head restraint according to their own body and comfort requirements. This may not be the best position to protect you in a crash. These adjustors, sensing a crash, will automatically move the seat and headrest to the optimal position to help reduce injury during a rear-end crash.

Adjustable Belts: Proper positioning of the safety belt

across your chest is critical to obtaining the benefits of buckling up. Some systems allow you to adjust the height of the belt so it crosses your chest properly.

Specifications

Drive: This indicates the type of drive the manufacturer offers. This could be two wheel drive in the front (FWD) or rear (RWD) or all or four wheel drive (AWD/4WD).

Engine: This is the engine size (liters) and type that is expected to be the most popular. The engine types specify V6 or V8 for six or eight cylinders and I4 for four in-line.

Transmission: This is the type of transmission expected to be the most popular. Most drivers today prefer automatic transmissions. The number listed with the transmission (5-sp.) is the number of gears or speeds. Then we list whether it's automatic or manual and if the transmission is a continuously variable transmission (CVT). CVT changes smoothly and efficiently between gears. This can provide better fuel economy than other transmissions by enabling the engine to run at its most efficient speed.

Tow Rating: Ratings of very low, low, average, high, and very high indicate the vehicle's relative ability to tow trailers or other loads. Some manufacturers do not provide a tow rating.

Head/Leg Room: This tells how roomy the front seat is. The values are given in inches

and rated in comparison to all other vehicles.

Interior Space: This tells how roomy the car's passenger area should feel. This value is given in cubic feet and rated in comparison to all other vehicles. Many SUVs do not provide interior space specifications.

Cargo Space: This gives you the cubic feet available for cargo. For minivans, the volume is behind the last row of seats. In cars, it's the trunk space. We rate the roominess of the cargo space compared to all trucks, SUVs and cars.

Wheelbase/Length: The wheelbase is the distance between the centers of the front and rear wheels and the length is the distance from front bumper to rear bumper. Wheelbase can affect the ride and length affects how big the car "feels."

DESTINATION CHARGES

TIP

Destination charges are a non-negotiable part of buying a new car, no matter where you purchase it. They are an important factor when comparing prices. You'll find the destination charges on the price sticker attached to the vehicle. According to automakers, destination charges are the cost of shipping a vehicle from its "final assembly point" to the dealership. But, the following table illustrates that there is little correlation between destination charges and where the cars are assembled:

Vehicle	Destination Charge*	Assembly Country
Chevrolet Silverado	$995	U.S.A.
Jeep Patriot	$995	U.S.A.
BMW 5 Series	$925	Germany
Kia Sorento	$850	South Korea

*Data based on 2014 model year cars.

Acura ILX

Ratings—10 Best, 1 Worst

Combo Crash Tests	5
Safety Features	1
Rollover	8
Preventive Maintenance	3
Repair Costs	6
Warranty	5
Fuel Economy	8
Complaints	7
Insurance Costs	8
OVERALL RATING	**6**

Acura ILX

Acura ILX

At-a-Glance

Status/Year Series Started	Unchanged/2013
Twins	Honda Civic
Body Styles	Sedan
Seating	5
Anti-Theft Device	Std. Pass. Immobil. & Alarm
Parking Index Rating	Easy
Where Made	Greensburg, IN
Fuel Factor	
MPG Rating (city/hwy)	Good-24/35
Driving Range (mi.)	Short-369
Fuel Type	Premium
Annual Fuel Cost	Low-$2,002
Gas Guzzler Tax	No
Greenhouse Gas Emissions (tons/yr.)	Low-6.6
Barrels of Oil Used per year	Average-11.8

How the Competition Rates

Competitors	Rating	Pg.
Audi A4	6	87
Cadillac ATS	9	105
Mercedes-Benz C-Class	4	203

Price Range

Price Range	Retail	Markup
Base 2.0	$26,900	8%
Base 2.4 w/Prem Pkg	$29,200	8%
Base 2.0 w/ Prem Pkg	$29,200	8%
Base 2.0 w/Tech Pkg	$31,600	8%

Safety Checklist

Crash Tests:
Frontal . . . . Average
Side . . . . Poor

Airbags:
Head . . . . Fr. & Rr. Roof Curtain
Torso . . . . Front Torso from Seat
Pelvis . . . . None
Roll Sensing . . . . No
Knee Bolster . . . . None

Crash Avoidance:
Collision Avoidance . . . . None
Blind Spot Detection . . . . None
Lane Keeping Assist . . . . None
Backup Camera . . . . Standard
Pedestrian Crash Avoidance . . . . None

General:
Auto. Crash Notification . . . . None
Day Running Lamps . . . . Standard

Safety Belt/Restraint:
Dynamic Head Restraints . . . . None
Adjustable Belt . . . . Standard Front

Acura ILX

Specifications

Drive	FWD
Engine	2.0-liter I4
Transmission	5-sp. Automatic
Tow Rating (lbs.)	
Head/Leg Room (in.)	Cramped-37.9/42.3
Interior Space (cu. ft.)	Very Cramped-89.3
Cargo Space (cu. ft.)	Very Cramped-12.4
Wheelbase/Length (in.)	105.1/179.1

Ratings—10 Best, 1 Worst

Combo Crash Tests	8
Safety Features	9
Rollover	4
Preventive Maintenance	6
Repair Costs	5
Warranty	5
Fuel Economy	3
Complaints	–
Insurance Costs	10
OVERALL RATING	**8**

Acura MDX

Acura MDX

At-a-Glance

Status/Year Series Started	All New/2014
Twins	–
Body Styles	SUV
Seating	7
Anti-Theft Device	Std. Pass. Immobil. & Alarm
Parking Index Rating	Hard
Where Made	Lincoln, AL
Fuel Factor	
MPG Rating (city/hwy)	Poor-18/27
Driving Range (mi.)	Average-413
Fuel Type	Premium
Annual Fuel Cost	High-$2,642
Gas Guzzler Tax	No
Greenhouse Gas Emissions (tons/yr.)	High-8.7
Barrels of Oil Used per year	High-15.7

How the Competition Rates

Competitors	Rating	Pg.
BMW X5	–	99
Ford Explorer	4	138
Volvo XC90	–	270

Price Range

	Retail	Markup
Base	$42,290	9%
Base w/Tech Pkg	$46,565	9%
SH-AWD w Tech Pkg	$48,565	9%
SH-AWD Adavnace	$56,505	9%

Safety Checklist

Crash Tests:
Frontal	Very Good
Side	Average

Airbags:
Head	Fr. & Rr. Roof Curtain
Torso	Front Pelvis/Torso from Seat
Pelvis	Front Pelvis/Torso from Seat
Roll Sensing	Yes
Knee Bolster	Standard

Crash Avoidance:
Collision Avoidance	Optional CIB & DBS
Blind Spot Detection	Optional
Lane Keeping Assist	Optional
Backup Camera	Standard
Pedestrian Crash Avoidance	None

General:
Auto. Crash Notification	None
Day Running Lamps	Standard

Safety Belt/Restraint:
Dynamic Head Restraints	Standard Front
Adjustable Belt	Standard Front

Acura MDX

Specifications

Drive	AWD
Engine	3.5-liter V6
Transmission	6-sp. Automatic
Tow Rating (lbs.)	
Head/Leg Room (in.)	Very Cramped-38.1/41.4
Interior Space (cu. ft.)	Very Roomy-132.3
Cargo Space (cu. ft.)	Cramped-15.8
Wheelbase/Length (in.)	111/193.6

Ratings—10 Best, 1 Worst	
Combo Crash Tests	9
Safety Features	2
Rollover	4
Preventive Maintenance	6
Repair Costs	6
Warranty	5
Fuel Economy	4
Complaints	6
Insurance Costs	10
OVERALL RATING	**7**

Acura RDX

Acura RDX

At-a-Glance

Status/Year Series Started	Unchanged/2013
Twins	—
Body Styles	SUV
Seating	5
Anti-Theft Device	Std. Pass. Immobil. & Alarm
Parking Index Rating	Hard
Where Made	East Liberty, OH
Fuel Factor	
MPG Rating (city/hwy)	Poor-19/27
Driving Range (mi.)	Very Short-351
Fuel Type	Premium
Annual Fuel Cost	High-$2,552
Gas Guzzler Tax	No
Greenhouse Gas Emissions (tons/yr.)	Average-8.6
Barrels of Oil Used per year	High-14.3

How the Competition Rates

Competitors	Rating	Pg.
Buick Encore	9	101
Lexus RX	5	193
Volkswagen Tiguan	2	265

Price Range	Retail	Markup
FWD	$34,520	8%
AWD	$35,920	8%
FWD w/Tech Pkg	$38,220	8%
AWD w/Tech Pkg	$39,620	8%

Safety Checklist

Crash Tests:
Frontal . . . . Very Good
Side . . . . Average
Airbags:
Head . . . . Fr. & Rr. Roof Curtain
Torso . . . . Front Tosro from Seat
Pelvis . . . . None
Roll Sensing . . . . .Yes
Knee Bolster . . . . None
Crash Avoidance:
Collision Avoidance . . . . None
Blind Spot Detection . . . . None
Lane Keeping Assist . . . . None
Backup Camera . . . . Standard
Pedestrian Crash Avoidance . . . . None
General:
Auto. Crash Notification . . . . None
Day Running Lamps . . . . Standard
Safety Belt/Restraint:
Dynamic Head Restraints . . . . None
Adjustable Belt . . . . .Standard Front

Acura RDX

Specifications

Drive	AWD
Engine	3.5-liter V6
Transmission	6-sp. Automatic
Tow Rating (lbs.)	Very Low-1500
Head/Leg Room (in.)	Cramped-38.7/42
Interior Space (cu. ft.)	Roomy-103.5
Cargo Space (cu. ft.)	Roomy-26.1
Wheelbase/Length (in.)	105.7/183.5

Ratings—10 Best, 1 Worst

Combo Crash Tests	–
Safety Features	8
Rollover	9
Preventive Maintenance	4
Repair Costs	2
Warranty	5
Fuel Economy	5
Complaints	–
Insurance Costs	5
OVERALL RATING	**–**

Acura RLX

Acura RLX

At-a-Glance

Status/Year Series Started	All New/2014
Twins	–
Body Styles	Sedan
Seating	5
Anti-Theft Device	Std. Pass. Immobil. & Alarm
Parking Index Rating	Very Hard
Where Made	Saitama, Japan
Fuel Factor	
MPG Rating (city/hwy)	Average-20/31
Driving Range (mi.)	Long-440
Fuel Type	Premium
Annual Fuel Cost	High-$2,351
Gas Guzzler Tax	No
Greenhouse Gas Emissions (tons/yr.)	Low-6.7
Barrels of Oil Used per year	High-13.7

How the Competition Rates

Competitors	Rating	Pg.
Buick LaCrosse	7	102
Chevrolet Impala	8	113
Lexus LS	–	192

Price Range

	Retail	Markup
Base	$48,450	8%
Technology Package	$54,450	8%
Audio Package	$56,950	8%
Advance Package	$60,450	8%

Safety Checklist

Crash Tests:
Frontal . . . .
Side . . . .
Airbags:
Head . . . . Fr. & Rr. Roof Curtain
Torso . . . . Front Pelvis/Torso from Seat
Pelvis . . . . Front Pelvis/Torso from Seat
Roll Sensing . . . . Yes
Knee Bolster . . . . Standard
Crash Avoidance:
Collision Avoidance . . . . . . Optional CIB & DBS
Blind Spot Detection . . . . Optional
Lane Keeping Assist . . . . Optional
Backup Camera . . . . Standard
Pedestrian Crash Avoidance . . . . None
General:
Auto. Crash Notification . . . . None
Day Running Lamps . . . . Standard
Safety Belt/Restraint:
Dynamic Head Restraints . . . . None
Adjustable Belt . . . . Standard Front

Acura RLX

Specifications

Drive	FWD
Engine	3.5-liter V6
Transmission	6-sp. Automatic
Tow Rating (lbs.)	
Head/Leg Room (in.)	Cramped-37.6/42.3
Interior Space (cu. ft.)	Average-102.1
Cargo Space (cu. ft.)	Cramped-15.3
Wheelbase/Length (in.)	112.2/196.1

Ratings—10 Best, 1 Worst	
Combo Crash Tests	1
Safety Features	2
Rollover	10
Preventive Maintenance	3
Repair Costs	4
Warranty	5
Fuel Economy	5
Complaints	8
Insurance Costs	8
OVERALL RATING	**3**

Acura TL

Acura TL

At-a-Glance

Status/Year Series Started	Unchanged/2009
Twins	Honda Accord
Body Styles	Sedan
Seating	5
Anti-Theft Device	Std. Pass. Immobil. & Alarm
Parking Index Rating	Hard
Where Made	Marysville, OH
Fuel Factor	
MPG Rating (city/hwy)	Average-20/29
Driving Range (mi.)	Long-430
Fuel Type	Premium
Annual Fuel Cost	High-$2,407
Gas Guzzler Tax	No
Greenhouse Gas Emissions (tons/yr.)	Average-7.9
Barrels of Oil Used per year	High-14.3

How the Competition Rates

Competitors	Rating	Pg.
Cadillac CTS	–	106
Hyundai Sonata	7	161
Lexus ES	6	188

Price Range	Retail	Markup
Base	$36,030	8%
Special Edition	$37,530	8%
SH-AWD	$39,580	8%
SH-AWD w/Advance Package	$45,540	8%

Safety Checklist

Crash Tests:
Frontal . . . . Very Poor
Side . . . . Very Poor

Airbags:
Head . . . . Fr. & Rr. Roof Curtain
Torso . . . . Front Pelvis/Torso from Seat
Pelvis . . . . Front Pelvis/Torso from Seat
Roll Sensing . . . . No
Knee Bolster . . . . None

Crash Avoidance:
Collision Avoidance . . . . None
Blind Spot Detection . . . . Optional
Lane Keeping Assist . . . . None
Backup Camera . . . . Optional
Pedestrian Crash Avoidance . . . . None

General:
Auto. Crash Notification . . . . None
Day Running Lamps . . . . Standard

Safety Belt/Restraint:
Dynamic Head Restraints . . . . . . Standard Front
Adjustable Belt . . . . Standard Front

Acura TL

Specifications

Drive	FWD
Engine	3.5-liter V6
Transmission	6-sp. Automatic
Tow Rating (lbs.)	
Head/Leg Room (in.)	Cramped-38.4/42.5
Interior Space (cu. ft.)	Average-98.2
Cargo Space (cu. ft.)	Cramped-13.1
Wheelbase/Length (in.)	109.3/194

Ratings—10 Best, 1 Worst

Combo Crash Tests	–
Safety Features	2
Rollover	9
Preventive Maintenance	5
Repair Costs	6
Warranty	5
Fuel Economy	6
Complaints	9
Insurance Costs	5
OVERALL RATING	**–**

Acura TSX

At-a-Glance

Status/Year Series Started	Unchanged/2009
Twins	–
Body Styles	Sedan, Wagon
Seating	5
Anti-Theft Device	Std. Pass. Immobil. & Alarm
Parking Index Rating	Easy
Where Made	Sayama, Japan
Fuel Factor	
MPG Rating (city/hwy)	Average-22/31
Driving Range (mi.)	Very Long-468
Fuel Type	Premium
Annual Fuel Cost	Average-$2,211
Gas Guzzler Tax	No
Greenhouse Gas Emissions (tons/yr.)	Low-7.0
Barrels of Oil Used per year	Average-12.7

How the Competition Rates

Competitors	Rating	Pg.
Chrysler 200	2	122
Hyundai Accent	6	155
Lexus IS	7	191

Price Range	Retail	Markup
Base	$30,635	8%
Special Edition	$31,635	8%
Sport Wagon	$31,985	8%
V6 w/ Tech Package	$39,275	8%

Acura TSX

Safety Checklist

Crash Tests:
  Frontal . . . .
  Side . . . .

Airbags:
  Head . . . . Fr. & Rr. Roof Curtain
  Torso . . . . .Front Pelvis/Torso from Seat
  Pelvis . . . . .Front Pelvis/Torso from Seat
  Roll Sensing . . . . No
  Knee Bolster . . . . None

Crash Avoidance:
  Collision Avoidance . . . . None
  Blind Spot Detection . . . . None
  Lane Keeping Assist . . . . None
  Backup Camera . . . . None
  Pedestrian Crash Avoidance . . . . None

General:
  Auto. Crash Notification . . . . None
  Day Running Lamps . . . . Standard

Safety Belt/Restraint:
  Dynamic Head Restraints . . . . . .Standard Front
  Adjustable Belt . . . . .Standard Front

Acura TSX Sport Wagon

Specifications

Drive	FWD
Engine	2.4-liter I4
Transmission	5-sp. Automatic
Tow Rating (lbs.)	
Head/Leg Room (in.)	Cramped-37.6/42.4
Interior Space (cu. ft.)	Cramped-94.5
Cargo Space (cu. ft.)	Cramped-14
Wheelbase/Length (in.)	106.4/185.6

Ratings—10 Best, 1 Worst	
Combo Crash Tests	6
Safety Features	1
Rollover	9
Preventive Maintenance	5
Repair Costs	4
Warranty	7
Fuel Economy	5
Complaints	7
Insurance Costs	5
OVERALL RATING	**6**

Audi A4

At-a-Glance

Audi A4

Status/Year Series Started	Unchanged/2009
Twins	—
Body Styles	Sedan
Seating	5
Anti-Theft Device	Std. Pass. Immobil. & Alarm
Parking Index Rating	Average
Where Made	Ingolstadt, Germany
Fuel Factor	
MPG Rating (city/hwy)	Average-20/29
Driving Range (mi.)	Short-374
Fuel Type	Premium
Annual Fuel Cost	High-$2,407
Gas Guzzler Tax	No
Greenhouse Gas Emissions (tons/yr.)	Low-6.8
Barrels of Oil Used per year	Average-12.2

How the Competition Rates

Competitors	Rating	Pg.
BMW 3 Series	10	92
Cadillac ATS	9	105
Mercedes-Benz C-Class	4	203

Price Range	Retail	Markup
Premium	$33,800	8%
Premium Plus	$37,300	8%
Prestige Quattro	$43,500	8%
Prestige S-Line	$45,450	8%

Safety Checklist

Crash Tests:
Frontal	Good
Side	Poor

Airbags:
Head	Fr.& Rr. Roof Curtain
Torso	Std. Fr. & Opt. Rr. Torso from Seat
Pelvis	Std. Fr. & Opt. Rr. Pelvis/Torso from Seat
Roll Sensing	No
Knee Bolster	None

Crash Avoidance:
Collision Avoidance	Optional CIB & DBS
Blind Spot Detection	Optional
Lane Keeping Assist	None
Backup Camera	Optional
Pedestrian Crash Avoidance	None

General:
Auto. Crash Notification	None
Day Running Lamps	Standard

Safety Belt/Restraint:
Dynamic Head Restraints	None
Adjustable Belt	Standard Front

Audi A4

Specifications

Drive	AWD
Engine	2.0-liter I4
Transmission	8-sp. Automatic
Tow Rating (lbs.)	
Head/Leg Room (in.)	Very Cramped-38/41.3
Interior Space (cu. ft.)	Cramped-91
Cargo Space (cu. ft.)	Very Cramped-12.4
Wheelbase/Length (in.)	110.6/185.1

Ratings—10 Best, 1 Worst

Combo Crash Tests	–
Safety Features	4
Rollover	10
Preventive Maintenance	5
Repair Costs	4
Warranty	7
Fuel Economy	5
Complaints	9
Insurance Costs	3
OVERALL RATING	**–**

Audi A5

At-a-Glance

Status/Year Series Started	Unchanged/2008
Twins	–
Body Styles	Coupe, Convertible
Seating	4
Anti-Theft Device	Std. Pass. Immobil. & Alarm
Parking Index Rating	Average
Where Made	Ingolstadt, Germany
Fuel Factor	
MPG Rating (city/hwy)	Average-20/29
Driving Range (mi.)	Short-374
Fuel Type	Premium
Annual Fuel Cost	High-$2,407
Gas Guzzler Tax	No
Greenhouse Gas Emissions (tons/yr.)	Low-6.8
Barrels of Oil Used per year	Average-12.2

How the Competition Rates

Competitors	Rating	Pg.
BMW 3 Series	10	92
Cadillac CTS	–	106
Lincoln MKS	3	194

Price Range

Price Range	Retail	Markup
Premium	$39,000	8%
Premium Plus	$43,300	8%
Prestige Cabrio	$53,700	8%
Prestige S-Line Cabrio	$56,750	8%

Audi A5

Safety Checklist

Crash Tests:
Frontal	
Side	

Airbags:
Head	Fr. & Rr. Roof Curtain
Torso	Front Pelvis/Torso from Seat
Pelvis	Front Pelvis/Torso from Seat
Roll Sensing	No
Knee Bolster	Standard

Crash Avoidance:
Collision Avoidance	Optional CIB & DBS
Blind Spot Detection	Optional
Lane Keeping Assist	None
Backup Camera	Optional
Pedestrian Crash Avoidance	None

General:
Auto. Crash Notification	None
Day Running Lamps	Standard

Safety Belt/Restraint:
Dynamic Head Restraints	None
Adjustable Belt	None

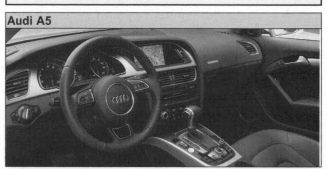

Audi A5

Specifications

Drive	AWD
Engine	2.0-liter I4
Transmission	8-sp. Automatic
Tow Rating (lbs.)	
Head/Leg Room (in.)	Very Cramped-37.5/41.3
Interior Space (cu. ft.)	Very Cramped-84
Cargo Space (cu. ft.)	Very Cramped-12.2
Wheelbase/Length (in.)	108.3/182.1

Ratings—10 Best, 1 Worst

Combo Crash Tests	–
Safety Features	5
Rollover	9
Preventive Maintenance	5
Repair Costs	3
Warranty	7
Fuel Economy	3
Complaints	8
Insurance Costs	3
OVERALL RATING	**–**

Audi A6

At-a-Glance

Status/Year Series Started	Unchanged/2012
Twins	–
Body Styles	Sedan
Seating	5
Anti-Theft Device	Std. Pass. Immobil. & Alarm
Parking Index Rating	Hard
Where Made	Neckarsulm, Germany
Fuel Factor	
MPG Rating (city/hwy)	Poor-18/27
Driving Range (mi.)	Long-419
Fuel Type	Premium
Annual Fuel Cost	High-$2,642
Gas Guzzler Tax	No
Greenhouse Gas Emissions (tons/yr.)	Average-8.3
Barrels of Oil Used per year	High-15

How the Competition Rates

Competitors	Rating	Pg.
BMW 7 Series	–	96
Cadillac XTS	10	108
Volvo S80	–	268

Price Range

Price Range	Retail	Markup
Premium	$43,100	8%
Premium Plus	$47,400	8%
Prestige	$57,900	8%
Prestige TDI	$60,300	8%

Audi A6

Safety Checklist

Crash Tests:
Frontal . . . .
Side . . . .

Airbags:
Head . . . . Fr. & Rr. Roof Curtain
Torso . . . . . . Std. Fr. & Opt. Rr. Torso from Seat
Pelvis Std. Fr. & Opt. Rr. Pelvis/Torso from Seat
Roll Sensing . . . . Yes
Knee Bolster . . . . Standard

Crash Avoidance:
Collision Avoidance . . . . . . Optional CIB & DBS
Blind Spot Detection . . . . Optional
Lane Keeping Assist . . . . Optional
Backup Camera . . . . Optional
Pedestrian Crash Avoidance . . . . None

General:
Auto. Crash Notification . . . . None
Day Running Lamps . . . . Standard

Safety Belt/Restraint:
Dynamic Head Restraints . . . . -
Adjustable Belt . . . . Standard Front

Audi A6

Specifications

Drive	AWD
Engine	3.0-liter V6
Transmission	8-sp Automatic
Tow Rating (lbs.)	
Head/Leg Room (in.)	Very Cramped-37.2/41.3
Interior Space (cu. ft.)	Average-98
Cargo Space (cu. ft.)	Cramped-14.1
Wheelbase/Length (in.)	114.7/193.9

Ratings—10 Best, 1 Worst

Combo Crash Tests	–
Safety Features	3
Rollover	4
Preventive Maintenance	5
Repair Costs	4
Warranty	7
Fuel Economy	4
Complaints	9
Insurance Costs	8
OVERALL RATING	**–**

Audi Q5

Audi Q5

At-a-Glance

Status/Year Series Started	Unchanged/2009
Twins	–
Body Styles	SUV
Seating	5
Anti-Theft Device	Std. Pass. Immobil. & Alarm
Parking Index Rating	Average
Where Made	Ingolstadt, Germany
Fuel Factor	
MPG Rating (city/hwy)	Poor-20/28
Driving Range (mi.)	Very Long-454
Fuel Type	Premium
Annual Fuel Cost	High-$2,438
Gas Guzzler Tax	No
Greenhouse Gas Emissions (tons/yr.)	Average-8
Barrels of Oil Used per year	High-14.3

How the Competition Rates

Competitors	Rating	Pg.
Cadillac SRX	8	107
Lexus RX	5	193
Volvo XC60	10	269

Price Range	Retail	Markup
2.0T Premium	$37,300	8%
3.0T Premium Plus	$44,400	8%
TDI Premium Plus S-Line	$50,000	8%
Prestige S-Line51059	$54,900	8%

Safety Checklist

Crash Tests:
  Frontal . . . .
  Side . . . .

Airbags:
  Head . . . . Fr. & Rr. Roof Curtain
  Torso Std. Fr. & Opt. Rr. Pelvis/Torso from Seat
  Pelvis Std. Fr. & Opt. Rr. Pelvis/Torso from Seat
  Roll Sensing . . . . Yes
  Knee Bolster . . . . None

Crash Avoidance:
  Collision Avoidance . . . . . . Optional CIB & DBS
  Blind Spot Detection . . . . Optional
  Lane Keeping Assist . . . . None
  Backup Camera . . . . Optional
  Pedestrian Crash Avoidance . . . . None

General:
  Auto. Crash Notification . . . . None
  Day Running Lamps . . . . Standard

Safety Belt/Restraint:
  Dynamic Head Restraints . . . . None
  Adjustable Belt . . . . Standard Front

Audi Q5

Specifications

Drive	AWD
Engine	2.0-liter I4
Transmission	8-sp. Automatic
Tow Rating (lbs.)	Low-4400
Head/Leg Room (in.)	Cramped-39.4/41
Interior Space (cu. ft.)	Average-101.5
Cargo Space (cu. ft.)	Roomy-29.1
Wheelbase/Length (in.)	110.5/182.6

Ratings—10 Best, 1 Worst

Combo Crash Tests	–
Safety Features	4
Rollover	4
Preventive Maintenance	3
Repair Costs	1
Warranty	7
Fuel Economy	2
Complaints	9
Insurance Costs	8
OVERALL RATING	**–**

Audi Q7

Audi Q7

At-a-Glance

Status/Year Series Started........ Unchanged/2007
Twins .... –
Body Styles .... SUV
Seating 7
Anti-Theft Device ...... Std. Pass. Immobil. & Alarm
Parking Index Rating .... Very Hard
Where Made................. Bratislava, Slovakia
Fuel Factor
  MPG Rating (city/hwy).......... Very Poor-16/22
  Driving Range (mi.) .... Very Long-481
  Fuel Type....................... Premium
  Annual Fuel Cost .... Very High-$3,068
  Gas Guzzler Tax .... No
  Greenhouse Gas Emissions (tons/yr.).... High-10.1
  Barrels of Oil Used per year .... Very High-18.3

How the Competition Rates

Competitors	Rating	Pg.
BMW X5	–	99
Hyundai Genesis	–	158
Land Rover Range Rover	–	184

Price Range

Price Range	Retail	Markup
Premium	$47,700	8%
Premium Plus	$53,700	8%
Prestige S-Line	$60,900	8%
Prestige TDI	$64,900	8%

Safety Checklist

Crash Tests:
  Frontal................................
  Side..................................
Airbags:
  Head .... Fr. & Rr. Roof Curtain
  Torso.......... Front Pelvis/Torso from Seat
  Pelvis .... Front Pelvis/Torso from Seat
  Roll Sensing .... Yes
  Knee Bolster .... None
Crash Avoidance:
  Collision Avoidance..... Warning Only Optional
  Blind Spot Detection .... Optional
  Lane Keeping Assist................ None
  Backup Camera .... Optional
  Pedestrian Crash Avoidance .... None
General:
  Auto. Crash Notification .... None
  Day Running Lamps............. Standard
Safety Belt/Restraint:
  Dynamic Head Restraints............ None
  Adjustable Belt .... Standard Front

Audi Q7

Specifications

Drive................................. 4WD
Engine 3.0-liter V6
Transmission .... 8-sp. Automatic
Tow Rating (lbs.) Low-5500
Head/Leg Room (in.) Cramped-39.5/41.3
Interior Space (cu. ft.)........ Very Roomy-133.2
Cargo Space (cu. ft.) .... Very Cramped-10.9
Wheelbase/Length (in.) 118.2/200.3

BMW 3 Series

Compact

Ratings—10 Best, 1 Worst	
Combo Crash Tests	7
Safety Features	8
Rollover	9
Preventive Maintenance	10
Repair Costs	3
Warranty	9
Fuel Economy	7
Complaints	3
Insurance Costs	8
OVERALL RATING	**10**

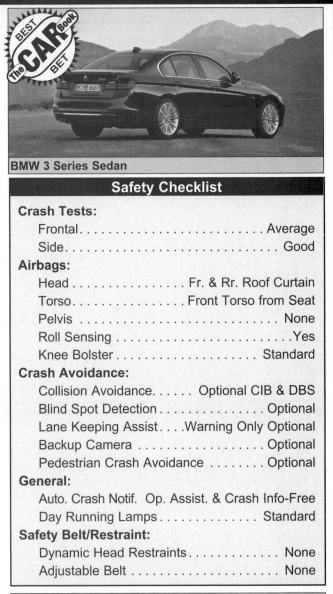

BMW 3 Series Sedan

BMW 3 Series Convertible

At-a-Glance

Status/Year Series Started	Unchanged/2013
Twins	–
Body Styles	Sedan, Wagon, Convertible
Seating	5
Anti-Theft Device	Std. Pass. Immobil.
Parking Index Rating	Average
Where Made	Munich, Germany
Fuel Factor	
MPG Rating (city/hwy)	Good-23/35
Driving Range (mi.)	Short-388
Fuel Type	Premium
Annual Fuel Cost	Low-$2,057
Gas Guzzler Tax	No
Greenhouse Gas Emissions (tons/yr.)	Low-6.6
Barrels of Oil Used per year	Average-11.8

How the Competition Rates

Competitors	Rating	Pg.
Audi A4	6	87
Lexus IS	7	191
Mercedes-Benz C-Class	4	203

Price Range	Retail	Markup
320i	$32,550	9%
328i	$37,100	9%
335i	$43,200	9%
335i Hybrid	$49,700	9%

Safety Checklist

Crash Tests:
Frontal	Average
Side	Good

Airbags:
Head	Fr. & Rr. Roof Curtain
Torso	Front Torso from Seat
Pelvis	None
Roll Sensing	Yes
Knee Bolster	Standard

Crash Avoidance:
Collision Avoidance	Optional CIB & DBS
Blind Spot Detection	Optional
Lane Keeping Assist	Warning Only Optional
Backup Camera	Optional
Pedestrian Crash Avoidance	Optional

General:
Auto. Crash Notif.	Op. Assist. & Crash Info-Free
Day Running Lamps	Standard

Safety Belt/Restraint:
Dynamic Head Restraints	None
Adjustable Belt	None

BMW 3 Series Couope

Specifications

Drive	RWD
Engine	2.0-liter I4
Transmission	8-sp. Automatic
Tow Rating (lbs.)	
Head/Leg Room (in.)	Average-40.3/42
Interior Space (cu. ft.)	Cramped-96
Cargo Space (cu. ft.)	Average-17
Wheelbase/Length (in.)	110.6/182

Ratings—10 Best, 1 Worst

Combo Crash Tests	–
Safety Features	5
Rollover	10
Preventive Maintenance	10
Repair Costs	3
Warranty	9
Fuel Economy	7
Complaints	–
Insurance Costs	5
OVERALL RATING	**–**

BMW 4 Series Coupe

BMW 4 Series Cabrio

At-a-Glance

Status/Year Series Started. . . . . All New/2014
Twins . . . . –
Body Styles . . . . Coupe, Convertible
Seating 4
Anti-Theft Device . . . . Std. Pass. Immobil.
Parking Index Rating . . . . Average
Where Made. . . . . .Munich, Germany
Fuel Factor
  MPG Rating (city/hwy) Good-23/35
  Driving Range (mi.) Long-432
  Fuel Type . . . . .Premium
  Annual Fuel Cost . . . . Low-$2,057
  Gas Guzzler Tax . . . . .No
  Greenhouse Gas Emissions (tons/yr.). Low-6.7
  Barrels of Oil Used per year Average-12.2

How the Competition Rates

Competitors	Rating	Pg.
Audi A4	6	87
Cadillac ATS	9	105
Lexus IS	7	191

Price Range

Price Range	Retail	Markup
428i	$40,500	9%
428xi	$42,500	9%
435i	$46,000	9%
435xi	$48,000	9%

Safety Checklist

Crash Tests:
  Frontal. . . . .
  Side. . . . .
Airbags:
  Head . . . . Fr. & Rr. Roof Curtain
  Torso. . . . . .Front Torso from Seat
  Pelvis . . . . None
  Roll Sensing . . . . .Yes
  Knee Bolster . . . . Standard
Crash Avoidance:
  Collision Avoidance. . . . .Warning Only Optional
  Blind Spot Detection . . . . Optional
  Lane Keeping Assist. . . .Warning Only Optional
  Backup Camera . . . . Optional
  Pedestrian Crash Avoidance . . . . Optional
General:
  Auto. Crash Notif. Op. Assist. & Crash Info-Free
  Day Running Lamps . . . . Standard
Safety Belt/Restraint:
  Dynamic Head Restraints. . . . . None
  Adjustable Belt . . . . None

BMW 4 Series

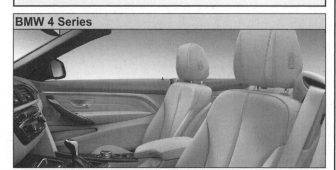

Specifications

Drive. . . . . .RWD
Engine 2.0-liter I4
Transmission . . . . 6-sp. Manual
Tow Rating (lbs.) . . . .
Head/Leg Room (in.) Average-39.8/42.2
Interior Space (cu. ft.). Cramped-92
Cargo Space (cu. ft.) Cramped-15.7
Wheelbase/Length (in.) 110.6/182.6

Ratings—10 Best, 1 Worst

Combo Crash Tests	9
Safety Features	8
Rollover	10
Preventive Maintenance	10
Repair Costs	2
Warranty	9
Fuel Economy	5
Complaints	2
Insurance Costs	5
OVERALL RATING	**9**

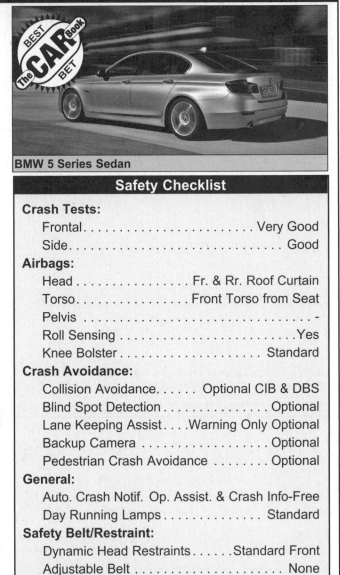

BMW 5 Series Sedan

BMW 5 Series Wagon

At-a-Glance

Status/Year Series Started........ Unchanged/2011
Twins . . . . –
Body Styles . . . . Sedan, Wagon
Seating 5
Anti-Theft Device . . . . Std. Pass. Immobil.
Parking Index Rating . . . . .Very Hard
Where Made. . . . . Dingolfing, Germany
Fuel Factor
  MPG Rating (city/hwy) Average-20/30
  Driving Range (mi.) Long-435
  Fuel Type. . . . . .Premium
  Annual Fuel Cost . . . . High-$2,378
  Gas Guzzler Tax . . . . .No
  Greenhouse Gas Emissions (tons/yr.). . Average-7.6
  Barrels of Oil Used per year High-13.7

How the Competition Rates

Competitors	Rating	Pg.
Acura TL	3	85
Lexus GS	–	189
Mercedes-Benz E-Class	4	205

Price Range	Retail	Markup
528i	$49,500	9%
535i	$55,100	9%
535xi	$57,400	9%
550i	$63,900	9%

Safety Checklist

Crash Tests:
  Frontal. . . . . Very Good
  Side. . . . . Good
Airbags:
  Head . . . . Fr. & Rr. Roof Curtain
  Torso. . . . . Front Torso from Seat
  Pelvis . . . . -
  Roll Sensing . . . . .Yes
  Knee Bolster . . . . Standard
Crash Avoidance:
  Collision Avoidance. . . . . . Optional CIB & DBS
  Blind Spot Detection . . . . Optional
  Lane Keeping Assist. . . .Warning Only Optional
  Backup Camera . . . . Optional
  Pedestrian Crash Avoidance . . . . Optional
General:
  Auto. Crash Notif. Op. Assist. & Crash Info-Free
  Day Running Lamps . . . . Standard
Safety Belt/Restraint:
  Dynamic Head Restraints. . . . . .Standard Front
  Adjustable Belt . . . . None

BMW 5 Series

Specifications

Drive. . . . . .RWD
Engine 3.0-liter I6
Transmission . . . . .8-sp. Automatic
Tow Rating (lbs.) . . . . Very Low-1653
Head/Leg Room (in.) Average-40.5/41.4
Interior Space (cu. ft.). Average-102
Cargo Space (cu. ft.) Average-18.36
Wheelbase/Length (in.) 116.9/193.2

Ratings—10 Best, 1 Worst

Combo Crash Tests	–
Safety Features	9
Rollover	10
Preventive Maintenance	10
Repair Costs	1
Warranty	9
Fuel Economy	6
Complaints	10
Insurance Costs	3

OVERALL RATING   –

BMW 6 Series Cabrio

At-a-Glance

Status/Year Series Started	Unchanged/2012
Twins	–
Body Styles	Sedan, Coupe, Convertible
Seating	4
Anti-Theft Device	Std. Pass. Immobil.
Parking Index Rating	Hard
Where Made	Dingolfing, Germany
Fuel Factor	
MPG Rating (city/hwy)	Average-22/32
Driving Range (mi.)	Very Long-474
Fuel Type	Premium
Annual Fuel Cost	Average-$2,186
Gas Guzzler Tax	No
Greenhouse Gas Emissions (tons/yr.)	Low-7.2
Barrels of Oil Used per year	Average-13.2

How the Competition Rates

Competitors	Rating	Pg.
Cadillac CTS	–	106
Lexus ES	6	188
Mercedes-Benz E-Class	4	205

Price Range

	Retail	Markup
640i	$74,900	9%
640i Gran Coupe	$77,100	9%
650xi	$89,200	9%
650i Convertible	$93,700	9%

BMW 6 Series Coupe

Safety Checklist

Crash Tests:
  Frontal . . . .
  Side . . . .
Airbags:
  Head . . . . Fr. & Rr. Roof Curtain
  Torso . . . . Front Torso from Seat
  Pelvis . . . . None
  Roll Sensing . . . . Yes
  Knee Bolster . . . . Standard
Crash Avoidance:
  Collision Avoidance . . . . . . Optional CIB & DBS
  Blind Spot Detection . . . . Optional
  Lane Keeping Assist . . . . Warning Only Optional
  Backup Camera . . . . Standard
  Pedestrian Crash Avoidance . . . . Optional
General:
  Auto. Crash Notif. Op. Assist. & Crash Info-Free
  Day Running Lamps . . . . Standard
Safety Belt/Restraint:
  Dynamic Head Restraints . . . . . . Standard Front
  Adjustable Belt . . . . None

BMW 6 Series

Specifications

Drive	RWD
Engine	3.0-liter V6
Transmission	8-sp. Automatic
Tow Rating (lbs.)	
Head/Leg Room (in.)	Average-40/42.1
Interior Space (cu. ft.)	Very Cramped-87
Cargo Space (cu. ft.)	Cramped-16.2
Wheelbase/Length (in.)	112.4/192.7

Ratings—10 Best, 1 Worst

Combo Crash Tests	–
Safety Features	9
Rollover	9
Preventive Maintenance	10
Repair Costs	1
Warranty	9
Fuel Economy	3
Complaints	5
Insurance Costs	1

OVERALL RATING   –

BMW 7 Series Sedan

BMW 7 Series Sedan

At-a-Glance

Status/Year Series Started. Unchanged/2011
Twins . . . . –
Body Styles . . . . .Sedan
Seating 5
Anti-Theft Device . . . . Std. Pass. Immobil.
Parking Index Rating . . . . .Very Hard
Where Made. . . . . Dingolfing, Germany
Fuel Factor
   MPG Rating (city/hwy) Poor-17/25
   Driving Range (mi.) Average-419
   Fuel Type. . . . . .Premium
   Annual Fuel Cost . . . . Very High-$2,817
   Gas Guzzler Tax . . . . .No
   Greenhouse Gas Emissions (tons/yr.). High-9.1
   Barrels of Oil Used per year High-16.5

How the Competition Rates

Competitors	Rating	Pg.
Cadillac XTS	10	108
Jaguar XF	–	171
Mercedes-Benz S-Class	–	209

Price Range	Retail	Markup
740i	$74,000	9%
750i	$87,300	9%
750xi	$90,300	9%
760Li	$141,200	9%

Safety Checklist

Crash Tests:
   Frontal . . . .
   Side . . . .
Airbags:
   Head . . . . Fr. & Rr. Roof Curtain
   Torso. . . . . Front Torso from Seat
   Pelvis . . . . None
   Roll Sensing . . . . .Yes
   Knee Bolster . . . . Standard
Crash Avoidance:
   Collision Avoidance. . . . . . Optional CIB & DBS
   Blind Spot Detection . . . . Optional
   Lane Keeping Assist . . . .Warning Only Optional
   Backup Camera . . . . Standard
   Pedestrian Crash Avoidance . . . . Optional
General:
   Auto. Crash Notif. Op. Assist. & Crash Info-Free
   Day Running Lamps . . . . Standard
Safety Belt/Restraint:
   Dynamic Head Restraints . . . . . .Standard Front
   Adjustable Belt . . . . None

BMW 7 Series

Specifications

Drive. . . . . .RWD
Engine 4.4-liter V8
Transmission . . . . .8-sp. Automatic
Tow Rating (lbs.) Low-4629
Head/Leg Room (in.) Roomy-40.6/42.1
Interior Space (cu. ft.). Roomy-107
Cargo Space (cu. ft.) Average-17.7
Wheelbase/Length (in.) 120.9/200

Ratings—10 Best, 1 Worst

Combo Crash Tests	–
Safety Features	4
Rollover	5
Preventive Maintenance	10
Repair Costs	2
Warranty	9
Fuel Economy	6
Complaints	8
Insurance Costs	8
OVERALL RATING	**–**

BMW X1

BMW X1

At-a-Glance

Status/Year Series Started	Unchanged/2013
Twins	–
Body Styles	SUV
Seating	5
Anti-Theft Device	Std. Pass. Immobil.
Parking Index Rating	Average
Where Made	Leipzig, Germany
Fuel Factor	
MPG Rating (city/hwy)	Average-22/33
Driving Range (mi.)	Long-430
Fuel Type	Premium
Annual Fuel Cost	Average-$2,162
Gas Guzzler Tax	No
Greenhouse Gas Emissions (tons/yr.)	Low-7.1
Barrels of Oil Used per year	Average-12.7

How the Competition Rates

Competitors	Rating	Pg.
Acura RDX	7	83
Buick Encore	9	101
Volkswagen Tiguan	2	265

Price Range	Retail	Markup
sDrive28i	$30,800	9%
XDrive28i	$32,500	9%
XDrive35i	$38,600	9%
	–	

Safety Checklist

Crash Tests:
  Frontal . . . .
  Side . . . .
Airbags:
  Head . . . . Fr. & Rr. Roof Curtain
  Torso . . . . Front Tosro from Seat
  Pelvis . . . . -
  Roll Sensing . . . . Yes
  Knee Bolster . . . . None
Crash Avoidance:
  Collision Avoidance . . . . None
  Blind Spot Detection . . . . None
  Lane Keeping Assist . . . . None
  Backup Camera . . . . Optional
  Pedestrian Crash Avoidance . . . . None
General:
  Auto. Crash Notif. Op. Assist. & Crash Info-Free
  Day Running Lamps . . . . Standard
Safety Belt/Restraint:
  Dynamic Head Restraints . . . . . . Standard Front
  Adjustable Belt . . . . None

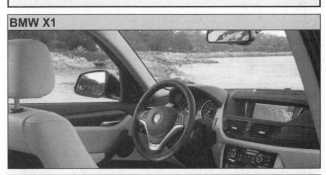

BMW X1

Specifications

Drive	AWD
Engine	2.0-liter I4
Transmission	8-sp. Automatic
Tow Rating (lbs.)	
Head/Leg Room (in.)	Roomy-41.3/41.4
Interior Space (cu. ft.)	Average-98
Cargo Space (cu. ft.)	Roomy-25
Wheelbase/Length (in.)	108.7/176.5

Ratings—10 Best, 1 Worst

Combo Crash Tests	–
Safety Features	6
Rollover	4
Preventive Maintenance	10
Repair Costs	2
Warranty	9
Fuel Economy	4
Complaints	5
Insurance Costs	8
OVERALL RATING	**–**

BMW X3

At-a-Glance

Status/Year Series Started	Unchanged/2011
Twins	–
Body Styles	SUV
Seating	5
Anti-Theft Device	Std. Pass. Immobil.
Parking Index Rating	Hard
Where Made	Spartanburg, SC
Fuel Factor	
MPG Rating (city/hwy)	Poor-19/26
Driving Range (mi.)	Short-383
Fuel Type	Premium
Annual Fuel Cost	High-$2,588
Gas Guzzler Tax	No
Greenhouse Gas Emissions (tons/yr.)	High-8.8
Barrels of Oil Used per year	High-15.7

How the Competition Rates

Competitors	Rating	Pg.
Audi Q5	–	90
Land Rover Range Rover	–	184
Porsche Cayenne	–	230

Price Range

	Retail	Markup
XDrive28i	$39,600	9%
XDrive35i	$44,700	9%

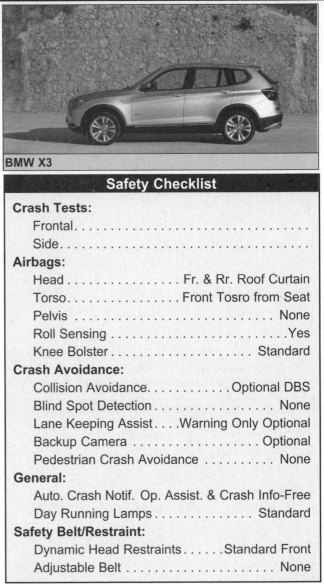

BMW X3

Safety Checklist

Crash Tests:
Frontal . . . .
Side . . . .

Airbags:
Head . . . . Fr. & Rr. Roof Curtain
Torso . . . . Front Tosro from Seat
Pelvis . . . . None
Roll Sensing . . . . .Yes
Knee Bolster . . . . Standard

Crash Avoidance:
Collision Avoidance . . . . .Optional DBS
Blind Spot Detection . . . . None
Lane Keeping Assist . . . .Warning Only Optional
Backup Camera . . . . Optional
Pedestrian Crash Avoidance . . . . None

General:
Auto. Crash Notif. Op. Assist. & Crash Info-Free
Day Running Lamps . . . . Standard

Safety Belt/Restraint:
Dynamic Head Restraints . . . . . .Standard Front
Adjustable Belt . . . . None

BMW X3

Specifications

Drive	AWD
Engine	3.0-liter V6
Transmission	8-sp. Automatic
Tow Rating (lbs.)	
Head/Leg Room (in.)	Cramped-40.7/39.9
Interior Space (cu. ft.)	Very Cramped-90.1
Cargo Space (cu. ft.)	Roomy-27.6
Wheelbase/Length (in.)	110.6/183

Ratings—10 Best, 1 Worst

Combo Crash Tests	–
Safety Features	8
Rollover	3
Preventive Maintenance	10
Repair Costs	1
Warranty	9
Fuel Economy	3
Complaints	–
Insurance Costs	3
OVERALL RATING	**–**

BMW X5

BMW X5

At-a-Glance

Status/Year Series Started	All New/2014
Twins	–
Body Styles	SUV
Seating	5/7
Anti-Theft Device	Std. Pass. Immobil.
Parking Index Rating	Very Hard
Where Made	Spartanburg, SC
Fuel Factor	
MPG Rating (city/hwy)	Poor-18/27
Driving Range (mi.)	Very Long-474
Fuel Type	Premium
Annual Fuel Cost	High-$2,642
Gas Guzzler Tax	No
Greenhouse Gas Emissions (tons/yr.)	High-8.7
Barrels of Oil Used per year	High-15.7

How the Competition Rates

Competitors	Rating	Pg.
Audi Q7	–	91
Cadillac SRX	8	107
Volvo XC90	–	270

Price Range

	Retail	Markup
sDrive35i	$52,800	9%
XDrive35i	$55,100	9%
XDrive50i	$68,200	9%
	–	

Safety Checklist

Crash Tests:
Frontal . . . .
Side . . . .
Airbags:
Head . . . . Fr. & Rr. Roof Curtain
Torso . . . . Front Torso from Seat
Pelvis . . . . None
Roll Sensing . . . . .Yes
Knee Bolster . . . . Standard
Crash Avoidance:
Collision Avoidance. . . . . . Optional CIB & DBS
Blind Spot Detection . . . . Optional
Lane Keeping Assist . . . .Warning Only Optional
Backup Camera . . . . Optional
Pedestrian Crash Avoidance . . . . Optional
General:
Auto. Crash Notif. Op. Assist. & Crash Info-Free
Day Running Lamps . . . . Standard
Safety Belt/Restraint:
Dynamic Head Restraints . . . . Optional
Adjustable Belt . . . . None

BMW X5

Specifications

Drive	AWD
Engine	3.0-liter I6
Transmission	8-sp. Automatic
Tow Rating (lbs.)	
Head/Leg Room (in.)	Cramped-40.5/40.4
Interior Space (cu. ft.)	
Cargo Space (cu. ft.)	Roomy-23
Wheelbase/Length (in.)	115.5/193.2

Buick Enclave

Buick Enclave — Large SUV

Buick Enclave

Ratings—10 Best, 1 Worst

Combo Crash Tests	9
Safety Features	6
Rollover	4
Preventive Maintenance	6
Repair Costs	2
Warranty	6
Fuel Economy	2
Complaints	6
Insurance Costs	10
OVERALL RATING	**7**

Buick Enclave

At-a-Glance

Status/Year Series Started........ Unchanged/2008
Twins .... –
Body Styles .... SUV
Seating 7/8
Anti-Theft Device ...... Std. Pass. Immobil. & Alarm
Parking Index Rating ....Very Hard
Where Made.....................Lansing, MI
Fuel Factor
  MPG Rating (city/hwy)..........Very Poor-17/24
  Driving Range (mi.) Long-431
  Fuel Type.......................Regular
  Annual Fuel Cost .... High-$2,629
  Gas Guzzler Tax ....No
  Greenhouse Gas Emissions (tons/yr.)..... High-9.7
  Barrels of Oil Used per year High-17.3

How the Competition Rates

Competitors	Rating	Pg.
Acura MDX	8	82
Audi Q7	–	91
Lexus GX	–	190

Price Range

	Retail	Markup
Convenience FWD	$38,740	5%
Convenience AWD	$40,740	5%
Leather	$42,755	5%
Premium AWD	$48,315	5%

Safety Checklist

Crash Tests:
  Frontal........................... Good
  Side........................... Very Good
Airbags:
  Head .... Fr. & Rr. Roof Curtain
  Torso..........Front Pelvis/Torso from Seat
  Pelvis ....Front Pelvis/Torso from Seat
  Roll Sensing ....Yes
  Knee Bolster .... None
Crash Avoidance:
  Collision Avoidance.....Warning Only Optional
  Blind Spot Detection .... Optional
  Lane Keeping Assist....Warning Only Optional
  Backup Camera .... Standard
  Pedestrian Crash Avoidance .... None
General:
  Auto. Crash Notif. .Op. Assist. & Crash Info-Fee
  Day Running Lamps .... Standard
Safety Belt/Restraint:
  Dynamic Head Restraints............ None
  Adjustable Belt .... Standard

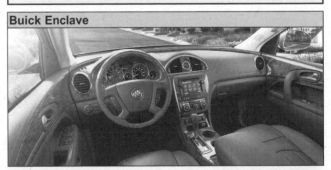
Buick Enclave

Specifications

Drive................................... FWD
Engine 3.6-liter V6
Transmission ....6-sp. Automatic
Tow Rating (lbs.) Low-4500
Head/Leg Room (in.) Average-40.4/41.3
Interior Space (cu. ft.)......... Very Roomy-151.1
Cargo Space (cu. ft.) Roomy-23.3
Wheelbase/Length (in.) 119/201.9

Ratings—10 Best, 1 Worst	
Combo Crash Tests	8
Safety Features	9
Rollover	2
Preventive Maintenance	–
Repair Costs	–
Warranty	6
Fuel Economy	6
Complaints	10
Insurance Costs	8
OVERALL RATING	**9**

Buick Encore

Buick Encore

At-a-Glance

Status/Year Series Started	Unchanged/2013
Twins	–
Body Styles	SUV
Seating	4
Anti-Theft Device	Std. Pass. Immobil. & Alarm
Parking Index Rating	Easy
Where Made	Bupyong, South Korea
Fuel Factor	
MPG Rating (city/hwy)	Average-23/30
Driving Range (mi.)	Very Short-360
Fuel Type	Regular
Annual Fuel Cost	Low-$2,002
Gas Guzzler Tax	No
Greenhouse Gas Emissions (tons/yr.)	Low-7.1
Barrels of Oil Used per year	Average-12.7

How the Competition Rates

Competitors	Rating	Pg.
Ford Escape	5	136
Honda CR-V	6	150
Mazda CX-5	6	196

Price Range	Retail	Markup
Base FWD	$24,160	4%
Convenience AWD	$27,285	4%
Leather	$27,485	4%
Premium AWD	$30,465	4%

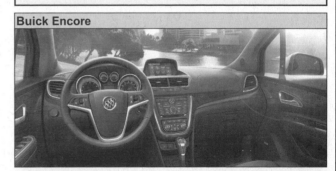
Buick Encore

Safety Checklist

Crash Tests:
Frontal . . . . Very Good
Side . . . . Average
Airbags:
Head . . . . Fr. & Rr. Roof Curtain
Torso . . . . Fr. & Rr. Pelvis/Torso from Seat
Pelvis . . . . Fr. & Rr. Pelvis/Torso from Seat
Roll Sensing . . . . .Yes
Knee Bolster . . . . Standard
Crash Avoidance:
Collision Avoidance. . . . .Warning Only Optional
Blind Spot Detection . . . . Optional
Lane Keeping Assist. . . .Warning Only Optional
Backup Camera . . . . Standard
Pedestrian Crash Avoidance . . . . None
General:
Auto. Crash Notif. .Op. Assist. & Crash Info-Fee
Day Running Lamps . . . . Standard
Safety Belt/Restraint:
Dynamic Head Restraints . . . . None
Adjustable Belt . . . . .Std. Front & Opt. Rear

Specifications

Drive	AWD
Engine	1.4-liter I4
Transmission	6-sp. Automatic
Tow Rating (lbs.)	
Head/Leg Room (in.)	Cramped-39.6/40.8
Interior Space (cu. ft.)	Cramped-92.8
Cargo Space (cu. ft.)	Average-18.8
Wheelbase/Length (in.)	100.6/168.4

Ratings—10 Best, 1 Worst

Combo Crash Tests	9
Safety Features	8
Rollover	7
Preventive Maintenance	5
Repair Costs	3
Warranty	6
Fuel Economy	4
Complaints	5
Insurance Costs	5
OVERALL RATING	**8**

Buick LaCrosse

Buick LaCrosse

At-a-Glance

Status/Year Series Started Appearance Change/2010
Twins . . . . –
Body Styles . . . . .Sedan
Seating 5
Anti-Theft Device . . . . . . Std. Pass. Immobil. & Alarm
Parking Index Rating . . . . Average
Where Made. . . . . Fairfax, KS
Fuel Factor
  MPG Rating (city/hwy) Poor-18/28
  Driving Range (mi.) . . . . .Very Short-337
  Fuel Type. . . . . .Regular
  Annual Fuel Cost . . . . High-$2,399
  Gas Guzzler Tax . . . . .No
  Greenhouse Gas Emissions (tons/yr.). High-8.8
  Barrels of Oil Used per year High-15.7

How the Competition Rates

Competitors	Rating	Pg.
Acura TL	3	85
Cadillac XTS	10	108
Volvo S80	–	268

Price Range

Price Range	Retail	Markup
Base	$33,135	4%
Leather	$35,210	4%
Premium I	$38,810	4%
Premium AWD	$39,885	4%

Safety Checklist

Crash Tests:
Frontal. . . . . Very Good
Side. . . . . Good
Airbags:
Head . . . . Fr. & Rr. Roof Curtain
Torso. . . . . Fr. & Rr. Pelvis/Torso from Seat
Pelvis . . . . Fr. & Rr. Pelvis/Torso from Seat
Roll Sensing . . . . .Yes
Knee Bolster . . . . None
Crash Avoidance:
Collision Avoidance. . . . .Warning Only Optional
Blind Spot Detection . . . . Optional
Lane Keeping Assist. . . .Warning Only Optional
Backup Camera . . . . Standard
Pedestrian Crash Avoidance . . . . None
General:
Auto. Crash Notif. .Op. Assist. & Crash Info-Fee
Day Running Lamps . . . . Standard
Safety Belt/Restraint:
Dynamic Head Restraints. . . . . None
Adjustable Belt . . . . Standard Front & Rear

Buick LaCrosse

Specifications

Drive. . . . . FWD
Engine 3.6-liter V6
Transmission . . . . .6-sp. Automatic
Tow Rating (lbs.) . . . . Very Low-1000
Head/Leg Room (in.) . . . . . . Very Cramped-38/41.7
Interior Space (cu. ft.). Average-99
Cargo Space (cu. ft.) Cramped-13.3
Wheelbase/Length (in.) 111.7/197

Ratings—10 Best, 1 Worst

Combo Crash Tests	6
Safety Features	6
Rollover	8
Preventive Maintenance	5
Repair Costs	6
Warranty	6
Fuel Economy	5
Complaints	8
Insurance Costs	3
OVERALL RATING	**7**

Buick Regal

At-a-Glance

Status/Year Series Started Appearance Change/2011
Twins . . . . –
Body Styles . . . . .Sedan
Seating 5
Anti-Theft Device . . . . . . Std. Pass. Immobil. & Alarm
Parking Index Rating . . . . Hard
Where Made. . . . . Oshawa, Ontario
Fuel Factor
  MPG Rating (city/hwy) Average-19/31
  Driving Range (mi.) . . . . Very Long-458
  Fuel Type . . . . .Regular
  Annual Fuel Cost . . . . Average-$2,236
  Gas Guzzler Tax . . . . .No
  Greenhouse Gas Emissions (tons/yr.) . . Average-8.0
  Barrels of Oil Used per year High-14.3

How the Competition Rates

Competitors	Rating	Pg.
Dodge Avenger	3	125
Hyundai Azera	–	156
Lincoln MKZ	4	195

Price Range	Retail	Markup
Base	$29,690	4%
Premium I	$31,560	4%
Premium II AWD	$35,935	4%
GS AWD	$39,270	4%

Buick Regal

Safety Checklist

Crash Tests:
  Frontal. . . . . Average
  Side. . . . . Average
Airbags:
  Head . . . . Fr. & Rr. Roof Curtain
  Torso. . . . . .Front Pelvis/Torso from Seat
  Pelvis . . . . .Front Pelvis/Torso from Seat
  Roll Sensing . . . . .Yes
  Knee Bolster . . . . None
Crash Avoidance:
  Collision Avoidance. . . . .Warning Only Optional
  Blind Spot Detection . . . . Optional
  Lane Keeping Assist. . . .Warning Only Optional
  Backup Camera . . . . Standard
  Pedestrian Crash Avoidance . . . . None
General:
  Auto. Crash Notif. .Op. Assist. & Crash Info-Fee
  Day Running Lamps . . . . Standard
Safety Belt/Restraint:
  Dynamic Head Restraints . . . . None
  Adjustable Belt . . . . Standard Front & Rear

Buick Regal

Specifications

Drive. . . . . FWD
Engine 2.4-liter I4
Transmission . . . . 6-sp. Auto w/Overdrive
Tow Rating (lbs.) . . . .
Head/Leg Room (in.) Cramped-38.8/42.1
Interior Space (cu. ft.). Cramped-96.8
Cargo Space (cu. ft.) . . . . .Very Cramped-11.1
Wheelbase/Length (in.) 107.8/190.2

Ratings—10 Best, 1 Worst	
Combo Crash Tests	10
Safety Features	9
Rollover	7
Preventive Maintenance	7
Repair Costs	7
Warranty	6
Fuel Economy	6
Complaints	8
Insurance Costs	5
OVERALL RATING	**10**

Buick Verano

Buick Verano

At-a-Glance

Status/Year Series Started	Unchanged/2012
Twins	Chevrolet Cruze
Body Styles	Sedan
Seating	5
Anti-Theft Device	Std. Pass. Immobil. & Alarm
Parking Index Rating	Easy
Where Made	Orion Township, MI
Fuel Factor	
MPG Rating (city/hwy)	Average-21/32
Driving Range (mi.)	Short-388
Fuel Type	Regular
Annual Fuel Cost	Average-$2,071
Gas Guzzler Tax	No
Greenhouse Gas Emissions (tons/yr.)	Average-7.4
Barrels of Oil Used per year	Average-13.2

How the Competition Rates

Competitors	Rating	Pg.
Acura ILX	6	81
Dodge Dart	9	128
Lexus IS	7	191

Price Range	Retail	Markup
Base	$23,700	4%
Convenience	$24,870	4%
Leather	$26,900	4%
Turbo	$29,065	4%

Safety Checklist

Crash Tests:
Frontal	Very Good
Side	Very Good

Airbags:
Head	Fr. & Rr. Roof Curtain
Torso	Fr. & Rr. Pelvis/Torso from Seat
Pelvis	Fr. & Rr. Pelvis/Torso from Seat
Roll Sensing	Yes
Knee Bolster	Standard

Crash Avoidance:
Collision Avoidance	Warning Only Optional
Blind Spot Detection	Optional
Lane Keeping Assist	Warning Only Optional
Backup Camera	Standard
Pedestrian Crash Avoidance	None

General:
Auto. Crash Notif.	Op. Assist. & Crash Info-Fee
Day Running Lamps	Standard

Safety Belt/Restraint:
Dynamic Head Restraints	None
Adjustable Belt	Standard Front & Rear

Buick Verano

Specifications

Drive	FWD
Engine	2.4-liter I4
Transmission	6-sp. Automatic
Tow Rating (lbs.)	Very Low-1000
Head/Leg Room (in.)	Cramped-38.3/42
Interior Space (cu. ft.)	Cramped-95
Cargo Space (cu. ft.)	Cramped-14.3
Wheelbase/Length (in.)	105.7/183.9

Ratings—10 Best, 1 Worst	–
Combo Crash Tests	9
Safety Features	7
Rollover	9
Preventive Maintenance	10
Repair Costs	3
Warranty	9
Fuel Economy	6
Complaints	1
Insurance Costs	5
OVERALL RATING	**9**

Cadillac ATS

Cadillac ATS

At-a-Glance

Status/Year Series Started	Unchanged/2013
Twins	–
Body Styles	Sedan
Seating	5
Anti-Theft Device	Std. Pass. Immobil. & Alarm
Parking Index Rating	Easy
Where Made	Lansing, MI
Fuel Factor	
MPG Rating (city/hwy)	Average-22/33
Driving Range (mi.)	Average-414
Fuel Type	Regular
Annual Fuel Cost	Low-$1,988
Gas Guzzler Tax	No
Greenhouse Gas Emissions (tons/yr.)	Low-7.0
Barrels of Oil Used per year	Average-12.7

How the Competition Rates

Competitors	Rating	Pg.
Acura ILX	6	81
Infiniti Q50	6	164
Mercedes-Benz C-Class	4	203

Price Range

Price Range	Retail	Markup
Base 2.5L	$33,065	6%
Luxury 2.0T	$39,095	6%
Performance 3.6L AWD	$46,095	7%
Premium 3.6L AWD	$48,195	7%

Safety Checklist

Crash Tests:
Frontal	Very Good
Side	Good

Airbags:
Head	Fr. & Rr. Roof Curtain
Torso	Front Pelvis/Torso from Seat
Pelvis	Front Pelvis/Torso from Seat
Roll Sensing	Yes
Knee Bolster	Standard

Crash Avoidance:
Collision Avoidance	Optional CIB
Blind Spot Detection	Optional
Lane Keeping Assist	Warning Only Optional
Backup Camera	Standard
Pedestrian Crash Avoidance	None

General:
Auto. Crash Notif.	Op. Assist. & Crash Info-Fee
Day Running Lamps	Standard

Safety Belt/Restraint:
Dynamic Head Restraints	None
Adjustable Belt	Standard Rear

Cadillac ATS

Specifications

Drive	RWD
Engine	2.5-liter I4
Transmission	6-sp. Auto W/overdrive
Tow Rating (lbs.)	Very Low-1000
Head/Leg Room (in.)	Cramped-38.6/42.5
Interior Space (cu. ft.)	Very Cramped-90.9
Cargo Space (cu. ft.)	Very Cramped-10.4
Wheelbase/Length (in.)	109.3/182.8

Ratings—10 Best, 1 Worst

Combo Crash Tests	–
Safety Features	7
Rollover	8
Preventive Maintenance	10
Repair Costs	3
Warranty	9
Fuel Economy	3
Complaints	–
Insurance Costs	8
OVERALL RATING	**–**

Cadillac CTS Coupe

At-a-Glance

Status/Year Series Started	All New/2014
Twins	–
Body Styles	Sedan, Coupe, Wagon
Seating	5
Anti-Theft Device	Std. Pass. Immobil. & Opt. Pass. Alarm
Parking Index Rating	Hard
Where Made	Lansing, MI

Fuel Factor

MPG Rating (city/hwy)	Poor-18/27
Driving Range (mi.)	Average-402
Fuel Type	Regular
Annual Fuel Cost	High-$2,430
Gas Guzzler Tax	No
Greenhouse Gas Emissions (tons/yr.)	Average-8.3
Barrels of Oil Used per year	High-15.0

How the Competition Rates

Competitors	Rating	Pg.
Acura TL	3	85
Infiniti Q50	6	164
Lexus ES	6	188

Price Range

	Retail	Markup
2.0T Base	$45,100	6%
Vsport	$59,070	7%
V Wagon	$63,600	7%
3.6L Premium	$64,500	7%

Cadillac CTS Sedan

Safety Checklist

Crash Tests:
Frontal . . . .
Side . . . .

Airbags:
Head . . . . Fr. & Rr. Roof Curtain
Torso . . . . Front Pelvis/Torso from Seat
Pelvis . . . . Front Pelvis/Torso from Seat
Roll Sensing . . . . Yes
Knee Bolster . . . . Standard

Crash Avoidance:
Collision Avoidance . . . . Optional CIB
Blind Spot Detection . . . . Optional
Lane Keeping Assist . . . . Warning Only Optional
Backup Camera . . . . Optional
Pedestrian Crash Avoidance . . . . None

General:
Auto. Crash Notif. . Op. Assist. & Crash Info-Fee
Day Running Lamps . . . . Standard

Safety Belt/Restraint:
Dynamic Head Restraints . . . . None
Adjustable Belt . . . . Standard Front & Rear

Cadillac CTS Sport Wagon

Specifications

Drive	RWD
Engine	3.6-liter V6
Transmission	6-sp. Auto. w/Overdrive
Tow Rating (lbs.)	Very Low-1000
Head/Leg Room (in.)	Average-39.2/42.6
Interior Space (cu. ft.)	Cramped-97
Cargo Space (cu. ft.)	Cramped-13.7
Wheelbase/Length (in.)	114.6/195.5

Ratings—10 Best, 1 Worst

Combo Crash Tests	7
Safety Features	8
Rollover	3
Preventive Maintenance	10
Repair Costs	5
Warranty	9
Fuel Economy	2
Complaints	6
Insurance Costs	8
OVERALL RATING	**8**

Cadillac SRX

At-a-Glance

Status/Year Series Started	Unchanged/2010
Twins	–
Body Styles	SUV
Seating	5
Anti-Theft Device	Std. Pass. Immobil. & Alarm
Parking Index Rating	Very Hard
Where Made	Ramos Arizpe, Mexico

Fuel Factor

MPG Rating (city/hwy)	Very Poor-17/24
Driving Range (mi.)	Average-411
Fuel Type	Regular
Annual Fuel Cost	High-$2,629
Gas Guzzler Tax	No
Greenhouse Gas Emissions (tons/yr.)	High-9.6
Barrels of Oil Used per year	High-17.3

How the Competition Rates

Competitors	Rating	Pg.
Acura RDX	7	83
Lexus RX	5	193
Volvo XC60	10	269

Price Range

	Retail	Markup
Base	$37,505	6%
Luxury	$42,880	6%
Performance AWD	$48,065	7%
Premium AWD	$50,955	7%

BEST CAR Book BET

Cadillac SRX

Safety Checklist

Crash Tests:

Frontal	Good
Side	Good

Airbags:

Head	Fr. & Rr. Roof Curtain
Torso	Front Pelvis/Torso from Seat
Pelvis	Front Pelvis/Torso from Seat
Roll Sensing	Yes
Knee Bolster	None

Crash Avoidance:

Collision Avoidance	Optional CIB & DBS
Blind Spot Detection	Optional
Lane Keeping Assist	Warning Only Optional
Backup Camera	Standard
Pedestrian Crash Avoidance	None

General:

Auto. Crash Notif.	Op. Assist. & Crash Info-Fee
Day Running Lamps	Standard

Safety Belt/Restraint:

Dynamic Head Restraints	None
Adjustable Belt	Standard Front & Rear

Cadillac SRX

Specifications

Drive	FWD
Engine	3.6-liter V6
Transmission	6-sp. Auto. w/Overdrive
Tow Rating (lbs.)	Very Low-3500
Head/Leg Room (in.)	Cramped-39.7/41.2
Interior Space (cu. ft.)	Average-100.6
Cargo Space (cu. ft.)	Roomy-29.9
Wheelbase/Length (in.)	110.5/190.3

Ratings—10 Best, 1 Worst

Combo Crash Tests	10
Safety Features	8
Rollover	7
Preventive Maintenance	10
Repair Costs	3
Warranty	9
Fuel Economy	4
Complaints	9
Insurance Costs	8
OVERALL RATING	**10**

Cadillac XTS

Cadillac XTS

Cadillac XTS

At-a-Glance

Status/Year Series Started........ Unchanged/2013
Twins . . . . –
Body Styles . . . . .Sedan
Seating 5
Anti-Theft Device . . . . . . Std. Pass. Immobil. & Alarm
Parking Index Rating . . . . Hard
Where Made. . . . . Oshawa, Ontario
Fuel Factor
  MPG Rating (city/hwy) Poor-18/28
  Driving Range (mi.) Average-407
  Fuel Type . . . . .Regular
  Annual Fuel Cost . . . . High-$2,399
  Gas Guzzler Tax . . . . .No
  Greenhouse Gas Emissions (tons/yr.) High-8.8
  Barrels of Oil Used per year High-15.7

How the Competition Rates

Competitors	Rating	Pg.
BMW 7 Series	–	96
Jaguar XF	–	171
Lincoln MKS	3	194

Price Range

Price Range	Retail	Markup
Base	$44,600	6%
Luxury	$49,510	6%
Premium	$54,455	7%
Platinum Vsport	$69,095	7%

Safety Checklist

Crash Tests:
  Frontal. . . . . Very Good
  Side. . . . . . . : . . . . Very Good
Airbags:
  Head . . . . Fr. & Rr. Roof Curtain
  Torso. . . . . Fr. & Rr. Torso from Seat
  Pelvis . . . . .Front Pelvis/Torso from Seat
  Roll Sensing . . . . .Yes
  Knee Bolster . . . . Standard
Crash Avoidance:
  Collision Avoidance. . . . . Optional CIB
  Blind Spot Detection . . . . Optional
  Lane Keeping Assist . . . .Warning Only Optional
  Backup Camera . . . . Standard
  Pedestrian Crash Avoidance . . . . None
General:
  Auto. Crash Notif. . .Op. Assist. & Crash Info-Fee
  Day Running Lamps . . . . Standard
Safety Belt/Restraint:
  Dynamic Head Restraints. . . . . None
  Adjustable Belt . . . . . . : Standard Front & Rear

Specifications

Drive . . . . FWD
Engine 3.6-liter V6
Transmission . . . . .6-sp. Automatic
Tow Rating (lbs.) . . . . Very Low-1000
Head/Leg Room (in.) . . . . . . Very Roomy-40.1/45.8
Interior Space (cu. ft.). Roomy-104.2
Cargo Space (cu. ft.) Average-18
Wheelbase/Length (in.) 111.7/202

Ratings—10 Best, 1 Worst

Combo Crash Tests	10
Safety Features	4
Rollover	10
Preventive Maintenance	5
Repair Costs	7
Warranty	8
Fuel Economy	4
Complaints	6
Insurance Costs	1
OVERALL RATING	**8**

The CAR Book BEST BET

Chevrolet Camaro

Chevrolet Camaro Convertible

At-a-Glance

Status/Year Series Started Appearance Change/2010
Twins .... –
Body Styles .... Coupe, Convertible
Seating 4
Anti-Theft Device ...... Std. Pass. Immobil. & Alarm
Parking Index Rating .... Hard
Where Made.................. Oshawa, Ontario
Fuel Factor
  MPG Rating (city/hwy) Poor-19/30
  Driving Range (mi.) .... –
  Fuel Type........................... Regular
  Annual Fuel Cost .... Average-$2,261
  Gas Guzzler Tax .... No
  Greenhouse Gas Emissions (tons/yr.)..... High-8.8
  Barrels of Oil Used per year High-15.7

How the Competition Rates

Competitors	Rating	Pg.
Dodge Challenger	5	126
Ford Mustang	2	144
Mazda MX-5 Miata	–	202

Price Range	Retail	Markup
1LS	$23,455	4%
2LT	$28,955	4%
1SS	$32,955	4%
ZL1	$54,955	4%

Safety Checklist

Crash Tests:
  Frontal......................... Very Good
  Side........................... Very Good
Airbags:
  Head .... Fr. & Rr. Roof Curtain
  Torso........... Front Pelvis/Torso from Seat
  Pelvis .... Front Pelvis/Torso from Seat
  Roll Sensing .... Yes
  Knee Bolster .... None
Crash Avoidance:
  Collision Avoidance................. None
  Blind Spot Detection .... None
  Lane Keeping Assist................ None
  Backup Camera .... Optional
  Pedestrian Crash Avoidance .... None
General:
  Auto. Crash Notif. .Op. Assist. & Crash Info-Fee
  Day Running Lamps .... Standard
Safety Belt/Restraint:
  Dynamic Head Restraints............ None
  Adjustable Belt .... Standard Rear

Chevrolet Camaro

Specifications

Drive................................. RWD
Engine 3.6-liter V6
Transmission .... 6-sp. Automatic
Tow Rating (lbs.) ....
Head/Leg Room (in.) ..... Very Cramped-37.4/42.4
Interior Space (cu. ft.)............. Cramped-93
Cargo Space (cu. ft.) .... Very Cramped-11.3
Wheelbase/Length (in.) 112.3/192.3

Chevrolet Corvette

Ratings—10 Best, 1 Worst

Combo Crash Tests	–
Safety Features	1
Rollover	10
Preventive Maintenance	6
Repair Costs	1
Warranty	8
Fuel Economy	3
Complaints	–
Insurance Costs	10

OVERALL RATING — –

Chevrolet Corvette

Chevrolet Corvette

At-a-Glance

Status/Year Series Started	All New/2014
Twins	–
Body Styles	Coupe, Convertible
Seating	2
Anti-Theft Device	Std. Pass. Immobil. & Alarm
Parking Index Rating	Average
Where Made	Bowling Green, KY
Fuel Factor	
MPG Rating (city/hwy)	Poor-16/28
Driving Range (mi.)	Short-367
Fuel Type	Regular
Annual Fuel Cost	High-$2,595
Gas Guzzler Tax	No
Greenhouse Gas Emissions (tons/yr.)	High-9.1
Barrels of Oil Used per year	High-16.5

How the Competition Rates

Competitors	Rating	Pg.
Dodge Challenger	5	126
Ford Mustang	2	144
Mazda MX-5 Miata	–	202

Price Range

Price Range	Retail	Markup
Base Coupe	$51,000	10%
Z51 Coupe	$53,800	10%
Base Convertible	$56,000	10%
Z51 Convertible	$58,800	10%

Safety Checklist

Crash Tests:
Frontal . . . . ·
Side . . . . ·

Airbags:
Head . . . . Front Head/Torso from Seat
Torso . . . . Front Head/Torso from Seat
Pelvis . . . . None
Roll Sensing . . . . No
Knee Bolster . . . . None

Crash Avoidance:
Collision Avoidance . . . . None
Blind Spot Detection . . . . None
Lane Keeping Assist . . . . None
Backup Camera . . . . Standard
Pedestrian Crash Avoidance . . . . None

General:
Auto. Crash Notif. .Op. Assist. & Crash Info-Fee
Day Running Lamps . . . . Standard

Safety Belt/Restraint:
Dynamic Head Restraints . . . . None
Adjustable Belt . . . . None

Chevrolet Corvette

Specifications

Drive	RWD
Engine	6.2-liter V8
Transmission	6-sp. Automatic
Tow Rating (lbs.)	
Head/Leg Room (in.)	Cramped-38/43
Interior Space (cu. ft.)	Very Cramped-52
Cargo Space (cu. ft.)	Cramped-15
Wheelbase/Length (in.)	106.7/177

Chevrolet Cruze Compact

Ratings—10 Best, 1 Worst

Combo Crash Tests	8
Safety Features	8
Rollover	8
Preventive Maintenance	5
Repair Costs	9
Warranty	8
Fuel Economy	7
Complaints	5
Insurance Costs	1
OVERALL RATING	**9**

Chevrolet Cruze

Chevrolet Cruze

At-a-Glance

Status/Year Series Started	Unchanged/2010
Twins	Buick Verano
Body Styles	Sedan
Seating	5
Anti-Theft Device	Std. Pass. Immobil. & Alarm
Parking Index Rating	Easy
Where Made	Lordstown, OH
Fuel Factor	
MPG Rating (city/hwy)	Good-22/35
Driving Range (mi.)	Average-412
Fuel Type	Regular
Annual Fuel Cost	Low-$1,948
Gas Guzzler Tax	No
Greenhouse Gas Emissions (tons/yr.)	Low-6.8
Barrels of Oil Used per year	Average-12.2

How the Competition Rates

Competitors	Rating	Pg.
Ford Focus	5	142
Honda Civic	6	148
Toyota Corolla	7	247

Price Range	Retail	Markup
LS	$18,355	4%
Eco	$21,030	4%
2LT	$22,480	4%
LTZ	$23,705	5%

Safety Checklist

Crash Tests:
Frontal .... Good
Side .... Good

Airbags:
Head .... Fr. & Rr. Roof Curtain
Torso .... Fr. & Rr. Pelvis/Torso from Seat
Pelvis .... Fr. & Rr. Pelvis/Torso from Seat
Roll Sensing .... Yes
Knee Bolster .... Standard

Crash Avoidance:
Collision Avoidance .... None
Blind Spot Detection .... Optional
Lane Keeping Assist .... None
Backup Camera .... Optional
Pedestrian Crash Avoidance .... None

General:
Auto. Crash Notif. .Op. Assist. & Crash Info-Fee
Day Running Lamps .... Standard

Safety Belt/Restraint:
Dynamic Head Restraints .... None
Adjustable Belt .... Standard Front & Rear

Chevrolet Cruze

Specifications

Drive	FWD
Engine	1.8-liter I4
Transmission	6-sp. Automatic
Tow Rating (lbs.)	Very Low-1000
Head/Leg Room (in.)	Average-39.3/42.3
Interior Space (cu. ft.)	Cramped-95
Cargo Space (cu. ft.)	Cramped-15
Wheelbase/Length (in.)	105.7/181

Ratings—10 Best, 1 Worst	Equinox	Terrain
Combo Crash Tests	3	3
Safety Features	5	4
Rollover	3	3
Preventive Maintenance	5	5
Repair Costs	5	5
Warranty	8	6
Fuel Economy	6	6
Complaints	4	7
Insurance Costs	5	5
OVERALL RATING	**3**	**3**

Chevrolet Equinox

Safety Checklist

Crash Tests:
Frontal . . . . Poor
Side . . . . Poor

Airbags:
Head . . . . Fr. & Rr. Roof Curtain
Torso . . . . Front Pelvis/Torso from Seat
Pelvis . . . . Front Pelvis/Torso from Seat
Roll Sensing . . . . Yes
Knee Bolster . . . . None

Crash Avoidance:
Collision Avoidance . . . . . Warning Only Optional
Blind Spot Detection . . . . None
Lane Keeping Assist . . . . Warning Only Optional
Backup Camera . . . . Optional
Pedestrian Crash Avoidance . . . . None

General:
Auto. Crash Notif. . Op. Assist. & Crash Info-Fee
Day Running Lamps . . . . Standard

Safety Belt/Restraint:
Dynamic Head Restraints . . . . None
Adjustable Belt . . . . Standard Front & Rear

GMC Terrain

At-a-Glance

Status/Year Series Started Unchanged/2005
Twins . . . . GMC Terrain
Body Styles . . . . SUV
Seating 5
Anti-Theft Device . . . . . . Std. Pass. Immobil. & Alarm
Parking Index Rating . . . . Very Hard
Where Made . . . . . . Ontario, Canada / Spring Hill, TN
Fuel Factor
  MPG Rating (city/hwy) Average-22/32
  Driving Range (mi.) . . . . Very Long-481
  Fuel Type . . . . Regular
  Annual Fuel Cost . . . . Low-$2,010
  Gas Guzzler Tax . . . . No
  Greenhouse Gas Emissions (tons/yr.) Low-7.1
  Barrels of Oil Used per year Average-12.7

How the Competition Rates

Competitors	Rating	Pg.
Dodge Journey	–	131
Ford Explorer	4	138
Hyundai Santa Fe	–	159

Price Range	Retail	Markup
LS FWD	$24,360	5%
LT	$26,020	5%
2LT AWD	$29,640	5%
LTZ AWD	$33,335	5%

Chevrolet Equinox

Specifications

Drive . . . . FWD
Engine 2.4-liter I4
Transmission . . . . 6-sp. Automatic
Tow Rating (lbs.) . . . . Very Low-1500
Head/Leg Room (in.) Average-40.9/41.2
Interior Space (cu. ft.) Average-99.7
Cargo Space (cu. ft.) Roomy-31.4
Wheelbase/Length (in.) 112.5/187.8

Chevrolet Impala — Large

Ratings—10 Best, 1 Worst

Combo Crash Tests	6
Safety Features	8
Rollover	6
Preventive Maintenance	5
Repair Costs	6
Warranty	8
Fuel Economy	4
Complaints	–
Insurance Costs	10
OVERALL RATING	**8**

Chevrolet Impala

Chevrolet Impala

At-a-Glance

Status/Year Series Started	All New/2014
Twins	–
Body Styles	Sedan
Seating	5
Anti-Theft Device	Std. Pass. Immobil. & Opt. Pass. Alarm
Parking Index Rating	Hard
Where Made	Hamtramck, MI / Oshawa, Ontario

Fuel Factor

MPG Rating (city/hwy)	Poor-19/29
Driving Range (mi.)	Average-416
Fuel Type	Regular
Annual Fuel Cost	Average-$2,288
Gas Guzzler Tax	No
Greenhouse Gas Emissions (tons/yr.)	High-8.8
Barrels of Oil Used per year	High-15.7

How the Competition Rates

Competitors	Rating	Pg.
Dodge Charger	6	127
Ford Taurus	4	145
Toyota Avalon	7	245

Price Range

	Retail	Markup
LS	$26,725	4%
LT	$28,975	5%
LTZ	$33,745	6%
2LZ	$35,770	6%

Safety Checklist

Crash Tests:
Frontal	Good
Side	Poor

Airbags:
Head	Fr. & Rr. Roof Curtain
Torso	Fr. & Rr. Torso from Seat
Pelvis	Front Pelvis/Torso from Seat
Roll Sensing	Yes
Knee Bolster	Standard

Crash Avoidance:
Collision Avoidance	Optional CIB
Blind Spot Detection	Optional
Lane Keeping Assist	Warning Only Optional
Backup Camera	Optional
Pedestrian Crash Avoidance	None

General:
Auto. Crash Notif.	Op. Assist. & Crash Info-Fee
Day Running Lamps	Standard

Safety Belt/Restraint:
Dynamic Head Restraints	None
Adjustable Belt	Standard Front & Rear

Chevrolet Impala

Specifications

Drive	FWD
Engine	3.6-liter V6
Transmission	6-sp. Automatic
Tow Rating (lbs.)	Very Low-1000
Head/Leg Room (in.)	Very Roomy-39.9/45.8
Interior Space (cu. ft.)	Roomy-105
Cargo Space (cu. ft.)	Average-18.8
Wheelbase/Length (in.)	111.7/201.3

113

Ratings—10 Best, 1 Worst

Combo Crash Tests	–
Safety Features	8
Rollover	8
Preventive Maintenance	5
Repair Costs	7
Warranty	8
Fuel Economy	8
Complaints	6
Insurance Costs	1
OVERALL RATING	**–**

Chevrolet Malibu

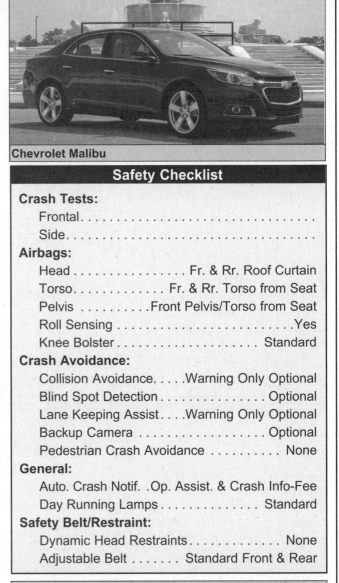
Chevrolet Malibu

At-a-Glance

Status/Year Series Started Appearance Change/2013
Twins . . . . –
Body Styles . . . . Sedan
Seating 5
Anti-Theft Device . . . . . . Std. Pass. Immobil. & Alarm
Parking Index Rating . . . . Average
Where Made . . . . Fairfax, KS / Hamtramck, MI
Fuel Factor
  MPG Rating (city/hwy) Good-25/36
  Driving Range (mi.) . . . . Very Long-536
  Fuel Type . . . . Regular
  Annual Fuel Cost . . . . Low-$1,775
  Gas Guzzler Tax . . . . No
  Greenhouse Gas Emissions (tons/yr.) . Very Low-6.3
  Barrels of Oil Used per year Low-11.4

How the Competition Rates

Competitors	Rating	Pg.
Ford Fusion	5	143
Honda Accord	7	147
Toyota Camry	6	246

Price Range	Retail	Markup
LS	$22,140	4%
Eco	$25,845	5%
LTZ	$27,690	6%
2LZ	$29,850	6%

Safety Checklist

Crash Tests:
  Frontal . . . .
  Side . . . .
Airbags:
  Head . . . . Fr. & Rr. Roof Curtain
  Torso . . . . Fr. & Rr. Torso from Seat
  Pelvis . . . . Front Pelvis/Torso from Seat
  Roll Sensing . . . . Yes
  Knee Bolster . . . . Standard
Crash Avoidance:
  Collision Avoidance . . . . . Warning Only Optional
  Blind Spot Detection . . . . Optional
  Lane Keeping Assist . . . . Warning Only Optional
  Backup Camera . . . . Optional
  Pedestrian Crash Avoidance . . . . None
General:
  Auto. Crash Notif. . Op. Assist. & Crash Info-Fee
  Day Running Lamps . . . . Standard
Safety Belt/Restraint:
  Dynamic Head Restraints . . . . None
  Adjustable Belt . . . . Standard Front & Rear

Chevrolet Malibu

Specifications

Drive . . . . FWD
Engine 2.4-liter I4
Transmission . . . . 6-sp. Automatic
Tow Rating (lbs.) . . . .
Head/Leg Room (in.) Cramped-39/42.1
Interior Space (cu. ft.) Average-100.3
Cargo Space (cu. ft.) Average-16.3
Wheelbase/Length (in.) 107.8/191.5

Ratings—10 Best, 1 Worst

Combo Crash Tests	10
Safety Features	5
Rollover	3
Preventive Maintenance	5
Repair Costs	6
Warranty	8
Fuel Economy	2
Complaints	–
Insurance Costs	10
OVERALL RATING	**8**

Chevrolet Silverado

Chevrolet Silverado

At-a-Glance

Status/Year Series Started. . . . . All New/2014
Twins . . . . –
Body Styles . . . . Pickup
Seating 5/6
Anti-Theft Device . . . Std. Pass. Immobil. & Opt. Pass. Alarm
Parking Index Rating . . . . Very Hard
Where Made. . . . . Fort Wayne, IN
Fuel Factor
  MPG Rating (city/hwy) . . . . .Very Poor-16/22
  Driving Range (mi.) . . . . Very Long-474
  Fuel Type . . . . .Regular
  Annual Fuel Cost . . . . Very High-$2,821
  Gas Guzzler Tax . . . . .No
  Greenhouse Gas Emissions (tons/yr.)Very High-10.2
  Barrels of Oil Used per year . . . . . . .Very High-18.3

How the Competition Rates

Competitors	Rating	Pg.
Ford F-150	1	139
Ram 1500	5	231
Toyota Tundra	–	257

Price Range

	Retail	Markup
W/T	$27,530	4%
LT Dbl Cab	$35,250	8%
LTZ Crew Cab	$42,870	8%
LTZ Z71 Crew Cab	$43,650	8%

Safety Checklist

Crash Tests:
  Frontal. . . . . Very Good
  Side. . . . . Very Good
Airbags:
  Head . . . . Fr. & Rr. Roof Curtain
  Torso. . . . . .Front Pelvis/Torso from Seat
  Pelvis . . . . .Front Pelvis/Torso from Seat
  Roll Sensing . . . . .Yes
  Knee Bolster . . . . None
Crash Avoidance:
  Collision Avoidance. . . . .Warning Only Optional
  Blind Spot Detection . . . . None
  Lane Keeping Assist. . . .Warning Only Optional
  Backup Camera . . . . Optional
  Pedestrian Crash Avoidance . . . . None
General:
  Auto. Crash Notif. . .Op. Assist. & Crash Info-Fee
  Day Running Lamps . . . . Standard
Safety Belt/Restraint:
  Dynamic Head Restraints . . . . None
  Adjustable Belt . . . . .Std. Front & Opt. Rear

Chevrolet Silverado

Specifications

Drive. 4WD
Engine 5.3-liter V8
Transmission . . . . .6-sp. Automatic
Tow Rating (lbs.) . . . . .Very High-9900
Head/Leg Room (in.) . . . . . . Very Roomy-42.8/45.2
Interior Space (cu. ft.). . . . .
Cargo Space (cu. ft.) . . . . .Very Roomy-61
Wheelbase/Length (in.) 143/230

Chevrolet Sonic Subcompact

Ratings—10 Best, 1 Worst

Combo Crash Tests	9
Safety Features	8
Rollover	6
Preventive Maintenance	9
Repair Costs	10
Warranty	8
Fuel Economy	8
Complaints	5
Insurance Costs	1
OVERALL RATING	**10**

Chevrolet Sonic

Chevrolet Sonic

At-a-Glance

Status/Year Series Started	Unchanged/2012
Twins	–
Body Styles	Hatchback
Seating	5
Anti-Theft Device	Std. Pass. Immobil. & Alarm
Parking Index Rating	Very Easy
Where Made	Orion Township, MI
Fuel Factor	
MPG Rating (city/hwy)	Good-26/35
Driving Range (mi.)	Very Short-359
Fuel Type	Regular
Annual Fuel Cost	Very Low-$1,750
Gas Guzzler Tax	No
Greenhouse Gas Emissions (tons/yr.)	Low-6.6
Barrels of Oil Used per year	Average-11.8

How the Competition Rates

Competitors	Rating	Pg.
Ford Fiesta	–	140
Mazda Mazda2	–	198
Toyota Yaris	6	259

Price Range

Price Range	Retail	Markup
LS	$15,420	3%
LT Hatchback	$17,665	4%
LTZ	$18,725	5%
RS	$21,610	5%

Safety Checklist

Crash Tests:
Frontal . . . . Very Good
Side . . . . Good
Airbags:
Head . . . . Fr. & Rr. Roof Curtain
Torso . . . . Fr. & Rr. Pelvis/Torso from Seat
Pelvis . . . . . . Fr. & Rr. Pelvis/Torso from Seat
Roll Sensing . . . . Yes
Knee Bolster . . . . Standard
Crash Avoidance:
Collision Avoidance . . . . . Warning Only Optional
Blind Spot Detection . . . . None
Lane Keeping Assist . . . . Warning Only Optional
Backup Camera . . . . Optional
Pedestrian Crash Avoidance . . . . None
General:
Auto. Crash Notif. . Op. Assist. & Crash Info-Fee
Day Running Lamps . . . . Standard
Safety Belt/Restraint:
Dynamic Head Restraints . . . . None
Adjustable Belt . . . . Std. Front & Opt. Rear

Chevrolet Sonic

Specifications

Drive	FWD
Engine	1.8-liter I4
Transmission	6-sp. Manual
Tow Rating (lbs.)	
Head/Leg Room (in.)	Cramped-38.7/41.8
Interior Space (cu. ft.)	Very Cramped-90.3
Cargo Space (cu. ft.)	Cramped-14.9
Wheelbase/Length (in.)	99.4/173.1

Chevrolet Spark

Ratings—10 Best, 1 Worst

Combo Crash Tests	3
Safety Features	7
Rollover	3
Preventive Maintenance	8
Repair Costs	6
Warranty	8
Fuel Economy	9
Complaints	–
Insurance Costs	3
OVERALL RATING	**6**

Chevrolet Spark

At-a-Glance

Status/Year Series Started........ Unchanged/2014
Twins ....–
Body Styles .... Hatchback
Seating 2
Anti-Theft Device . . . Std. Pass. Immobil. & Opt. Pass. Alarm
Parking Index Rating .... .Very Easy
Where Made..................... South Korea
Fuel Factor
  MPG Rating (city/hwy) .... Very Good-30/39
  Driving Range (mi.) .... .Very Short-308
  Fuel Type............................Regular
  Annual Fuel Cost .... Very Low-$1,537
  Gas Guzzler Tax ....No
  Greenhouse Gas Emissions (tons/yr.). Very Low-5.4
  Barrels of Oil Used per year Low-9.7

How the Competition Rates

Competitors	Rating	Pg.
Fiat 500	4	132
Mazda Mazda2	–	198
Smart ForTwo	–	236

Price Range	Retail	Markup
LS	$13,480	3%
1LT	$14,995	4%
2LT	$16,385	4%
2LT EV	$27,820	4%

Chevrolet Spark

Safety Checklist

Crash Tests:
  Frontal............................Poor
  Side..............................Poor
Airbags:
  Head .... Fr. & Rr. Roof Curtain
  Torso........ Fr. & Rr. Pelvis/Torso from Seat
  Pelvis .... Fr. & Rr. Pelvis/Torso from Seat
  Roll Sensing ....Yes
  Knee Bolster .... Standard
Crash Avoidance:
  Collision Avoidance.................. None
  Blind Spot Detection................. None
  Lane Keeping Assist................. None
  Backup Camera .... None
  Pedestrian Crash Avoidance .... None
General:
  Auto. Crash Notif. .Op. Assist. & Crash Info-Fee
  Day Running Lamps............. Standard
Safety Belt/Restraint:
  Dynamic Head Restraints............. None
  Adjustable Belt ....Std. Front & Opt. Rear

Chevrolet Spark

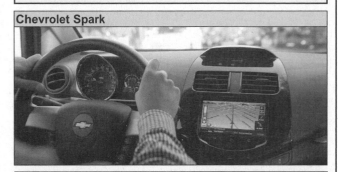

Specifications

Drive.....................................FWD
Engine 1.2-liter I4
Transmission ....CVT
Tow Rating (lbs.) ....
Head/Leg Room (in.) Average-39.4/42
Interior Space (cu. ft.).........Very Cramped-86.3
Cargo Space (cu. ft.) .... Very Cramped-11.4
Wheelbase/Length (in.) 93.5/114.7

Chev. Suburban/Cad. Escalade ESV/GMC Yukon XL Large SUV

Ratings—10 Best, 1 Worst	Suburban	Escalade ESV	Yukon XL
Combo Crash Tests	9	5	9
Safety Features	3	6	5
Rollover	1	1	1
Preventive Maintenance	5	10	5
Repair Costs	2	3	4
Warranty	8	9	6
Fuel Economy	1	1	1
Complaints	8	10	8
Insurance Costs	10	5	10
OVERALL RATING	**6**	**6**	**7**

Chevrolet Suburban

Safety Checklist

Crash Tests:
Frontal . . . . Good
Side . . . . Very Good

Airbags:
Head . . . . Fr & Rr. Roof Curtain
Torso . . . . Front Pelvis/Torso from Seat
Pelvis . . . . Front Pelvis/Torso from Seat
Roll Sensing . . . . Yes
Knee Bolster . . . . None

Crash Avoidance:
Collision Avoidance . . . . None
Blind Spot Detection . . . . Optional
Lane Keeping Assist . . . . None
Backup Camera . . . . Standard
Pedestrian Crash Avoidance . . . . None

General:
Auto. Crash Notif. .Op. Assist. & Crash Info-Fee
Day Running Lamps . . . . Standard

Safety Belt/Restraint:
Dynamic Head Restraints . . . . None
Adjustable Belt . . . . Standard Front & Rear

Cadillac Escalade ESV

At-a-Glance

Status/Year Series Started Unchanged/2007
Twins . . . . . . Cadillac Escalade ESV, GMC Yukon XL
Body Styles . . . . SUV
Seating 9
Anti-Theft Device . . . . . . Std. Pass. Immobil. & Alarm
Parking Index Rating . . . . Very Hard
Where Made . . . . Arlington, TX
Fuel Factor
  MPG Rating (city/hwy) . . . . Very Poor-15/21
  Driving Range (mi.) . . . . Very Long-542
  Fuel Type . . . . Regular
  Annual Fuel Cost . . . . Very High-$2,989
  Gas Guzzler Tax . . . . No
  Greenhouse Gas Emissions (tons/yr.) Very High-10.8
  Barrels of Oil Used per year . . . . Very High-19.4

How the Competition Rates

Competitors	Rating	Pg.
Dodge Durango	7	129
Ford Expedition	2	137
Nissan Armada	–	217

Price Range	Retail	Markup
LS 2WD	$45,065	8%
LS 4WD	$47,910	8%
LT 4WD	$51,060	8%
LTZ 4WD	$59,900	8%

GMC Yukon XL

Specifications

Drive 4WD
Engine 5.3-liter V8
Transmission . . . . 6-sp. Automatic
Tow Rating (lbs.) High-8000
Head/Leg Room (in.) Average-41.1/41.3
Interior Space (cu. ft.) . . . . Very Roomy-137.4
Cargo Space (cu. ft.) . . . . Very Roomy-45.8
Wheelbase/Length (in.) 130/222.4

Chev. Tahoe/Cadillac Escalade/GMC Yukon   Large SUV

Ratings—10 Best, 1 Worst

Ratings—10 Best, 1 Worst	Tahoe	Escalade	Yukon
Combo Crash Tests	9	9	9
Safety Features	5	5	5
Rollover	1	1	1
Preventive Maintenance	5	10	5
Repair Costs	5	2	6
Warranty	8	9	6
Fuel Economy	1	1	1
Complaints	8	9	9
Insurance Costs	10	8	10
OVERALL RATING	**7**	**8**	**7**

Chevrolet Tahoe

Cadillac Escalade

At-a-Glance

Status/Year Series Started Unchanged/2007
Twins . . . . .Cadillac Escalade, GMC Yukon
Body Styles . . . . SUV
Seating 9
Anti-Theft Device . . . . . . Std. Pass. Immobil. & Alarm
Parking Index Rating . . . . .Very Hard
Where Made. . . . . Arlington, TX
Fuel Factor
　MPG Rating (city/hwy) . . . . .Very Poor-15/21
　Driving Range (mi.) Long-448
　Fuel Type. . . . . .Regular
　Annual Fuel Cost . . . . .Very High-$2,989
　Gas Guzzler Tax . . . . .No
　Greenhouse Gas Emissions (tons/yr.)Very High-10.8
　Barrels of Oil Used per year . . . . . . .Very High-19.4

How the Competition Rates

Competitors	Rating	Pg.
Ford Expedition	2	137
Nissan Armada	–	217
Toyota Sequoia	–	254

Price Range

Price Range	Retail	Markup
LS 2WD	$41,600	8%
LS 4WD	$45,660	8%
LT 4WD	$48,990	8%
LTZ 4WD	$57,860	8%

Safety Checklist

Crash Tests:
　Frontal. . . . . Good
　Side. . . . . Very Good
Airbags:
　Head . . . . Fr. & Rr. Roof Curtain
　Torso. . . . . .Front Pelvis/Torso from Seat
　Pelvis . . . . .Front Pelvis/Torso from Seat
　Roll Sensing . . . . .Yes
　Knee Bolster . . . . None
Crash Avoidance:
　Collision Avoidance. . . . . None
　Blind Spot Detection . . . . Optional
　Lane Keeping Assist. . . . . None
　Backup Camera . . . . Standard
　Pedestrian Crash Avoidance . . . . None
General:
　Auto. Crash Notif. .Op. Assist. & Crash Info-Fee
　Day Running Lamps . . . . Standard
Safety Belt/Restraint:
　Dynamic Head Restraints. . . . . None
　Adjustable Belt . . . . Standard Front & Rear

GMC Yukon

Specifications

Drive. 4WD
Engine 5.3-liter V8
Transmission . . . . 6sp. Automatic
Tow Rating (lbs.) High-8200
Head/Leg Room (in.) Average-41.1/41.3
Interior Space (cu. ft.). Roomy-108.9
Cargo Space (cu. ft.) Average-16.9
Wheelbase/Length (in.) 116/202

Ratings—10 Best, 1 Worst	Traverse	Acadia
Combo Crash Tests	9	9
Safety Features	6	6
Rollover	4	4
Preventive Maintenance	6	6
Repair Costs	4	3
Warranty	8	6
Fuel Economy	2	2
Complaints	8	4
Insurance Costs	10	10
OVERALL RATING	9	7

Chevrolet Traverse

GMC Acadia

At-a-Glance

Status/Year Series Started Unchanged/2009
Twins . . . . .GMC Acadia
Body Styles . . . . SUV
Seating 7/8
Anti-Theft Device . . . . . . Std. Pass. Immobil. & Alarm
Parking Index Rating . . . . .Very Hard
Where Made. . . . . .Lansing, MI
Fuel Factor
  MPG Rating (city/hwy) . . . . .Very Poor-17/24
  Driving Range (mi.) Long-431
  Fuel Type . . . . .Regular
  Annual Fuel Cost . . . . High-$2,629
  Gas Guzzler Tax . . . . .No
  Greenhouse Gas Emissions (tons/yr.) High-9.7
  Barrels of Oil Used per year High-17.3

How the Competition Rates

Competitors	Rating	Pg.
Ford Flex	–	141
Honda Pilot	2	153
Toyota Highlander	–	249

Price Range

Price Range	Retail	Markup
LS FWD	$30,795	4%
LT FWD	$34,010	5%
2LT AWD	$38,865	5%
LTZ	$43,255	6%

Safety Checklist

Crash Tests:
  Frontal. . . . . Good
  Side. Very Good
Airbags:
  Head . . . . Fr. & Rr. Roof Curtain
  Torso. . . . . .Front Pelvis/Torso from Seat
  Pelvis . . . . .Front Pelvis/Torso from Seat
  Roll Sensing . . . . .Yes
  Knee Bolster . . . . None
Crash Avoidance:
  Collision Avoidance. . . . .Warning Only Optional
  Blind Spot Detection . . . . Optional
  Lane Keeping Assist . . . .Warning Only Optional
  Backup Camera . . . . Optional
  Pedestrian Crash Avoidance . . . . None
General:
  Auto. Crash Notif. .Op. Assist. & Crash Info-Fee
  Day Running Lamps . . . . Standard
Safety Belt/Restraint:
  Dynamic Head Restraints. . . . . None
  Adjustable Belt . . . . Standard Front & Rear

Chevrolet Traverse

Specifications

Drive. . . . . FWD
Engine 3.6-liter V6
Transmission . . . . .6-sp. Automatic
Tow Rating (lbs.) Low-5200
Head/Leg Room (in.) Average-40.4/41.3
Interior Space (cu. ft.). . . . . Very Roomy-150.8
Cargo Space (cu. ft.) Roomy-24.4
Wheelbase/Length (in.) 118.9/203.7

Chevrolet Volt Compact

Chevrolet Volt

Ratings—10 Best, 1 Worst

Combo Crash Tests	4
Safety Features	6
Rollover	10
Preventive Maintenance	7
Repair Costs	8
Warranty	8
Fuel Economy	10
Complaints	1
Insurance Costs	8
OVERALL RATING	**9**

Chevrolet Volt

At-a-Glance

Status/Year Series Started	Unchanged/2011
Twins	–
Body Styles	Sedan
Seating	5
Anti-Theft Device	Std. Pass. Immobil. & Alarm
Parking Index Rating	Easy
Where Made	Hamtramck, MI
Fuel Factor	
MPG Rating (city/hwy)	Very Good-35/40
Driving Range (mi.)	Very Short-345
Fuel Type	Regular
Annual Fuel Cost	Very Low-$1,387
Gas Guzzler Tax	No
Greenhouse Gas Emissions (tons/yr.)	Very Low-3.6
Barrels of Oil Used per year	Very Low-3.1

How the Competition Rates

Competitors	Rating	Pg.
Ford C-MAX	4	134
Nissan Leaf	4	220
Toyota Prius	5	250

Price Range

	Retail	Markup
Hatchback	$34,185	4%

Safety Checklist

Crash Tests:
Frontal . . . . Average
Side . . . . Poor

Airbags:
Head . . . . Fr. & Rr. Roof Curtain
Torso . . . . Front Pelvis/Torso from Seat
Pelvis . . . . Front Pelvis/Torso from Seat
Roll Sensing . . . . .Yes
Knee Bolster . . . . Standard

Crash Avoidance:
Collision Avoidance . . . . .Warning Only Optional
Blind Spot Detection . . . . None
Lane Keeping Assist . . . .Warning Only Optional
Backup Camera . . . . Optional
Pedestrian Crash Avoidance . . . . None

General:
Auto. Crash Notif. .Op. Assist. & Crash Info-Fee
Day Running Lamps . . . . Standard

Safety Belt/Restraint:
Dynamic Head Restraints . . . . None
Adjustable Belt . . . . None

Chevrolet Volt

Specifications

Drive	FWD
Engine	1.4-liter I4
Transmission	CVT
Tow Rating (lbs.)	
Head/Leg Room (in.)	Very Cramped-37.8/42.05
Interior Space (cu. ft.)	Very Cramped-90.3
Cargo Space (cu. ft.)	Very Cramped-10.6
Wheelbase/Length (in.)	105.7/177.1

Chrysler 200

Ratings—10 Best, 1 Worst

Combo Crash Tests	1
Safety Features	1
Rollover	7
Preventive Maintenance	6
Repair Costs	9
Warranty	8
Fuel Economy	5
Complaints	3
Insurance Costs	3
OVERALL RATING	**2**

Chrysler 200

At-a-Glance

Status/Year Series Started........ Unchanged/2011
Twins . . . . Dodge Avenger
Body Styles . . . . .Sedan, Convertible
Seating 5
Anti-Theft Device . . . . . . Std. Pass. Immobil. & Alarm
Parking Index Rating . . . . Average
Where Made. . . . . Sterling Heights, MI
Fuel Factor
  MPG Rating (city/hwy) Average-20/31
  Driving Range (mi.) Average-402
  Fuel Type . . . . .Regular
  Annual Fuel Cost . . . . Average-$2,162
  Gas Guzzler Tax . . . . .No
  Greenhouse Gas Emissions (tons/yr.). . Average-7.6
  Barrels of Oil Used per year High-13.7

How the Competition Rates

Competitors	Rating	Pg.
Chevrolet Malibu	–	114
Ford Fusion	5	143
Nissan Maxima	2	221

Price Range

Price Range	Retail	Markup
LX	$21,195	2%
Touring	$22,665	4%
Limited	$25,355	5%
S Convertible	$33,195	5%

Safety Checklist

Crash Tests:
  Frontal . . . . .Very Poor
  Side . . . . .Very Poor
Airbags:
  Head . . . . Fr. & Rr. Roof Curtain
  Torso . . . . Front Tosro from Seat
  Pelvis . . . . None
  Roll Sensing . . . . No
  Knee Bolster . . . . None
Crash Avoidance:
  Collision Avoidance. . . . . None
  Blind Spot Detection . . . . None
  Lane Keeping Assist. . . . . None
  Backup Camera . . . . None
  Pedestrian Crash Avoidance . . . . None
General:
  Auto. Crash Notification . . . . None
  Day Running Lamps . . . . Optional
Safety Belt/Restraint:
  Dynamic Head Restraints . . . . None
  Adjustable Belt . . . . .Standard Front

Chrysler 200

Specifications

Drive . . . . FWD
Engine 2.4-liter I4
Transmission . . . . 6-sp. Auto w/Overdrive
Tow Rating (lbs.) . . . . Very Low-1000
Head/Leg Room (in.) Average-40.1/42.4
Interior Space (cu. ft.) Average-100.3
Cargo Space (cu. ft.) Cramped-13.6
Wheelbase/Length (in.) 108.9/191.7

Ratings—10 Best, 1 Worst

Combo Crash Tests	5
Safety Features	3
Rollover	7
Preventive Maintenance	5
Repair Costs	6
Warranty	8
Fuel Economy	2
Complaints	5
Insurance Costs	3
OVERALL RATING	**4**

Chrysler 300

Chrysler 300

At-a-Glance

Status/Year Series Started	Unchanged/2011
Twins	Dodge Charger
Body Styles	Sedan
Seating	5
Anti-Theft Device	Std. Pass. Immobil. & Alarm
Parking Index Rating	Very Hard
Where Made	Brampton, Ontario
Fuel Factor	
MPG Rating (city/hwy)	Very Poor-15/25
Driving Range (mi.)	Very Short-349
Fuel Type	Regular
Annual Fuel Cost	Very High-$2,813
Gas Guzzler Tax	No
Greenhouse Gas Emissions (tons/yr.)	Very High-10.2
Barrels of Oil Used per year	Very High-18.3

How the Competition Rates

Competitors	Rating	Pg.
Buick LaCrosse	7	102
Chevrolet Impala	8	113
Lincoln MKS	3	194

Price Range	Retail	Markup
Base	$30,545	4%
S V6	$33,545	4%
C V8	$38,745	5%
SRT8	$48,495	4%

Safety Checklist

Crash Tests:
- Frontal . . . . Good
- Side . . . . Poor

Airbags:
- Head . . . . Fr. & Rr. Roof Curtain
- Torso . . . . Front Pelvis/Torso from Seat
- Pelvis . . . . Front Pelvis/Torso from Seat
- Roll Sensing . . . . No
- Knee Bolster . . . . Standard

Crash Avoidance:
- Collision Avoidance . . . . . Warning Only Optional
- Blind Spot Detection . . . . Optional
- Lane Keeping Assist . . . . None
- Backup Camera . . . . Optional
- Pedestrian Crash Avoidance . . . . None

General:
- Auto. Crash Notification . . . . None
- Day Running Lamps . . . . Optional

Safety Belt/Restraint:
- Dynamic Head Restraints . . . . None
- Adjustable Belt . . . . Standard Front

Chrysler 300

Specifications

Drive	RWD
Engine	5.7-liter V8
Transmission	5 sp. Auto w/Overdrive
Tow Rating (lbs.)	Very Low-1000
Head/Leg Room (in.)	Cramped-38.6/41.8
Interior Space (cu. ft.)	Roomy-122.6
Cargo Space (cu. ft.)	Average-16.3
Wheelbase/Length (in.)	120.2/198.6

Chrysler Town and Country — Minivan

Ratings—10 Best, 1 Worst

Combo Crash Tests	–
Safety Features	5
Rollover	4
Preventive Maintenance	9
Repair Costs	7
Warranty	8
Fuel Economy	3
Complaints	3
Insurance Costs	8
OVERALL RATING	**–**

Chrysler Town and Country

At-a-Glance

Status/Year Series Started Unchanged/2008
Twins .Dodge Grand Caravan
Body Styles . . . . .Minivan
Seating 7
Anti-Theft Device . . . . . . Std. Pass. Immobil. & Alarm
Parking Index Rating . . . . .Very Hard
Where Made. . . . . Windsor, Ontario
Fuel Factor
  MPG Rating (city/hwy) Poor-17/25
  Driving Range (mi.) Average-397
  Fuel Type. . . . . .Regular
  Annual Fuel Cost . . . . High-$2,591
  Gas Guzzler Tax . . . . .No
  Greenhouse Gas Emissions (tons/yr.). High-9.1
  Barrels of Oil Used per year High-16.5

How the Competition Rates

Competitors	Rating	Pg.
Honda Odyssey	–	152
Nissan Quest	–	224
Toyota Sienna	2	255

Price Range

Price Range	Retail	Markup
Touring	$30,765	4%
S	$32,195	4%
Touring L	$33,995	5%
Limited	$41,295	5%

Chrysler Town and Country

Safety Checklist

Crash Tests:
  Frontal. . . . .
  Side. . . . .
Airbags:
  Head . . . . Fr. & Rr. Roof Curtain
  Torso. . . . . .Front Pelvis/Torso from Seat
  Pelvis . . . . .Front Pelvis/Torso from Seat
  Roll Sensing . . . . .Yes
  Knee Bolster . . . . Standard
Crash Avoidance:
  Collision Avoidance. . . . . None
  Blind Spot Detection . . . . Optional
  Lane Keeping Assist. . . . . None
  Backup Camera . . . . Optional
  Pedestrian Crash Avoidance . . . . None
General:
  Auto. Crash Notification . . . . None
  Day Running Lamps . . . . Optional
Safety Belt/Restraint:
  Dynamic Head Restraints. . . . . .Standard Front
  Adjustable Belt . . . . Standard Front & Rear

Chrysler Town and Country

Specifications

Drive. . . . . FWD
Engine 3.6-liter V6
Transmission . . . . 6-sp. Auto w/Overdrive
Tow Rating (lbs.) Low-3600
Head/Leg Room (in.) Cramped-39.8/40.7
Interior Space (cu. ft.). . . . . Very Roomy-163.5
Cargo Space (cu. ft.) Roomy-33
Wheelbase/Length (in.) 121.2/202.8

Ratings—10 Best, 1 Worst

Combo Crash Tests	2
Safety Features	1
Rollover	7
Preventive Maintenance	6
Repair Costs	9
Warranty	8
Fuel Economy	5
Complaints	3
Insurance Costs	3
OVERALL RATING	**3**

Dodge Avenger

Dodge Avenger

Safety Checklist

Crash Tests:
Frontal . . . . Poor
Side . . . . Very Poor

Airbags:
Head . . . . Fr. & Rr. Roof Curtain
Torso . . . . Front Tosro from Seat
Pelvis . . . . None
Roll Sensing . . . . No
Knee Bolster . . . . None

Crash Avoidance:
Collision Avoidance. . . . . None
Blind Spot Detection . . . . None
Lane Keeping Assist . . . . None
Backup Camera . . . . None
Pedestrian Crash Avoidance . . . . None

General:
Auto. Crash Notification . . . . None
Day Running Lamps . . . . Optional

Safety Belt/Restraint:
Dynamic Head Restraints . . . . None
Adjustable Belt . . . . Standard Front

At-a-Glance

Status/Year Series Started Unchanged/2008
Twins . . . . Chrysler 200
Body Styles . . . . Sedan
Seating 5
Anti-Theft Device . . . . . . Std. Pass. Immobil. & Alarm
Parking Index Rating . . . . Average
Where Made. . . . . Sterling Heights, MI
Fuel Factor
  MPG Rating (city/hwy) Average-21/30
  Driving Range (mi.) Average-410
  Fuel Type. . . . . Regular
  Annual Fuel Cost . . . . Average-$2,119
  Gas Guzzler Tax . . . . No
  Greenhouse Gas Emissions (tons/yr.) . . Average-7.6
  Barrels of Oil Used per year High-13.7

How the Competition Rates

Competitors	Rating	Pg.
Chevrolet Impala	8	113
Ford Fusion	5	143
Nissan Maxima	2	221

Price Range

	Retail	Markup
SE	$19,895	2%
SXT	$22,695	4%
R/T	$25,795	5%

Dodge Avenger

Specifications

Drive . . . . FWD
Engine 2.4-liter I4
Transmission . . . . 4-sp. Auto w/Overdrive
Tow Rating (lbs.) . . . . Very Low-1000
Head/Leg Room (in.) Average-40/42.4
Interior Space (cu. ft.) Average-100.2
Cargo Space (cu. ft.) Cramped-13.5
Wheelbase/Length (in.) 108.9/192.6

Ratings—10 Best, 1 Worst

Combo Crash Tests	6
Safety Features	1
Rollover	7
Preventive Maintenance	6
Repair Costs	9
Warranty	8
Fuel Economy	3
Complaints	4
Insurance Costs	1
OVERALL RATING	**5**

Dodge Challenger

Dodge Challenger

At-a-Glance

Status/Year Series Started Unchanged/2009
Twins . . . . —
Body Styles . . . . .Coupe
Seating 5
Anti-Theft Device . . . . . . Std. Pass. Immobil. & Alarm
Parking Index Rating . . . . Hard
Where Made . . . . Brampton, Ontario
Fuel Factor
  MPG Rating (city/hwy) Poor-18/27
  Driving Range (mi.) Average-404
  Fuel Type . . . . .Regular
  Annual Fuel Cost . . . . High-$2,430
  Gas Guzzler Tax . . . . .No
  Greenhouse Gas Emissions (tons/yr.) High-9.8
  Barrels of Oil Used per year High-15.7

How the Competition Rates

Competitors	Rating	Pg.
Chevrolet Camaro	8	109
Ford Mustang	2	144
Mazda MX-5 Miata	–	202

Price Range

	Retail	Markup
SXT	$26,295	4%
R/T	$30,495	5%
SRT8 Core	$38,995	3%
SRT8	$44,195	4%

Safety Checklist

Crash Tests:
  Frontal . . . . Good
  Side . . . . Poor*
Airbags:
  Head . . . . Fr. & Rr. Roof Curtain
  Torso . . . . .Front Pelvis/Torso from Seat
  Pelvis . . . . .Front Pelvis/Torso from Seat
  Roll Sensing . . . . No
  Knee Bolster . . . . None
Crash Avoidance:
  Collision Avoidance . . . . None
  Blind Spot Detection . . . . None
  Lane Keeping Assist . . . . None
  Backup Camera . . . . None
  Pedestrian Crash Avoidance . . . . None
General:
  Auto. Crash Notification . . . . None
  Day Running Lamps . . . . Optional
Safety Belt/Restraint:
  Dynamic Head Restraints . . . . . .Standard Front
  Adjustable Belt . . . . None

Dodge Challenger

Specifications

Drive . . . . RWD
Engine 3.6-liter V6
Transmission . . . . 5-sp. Auto w/Overdrive
Tow Rating (lbs.) . . . . Very Low-1000
Head/Leg Room (in.) Average-39.3/42
Interior Space (cu. ft.) Cramped-91.5
Cargo Space (cu. ft.) Cramped-16.2
Wheelbase/Length (in.) 116/197.7

*Additional injury potential in side test. See footnote on page 24.

Ratings—10 Best, 1 Worst

Combo Crash Tests	6
Safety Features	4
Rollover	9
Preventive Maintenance	8
Repair Costs	8
Warranty	8
Fuel Economy	3
Complaints	4
Insurance Costs	1
OVERALL RATING	**6**

Dodge Charger

Dodge Charger

At-a-Glance

Status/Year Series Started	Unchanged/2006
Twins	Chrysler 300
Body Styles	Sedan
Seating	5
Anti-Theft Device	Std. Pass. Immobil. & Alarm
Parking Index Rating	Hard
Where Made	Brampton, Ontario
Fuel Factor	
MPG Rating (city/hwy)	Poor-18/27
Driving Range (mi.)	Average-404
Fuel Type	Regular
Annual Fuel Cost	High-$2,430
Gas Guzzler Tax	No
Greenhouse Gas Emissions (tons/yr.)	High-8.8
Barrels of Oil Used per year	High-15.7

How the Competition Rates

Competitors	Rating	Pg.
Chrysler 300	4	123
Ford Taurus	4	145
Lincoln MKS	3	194

Price Range	Retail	Markup
SE	$26,295	4%
SXT	$29,295	4%
R/T AWD	$32,995	5%
SRT8 Super Bee	$42,895	3%

Dodge Charger

Safety Checklist

Crash Tests:
Frontal . . . . Good
Side . . . . Average

Airbags:
Head . . . . Fr. & Rr. Roof Curtain
Torso . . . . Front Pelvis/Torso from Seat
Pelvis . . . . Front Pelvis/Torso from Seat
Roll Sensing . . . . No
Knee Bolster . . . . Standard

Crash Avoidance:
Collision Avoidance . . . . . Warning Only Optional
Blind Spot Detection . . . . Optional
Lane Keeping Assist . . . . None
Backup Camera . . . . Optional
Pedestrian Crash Avoidance . . . . None

General:
Auto. Crash Notification . . . . None
Day Running Lamps . . . . Optional

Safety Belt/Restraint:
Dynamic Head Restraints . . . . . . Standard Front
Adjustable Belt . . . . Standard Front

Dodge Charger

Specifications

Drive	RWD
Engine	3.6-liter V6
Transmission	5-sp. Auto w/Overdrive
Tow Rating (lbs.)	Very Low-1000
Head/Leg Room (in.)	Cramped-38.6/41.8
Interior Space (cu. ft.)	Roomy-104.7
Cargo Space (cu. ft.)	Average-16.5
Wheelbase/Length (in.)	120.2/199.9

Dodge Dart

Ratings—10 Best, 1 Worst

Combo Crash Tests	8
Safety Features	4
Rollover	8
Preventive Maintenance	6
Repair Costs	9
Warranty	8
Fuel Economy	8
Complaints	–
Insurance Costs	3
OVERALL RATING	**9**

Dodge Dart

Dodge Dart

At-a-Glance

Status/Year Series Started Unchanged/2013
Twins . . . . –
Body Styles . . . . Sedan
Seating 5
Anti-Theft Device . . . . . . Std. Pass. Immobil. & Alarm
Parking Index Rating . . . . Easy
Where Made . . . . Belvidere, IL
Fuel Factor
  MPG Rating (city/hwy) Good-25/36
  Driving Range (mi.) Average-412
  Fuel Type . . . . .Regular
  Annual Fuel Cost . . . . Low-$1,775
  Gas Guzzler Tax . . . . .No
  Greenhouse Gas Emissions (tons/yr.) Low-6.8
  Barrels of Oil Used per year Average-12.2

How the Competition Rates

Competitors	Rating	Pg.
Chevrolet Cruze	9	111
Ford Focus	5	142
Volkswagen Jetta	6	263

Price Range

	Retail	Markup
SE	$15,995	0%
SXT	$18,495	2%
GT	$20,995	2%
Limited	$22,995	3%

Safety Checklist

Crash Tests:
  Frontal . . . . Good
  Side . . . . Very Good
Airbags:
  Head . . . . Fr. & Rr. Roof Curtain
  Torso . . . . Front Pelvis/Torso from Seat
  Pelvis . . . . Fr. & Rr. Pelvis/Torso from Seat
  Roll Sensing . . . . No
  Knee Bolster . . . . Standard
Crash Avoidance:
  Collision Avoidance . . . . None
  Blind Spot Detection . . . . Optional
  Lane Keeping Assist . . . . None
  Backup Camera . . . . Optional
  Pedestrian Crash Avoidance . . . . None
General:
  Auto. Crash Notification . . . . None
  Day Running Lamps . . . . Optional
Safety Belt/Restraint:
  Dynamic Head Restraints . . . . . .Standard Front
  Adjustable Belt . . . . .Standard Front

Dodge Dart

Specifications

Drive . . . . FWD
Engine 2.0-liter I4
Transmission . . . . 6-sp. Manual
Tow Rating (lbs.) . . . . Very Low-1000
Head/Leg Room (in.) Cramped-38.6/42.2
Interior Space (cu. ft.) Cramped-97.2
Cargo Space (cu. ft.) Cramped-13.1
Wheelbase/Length (in.) 106.4/183.9

Ratings—10 Best, 1 Worst

Combo Crash Tests	5
Safety Features	7
Rollover	2
Preventive Maintenance	8
Repair Costs	9
Warranty	8
Fuel Economy	2
Complaints	4
Insurance Costs	8
OVERALL RATING	**7**

Dodge Durango

Dodge Durango

At-a-Glance

Status/Year Series Started Appearance Change/2011	
Twins	–
Body Styles	SUV
Seating	6/7
Anti-Theft Device	Std. Pass. Immobil. & Alarm
Parking Index Rating	Hard
Where Made	Detroit, MI
Fuel Factor	
MPG Rating (city/hwy)	Very Poor-17/24
Driving Range (mi.)	Very Long-481
Fuel Type	Regular
Annual Fuel Cost	High-$2,629
Gas Guzzler Tax	No
Greenhouse Gas Emissions (tons/yr.)	High-9.7
Barrels of Oil Used per year	High-17.3

How the Competition Rates

Competitors	Rating	Pg.
Chevrolet Tahoe	7	119
Ford Expedition	2	137
Toyota 4Runner	–	244

Price Range

Price Range	Retail	Markup
SXT	$29,795	2%
Limited	$35,995	5%
R/T AWD	$41,395	5%
Citadel AWD	$43,395	5%

Dodge Durango

Safety Checklist

Crash Tests:
Frontal	Poor
Side	Good

Airbags:
Head	Fr. & Rr. Roof Curtain
Torso	Front Pelvis/Torso from Seat
Pelvis	Front Pelvis/Torso from Seat
Roll Sensing	Yes
Knee Bolster	Standard

Crash Avoidance:
Collision Avoidance	Optional CIB & DBS
Blind Spot Detection	Optional
Lane Keeping Assist	None
Backup Camera	Optional
Pedestrian Crash Avoidance	None

General:
Auto. Crash Notification	None
Day Running Lamps	Optional

Safety Belt/Restraint:
Dynamic Head Restraints	Standard Front
Adjustable Belt	Standard Front

Dodge Durango

Specifications

Drive	AWD
Engine	3.6-liter V6
Transmission	8-sp. Automatic
Tow Rating (lbs.)	Average-6200
Head/Leg Room (in.)	Cramped-39.9/40.3
Interior Space (cu. ft.)	
Cargo Space (cu. ft.)	Average-17.2
Wheelbase/Length (in.)	119.8/201.2

Dodge Grand Caravan   Minivan

Ratings—10 Best, 1 Worst

Combo Crash Tests	3
Safety Features	5
Rollover	4
Preventive Maintenance	8
Repair Costs	8
Warranty	8
Fuel Economy	3
Complaints	4
Insurance Costs	8
OVERALL RATING	**6**

Dodge Grand Caravan

Dodge Grand Caravan

At-a-Glance

Status/Year Series Started. Unchanged/2008
Twins . . . . .Chrysler Town and Country
Body Styles . . . . .Minivan
Seating 7
Anti-Theft Device . . . . Std. Pass. Immobil.
Parking Index Rating . . . . .Very Hard
Where Made. . . . . Windsor, Ontario
Fuel Factor
  MPG Rating (city/hwy) Poor-17/25
  Driving Range (mi.) Average-397
  Fuel Type. . . . . .Regular
  Annual Fuel Cost . . . . High-$2,591
  Gas Guzzler Tax . . . . .No
  Greenhouse Gas Emissions (tons/yr.). High-9.1
  Barrels of Oil Used per year High-16.5

How the Competition Rates

Competitors	Rating	Pg.
Honda Odyssey	–	152
Nissan Quest	–	224
Toyota Sienna	2	255

Price Range

Price Range	Retail	Markup
SE	$19,995	1%
SXT	$26,695	5%
R/T	$29,995	5%

Safety Checklist

Crash Tests:
  Frontal. . . . . Average
  Side. . . . . .Very Poor
Airbags:
  Head . . . . Fr. & Rr. Roof Curtain
  Torso. . . . . .Front Pelvis/Torso from Seat
  Pelvis . . . . .Front Pelvis/Torso from Seat
  Roll Sensing . . . . .Yes
  Knee Bolster . . . . Standard
Crash Avoidance:
  Collision Avoidance. . . . . None
  Blind Spot Detection . . . . Optional
  Lane Keeping Assist. . . . . None
  Backup Camera . . . . Optional
  Pedestrian Crash Avoidance . . . . None
General:
  Auto. Crash Notification . . . . None
  Day Running Lamps. . . . . Optional
Safety Belt/Restraint:
  Dynamic Head Restraints. . . . . .Standard Front
  Adjustable Belt . . . . Standard Front & Rear

Dodge Grand Caravan

Specifications

Drive. . . . . FWD
Engine 3.6-liter V6
Transmission . . . . 6-sp. w/Overdrive
Tow Rating (lbs.) Low-3600
Head/Leg Room (in.) Cramped-39.8/40.7
Interior Space (cu. ft.). . . . . Very Roomy-163.5
Cargo Space (cu. ft.). Roomy-33
Wheelbase/Length (in.) 121.2/202.8

Ratings—10 Best, 1 Worst	
Combo Crash Tests	–
Safety Features	4
Rollover	3
Preventive Maintenance	5
Repair Costs	5
Warranty	8
Fuel Economy	3
Complaints	1
Insurance Costs	8
OVERALL RATING	**–**

Dodge Journey

Dodge Journey

At-a-Glance

Status/Year Series Started	Unchanged/2009
Twins	–
Body Styles	SUV
Seating	5/7
Anti-Theft Device	Std. Pass. Immobil. & Alarm
Parking Index Rating	Hard
Where Made	Toluca, Mexico
Fuel Factor	
MPG Rating (city/hwy)	Poor-17/25
Driving Range (mi.)	Average-407
Fuel Type	Regular
Annual Fuel Cost	High-$2,591
Gas Guzzler Tax	No
Greenhouse Gas Emissions (tons/yr.)	High-9.6
Barrels of Oil Used per year	High-17.3

How the Competition Rates

Competitors	Rating	Pg.
Chevrolet Equinox	3	112
Ford Edge	1	135
Nissan Murano	3	222

Price Range	Retail	Markup
SE	$19,495	1%
SXT	$23,295	4%
Limited AWD	$30,195	5%
R/T AWD	$30,795	5%

Safety Checklist

Crash Tests:
Frontal	
Side	

Airbags:
Head	Fr.& Rr. Roof Curtain
Torso	Front Tosro from Seat
Pelvis	None
Roll Sensing	Yes
Knee Bolster	Standard

Crash Avoidance:
Collision Avoidance	None
Blind Spot Detection	None
Lane Keeping Assist	None
Backup Camera	Optional
Pedestrian Crash Avoidance	None

General:
Auto. Crash Notification	None
Day Running Lamps	Optional

Safety Belt/Restraint:
Dynamic Head Restraints	Standard Front
Adjustable Belt	Standard Front

Dodge Journey

Specifications

Drive	FWD
Engine	3.6-liter V6
Transmission	6-sp. Auto w/Overdrive
Tow Rating (lbs.)	Very Low-2500
Head/Leg Room (in.)	Average-40.8/40.8
Interior Space (cu. ft.)	Average-99.6
Cargo Space (cu. ft.)	Very Cramped-10.7
Wheelbase/Length (in.)	113.8/192.4

Ratings—10 Best, 1 Worst

Combo Crash Tests	2
Safety Features	2
Rollover	5
Preventive Maintenance	9
Repair Costs	10
Warranty	4
Fuel Economy	8
Complaints	4
Insurance Costs	3
OVERALL RATING	**4**

Fiat 500

Fiat 500c

At-a-Glance

Status/Year Series Started	Unchanged/2012
Twins	–
Body Styles	Hatchback, Convertible
Seating	4
Anti-Theft Device	Std. Pass. Immobil. & Alarm
Parking Index Rating	Very Easy
Where Made	Toluca, Mexico

Fuel Factor

MPG Rating (city/hwy)	Good-27/34
Driving Range (mi.)	Very Short-312
Fuel Type	Regular
Annual Fuel Cost	Very Low-$1,729
Gas Guzzler Tax	No
Greenhouse Gas Emissions (tons/yr.)	Very Low-6.1
Barrels of Oil Used per year	Low-11.0

How the Competition Rates

Competitors	Rating	Pg.
Ford Fiesta	–	140
Mazda Mazda2	–	198
Mini Cooper	–	210

Price Range	Retail	Markup
Pop	$16,000	3%
Sport	$17,500	5%
Lounge	$18,500	3%
Abarth Cabriolet	$26,000	4%

Safety Checklist

Crash Tests:
Frontal	Very Poor
Side	Poor

Airbags:
Head	Fr. & Rr. Roof Curtain
Torso	Front Pelvis/Torso from Seat
Pelvis	Front Pelvis/Torso from Seat
Roll Sensing	No
Knee Bolster	Standard

Crash Avoidance:
Collision Avoidance	None
Blind Spot Detection	None
Lane Keeping Assist	None
Backup Camera	None
Pedestrian Crash Avoidance	None

General:
Auto. Crash Notification	None
Day Running Lamps	Optional

Safety Belt/Restraint:
Dynamic Head Restraints	Standard Front
Adjustable Belt	Standard Front & Rear

Fiat 500

Specifications

Drive	FWD
Engine	1.4-liter I4
Transmission	6-sp. Auto w/Overdrive
Tow Rating (lbs.)	
Head/Leg Room (in.)	Very Cramped-38.9/40.7
Interior Space (cu. ft.)	Very Cramped-75.6
Cargo Space (cu. ft.)	Very Cramped-9.5
Wheelbase/Length (in.)	90.6/139.6

Ratings—10 Best, 1 Worst

Combo Crash Tests	–
Safety Features	3
Rollover	2
Preventive Maintenance	10
Repair Costs	–
Warranty	4
Fuel Economy	8
Complaints	–
Insurance Costs	5
OVERALL RATING	**–**

Fiat 500L

Fiat 500L

At-a-Glance

Status/Year Series Started	All New/2014
Twins	–
Body Styles	Wagon
Seating	5
Anti-Theft Device	Std. Pass. Immobil. & Alarm
Parking Index Rating	Very Easy
Where Made	Kragujevac, Serbia
Fuel Factor	
MPG Rating (city/hwy)	Good-25/33
Driving Range (mi.)	Short-370
Fuel Type	Regular
Annual Fuel Cost	Low-$1,833
Gas Guzzler Tax	No
Greenhouse Gas Emissions (tons/yr.)	Low-6.8
Barrels of Oil Used per year	Average-12.2

How the Competition Rates

Competitors	Rating	Pg.
Ford Fiesta	–	140
Mini Cooper	–	210
Toyota Yaris	6	259

Price Range

	Retail	Markup
Pop	$19,100	1%
Easy	$20,195	3%
Trekking	$21,195	3%
Lounge	$24,195	4%

Safety Checklist

Crash Tests:
Frontal . . . .
Side . . . .

Airbags:
Head . . . . Fr. & Rr. Roof Curtain
Torso . . . . Front Pelvis/Torso from Seat
Pelvis . . . . Front Pelvis/Torso from Seat
Roll Sensing . . . . No
Knee Bolster . . . . Standard

Crash Avoidance:
Collision Avoidance. . . . . None
Blind Spot Detection . . . . None
Lane Keeping Assist. . . . . None
Backup Camera . . . . Optional
Pedestrian Crash Avoidance . . . . None

General:
Auto. Crash Notification . . . . None
Day Running Lamps . . . . Standard

Safety Belt/Restraint:
Dynamic Head Restraints . . . . . Standard Front
Adjustable Belt . . . . None

Fiat 500L

Specifications

Drive	FWD
Engine	1.4-liter I4
Transmission	6-sp. Manual
Tow Rating (lbs.)	
Head/Leg Room (in.)	Cramped-40.7/40
Interior Space (cu. ft.)	Average-98.8
Cargo Space (cu. ft.)	Average-21.3
Wheelbase/Length (in.)	102.8/167.3

Ratings—10 Best, 1 Worst

Combo Crash Tests	4
Safety Features	4
Rollover	5
Preventive Maintenance	3
Repair Costs	10
Warranty	3
Fuel Economy	10
Complaints	1
Insurance Costs	5
OVERALL RATING	**4**

Ford C-MAX

Ford C-MAX

At-a-Glance

Status/Year Series Started........ Unchanged/2013
Twins . . . . –
Body Styles . . . . Hatchback
Seating 5
Anti-Theft Device . . . . . . Std. Pass. Immobil. & Alarm
Parking Index Rating . . . . Average
Where Made. . . . . Wayne, MI
Fuel Factor
  MPG Rating (city/hwy) . . . . Very Good-43/43
  Driving Range (mi.) . . . . Very Long-581
  Fuel Type. . . . . .Regular
  Annual Fuel Cost . . . . Very Low-$1,197
  Gas Guzzler Tax . . . . .No
  Greenhouse Gas Emissions (tons/yr.). Very Low-4.2
  Barrels of Oil Used per year . . . . Very Low-7.6

How the Competition Rates

Competitors	Rating	Pg.
Chevrolet Volt	9	121
Nissan Leaf	4	220
Toyota Prius	5	250

Price Range

Price Range	Retail	Markup
SE Hybrid	$25,200	7%
SEL Hybrid	$28,365	7%
SEL Energi	$32,950	7%

Ford C-MAX

Safety Checklist

Crash Tests:
  Frontal. . . . . .Poor
  Side. . . . . Average
Airbags:
  Head . . . . Fr. & Rr. Roof Curtain
  Torso. . . . . .Front Pelvis/Torso from Seat
  Pelvis . . . . .Front Pelvis/Torso from Seat
  Roll Sensing . . . . .Yes
  Knee Bolster . . . . Standard
Crash Avoidance:
  Collision Avoidance. . . . . None
  Blind Spot Detection . . . . None
  Lane Keeping Assist . . . . None
  Backup Camera . . . . Optional
  Pedestrian Crash Avoidance . . . . None
General:
  Auto. Crash Notification . . . . . Dial Assist.-Free
  Day Running Lamps . . . . None
Safety Belt/Restraint:
  Dynamic Head Restraints. . . . . None
  Adjustable Belt . . . . .Standard Front

Ford C-MAX

Specifications

Drive. . . . . FWD
Engine 2.0-liter I4
Transmission . . . . .eCVT
Tow Rating (lbs.) . . . .
Head/Leg Room (in.) . . . . Very Roomy-41/43.1
Interior Space (cu. ft.). Average-99.7
Cargo Space (cu. ft.) Roomy-24.5
Wheelbase/Length (in.) 104.3/173.6

Ratings—10 Best, 1 Worst	Edge	MKX
Combo Crash Tests	2	2
Safety Features	3	3
Rollover	4	5
Preventive Maintenance	6	6
Repair Costs	4	3
Warranty	3	3
Fuel Economy	4	2
Complaints	5	8
Insurance Costs	8	10
OVERALL RATING	**1**	**2**

Ford Edge

Lincoln MKX

At-a-Glance

Status/Year Series Started........ Unchanged/2007
Twins . . . . .Lincoln MKX
Body Styles . . . . SUV
Seating 5
Anti-Theft Device . . . . . . Std. Pass. Immobil. & Alarm
Parking Index Rating . . . . Hard
Where Made . . . . .Oakville, Ontario
Fuel Factor
  MPG Rating (city/hwy) Poor-19/27
  Driving Range (mi.) Average-401
  Fuel Type . . . . .Regular
  Annual Fuel Cost . . . . Average-$2,347
  Gas Guzzler Tax . . . . .No
  Greenhouse Gas Emissions (tons/yr.) High-9.6
  Barrels of Oil Used per year High-17.3

How the Competition Rates

Competitors	Rating	Pg.
Chevrolet Equinox	3	112
Dodge Journey	–	131
Nissan Murano	3	222

Price Range

Price Range	Retail	Markup
SE FWD	$27,555	6%
SEL FWD	$31,100	7%
Limited AWD	$36,905	7%
Sport AWD	$39,050	7%

Safety Checklist

Crash Tests:
  Frontal . . . . .Very Poor
  Side . . . . Average
Airbags:
  Head . . . . Fr. & Rr. Roof Curtain
  Torso . . . . Front Tosro from Seat
  Pelvis . . . . None
  Roll Sensing . . . . .Yes
  Knee Bolster . . . . None
Crash Avoidance:
  Collision Avoidance . . . . .Warning Only Optional
  Blind Spot Detection . . . . Optional
  Lane Keeping Assist . . . . None
  Backup Camera . . . . Optional
  Pedestrian Crash Avoidance . . . . None
General:
  Auto. Crash Notification . . . . . Dial Assist.-Free
  Day Running Lamps . . . . None
Safety Belt/Restraint:
  Dynamic Head Restraints . . . . None
  Adjustable Belt . . . . .Standard Front

Ford Edge

Specifications

Drive . . . . FWD
Engine 3.5-liter V6
Transmission . . . . 6-sp. Automatic
Tow Rating (lbs.) . . . . Very Low-3500
Head/Leg Room (in.) Cramped-40/40.7
Interior Space (cu. ft.) Roomy-108.4
Cargo Space (cu. ft.) Roomy-32.2
Wheelbase/Length (in.) 111.2/184.2

Ratings—10 Best, 1 Worst

Combo Crash Tests	5
Safety Features	5
Rollover	3
Preventive Maintenance	6
Repair Costs	10
Warranty	3
Fuel Economy	6
Complaints	2
Insurance Costs	8
OVERALL RATING	**5**

Ford Escape

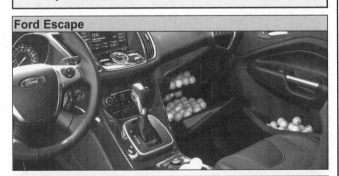

Ford Escape

Safety Checklist

Crash Tests:
Frontal . . . . Poor
Side . . . . Good
Airbags:
Head . . . . Fr. & Rr. Roof Curtain
Torso . . . . .Front Pelvis/Torso from Seat
Pelvis . . . . .Front Pelvis/Torso from Seat
Roll Sensing . . . . .Yes
Knee Bolster . . . . Standard
Crash Avoidance:
Collision Avoidance . . . . None
Blind Spot Detection . . . . Optional
Lane Keeping Assist . . . . None
Backup Camera . . . . Standard
Pedestrian Crash Avoidance . . . . None
General:
Auto. Crash Notification . . . . . Dial Assist.-Free
Day Running Lamps . . . . Optional
Safety Belt/Restraint:
Dynamic Head Restraints . . . . None
Adjustable Belt . . . . .Standard Front

Ford Escape

At-a-Glance

Status/Year Series Started Unchanged/2013
Twins . . . . –
Body Styles . . . . SUV
Seating 5
Anti-Theft Device . . . . . . Std. Pass. Immobil. & Alarm
Parking Index Rating . . . . Average
Where Made . . . . Louisville, Kentucky
Fuel Factor
  MPG Rating (city/hwy) Average-22/31
  Driving Range (mi.) Short-381
  Fuel Type . . . . .Regular
  Annual Fuel Cost . . . . Low-$2,033
  Gas Guzzler Tax . . . . .No
  Greenhouse Gas Emissions (tons/yr.) . . Average-7.4
  Barrels of Oil Used per year Average-13.2

How the Competition Rates

Competitors	Rating	Pg.
Honda CR-V	6	150
Jeep Compass	5	173
Toyota RAV4	5	253

Price Range

Price Range	Retail	Markup
S FWD	$22,700	6%
SE FWD	$25,550	7%
SE 4WD	$27,300	7%
Titanium 4WD	$30,850	7%

Specifications

Drive . . . . FWD
Engine 2.5-liter I4
Transmission . . . . .6-sp. Automatic
Tow Rating (lbs.) . . . . Very Low-1500
Head/Leg Room (in.) Roomy-39.9/43.1
Interior Space (cu. ft.) Average-98.1
Cargo Space (cu. ft.) . . . . Very Roomy-34.3
Wheelbase/Length (in.) 105.9/178.1

Ratings—10 Best, 1 Worst

	Expedition	Navigator
Combo Crash Tests	3	3
Safety Features	3	3
Rollover	2	2
Preventive Maintenance	4	4
Repair Costs	7	3
Warranty	3	3
Fuel Economy	1	1
Complaints	6	10
Insurance Costs	10	10
OVERALL RATING	**2**	**2**

Ford Expedition

Lincoln Navigator

At-a-Glance

Status/Year Series Started	Unchanged/2003
Twins	Lincoln Navigator
Body Styles	SUV
Seating	8
Anti-Theft Device	Std. Pass. Immobil. & Alarm
Parking Index Rating	Very Hard
Where Made	Louisville, Kentucky
Fuel Factor	
MPG Rating (city/hwy)	Very Poor-13/18
Driving Range (mi.)	Average-416
Fuel Type	Regular
Annual Fuel Cost	Very High-$3,463
Gas Guzzler Tax	No
Greenhouse Gas Emissions (tons/yr.)	Very High-12.2
Barrels of Oil Used per year	Very High-22.0

How the Competition Rates

Competitors	Rating	Pg.
Chevrolet Suburban	6	118
Nissan Armada	–	217
Toyota Sequoia	–	254

Price Range

	Retail	Markup
XL 2WD	$38,080	7%
XLT 2WD	$41,180	7%
Limited 4WD	$50,355	7%
King Ranch 4WD	$54,615	7%

Safety Checklist

Crash Tests:
Frontal	Very Poor
Side	Average

Airbags:
Head	Fr. & Rr. Roof Curtain
Torso	Front Tosro from Seat
Pelvis	None
Roll Sensing	Yes
Knee Bolster	None

Crash Avoidance:
Collision Avoidance	None
Blind Spot Detection	None
Lane Keeping Assist	None
Backup Camera	Optional
Pedestrian Crash Avoidance	None

General:
Auto. Crash Notification	Dial Assist.-Free
Day Running Lamps	None

Safety Belt/Restraint:
Dynamic Head Restraints	Standard Front
Adjustable Belt	Standard Front

Ford Expedition

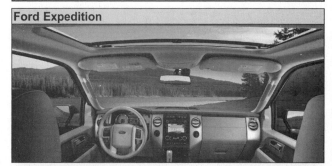

Specifications

Drive	4WD
Engine	5.4-liter V8
Transmission	6-sp. Auto w/ Overdrive
Tow Rating (lbs.)	Very High-9000
Head/Leg Room (in.)	Cramped-39.6/41.1
Interior Space (cu. ft.)	Very Roomy-160.3
Cargo Space (cu. ft.)	Average-18.6
Wheelbase/Length (in.)	119/206.5

Ratings—10 Best, 1 Worst

Combo Crash Tests	8
Safety Features	6
Rollover	3
Preventive Maintenance	5
Repair Costs	5
Warranty	3
Fuel Economy	2
Complaints	2
Insurance Costs	8
OVERALL RATING	**4**

Ford Explorer

At-a-Glance

Status/Year Series Started	Unchanged/2011
Twins	–
Body Styles	SUV
Seating	6/7
Anti-Theft Device	Std. Pass. Immobil. & Alarm
Parking Index Rating	Hard
Where Made	Chicago, IL
Fuel Factor	
MPG Rating (city/hwy)	Very Poor-17/23
Driving Range (mi.)	Very Short-358
Fuel Type	Regular
Annual Fuel Cost	High-$2,671
Gas Guzzler Tax	No
Greenhouse Gas Emissions (tons/yr.)	High-9.7
Barrels of Oil Used per year	High-17.3

How the Competition Rates

Competitors	Rating	Pg.
Dodge Journey	–	131
Nissan Pathfinder	3	223
Toyota Highlander	–	249

Price Range

Price Range	Retail	Markup
Base FWD	$29,600	6%
XLT FWD	$32,600	7%
Limited 4WD	$40,100	7%
Sport 4WD	$40,780	7%

Ford Explorer

Safety Checklist

Crash Tests:
Frontal	Very Good
Side	Good

Airbags:
Head	Fr. & Rr. Roof Curtain
Torso	Front Pelvis/Torso from Seat
Pelvis	Front Pelvis/Torso from Seat
Roll Sensing	Yes
Knee Bolster	Standard

Crash Avoidance:
Collision Avoidance	Warning Only Optional
Blind Spot Detection	Optional
Lane Keeping Assist	Optional
Backup Camera	Optional
Pedestrian Crash Avoidance	None

General:
Auto. Crash Notification	Dial Assist.-Free
Day Running Lamps	None

Safety Belt/Restraint:
Dynamic Head Restraints	None
Adjustable Belt	Standard Front

Ford Explorer

Specifications

Drive	AWD
Engine	3.5-liter V6
Transmission	6-sp. Automatic
Tow Rating (lbs.)	Low-5000
Head/Leg Room (in.)	Average-41.4/40.6
Interior Space (cu. ft.)	Very Roomy-151.7
Cargo Space (cu. ft.)	Average-21
Wheelbase/Length (in.)	112.6/197.1

Ratings—10 Best, 1 Worst

Combo Crash Tests	4
Safety Features	1
Rollover	1
Preventive Maintenance	2
Repair Costs	7
Warranty	3
Fuel Economy	1
Complaints	6
Insurance Costs	10
OVERALL RATING	**1**

Ford F-150

Ford F-150

At-a-Glance

Status/Year Series Started. Unchanged/2009
Twins . . . . –
Body Styles . . . . Pickup
Seating. 5/6
Anti-Theft Device . . . . . . Std. Pass. Immobil. & Alarm
Parking Index Rating . . . . .Very Hard
Where Made. . . . . Dearborn, MI
Fuel Factor
  MPG Rating (city/hwy) . . . . . . .Very Poor-15/21
  Driving Range (mi.) . . . . Very Long-620
  Fuel Type. Regular/E85
  Annual Fuel Cost . . . . Very High-$2,989
  Gas Guzzler Tax . . . . .No
  Greenhouse Gas Emissions (tons/yr.)Very High-14.1
  Barrels of Oil Used per year . . . . . . .Very High-25.3

How the Competition Rates

Competitors	Rating	Pg.
Chevrolet Silverado	8	115
Nissan Titan	–	227
Toyota Tundra	–	257

Price Range	Retail	Markup
XL Reg Cab 2WD 126	$23,670	8%
STX Supercab 145 4WD	$33,395	10%
Lariat Supercrew 4WD 145	$42,030	10%
Limited Supercrew 4WD	$52,895	10%

Ford F-150

Safety Checklist

Crash Tests:
  Frontal. . . . . Very Good
  Side. . . . . .Very Poor
Airbags:
  Head . . . . .Fr & Rr. Roof Curtain
  Torso. . . . . .Front Pelvis/Torso from Seat
  Pelvis . . . . .Front Pelvis/Torso from Seat
  Roll Sensing . . . . .Yes
  Knee Bolster . . . . None
Crash Avoidance:
  Collision Avoidance. . . . . None
  Blind Spot Detection . . . . None
  Lane Keeping Assist. . . . . None
  Backup Camera . . . . Optional
  Pedestrian Crash Avoidance . . . . None
General:
  Auto. Crash Notification . . . . . Dial Assist.-Free
  Day Running Lamps . . . . None
Safety Belt/Restraint:
  Dynamic Head Restraints . . . . None
  Adjustable Belt . . . . .Standard Front

Specifications

Drive. 4WD
Engine 5.0-liter V8
Transmission . . . . .6-sp. Automatic
Tow Rating (lbs.) High-7800
Head/Leg Room (in.) Average-41/41.4
Interior Space (cu. ft.). . . . .
Cargo Space (cu. ft.) . . . . Very Roomy-51.1
Wheelbase/Length (in.) 144.5/231.9

Ford Fiesta

Ratings—10 Best, 1 Worst

Combo Crash Tests	–
Safety Features	2
Rollover	5
Preventive Maintenance	7
Repair Costs	10
Warranty	3
Fuel Economy	9
Complaints	1
Insurance Costs	3
OVERALL RATING	–

Ford Fiesta

At-a-Glance

Status/Year Series Started Appearance Change/2011
Twins . . . . –
Body Styles . . . . Sedan, Hatchback
Seating 5
Anti-Theft Device . . . . . . Std. Pass. Immobil. & Alarm
Parking Index Rating . . . . .Very Easy
Where Made. . . . . Cuautitlán, Mexico
Fuel Factor
  MPG Rating (city/hwy) . . . . Very Good-29/39
  Driving Range (mi.) Average-407
  Fuel Type. . . . . .Regular
  Annual Fuel Cost . . . . Very Low-$1,569
  Gas Guzzler Tax . . . . .No
  Greenhouse Gas Emissions (tons/yr.). Very Low-5.7
  Barrels of Oil Used per year Low-10.3

How the Competition Rates

Competitors	Rating	Pg.
Chevrolet Sonic	10	116
Hyundai Accent	6	155
Toyota Yaris	6	259

Price Range	Retail	Markup
S Sedan	$14,000	4%
SE Hatchback	$16,050	4%
Titanium Sedan	$18,200	4%
ST Hatchback	$21,400	4%

Safety Checklist

Crash Tests:
  Frontal . . . .
  Side . . . .
Airbags:
  Head . . . . Fr. & Rr. Roof Curtain
  Torso . . . . .Front Pelvis/Torso from Seat
  Pelvis . . . . .Front Pelvis/Torso from Seat
  Roll Sensing . . . . No
  Knee Bolster . . . . Standard
Crash Avoidance:
  Collision Avoidance . . . . None
  Blind Spot Detection . . . . None
  Lane Keeping Assist . . . . None
  Backup Camera . . . . Optional
  Pedestrian Crash Avoidance . . . . None
General:
  Auto. Crash Notification . . . . . Dial Assist.-Free
  Day Running Lamps . . . . None
Safety Belt/Restraint:
  Dynamic Head Restraints . . . . None
  Adjustable Belt . . . . .Standard Front

Ford Fiesta

Specifications

Drive . . . . FWD
Engine 1.6-liter I4
Transmission . . . . .5-sp. Manual
Tow Rating (lbs.) . . . .
Head/Leg Room (in.) Average-39.1/42.2
Interior Space (cu. ft.) . . . . .Very Cramped-85.1
Cargo Space (cu. ft.) . . . . .Very Cramped-12.8
Wheelbase/Length (in.) 98/173.5

Ratings—10 Best, 1 Worst

Combo Crash Tests	–
Safety Features	3
Rollover	3
Preventive Maintenance	6
Repair Costs	4
Warranty	3
Fuel Economy	3
Complaints	4
Insurance Costs	5

OVERALL RATING — –

Ford Flex

Ford Flex

At-a-Glance

Status/Year Series Started	Unchanged/2009
Twins	–
Body Styles	SUV
Seating	6/7
Anti-Theft Device	Std. Pass. Immobil. & Alarm
Parking Index Rating	Very Hard
Where Made	Oakville, Ontario
Fuel Factor	
MPG Rating (city/hwy)	Poor-18/25
Driving Range (mi.)	Short-383
Fuel Type	Regular
Annual Fuel Cost	High-$2,498
Gas Guzzler Tax	No
Greenhouse Gas Emissions (tons/yr.)	High-9.1
Barrels of Oil Used per year	High-16.5

How the Competition Rates°

Competitors	Rating	Pg.
Chevrolet Traverse	9	120
Dodge Durango	7	129
Honda Pilot	2	153

Price Range

	Retail	Markup
SE FWD	$31,100	6%
SEL FWD	$33,500	7%
SEL AWD	$35,450	7%
Limited Ecoboost AWD	$44,020	7%

Safety Checklist

Crash Tests:
Frontal	....
Side	....

Airbags:
Head	Fr. & Rr. Roof Curtain
Torso	Front Tosro from Seat
Pelvis	None
Roll Sensing	Yes
Knee Bolster	None

Crash Avoidance:
Collision Avoidance	Warning Only Optional
Blind Spot Detection	Optional
Lane Keeping Assist	None
Backup Camera	Standard
Pedestrian Crash Avoidance	None

General:
Auto. Crash Notification	Dial Assist.-Free
Day Running Lamps	None

Safety Belt/Restraint:
Dynamic Head Restraints	None
Adjustable Belt	Standard Front

Ford Flex

Specifications

Drive	FWD
Engine	3.5-liter V6
Transmission	6-sp. Automatic
Tow Rating (lbs.)	Low-4500
Head/Leg Room (in.)	Roomy-41.8/40.8
Interior Space (cu. ft.)	Very Roomy-155.8
Cargo Space (cu. ft.)	Average-20
Wheelbase/Length (in.)	117.9/201.8

Ratings—10 Best, 1 Worst

Combo Crash Tests	6
Safety Features	2
Rollover	7
Preventive Maintenance	6
Repair Costs	10
Warranty	3
Fuel Economy	9
Complaints	1
Insurance Costs	3
OVERALL RATING	**5**

Ford Focus

Ford Focus

At-a-Glance

Status/Year Series Started Unchanged/2012
Twins . . . . —
Body Styles . . . . Sedan, Hatchback
Seating 5
Anti-Theft Device . . . . . . Std. Pass. Immobil. & Alarm
Parking Index Rating . . . . Easy
Where Made . . . . Wayne, MI
Fuel Factor
  MPG Rating (city/hwy) . . . . Very Good-27/37
  Driving Range (mi.) Short-381
  Fuel Type . . . . Regular
  Annual Fuel Cost . . . . Very Low-$1,674
  Gas Guzzler Tax . . . . No
  Greenhouse Gas Emissions (tons/yr.). Very Low-5.9
  Barrels of Oil Used per year Low-10.6

How the Competition Rates

Competitors	Rating	Pg.
Honda Civic	6	148
Kia Forte	5	178
Toyota Corolla	7	247

Price Range	Retail	Markup
S	$16,310	6%
SE Hatchback	$19,115	7%
ST Hatchback	$24,115	7%
Electric	$39,200	7%

Safety Checklist

Crash Tests:
  Frontal . . . . Average
  Side . . . . Average
Airbags:
  Head . . . . Fr. & Rr. Roof Curtain
  Torso . . . . Front Pelvis/Torso from Seat
  Pelvis . . . . Front Pelvis/Torso from Seat
  Roll Sensing . . . . No
  Knee Bolster . . . . Standard
Crash Avoidance:
  Collision Avoidance . . . . None
  Blind Spot Detection . . . . None
  Lane Keeping Assist . . . . None
  Backup Camera . . . . Optional
  Pedestrian Crash Avoidance . . . . None
General:
  Auto. Crash Notification . . . . . Dial Assist.-Free
  Day Running Lamps . . . . None
Safety Belt/Restraint:
  Dynamic Head Restraints . . . . None
  Adjustable Belt . . . . Standard Front

Ford Focus

Specifications

Drive . . . . FWD
Engine 2.0-liter I4
Transmission . . . . 6-sp. Automatic
Tow Rating (lbs.) . . . .
Head/Leg Room (in.) Average-38.3/43.7
Interior Space (cu. ft.) . . . . Very Cramped-90
Cargo Space (cu. ft.) Cramped-13.2
Wheelbase/Length (in.) 104.3/178.5

Ford Fusion Intermediate

Ratings—10 Best, 1 Worst

Combo Crash Tests	5
Safety Features	4
Rollover	8
Preventive Maintenance	5
Repair Costs	10
Warranty	3
Fuel Economy	7
Complaints	3
Insurance Costs	1
OVERALL RATING	**5**

Ford Fusion

Ford Fusion

At-a-Glance

Status/Year Series Started........ Unchanged/2013
Twins ....Lincoln MKZ
Body Styles ....Sedan
Seating 5
Anti-Theft Device ...... Std. Pass. Immobil. & Alarm
Parking Index Rating .... Hard
Where Made..... Hermosillo, Mexico / Flat Rock, MI
Fuel Factor
  MPG Rating (city/hwy)............. Good-22/34
  Driving Range (mi.) Long-432
  Fuel Type ....Regular
  Annual Fuel Cost .... Low-$1,967
  Gas Guzzler Tax ....No
  Greenhouse Gas Emissions (tons/yr.)..... Low-7.0
  Barrels of Oil Used per year Average-12.7

How the Competition Rates

Competitors	Rating	Pg.
Chevrolet Malibu	–	114
Hyundai Sonata	7	161
Toyota Camry	6	246

Price Range

Price Range	Retail	Markup
S	$21,900	7%
SE	$23,855	8%
SE Hybrid	$27,200	8%
Titanium Energi	$40,500	8%

Safety Checklist

Crash Tests:
  Frontal............................ Good
  Side..........................Very Poor
Airbags:
  Head .... Fr. & Rr. Roof Curtain
  Torso..........Front Pelvis/Torso from Seat
  Pelvis ....Front Pelvis/Torso from Seat
  Roll Sensing .... No
  Knee Bolster .... Standard
Crash Avoidance:
  Collision Avoidance.....Warning Only Optional
  Blind Spot Detection .... Optional
  Lane Keeping Assist............... Optional
  Backup Camera .... Optional
  Pedestrian Crash Avoidance .... None
General:
  Auto. Crash Notification ..... Dial Assist.-Free
  Day Running Lamps .... None
Safety Belt/Restraint:
  Dynamic Head Restraints............. None
  Adjustable Belt ....Standard Front

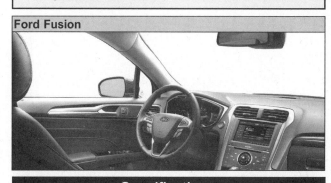
Ford Fusion

Specifications

Drive.................................. FWD
Engine 2.5-liter I4
Transmission ....6-sp. Automatic
Tow Rating (lbs.) ....
Head/Leg Room (in.) Roomy-39.2/44.3
Interior Space (cu. ft.)............Roomy-118.8
Cargo Space (cu. ft.) Cramped-16
Wheelbase/Length (in.) 112.2/191.7

Ratings—10 Best, 1 Worst

Combo Crash Tests	3
Safety Features	1
Rollover	10
Preventive Maintenance	2
Repair Costs	9
Warranty	3
Fuel Economy	4
Complaints	4
Insurance Costs	5
OVERALL RATING	**2**

Ford Mustang

At-a-Glance

Status/Year Series Started	Unchanged/2005
Twins	–
Body Styles	Coupe, Convertible
Seating	4
Anti-Theft Device	Std. Pass. Immobil. & Alarm
Parking Index Rating	Easy
Where Made	Flat Rock, MI
Fuel Factor	
MPG Rating (city/hwy)	Poor-19/29
Driving Range (mi.)	Very Short-360
Fuel Type	Regular
Annual Fuel Cost	Average-$2,288
Gas Guzzler Tax	No
Greenhouse Gas Emissions (tons/yr.)	Average-7.9
Barrels of Oil Used per year	High-14.3

How the Competition Rates

Competitors	Rating	Pg.
Chevrolet Camaro	8	109
Chevrolet Corvette	–	110
Dodge Challenger	5	126

Price Range

	Retail	Markup
Base	$22,200	6%
GT	$30,750	8%
GT Convertible	$35,750	8%
Shelby GT500	$54,650	10%

Ford Mustang

Safety Checklist

Crash Tests:
Frontal . . . . Average
Side . . . . .Very Poor

Airbags:
Head . . . . Front Head/Torso from Seat
Torso . . . . Front Head/Torso from Seat
Pelvis . . . . None
Roll Sensing . . . . No
Knee Bolster . . . . None

Crash Avoidance:
Collision Avoidance. . . . . None
Blind Spot Detection . . . . None
Lane Keeping Assist . . . . None
Backup Camera . . . . Optional
Pedestrian Crash Avoidance . . . . None

General:
Auto. Crash Notification . . . . . Dial Assist.-Free
Day Running Lamps . . . . None

Safety Belt/Restraint:
Dynamic Head Restraints . . . . None
Adjustable Belt . . . . None

Ford Mustang

Specifications

Drive	RWD
Engine	3.7-liter V6
Transmission	6-sp. Manual
Tow Rating (lbs.)	
Head/Leg Room (in.)	Cramped-38.5/42.4
Interior Space (cu. ft.)	Very Cramped-81
Cargo Space (cu. ft.)	Cramped-13.4
Wheelbase/Length (in.)	107.1/188.5

Ratings—10 Best, 1 Worst

Combo Crash Tests	7
Safety Features	4
Rollover	7
Preventive Maintenance	5
Repair Costs	4
Warranty	3
Fuel Economy	4
Complaints	6
Insurance Costs	1
OVERALL RATING	**4**

Ford Taurus

Ford Taurus

At-a-Glance

Status/Year Series Started	Unchanged/2010
Twins	—
Body Styles	Sedan
Seating	5
Anti-Theft Device	Std. Pass. Immobil. & Alarm
Parking Index Rating	Very Hard
Where Made	Chicago, IL
Fuel Factor	
MPG Rating (city/hwy)	Poor-19/29
Driving Range (mi.)	Long-427
Fuel Type	Regular
Annual Fuel Cost	Average-$2,288
Gas Guzzler Tax	No
Greenhouse Gas Emissions (tons/yr.)	Average-8.0
Barrels of Oil Used per year	High-14.3

How the Competition Rates

Competitors	Rating	Pg.
Chevrolet Malibu	–	114
Dodge Charger	6	127
Lincoln MKS	3	194

Price Range

	Retail	Markup
SE	$26,700	8%
SEL	$28,900	8%
Limited AWD	$36,050	8%
SHO AWD	$39,800	8%

Safety Checklist

Crash Tests:
Frontal . . . . Very Good
Side . . . . Poor
Airbags:
Head . . . . Fr. & Rr. Roof Curtain
Torso . . . . Front Tosro from Seat
Pelvis . . . . None
Roll Sensing . . . . Yes
Knee Bolster . . . . None
Crash Avoidance:
Collision Avoidance . . . . . Warning Only Optional
Blind Spot Detection . . . . Optional
Lane Keeping Assist . . . . Optional
Backup Camera . . . . Optional
Pedestrian Crash Avoidance . . . . None
General:
Auto. Crash Notification . . . . . Dial Assist.-Free
Day Running Lamps . . . . None
Safety Belt/Restraint:
Dynamic Head Restraints . . . . None
Adjustable Belt . . . . Standard Front

Ford Taurus

Specifications

Drive	FWD
Engine	3.5-liter V6
Transmission	6-sp. Automatic
Tow Rating (lbs.)	Very Low-1000
Head/Leg Room (in.)	Cramped-39/41.9
Interior Space (cu. ft.)	Average-102.2
Cargo Space (cu. ft.)	Average-20.1
Wheelbase/Length (in.)	112/202.9

Ratings—10 Best, 1 Worst

Combo Crash Tests	10
Safety Features	5
Rollover	3
Preventive Maintenance	5
Repair Costs	5
Warranty	6
Fuel Economy	2
Complaints	10
Insurance Costs	10
OVERALL RATING	**9**

GMC Sierra

GMC Sierra

At-a-Glance

Status/Year Series Started . . . . All New/2007
Twins . . . . –
Body Styles . . . . Pickup
Seating 5/6
Anti-Theft Device . . . Std. Pass. Immobil. & Opt. Pass. Alarm
Parking Index Rating . . . . Very Hard
Where Made. . . . . Fort Wayne, IN
Fuel Factor
  MPG Rating (city/hwy) . . . . .Very Poor-16/22
  Driving Range (mi.) . . . . Very Long-474
  Fuel Type. . . . . .Regular
  Annual Fuel Cost . . . . Very High-$2,821
  Gas Guzzler Tax . . . . .No
  Greenhouse Gas Emissions (tons/yr.)Very High-10.2
  Barrels of Oil Used per year . . . . . . .Very High-18.3

How the Competition Rates

Competitors	Rating	Pg.
Chevrolet Silverado	8	115
Ford F-150	1	139
Toyota Tundra	–	257

Price Range

	Retail	Markup
Base Reg Cab 119 2WD	$24,090	4%
Base Dbl Cab 143.5 4WD	$32,095	5%
SLE Crew Cab 143.5 4WD	$40,140	8%
SLT Crew Cab 153 4WD	$43,910	8%

Safety Checklist

Crash Tests:
  Frontal . . . . Very Good
  Side. . . . . Very Good
Airbags:
  Head . . . . Fr. & Rr. Roof Curtain
  Torso. . . . . .Front Pelvis/Torso from Seat
  Pelvis . . . . .Front Pelvis/Torso from Seat
  Roll Sensing . . . . .Yes
  Knee Bolster . . . . None
Crash Avoidance:
  Collision Avoidance. . . . .Warning Only Optional
  Blind Spot Detection . . . . None
  Lane Keeping Assist. . . .Warning Only Optional
  Backup Camera . . . . Optional
  Pedestrian Crash Avoidance . . . . None
General:
  Auto. Crash Notif. . .Op. Assist.and Crash Info-Fee
  Day Running Lamps . . . . Standard
Safety Belt/Restraint:
  Dynamic Head Restraints. . . . . None
  Adjustable Belt . . . . .Std. Front & Opt. Rear

GMC Sierra

Specifications

Drive 4WD
Engine 5.3-liter V8
Transmission . . . . .6-sp. Automatic
Tow Rating (lbs.) . . . . .Very High-9600
Head/Leg Room (in.) . . . . . . Very Roomy-42.8/45.2
Interior Space (cu. ft.). . . . .
Cargo Space (cu. ft.) . . . . Very Roomy-61
Wheelbase/Length (in.) 143.5/229.5

Honda Accord

Ratings—10 Best, 1 Worst	
Combo Crash Tests	7
Safety Features	4
Rollover	9
Preventive Maintenance	4
Repair Costs	9
Warranty	1
Fuel Economy	9
Complaints	2
Insurance Costs	8
OVERALL RATING	**7**

Honda Accord Coupe

Honda Accord Sedan

At-a-Glance

Status/Year Series Started	Unchanged/2013
Twins	Acura TL
Body Styles	Sedan, Coupe
Seating	5
Anti-Theft Device	Std. Pass. Immobil. & Alarm
Parking Index Rating	Hard
Where Made	Marysville, OH
Fuel Factor	
MPG Rating (city/hwy)	Very Good-27/36
Driving Range (mi.)	Very Long-523
Fuel Type	Regular
Annual Fuel Cost	Very Low-$1,691
Gas Guzzler Tax	No
Greenhouse Gas Emissions (tons/yr.)	Very Low-6.1
Barrels of Oil Used per year	Low-11.0

How the Competition Rates

Competitors	Rating	Pg.
Ford Fusion	5	143
Nissan Altima	6	216
Toyota Camry	6	246

Price Range	Retail	Markup
LX	$22,755	9%
Sport	$24,515	9%
Touring	$33,480	9%
Plug-In Hybrid	$39,780	9%

Safety Checklist

Crash Tests:
Frontal . . . . Average
Side . . . . Very Good
Airbags:
Head . . . . Fr. & Rr. Roof Curtain
Torso . . . . Front Pelvis/Torso from Seat
Pelvis . . . . Front Pelvis/Torso from Seat
Roll Sensing . . . . Yes
Knee Bolster . . . . None
Crash Avoidance:
Collision Avoidance . . . . . Warning Only Optional
Blind Spot Detection . . . . None
Lane Keeping Assist . . . . Warning Only Optional
Backup Camera . . . . Standard
Pedestrian Crash Avoidance . . . . None
General:
Auto. Crash Notification . . . . None
Day Running Lamps . . . . Standard
Safety Belt/Restraint:
Dynamic Head Restraints . . . . None
Adjustable Belt . . . . Standard Front

Honda Accord

Specifications

Drive	FWD
Engine	2.4-liter I4
Transmission	CVT
Tow Rating (lbs.)	
Head/Leg Room (in.)	Average-39.1/42.5
Interior Space (cu. ft.)	Roomy-103.2
Cargo Space (cu. ft.)	Cramped-15.8
Wheelbase/Length (in.)	109.3/191.4

Honda Civic | Compact

Ratings—10 Best, 1 Worst

Rating	
Combo Crash Tests	5
Safety Features	2
Rollover	7
Preventive Maintenance	7
Repair Costs	9
Warranty	1
Fuel Economy	10
Complaints	8
Insurance Costs	3
OVERALL RATING	**6**

Honda Civic Sedan

At-a-Glance

Status/Year Series Started Unchanged/2012
Twins . . . . Acura ILX
Body Styles . . . . Sedan, Coupe
Seating 5
Anti-Theft Device . . . . Std. Pass Immobil. & Opt. Pass Alarm
Parking Index Rating . . . . Easy
Where Made . . . . . . Greensburg, IN / Alliston, Ontario
Fuel Factor
  MPG Rating (city/hwy) . . . . Very Good-31/41
  Driving Range (mi.) . . . . Very Long-460
  Fuel Type . . . . .Regular
  Annual Fuel Cost . . . . Very Low-$1,478
  Gas Guzzler Tax . . . . .No
  Greenhouse Gas Emissions (tons/yr). Very Low-5.7
  Barrels of Oil Used per year Low-10.3

How the Competition Rates

Competitors	Rating	Pg.
Nissan Sentra	3	226
Subaru Impreza	–	239
Volkswagen Jetta	6	263

Price Range

Price Range	Retail	Markup
LX	$18,965	8%
EX	$20,815	8%
Si	$22,715	8%
GX w/Nav	$27,965	5%

Honda Civic Coupe

Safety Checklist

Crash Tests:
  Frontal . . . . Average
  Side . . . . Average
Airbags:
  Head . . . . Fr. & Rr. Roof Curtain
  Torso . . . . .Front Pelvis/Torso from Seat
  Pelvis . . . . .Front Pelvis/Torso from Seat
  Roll Sensing . . . . No
  Knee Bolster . . . . None
Crash Avoidance:
  Collision Avoidance . . . . None
  Blind Spot Detection . . . . None
  Lane Keeping Assist . . . . None
  Backup Camera . . . . Standard
  Pedestrian Crash Avoidance . . . . None
General:
  Auto. Crash Notification . . . . None
  Day Running Lamps . . . . Standard
Safety Belt/Restraint:
  Dynamic Head Restraints . . . . None
  Adjustable Belt . . . . .Standard Front

Honda Civic

Specifications

Drive . . . . FWD
Engine 1.8-liter I4
Transmission . . . . .5-sp. Automatic
Tow Rating (lbs.) . . . .
Head/Leg Room (in.) Cramped-39/42
Interior Space (cu. ft.) Cramped-94.6
Cargo Space (cu. ft.) . . . . .Very Cramped-12.5
Wheelbase/Length (in.) 105.1/179.4

Honda Crosstour

Small SUV

Ratings—10 Best, 1 Worst	
Combo Crash Tests	–
Safety Features	5
Rollover	7
Preventive Maintenance	4
Repair Costs	7
Warranty	1
Fuel Economy	6
Complaints	–
Insurance Costs	8
OVERALL RATING	**–**

Honda Crosstour

Honda Crosstour

At-a-Glance

Status/Year Series Started	Unchanged/2014
Twins	–
Body Styles	SUV
Seating	5
Anti-Theft Device	Std. Pass. Immobil. & Alarm
Parking Index Rating	Very Hard
Where Made	East Liberty, OH
Fuel Factor	
MPG Rating (city/hwy)	Average-22/31
Driving Range (mi.)	Very Long-468
Fuel Type	Regular
Annual Fuel Cost	Low-$2,033
Gas Guzzler Tax	No
Greenhouse Gas Emissions (tons/yr.)	Average-8.3
Barrels of Oil Used per year	High-15.0

How the Competition Rates

Competitors	Rating	Pg.
Acura RDX	7	83
Subaru Forester	4	238
Toyota Venza	4	258

Price Range	Retail	Markup
EX 4 cyl.	$27,380	9%
EX 6 cyl.	$31,040	9%
EX-L	$33,690	9%
EX-L 4WD w/Nav	$37,240	9%

Safety Checklist

Crash Tests:
Frontal . . . .
Side . . . .
Airbags:
Head . . . . Fr. & Rr. Roof Curtain
Torso . . . . Front Pelvis/Torso from Seat
Pelvis . . . . Front Pelvis/Torso from Seat
Roll Sensing . . . . .Yes
Knee Bolster . . . . None
Crash Avoidance:
Collision Avoidance . . . . .Warning Only Optional
Blind Spot Detection . . . . None
Lane Keeping Assist . . . .Warning Only Optional
Backup Camera . . . . Standard
Pedestrian Crash Avoidance . . . . None
General:
Auto. Crash Notification . . . . None
Day Running Lamps . . . . Standard
Safety Belt/Restraint:
Dynamic Head Restraints . . . . . .Standard Front
Adjustable Belt . . . . .Standard Front

Honda Crosstour

Specifications

Drive	FWD
Engine	2.4-liter I4
Transmission	5-sp. Automatic
Tow Rating (lbs.)	Very Low-1000
Head/Leg Room (in.)	Average-39.5/42.2
Interior Space (cu. ft.)	Average-101.4
Cargo Space (cu. ft.)	Roomy-25.7
Wheelbase/Length (in.)	110.1/196.6

Ratings—10 Best, 1 Worst

Combo Crash Tests	6
Safety Features	2
Rollover	3
Preventive Maintenance	5
Repair Costs	9
Warranty	1
Fuel Economy	6
Complaints	8
Insurance Costs	8
OVERALL RATING	**6**

Honda CR-V

Honda CR-V

At-a-Glance

Status/Year Series Started Unchanged/2012
Twins . . . . –
Body Styles . . . . SUV
Seating 5
Anti-Theft Device . . . Std Pass. Immobil. & Opt. Pass. Alarm
Parking Index Rating . . . . Easy
Where Made . . . . . East Liberty, OH / Alliston, Ontario
Fuel Factor
  MPG Rating (city/hwy) Average-22/30
  Driving Range (mi.) Short-383
  Fuel Type . . . . .Regular
  Annual Fuel Cost . . . . Average-$2,058
  Gas Guzzler Tax . . . . .No
  Greenhouse Gas Emissions (tons/yr.) . . Average-7.4
  Barrels of Oil Used per year Average-13.2

How the Competition Rates

Competitors	Rating	Pg.
Ford Escape	5	136
Jeep Compass	5	173
Toyota RAV4	5	253

Price Range

	Retail	Markup
LX 2WD	$22,945	7%
EX AWD	$26,295	7%
EX-L AWD	$28,945	7%
EX-L AWD w/Nav	$30,445	7%

Safety Checklist

Crash Tests:
  Frontal . . . . Good
  Side . . . . Average
Airbags:
  Head . . . . Fr. & Rr. Roof Curtain
  Torso . . . . Front Tosro from Seat
  Pelvis . . . . None
  Roll Sensing . . . . .Yes
  Knee Bolster . . . . None
Crash Avoidance:
  Collision Avoidance . . . . None
  Blind Spot Detection . . . . None
  Lane Keeping Assist . . . . None
  Backup Camera . . . . Standard
  Pedestrian Crash Avoidance . . . . None
General:
  Auto. Crash Notification . . . . None
  Day Running Lamps . . . . Standard
Safety Belt/Restraint:
  Dynamic Head Restraints . . . . None
  Adjustable Belt . . . . .Standard Front

Honda CR-V

Specifications

Drive 4WD
Engine 2.4-liter I4
Transmission . . . . .5-sp. Automatic
Tow Rating (lbs.) . . . . Very Low-1500
Head/Leg Room (in.) Cramped-39.9/41.3
Interior Space (cu. ft.) Roomy-104.1
Cargo Space (cu. ft.) . . . . Very Roomy-37.2
Wheelbase/Length (in.) 103.1/178.3

Honda Insight
Compact

Ratings—10 Best, 1 Worst	
Combo Crash Tests	–
Safety Features	1
Rollover	7
Preventive Maintenance	4
Repair Costs	6
Warranty	1
Fuel Economy	10
Complaints	7
Insurance Costs	1
OVERALL RATING	**–**

Honda Insight

Honda Insight

At-a-Glance

Status/Year Series Started	Unchanged/2010
Twins	–
Body Styles	Hatchback
Seating	5
Anti-Theft Device	Std. Pass. Immobil.
Parking Index Rating	Easy
Where Made	Suzuka, Japan
Fuel Factor	
MPG Rating (city/hwy)	Very Good-41/44
Driving Range (mi.)	Long-448
Fuel Type	Regular
Annual Fuel Cost	Very Low-$1,216
Gas Guzzler Tax	No
Greenhouse Gas Emissions (tons/yr.)	Very Low-4.4
Barrels of Oil Used per year	Very Low-7.8

How the Competition Rates

Competitors	Rating	Pg.
Ford C-MAX	4	134
Toyota Prius	5	250
Volkswagen Jetta	6	263

Price Range	Retail	Markup
Base	$18,600	5%
LX	$20,375	5%
EX	$22,065	5%
EX w/Nav	$23,790	5%

Safety Checklist

Crash Tests:
Frontal . . . .
Side . . . .
Airbags:
Head . . . . Fr. & Rr. Roof Curtain
Torso . . . . Front Tosro from Seat
Pelvis . . . . None
Roll Sensing . . . . No
Knee Bolster . . . . None
Crash Avoidance:
Collision Avoidance . . . . None
Blind Spot Detection . . . . None
Lane Keeping Assist . . . . None
Backup Camera . . . . Optional
Pedestrian Crash Avoidance . . . . None
General:
Auto. Crash Notification . . . . None
Day Running Lamps . . . . Standard
Safety Belt/Restraint:
Dynamic Head Restraints . . . . . Standard Front
Adjustable Belt . . . . Standard Front

Honda Insight

Specifications

Drive	RWD
Engine	1.3-liter I4
Transmission	CVT
Tow Rating (lbs.)	
Head/Leg Room (in.)	Cramped-38.4/42.3
Interior Space (cu. ft.)	Very Cramped-85
Cargo Space (cu. ft.)	Cramped-15.9
Wheelbase/Length (in.)	100.4/172.3

Honda Odyssey | Minivan

Ratings—10 Best, 1 Worst

Combo Crash Tests	–
Safety Features	6
Rollover	5
Preventive Maintenance	4
Repair Costs	8
Warranty	1
Fuel Economy	4
Complaints	5
Insurance Costs	10

OVERALL RATING — –

Honda Odyssey

Honda Odyssey

At-a-Glance

Status/Year Series Started Appearance Change/2005
Twins . . . . –
Body Styles . . . . .Minivan
Seating 7
Anti-Theft Device . . . . Std. Pass. Immobil.
Parking Index Rating . . . . Hard
Where Made. . . . . Lincoln, AL
Fuel Factor
  MPG Rating (city/hwy) Poor-19/28
  Driving Range (mi.) . . . . Very Long-466
  Fuel Type . . . . .Regular
  Annual Fuel Cost . . . . Average-$2,316
  Gas Guzzler Tax . . . . .No
  Greenhouse Gas Emissions (tons/yr.). . Average-8.3
  Barrels of Oil Used per year High-15.0

How the Competition Rates

Competitors	Rating	Pg.
Chrysler Town and Country	–	124
Nissan Quest	–	224
Toyota Sienna	2	255

Price Range

Price Range	Retail	Markup
LX	$28,825	9%
EX	$35,625	9%
Touring	$41,880	9%
Touring Elite	$44,450	9%

Safety Checklist

Crash Tests:
  Frontal . . . .
  Side . . . .
Airbags:
  Head . . . . Fr. & Rr. Roof Curtain
  Torso . . . . .Front Pelvis/Torso from Seat
  Pelvis . . . . .Front Pelvis/Torso from Seat
  Roll Sensing . . . . .Yes
  Knee Bolster . . . . None
Crash Avoidance:
  Collision Avoidance. . . . .Warning Only Optional
  Blind Spot Detection . . . . Optional
  Lane Keeping Assist . . . .Warning Only Optional
  Backup Camera . . . . Standard
  Pedestrian Crash Avoidance . . . . None
General:
  Auto. Crash Notification . . . . None
  Day Running Lamps . . . . Standard
Safety Belt/Restraint:
  Dynamic Head Restraints . . . . . .Standard Front
  Adjustable Belt . . . . Standard Front & Rear

Honda Odyssey

Specifications

Drive . . . . FWD
Engine 3.5-liter V6
Transmission . . . . .6-sp. Automatic
Tow Rating (lbs.) . . . . Very Low-3500
Head/Leg Room (in.) Cramped-39.7/40.9
Interior Space (cu. ft.). . . . . Very Roomy-172.6
Cargo Space (cu. ft.) . . . . Very Roomy-38.4
Wheelbase/Length (in.) 118.1/202.9

Honda Pilot — Mid-Size SUV

Honda Pilot

Ratings—10 Best, 1 Worst

Combo Crash Tests	2
Safety Features	5
Rollover	4
Preventive Maintenance	4
Repair Costs	7
Warranty	1
Fuel Economy	2
Complaints	6
Insurance Costs	10
OVERALL RATING	**2**

Honda Pilot

At-a-Glance

Status/Year Series Started	Unchanged/2009
Twins	–
Body Styles	SUV
Seating	8
Anti-Theft Device	Std. Pass. Immobil.
Parking Index Rating	Hard
Where Made	Lincoln, AL
Fuel Factor	
MPG Rating (city/hwy)	Very Poor-17/24
Driving Range (mi.)	Average-411
Fuel Type	Regular
Annual Fuel Cost	High-$2,629
Gas Guzzler Tax	No
Greenhouse Gas Emissions (tons/yr.)	High-9.2
Barrels of Oil Used per year	High-16.5

How the Competition Rates

Competitors	Rating	Pg.
Ford Explorer	4	138
Nissan Pathfinder	3	223
Toyota 4Runner	–	244

Price Range

Price Range	Retail	Markup
LX 2WD	$29,670	9%
EX 2WD	$31,920	9%
EX-L 4WD	$36,770	9%
Touring 4WD	$41,420	9%

Safety Checklist

Crash Tests:
- Frontal.............................Poor
- Side..........................Very Poor

Airbags:
- Head............... Fr. & Rr. Roof Curtain
- Torso.........Front Pelvis/Torso from Seat
- Pelvis ....Front Pelvis/Torso from Seat
- Roll Sensing ....Yes
- Knee Bolster .... None

Crash Avoidance:
- Collision Avoidance.................. None
- Blind Spot Detection .... None
- Lane Keeping Assist................ None
- Backup Camera .... Standard
- Pedestrian Crash Avoidance .... None

General:
- Auto. Crash Notification .... None
- Day Running Lamps .... Standard

Safety Belt/Restraint:
- Dynamic Head Restraints......Standard Front
- Adjustable Belt .... Standard Front & Rear

Honda Pilot

Specifications

Drive	4WD
Engine	3.5-liter V6
Transmission	5-sp. Automatic
Tow Rating (lbs.)	Low-4500
Head/Leg Room (in.)	Average-40/41.4
Interior Space (cu. ft.)	Very Roomy-153.7
Cargo Space (cu. ft.)	Average-18
Wheelbase/Length (in.)	109.2/191.4

Honda Ridgeline

Standard Pickup

Honda Ridgeline

Ratings—10 Best, 1 Worst

Combo Crash Tests	–
Safety Features	3
Rollover	4
Preventive Maintenance	5
Repair Costs	9
Warranty	1
Fuel Economy	1
Complaints	9
Insurance Costs	5
OVERALL RATING	**–**

Honda Ridgeline

At-a-Glance

Status/Year Series Started	Unchanged/2006
Twins	–
Body Styles	Pickup
Seating	5
Anti-Theft Device	Std. Pass. Immobil.
Parking Index Rating	Very Hard
Where Made	Lincoln, AL
Fuel Factor	
MPG Rating (city/hwy)	Very Poor-15/21
Driving Range (mi.)	Short-379
Fuel Type	Regular
Annual Fuel Cost	Very High-$2,989
Gas Guzzler Tax	No
Greenhouse Gas Emissions (tons/yr.)	Very High-10.8
Barrels of Oil Used per year	Very High-19.4

How the Competition Rates

Competitors	Rating	Pg.
Ford F-150	1	139
Nissan Titan	–	227
Toyota Tacoma	1	256

Price Range

Price Range	Retail	Markup
RT	$29,575	9%
Sport	$30,720	9%
RTS	$32,380	9%
RTL /Leather & Nav	$37,505	9%

Safety Checklist

Crash Tests:
- Frontal . . . .
- Side . . . .

Airbags:
- Head . . . . Fr. & Rr. Roof Curtain
- Torso . . . . Front Tosro from Seat
- Pelvis . . . . None
- Roll Sensing . . . . .Yes
- Knee Bolster . . . . None

Crash Avoidance:
- Collision Avoidance . . . . None
- Blind Spot Detection . . . . None
- Lane Keeping Assist . . . . None
- Backup Camera . . . . Standard
- Pedestrian Crash Avoidance . . . . None

General:
- Auto. Crash Notification . . . . None
- Day Running Lamps . . . . Standard

Safety Belt/Restraint:
- Dynamic Head Restraints . . . . . .Standard Front
- Adjustable Belt . . . . .Standard Front

Honda Ridgeline

Specifications

Drive	4WD
Engine	3.5-liter V6
Transmission	5-sp. Automatic
Tow Rating (lbs.)	Low-5000
Head/Leg Room (in.)	Average-40.7/40.8
Interior Space (cu. ft.)	Roomy-112
Cargo Space (cu. ft.)	Very Roomy-44.1
Wheelbase/Length (in.)	122/206.9

Hyundai Accent

Ratings—10 Best, 1 Worst

Combo Crash Tests	3
Safety Features	1
Rollover	6
Preventive Maintenance	6
Repair Costs	10
Warranty	10
Fuel Economy	9
Complaints	5
Insurance Costs	1
OVERALL RATING	**6**

Hyundai Accent

Hyundai Accent

At-a-Glance

Status/Year Series Started	Unchanged/2012
Twins	Kia Rio
Body Styles	Sedan, Hatchback
Seating	5
Anti-Theft Device	None
Parking Index Rating	Very Easy
Where Made	Ulsan, South Korea
Fuel Factor	
MPG Rating (city/hwy)	Very Good-27/37
Driving Range (mi.)	Very Short-350
Fuel Type	Regular
Annual Fuel Cost	Very Low-$1,674
Gas Guzzler Tax	No
Greenhouse Gas Emissions (tons/yr.)	Very Low-5.9
Barrels of Oil Used per year	Low-10.6

How the Competition Rates

Competitors	Rating	Pg.
Ford Fiesta	–	140
Nissan Versa	2	228
Toyota Yaris	6	259

Price Range

	Retail	Markup
GLS Manual	$14,545	3%
GLS	$15,545	3%
GS	$15,995	3%
SE	$17,095	3%

Safety Checklist

Crash Tests:
Frontal . . . . Average
Side . . . . Very Poor*

Airbags:
Head . . . . Fr. & Rr. Roof Curtain
Torso . . . . Front Pelvis/Torso from Seat
Pelvis . . . . Front Pelvis/Torso from Seat
Roll Sensing . . . . No
Knee Bolster . . . . None

Crash Avoidance:
Collision Avoidance. . . . . None
Blind Spot Detection . . . . None
Lane Keeping Assist . . . . None
Backup Camera . . . . None
Pedestrian Crash Avoidance . . . . None

General:
Auto. Crash Notification . . . . None
Day Running Lamps . . . . None

Safety Belt/Restraint:
Dynamic Head Restraints . . . . . . Standard Front
Adjustable Belt . . . . Standard Front

Hyundai Accent

Specifications

Drive	FWD
Engine	1.6-liter I4
Transmission	6-sp. Automatic
Tow Rating (lbs.)	
Head/Leg Room (in.)	Average-39.9/41.8
Interior Space (cu. ft.)	Very Cramped-90.1
Cargo Space (cu. ft.)	Average-21.2
Wheelbase/Length (in.)	101.2/162

*Additional injury potential in side test. See footnote on page 20.

Hyundai Azera

Intermediate

Ratings—10 Best, 1 Worst	
Combo Crash Tests	–
Safety Features	3
Rollover	9
Preventive Maintenance	4
Repair Costs	3
Warranty	10
Fuel Economy	4
Complaints	2
Insurance Costs	3
OVERALL RATING	**–**

Hyundai Azera

Hyundai Azera

At-a-Glance

Status/Year Series Started. Unchanged/2012
Twins . . . . –
Body Styles . . . . .Sedan
Seating. 5
Anti-Theft Device . Std. Pass. Immobil. & Active Alarm
Parking Index Rating . . . . Average
Where Made. . . . . .Asan, South Korea
Fuel Factor
  MPG Rating (city/hwy). Poor-19/29
  Driving Range (mi.) Average-416
  Fuel Type . . . . .Regular
  Annual Fuel Cost . . . . Average-$2,288
  Gas Guzzler Tax . . . . .No
  Greenhouse Gas Emissions (tons/yr.). . Average-8.0
  Barrels of Oil Used per year High-14.3

How the Competition Rates

Competitors	Rating	Pg.
Lexus ES	6	188
Nissan Maxima	2	221
Toyota Camry	6	246

Price Range	Retail	Markup
4D Sedan	$32,250	7%

Safety Checklist

Crash Tests:
  Frontal. . . . .
  Side. . . . .
Airbags:
  Head . . . . Fr. & Rr. Roof Curtain
  Torso. . . . . Fr. & Rr. Torso from Seat
  Pelvis . . . . .Front Pelvis/Torso from Seat
  Roll Sensing . . . . No
  Knee Bolster . . . . Standard
Crash Avoidance:
  Collision Avoidance. . . . . None
  Blind Spot Detection . . . . None
  Lane Keeping Assist. . . . . None
  Backup Camera . . . . Optional
  Pedestrian Crash Avoidance . . . . None
General:
  Auto. Crash Notification . . Operator Assist.-Fee
  Day Running Lamps . . . . Standard
Safety Belt/Restraint:
  Dynamic Head Restraints . . . . None
  Adjustable Belt . . . . .Standard Front

Hyundai Azera

Specifications

Drive. . . . . FWD
Engine 3.3-liter V6
Transmission . . . . .6-sp. Automatic
Tow Rating (lbs.) . . . .
Head/Leg Room (in.) . . . . . . Very Roomy-40.3/45.5
Interior Space (cu. ft.). Roomy-106
Cargo Space (cu. ft.) Cramped-16
Wheelbase/Length (in.) 112/193.3

Ratings—10 Best, 1 Worst

Combo Crash Tests	5
Safety Features	1
Rollover	8
Preventive Maintenance	3
Repair Costs	10
Warranty	10
Fuel Economy	9
Complaints	5
Insurance Costs	1
OVERALL RATING	**6**

Hyundai Elantra Coupe

Hyundai Elantra Sedan

At-a-Glance

Status/Year Series Started. Unchanged/2011
Twins . . . . –
Body Styles . . . . .Sedan, Coupe, Hatchback
Seating 5
Anti-Theft Device .Opt. Pass. Immobil. & Active Alarm
Parking Index Rating . . . . Easy
Where Made. . . . . Ulsan, South Korea
Fuel Factor
  MPG Rating (city/hwy) . . . . Very Good-28/38
  Driving Range (mi.) Average-407
  Fuel Type. . . . . .Regular
  Annual Fuel Cost . . . . Very Low-$1,620
  Gas Guzzler Tax . . . . .No
  Greenhouse Gas Emissions (tons/yr.). Low-6.8
  Barrels of Oil Used per year Average-12.2

How the Competition Rates

Competitors	Rating	Pg.
Honda Civic	6	148
Nissan Sentra	3	226
Toyota Corolla	7	247

Price Range

	Retail	Markup
GLS	$17,965	3%
GT	$19,545	4%
SE	$20,895	4%
Limited PZEV	$21,115	4%

Safety Checklist

Crash Tests:
  Frontal. . . . . Average
  Side. . . . . .Poor
Airbags:
  Head . . . . Fr. & Rr. Roof Curtain
  Torso. . . . . .Front Pelvis/Torso from Seat
  Pelvis . . . . .Front Pelvis/Torso from Seat
  Roll Sensing . . . . No
  Knee Bolster . . . . None
Crash Avoidance:
  Collision Avoidance. . . . . None
  Blind Spot Detection . . . . None
  Lane Keeping Assist. . . . . None
  Backup Camera . . . . Optional
  Pedestrian Crash Avoidance . . . . None
General:
  Auto. Crash Notification . . Operator Assist.-Fee
  Day Running Lamps . . . . Optional
Safety Belt/Restraint:
  Dynamic Head Restraints. . . . . None
  Adjustable Belt . . . . .Standard Front

Hyundai Elantra GT

Specifications

Drive. . . . . FWD
Engine 1.8-liter I4
Transmission . . . . .6-sp. Automatic
Tow Rating (lbs.) . . . .
Head/Leg Room (in.) Roomy-40/43.6
Interior Space (cu. ft.). Cramped-95.6
Cargo Space (cu. ft.) Cramped-14.8
Wheelbase/Length (in.) 106.3/179.1

Hyundai Genesis

Ratings—10 Best, 1 Worst

Combo Crash Tests	–
Safety Features	4
Rollover	9
Preventive Maintenance	3
Repair Costs	5
Warranty	10
Fuel Economy	3
Complaints	2
Insurance Costs	3
OVERALL RATING	**–**

Hyundai Genesis

Hyundai Genesis

At-a-Glance

Status/Year Series Started........ Unchanged/2009
Twins . . . .–
Body Styles . . . . Sedan, Coupe
Seating 5
Anti-Theft Device . Std. Pass. Immobil. & Active Alarm
Parking Index Rating . . . . Average
Where Made. . . . . Ulsan, South Korea
Fuel Factor
  MPG Rating (city/hwy) Poor-18/27
  Driving Range (mi.) Average-409
  Fuel Type. . . . . .Regular
  Annual Fuel Cost . . . . High-$2,430
  Gas Guzzler Tax . . . . .No
  Greenhouse Gas Emissions (tons/yr.). High-8.7
  Barrels of Oil Used per year High-15.7

How the Competition Rates

Competitors	Rating	Pg.
Acura TL	3	85
Lexus ES	6	188
Volkswagen CC	–	261

Price Range

Price Range	Retail	Markup
Base Coupe	$25,500	5%
Grand Touring Coupe	$32,000	7%
Sedan 3.8L V6	$34,200	7%
Sedan 5.0L R-Spec	$46,800	8%

Safety Checklist

Crash Tests:
  Frontal. . . . .
  Side. . . . .
Airbags:
  Head . . . . Fr. & Rr. Roof Curtain
  Torso. . . . . Fr. & Rr. Torso from Seat
  Pelvis . . . . .Front Pelvis/Torso from Seat
  Roll Sensing . . . . No
  Knee Bolster . . . . None
Crash Avoidance:
  Collision Avoidance. . . . . None
  Blind Spot Detection . . . . None
  Lane Keeping Assist. . . .Warning Only Optional
  Backup Camera . . . . Optional
  Pedestrian Crash Avoidance . . . . None
General:
  Auto. Crash Notification . . Operator Assist.-Fee
  Day Running Lamps . . . . Optional
Safety Belt/Restraint:
  Dynamic Head Restraints . . . . . .Standard Front
  Adjustable Belt . . . . .Standard Front

Hyundai Genesis

Specifications

Drive. . . . . FWD
Engine .3.8-liter V6
Transmission . . . . .8-sp. Automatic
Tow Rating (lbs.) . . . .
Head/Leg Room (in.) . . . . . . Very Roomy-40.4/44.3
Interior Space (cu. ft.). Roomy-109.4
Cargo Space (cu. ft.) Cramped-15.9
Wheelbase/Length (in.) 115.6/196.3

Ratings—10 Best, 1 Worst

Combo Crash Tests	–
Safety Features	4
Rollover	4
Preventive Maintenance	4
Repair Costs	8
Warranty	10
Fuel Economy	3
Complaints	1
Insurance Costs	8
OVERALL RATING	**–**

Hyundai Santa Fe

Hyundai Santa Fe

Hyundai Santa Fe

At-a-Glance

Status/Year Series Started	Unchanged/2013
Twins	–
Body Styles	SUV
Seating	7
Anti-Theft Device	Std. Pass. Immobil. & Active Alarm
Parking Index Rating	Average
Where Made	West Point, GA
Fuel Factor	
MPG Rating (city/hwy)	Poor-18/25
Driving Range (mi.)	Short-387
Fuel Type	Regular
Annual Fuel Cost	High-$2,498
Gas Guzzler Tax	No
Greenhouse Gas Emissions (tons/yr.)	High-8.7
Barrels of Oil Used per year	High-15.7

How the Competition Rates

Competitors	Rating	Pg.
Acura MDX	8	82
Nissan Rogue	–	225
Toyota Venza	4	258

Price Range

Price Range	Retail	Markup
Sport 2.4L FWD	$24,450	4%
Sport 2.0 AWD	$29,450	5%
GLS AWD	$30,100	5%
Limited AWD	$34,850	6%

Safety Checklist

Crash Tests:
Frontal . . . .
Side . . . .

Airbags:
Head . . . . Fr. & Rr. Roof Curtain
Torso . . . . Front Pelvis/Torso from Seat
Pelvis . . . . Front Pelvis/Torso from Seat
Roll Sensing . . . . Yes
Knee Bolster . . . . Standard

Crash Avoidance:
Collision Avoidance . . . . None
Blind Spot Detection . . . . Optional
Lane Keeping Assist . . . . None
Backup Camera . . . . Optional
Pedestrian Crash Avoidance . . . . None

General:
Auto. Crash Notification . . Operator Assist.-Fee
Day Running Lamps . . . . None

Safety Belt/Restraint:
Dynamic Head Restraints . . . . None
Adjustable Belt . . . . Standard Front

Hyundai Santa Fe

Specifications

Drive	FWD
Engine	3.3-liter V6
Transmission	6-sp. Automatic
Tow Rating (lbs.)	Low-5000
Head/Leg Room (in.)	Cramped-39.6/41.3
Interior Space (cu. ft.)	Very Roomy-146.6
Cargo Space (cu. ft.)	Cramped-13.5
Wheelbase/Length (in.)	110.2/193.1

Hyundai Santa Fe Sport
Mid-Size SUV

Ratings—10 Best, 1 Worst

Combo Crash Tests	7
Safety Features	4
Rollover	5
Preventive Maintenance	4
Repair Costs	8
Warranty	10
Fuel Economy	4
Complaints	–
Insurance Costs	8
OVERALL RATING	**8**

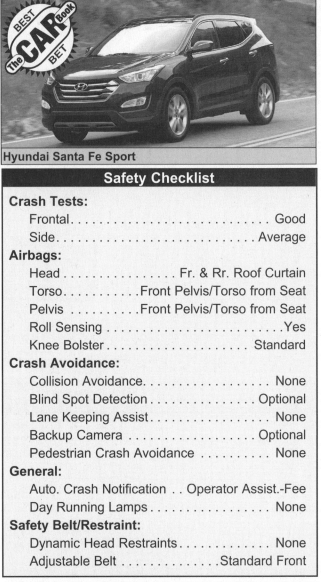

Hyundai Santa Fe Sport

Hyundai Santa Fe Sport

At-a-Glance

Status/Year Series Started........ Unchanged/2014
Twins . . . . –
Body Styles . . . . SUV
Seating 5
Anti-Theft Device . Std. Pass. Immobil. & Active Alarm
Parking Index Rating . . . . Easy
Where Made. . . . . West Point, GA
Fuel Factor
  MPG Rating (city/hwy) Poor-20/27
  Driving Range (mi.) Short-394
  Fuel Type . . . . .Regular
  Annual Fuel Cost . . . . Average-$2,272
  Gas Guzzler Tax . . . . .No
  Greenhouse Gas Emissions (tons/yr.). . Average-8.0
  Barrels of Oil Used per year High-14.3

How the Competition Rates

Competitors	Rating	Pg.
Ford Edge	1	135
Kia Sorento	5	181
Nissan Rogue	–	225

Price Range	Retail	Markup
2.4L FWD	$24,450	4%
2.4L AWD	$26,200	4%
2.0L FWD	$27,700	5%
2.0L AWD	$29,450	5%

Safety Checklist

Crash Tests:
  Frontal. . . . . Good
  Side. . . . . Average
Airbags:
  Head . . . . Fr. & Rr. Roof Curtain
  Torso. . . . . .Front Pelvis/Torso from Seat
  Pelvis . . . . .Front Pelvis/Torso from Seat
  Roll Sensing . . . . .Yes
  Knee Bolster . . . . Standard
Crash Avoidance:
  Collision Avoidance. . . . . None
  Blind Spot Detection . . . . Optional
  Lane Keeping Assist. . . . . None
  Backup Camera . . . . Optional
  Pedestrian Crash Avoidance . . . . None
General:
  Auto. Crash Notification . . Operator Assist.-Fee
  Day Running Lamps . . . . None
Safety Belt/Restraint:
  Dynamic Head Restraints . . . . None
  Adjustable Belt . . . . .Standard Front

Hyundai Santa Fe Sport

Specifications

Drive. . . . . FWD
Engine 2.4-liter I4
Transmission . . . . .6-sp. Automatic
Tow Rating (lbs.) . . . . Very Low-2000
Head/Leg Room (in.) Cramped-39.2/41.3
Interior Space (cu. ft.). Roomy-108
Cargo Space (cu. ft.) . . . . . Very Roomy-35.4
Wheelbase/Length (in.) 106.3/184.6

Ratings—10 Best, 1 Worst

Combo Crash Tests	7
Safety Features	3
Rollover	9
Preventive Maintenance	5
Repair Costs	9
Warranty	10
Fuel Economy	8
Complaints	2
Insurance Costs	1
OVERALL RATING	**7**

Hyundai Sonata

At-a-Glance

Status/Year Series Started Appearance Change/2011	
Twins	–
Body Styles	Sedan
Seating	5
Anti-Theft Device	Std. Pass. Immobil. & Active Alarm
Parking Index Rating	Easy
Where Made	Montgomery, AL
Fuel Factor	
MPG Rating (city/hwy)	Good-24/35
Driving Range (mi.)	Very Long-517
Fuel Type	Regular
Annual Fuel Cost	Low-$1,841
Gas Guzzler Tax	No
Greenhouse Gas Emissions (tons/yr.)	Low-6.5
Barrels of Oil Used per year	Average-11.8

How the Competition Rates

Competitors	Rating	Pg.
Mazda Mazda6	–	201
Toyota Camry	6	246
Volkswagen Passat	6	264

Price Range	Retail	Markup
GLS	$21,350	4%
SE 2.4	$25,750	6%
Limited 2.0 Turbo	$28,650	7%
Hybrid Limited	$30,550	7%

BEST BET — The CAR book

Hyundai Sonata

Safety Checklist

Crash Tests:
Frontal	Average
Side	Good

Airbags:
Head	Fr. & Rr. Roof Curtain
Torso	Front Pelvis/Torso from Seat
Pelvis	Front Pelvis/Torso from Seat
Roll Sensing	No
Knee Bolster	None

Crash Avoidance:
Collision Avoidance	None
Blind Spot Detection	Optional
Lane Keeping Assist	None
Backup Camera	Optional
Pedestrian Crash Avoidance	None

General:
Auto. Crash Notification	Operator Assist.-Fee
Day Running Lamps	Standard

Safety Belt/Restraint:
Dynamic Head Restraints	Standard Front
Adjustable Belt	Standard Front

Hyundai Sonata

Specifications

Drive	FWD
Engine	2.4-liter I4
Transmission	6-sp. Automatic
Tow Rating (lbs.)	
Head/Leg Room (in.)	Very Roomy-40/45.5
Interior Space (cu. ft.)	Roomy-103.8
Cargo Space (cu. ft.)	Average-16.4
Wheelbase/Length (in.)	110/189.8

Ratings—10 Best, 1 Worst

Combo Crash Tests	3
Safety Features	3
Rollover	3
Preventive Maintenance	4
Repair Costs	8
Warranty	10
Fuel Economy	5
Complaints	6
Insurance Costs	5
OVERALL RATING	**4**

Hyundai Tucson

Kia Sportage

At-a-Glance

Status/Year Series Started........ Unchanged/2010
Twins . . . . Kia Sportage
Body Styles . . . . SUV
Seating 5
Anti-Theft Device .Opt. Pass. Immobil. & Active Alarm
Parking Index Rating . . . . .Very Easy
Where Made. . . . . Ulsan, South Korea
Fuel Factor
  MPG Rating (city/hwy) Average-21/28
  Driving Range (mi.) . . . . Very Short-362
  Fuel Type . . . . .Regular
  Annual Fuel Cost . . . . Average-$2,174
  Gas Guzzler Tax .No
  Greenhouse Gas Emissions (tons/yr.). . Average-8.3
  Barrels of Oil Used per year High-15.0

How the Competition Rates

Competitors	Rating	Pg.
Ford Escape	5	136
Honda CR-V	6	150
Toyota RAV4	5	253

Price Range

Price Range	Retail	Markup
GL FWD	$20,395	4%
GLS FWD	$21,450	4%
GLS AWD	$22,950	4%
Limited AWD	$27,700	5%

Safety Checklist

Crash Tests:
Frontal. . . . . Poor
Side . . . . Poor
Airbags:
Head . . . . Fr. & Rr. Roof Curtain
Torso. . . . . .Front Pelvis/Torso from Seat
Pelvis . . . . .Front Pelvis/Torso from Seat
Roll Sensing . . . . .Yes
Knee Bolster . . . . None
Crash Avoidance:
Collision Avoidance. . . . . None
Blind Spot Detection . . . . None
Lane Keeping Assist. . . . . None
Backup Camera . . . . Optional
Pedestrian Crash Avoidance . . . . None
General:
Auto. Crash Notification . . Operator Assist.-Fee
Day Running Lamps. . . . . None
Safety Belt/Restraint:
Dynamic Head Restraints. . . . . Optional Front
Adjustable Belt . . . . .Standard Front

Hyundai Tucson

Specifications

Drive. . . . . FWD
Engine 2.4-liter I4
Transmission . . . . .6-sp. Automatic
Tow Rating (lbs.) . . . . Very Low-2000
Head/Leg Room (in.) Cramped-39.4/41.2
Interior Space (cu. ft.). Average-101.9
Cargo Space (cu. ft.) Roomy-25.7
Wheelbase/Length (in.) 103.9/173.2

Ratings—10 Best, 1 Worst

Combo Crash Tests	–
Safety Features	1
Rollover	10
Preventive Maintenance	5
Repair Costs	9
Warranty	10
Fuel Economy	8
Complaints	1
Insurance Costs	3

OVERALL RATING —

Hyundai Veloster

Hyundai Veloster

At-a-Glance

Status/Year Series Started	Unchanged/2012
Twins	–
Body Styles	Hatchback
Seating	4
Anti-Theft Device	Std. Pass. Immobil. & Active Alarm
Parking Index Rating	Very Easy
Where Made	Ulsan, South Korea
Fuel Factor	
MPG Rating (city/hwy)	Good-26/35
Driving Range (mi.)	Short-388
Fuel Type	Regular
Annual Fuel Cost	Very Low-$1,750
Gas Guzzler Tax	No
Greenhouse Gas Emissions (tons/yr.)	Low-6.8
Barrels of Oil Used per year	Average-12.2

How the Competition Rates

Competitors	Rating	Pg.
Chevrolet Sonic	10	116
Mini Cooper	–	210
Scion tC	6	233

Price Range

	Retail	Markup
Base Manual	$17,600	4%
Base AT	$18,850	4%
REMIX AT	$21,300	4%
Turbo AT	$23,100	5%

Safety Checklist

Crash Tests:
- Frontal ...
- Side ...

Airbags:
- Head ... Fr. & Rr. Roof Curtain
- Torso ... Front Pelvis/Torso from Seat
- Pelvis ... Front Pelvis/Torso from Seat
- Roll Sensing ... No
- Knee Bolster ... None

Crash Avoidance:
- Collision Avoidance ... None
- Blind Spot Detection ... None
- Lane Keeping Assist ... None
- Backup Camera ... Optional
- Pedestrian Crash Avoidance ... None

General:
- Auto. Crash Notification ... Operator Assist.-Fee
- Day Running Lamps ... None

Safety Belt/Restraint:
- Dynamic Head Restraints ... None
- Adjustable Belt ... None

Specifications

Drive	FWD
Engine	1.6-liter I4
Transmission	6-sp. Manual
Tow Rating (lbs.)	...
Head/Leg Room (in.)	Roomy-39/43.9
Interior Space (cu. ft.)	Very Cramped-89.8
Cargo Space (cu. ft.)	Cramped-15.5
Wheelbase/Length (in.)	104.3/166.1

Infiniti Q50

Intermediate

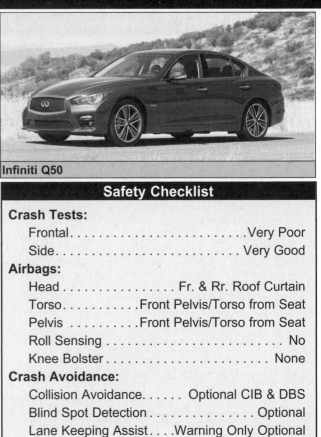

Infiniti Q50

Ratings—10 Best, 1 Worst	
Combo Crash Tests	5
Safety Features	4
Rollover	9
Preventive Maintenance	8
Repair Costs	2
Warranty	7
Fuel Economy	4
Complaints	–
Insurance Costs	5
OVERALL RATING	**6**

Infiniti Q50

Safety Checklist

Crash Tests:
Frontal . . . . Very Poor
Side . . . . Very Good
Airbags:
Head . . . . Fr. & Rr. Roof Curtain
Torso . . . . Front Pelvis/Torso from Seat
Pelvis . . . . Front Pelvis/Torso from Seat
Roll Sensing . . . . No
Knee Bolster . . . . None
Crash Avoidance:
Collision Avoidance . . . . . . Optional CIB & DBS
Blind Spot Detection . . . . Optional
Lane Keeping Assist . . . . Warning Only Optional
Backup Camera . . . . Standard
Pedestrian Crash Avoidance . . . . None
General:
Auto. Crash Notification . . Operator Assist.-Fee
Day Running Lamps . . . . Standard
Safety Belt/Restraint:
Dynamic Head Restraints . . . . None
Adjustable Belt . . . . Standard Front

At-a-Glance

Status/Year Series Started . . . . All New/2014
Twins . . . . –
Body Styles . . . . Sedan
Seating 5
Anti-Theft Device . . . . . . Std. Pass. Immobil. & Alarm
Parking Index Rating . . . . Average
Where Made . . . . Tochigi, Japan
Fuel Factor
  MPG Rating (city/hwy) Poor-19/27
  Driving Range (mi.) Long-438
  Fuel Type . . . . Premium
  Annual Fuel Cost . . . . High-$2,552
  Gas Guzzler Tax . . . . No
  Greenhouse Gas Emissions (tons/yr.) . . Average-8.0
  Barrels of Oil Used per year High-14.3

How the Competition Rates

Competitors	Rating	Pg.
BMW 3 Series	10	92
Lexus IS	7	191
Lincoln MKZ	4	195

Infiniti Q50

Specifications

Drive . . . . AWD
Engine 3.7-liter V6
Transmission . . . . 7-sp. Automatic
Tow Rating (lbs.) . . . .
Head/Leg Room (in.) . . . . . . Very Roomy-40.2/44.5
Interior Space (cu. ft.) Average-101.9
Cargo Space (cu. ft.) Cramped-13.5
Wheelbase/Length (in.) 112.2/188.3

Price Range	Retail	Markup
Base RWD	$36,700	8%
Premium RWD	$39,550	8%
Sport AWD	$45,000	8%
Hybrid Sport AWD	$48,150	8%

Ratings—10 Best, 1 Worst

Combo Crash Tests	–
Safety Features	2
Rollover	8
Preventive Maintenance	8
Repair Costs	2
Warranty	7
Fuel Economy	4
Complaints	10
Insurance Costs	3
OVERALL RATING	**–**

Infiniti Q60

Infiniti Q60

At-a-Glance

Status/Year Series Started Unchanged/2007
Twins . . . . –
Body Styles . . . . Coupe, Convertible
Seating 4
Anti-Theft Device . . . . . . Std. Pass. Immobil. & Alarm
Parking Index Rating . . . . Easy
Where Made. Tochigi, Japan
Fuel Factor
  MPG Rating (city/hwy) Poor-19/27
  Driving Range (mi.) Long-438
  Fuel Type . . . . .Premium
  Annual Fuel Cost . . . . High-$2,552
  Gas Guzzler Tax . . . . .No
  Greenhouse Gas Emissions (tons/yr.) . . Average-8.3
  Barrels of Oil Used per year High-16.5

How the Competition Rates

Competitors	Rating	Pg.
BMW 6 Series	–	95
Lexus GS	–	189
Mercedes-Benz C-Class	4	203

Price Range

	Retail	Markup
Coupe Journey	$40,850	8%
Coupe AWD	$42,500	8%
Convertible	$48,450	8%
IPL Coupe	$53,550	8%

Safety Checklist

Crash Tests:
  Frontal . . . . .Very Poor
  Side . . . . .Very Poor

Airbags:
  Head . . . . Fr. & Rr. Roof Curtain
  Torso . . . . Front Pelvis/Torso from Seat
  Pelvis . . . . Front Pelvis/Torso from Seat
  Roll Sensing . . . . No
  Knee Bolster . . . . None

Crash Avoidance:
  Collision Avoidance . . . . None
  Blind Spot Detection . . . . None
  Lane Keeping Assist . . . . None
  Backup Camera . . . . Standard
  Pedestrian Crash Avoidance . . . . None

General:
  Auto. Crash Notification . . . . None
  Day Running Lamps . . . . None

Safety Belt/Restraint:
  Dynamic Head Restraints . . . . . .Standard Front
  Adjustable Belt . . . . None

Infiniti Q60

Specifications

Drive . . . . .RWD
Engine 3.7-liter V6
Transmission . . . . .7-sp. Automatic
Tow Rating (lbs.) . . . .
Head/Leg Room (in.) Roomy-39.4/43.8
Interior Space (cu. ft.) . . . . Very Cramped-85
Cargo Space (cu. ft.) . . . . .Very Cramped-7.4
Wheelbase/Length (in.) 112.2/183.1

Ratings—10 Best, 1 Worst

Combo Crash Tests	5
Safety Features	5
Rollover	7
Preventive Maintenance	7
Repair Costs	2
Warranty	7
Fuel Economy	3
Complaints	2
Insurance Costs	5
OVERALL RATING	**4**

Infiniti Q70

Infiniti Q70

At-a-Glance

Status/Year Series Started	Unchanged/2011
Twins	–
Body Styles	Sedan
Seating	5
Anti-Theft Device	Std. Pass. Immobil. & Alarm
Parking Index Rating	Average
Where Made	Tochigi, Japan
Fuel Factor	
MPG Rating (city/hwy)	Poor-18/26
Driving Range (mi.)	Average-418
Fuel Type	Premium
Annual Fuel Cost	High-$2,678
Gas Guzzler Tax	No
Greenhouse Gas Emissions (tons/yr.)	High-8.7
Barrels of Oil Used per year	High-15.7

How the Competition Rates

Competitors	Rating	Pg.
BMW 7 Series	–	96
Jaguar XF	–	171
Mercedes-Benz S-Class	–	209

Price Range

	Retail	Markup

Safety Checklist

Crash Tests:
Frontal . . . . Poor
Side . . . . Good
Airbags:
Head . . . . Fr. & Rr. Roof Curtain
Torso . . . . Front Pelvis/Torso from Seat
Pelvis . . . . Front Pelvis/Torso from Seat
Roll Sensing . . . . No
Knee Bolster . . . . None
Crash Avoidance:
Collision Avoidance . . . . . . Optional CIB & DBS
Blind Spot Detection . . . . Optional
Lane Keeping Assist . . . . Warning Only Optional
Backup Camera . . . . Standard
Pedestrian Crash Avoidance . . . . None
General:
Auto. Crash Notification . . Operator Assist.-Fee
Day Running Lamps . . . . Standard
Safety Belt/Restraint:
Dynamic Head Restraints . . . . . Standard Front
Adjustable Belt . . . . Standard Front

Infiniti Q70

Specifications

Drive	RWD
Engine	3.6-liter V6
Transmission	7-sp. Automatic
Tow Rating (lbs.)	
Head/Leg Room (in.)	Roomy-39.1/44
Interior Space (cu. ft.)	Roomy-103.6
Cargo Space (cu. ft.)	Cramped-14.9
Wheelbase/Length (in.)	114.2/194.7

Ratings—10 Best, 1 Worst

Combo Crash Tests	–
Safety Features	4
Rollover	6
Preventive Maintenance	8
Repair Costs	5
Warranty	7
Fuel Economy	2
Complaints	9
Insurance Costs	8
OVERALL RATING	**–**

Infiniti QX50

At-a-Glance

Status/Year Series Started	Unchanged/2008
Twins	–
Body Styles	SUV
Seating	5
Anti-Theft Device	Std. Pass. Immobil. & Alarm
Parking Index Rating	Easy
Where Made	Tochigi, Japan
Fuel Factor	
MPG Rating (city/hwy)	Very Poor-17/24
Driving Range (mi.)	Short-391
Fuel Type	Premium
Annual Fuel Cost	Very High-$2,859
Gas Guzzler Tax	No
Greenhouse Gas Emissions (tons/yr.)	High-9.2
Barrels of Oil Used per year	High-16.5

How the Competition Rates

Competitors	Rating	Pg.
Acura RDX	7	83
BMW X1	–	97
Volvo XC60	10	269

Price Range

Price Range	Retail	Markup
Base RWD	$34,400	8%
Base AWD	$35,800	8%
Journey RWD	$36,750	8%
Journey AWD	$38,150	8%

Infiniti QX50

Safety Checklist

Crash Tests:
Frontal . . . .
Side . . . .

Airbags:
Head . . . . Fr. & Rr. Roof Curtain
Torso . . . . .Front Pelvis/Torso from Seat
Pelvis . . . . .Front Pelvis/Torso from Seat
Roll Sensing . . . . No
Knee Bolster . . . . None

Crash Avoidance:
Collision Avoidance . . . . . . Optional CIB & DBS
Blind Spot Detection . . . . Optional
Lane Keeping Assist . . . .Warning Only Optional
Backup Camera . . . . Standard
Pedestrian Crash Avoidance . . . . None

General:
Auto. Crash Notification . . . . None
Day Running Lamps . . . . None

Safety Belt/Restraint:
Dynamic Head Restraints . . . . . .Standard Front
Adjustable Belt . . . . .Standard Front

Infiniti QX50

Specifications

Drive	AWD
Engine	3.7-liter V6
Transmission	7-sp. Automatic
Tow Rating (lbs.)	
Head/Leg Room (in.)	Very Roomy-40.5/44.3
Interior Space (cu. ft.)	Cramped-92
Cargo Space (cu. ft.)	Average-18.6
Wheelbase/Length (in.)	110.2/182.3

Infiniti QX60   Mid-Size SUV

Ratings—10 Best, 1 Worst

Combo Crash Tests	6
Safety Features	6
Rollover	4
Preventive Maintenance	7
Repair Costs	1
Warranty	7
Fuel Economy	3
Complaints	1
Insurance Costs	5
OVERALL RATING	**3**

Infiniti QX60

At-a-Glance

Status/Year Series Started. Unchanged/2013
Twins . . . . .Nissan Pathfinder
Body Styles . . . . SUV
Seating 7
Anti-Theft Device . . . . . . Std. Pass. Immobil. & Alarm
Parking Index Rating . . . . Hard
Where Made. . . . . Smyrna, TN
Fuel Factor
  MPG Rating (city/hwy). Poor-19/25
  Driving Range (mi.) Average-415
  Fuel Type. .Premium
  Annual Fuel Cost . . . . High-$2,627
  Gas Guzzler Tax . . . . .No
  Greenhouse Gas Emissions (tons/yr.). High-8.7
  Barrels of Oil Used per year High-15.7

How the Competition Rates

Competitors	Rating	Pg.
Land Rover Range Rover	–	184
Lexus RX	5	193
Mercedes-Benz M-Class	5	208

Price Range	Retail	Markup
FWD	$41,550	8%
AWD	$42,950	8%

Infiniti QX60

Infiniti QX60

Safety Checklist

Crash Tests:
  Frontal. . . . . Average
  Side. . . . . Good
Airbags:
  Head . . . . Fr. & Rr. Roof Curtain
  Torso. . . . . .Front Pelvis/Torso from Seat
  Pelvis . . . . .Front Pelvis/Torso from Seat
  Roll Sensing . . . . .Yes
  Knee Bolster . . . . None
Crash Avoidance:
  Collision Avoidance. . . . . . Optional CIB & DBS
  Blind Spot Detection . . . . Optional
  Lane Keeping Assist . . . .Warning Only Optional
  Backup Camera . . . . Standard
  Pedestrian Crash Avoidance . . . . None
General:
  Auto. Crash Notification . . Operator Assist.-Fee
  Day Running Lamps. . . . . None
Safety Belt/Restraint:
  Dynamic Head Restraints. . . . . None
  Adjustable Belt . . . . Standard Front & Rear

Specifications

Drive. . . . . AWD
Engine 3.5-liter V6
Transmission . . . . .CVT
Tow Rating (lbs.) . . . .
Head/Leg Room (in.) Roomy-40.7/42.3
Interior Space (cu. ft.). . . . . Very Roomy-149.8
Cargo Space (cu. ft.) Cramped-15.8
Wheelbase/Length (in.) 114.2/196.4

Ratings—10 Best, 1 Worst	
Combo Crash Tests	–
Safety Features	6
Rollover	4
Preventive Maintenance	7
Repair Costs	1
Warranty	7
Fuel Economy	2
Complaints	10
Insurance Costs	8
OVERALL RATING	**–**

Infiniti QX70

Infiniti QX70

At-a-Glance

Status/Year Series Started	Unchanged/2009
Twins	–
Body Styles	SUV
Seating	5
Anti-Theft Device	Std. Pass. Immobil. & Alarm
Parking Index Rating	Average
Where Made	Tochigi, Japan
Fuel Factor	
MPG Rating (city/hwy)	Very Poor-16/22
Driving Range (mi.)	Long-434
Fuel Type	Premium
Annual Fuel Cost	Very High-$3,068
Gas Guzzler Tax	No
Greenhouse Gas Emissions (tons/yr.)	Very High-10.2
Barrels of Oil Used per year	Very High-18.3

How the Competition Rates

Competitors	Rating	Pg.
Acura MDX	8	82
Nissan Murano	3	222
Porsche Cayenne	–	230

Price Range	Retail	Markup
V6 RWD	$44,950	8%
V6 AWD	$46,400	8%
V8 AWD	$61,500	8%

Safety Checklist

Crash Tests:
Frontal . . . .
Side . . . .

Airbags:
Head . . . . Fr. & Rr. Roof Curtain
Torso . . . . Front Pelvis/Torso from Seat
Pelvis . . . . Front Pelvis/Torso from Seat
Roll Sensing . . . . Yes
Knee Bolster . . . . None

Crash Avoidance:
Collision Avoidance . . . . . . Optional CIB & DBS
Blind Spot Detection . . . . None
Lane Keeping Assist . . . . Warning Only Optional
Backup Camera . . . . Standard
Pedestrian Crash Avoidance . . . . None

General:
Auto. Crash Notification . . . . None
Day Running Lamps . . . . None

Safety Belt/Restraint:
Dynamic Head Restraints . . . . . . Standard Front
Adjustable Belt . . . . Standard Front

Infiniti QX70

Specifications

Drive	AWD
Engine	3.7-liter V6
Transmission	7-sp. Automatic
Tow Rating (lbs.)	Very Low-2000
Head/Leg Room (in.)	Very Roomy-39.3/44.7
Interior Space (cu. ft.)	Average-102.5
Cargo Space (cu. ft.)	Roomy-24.8
Wheelbase/Length (in.)	113.6/191.3

Ratings—10 Best, 1 Worst

Combo Crash Tests	–
Safety Features	7
Rollover	2
Preventive Maintenance	3
Repair Costs	4
Warranty	7
Fuel Economy	1
Complaints	9
Insurance Costs	8
OVERALL RATING	–

Infiniti QX80

Infiniti QX80

At-a-Glance

Status/Year Series Started........ Unchanged/2011
Twins . . . . –
Body Styles . . . . SUV
Seating 7/8
Anti-Theft Device . . . . . . Std. Pass. Immobil. & Alarm
Parking Index Rating . . . . .Very Hard
Where Made. Kyushu, Japan
Fuel Factor
  MPG Rating (city/hwy). . . . . .Very Poor-14/20
  Driving Range (mi.) Long-421
  Fuel Type . . . . .Premium
  Annual Fuel Cost . . . . Very High-$3,457
  Gas Guzzler Tax . . . . .No
  Greenhouse Gas Emissions (tons/yr.)Very High-11.5
  Barrels of Oil Used per year . . . . . . .Very High-20.6

How the Competition Rates

Competitors	Rating	Pg.
Audi Q7	–	91
Mercedes-Benz GL-Class	–	206
Toyota Sequoia	–	254

Price Range	Retail	Markup
2WD	$61,350	8%
4WD	$64,450	8%

Safety Checklist

Crash Tests:
  Frontal. . . . .
  Side. . . . .
Airbags:
  Head . . . . Fr. & Rr. Roof Curtain
  Torso. . . . . .Front Pelvis/Torso from Seat
  Pelvis . . . . .Front Pelvis/Torso from Seat
  Roll Sensing . . . . .Yes
  Knee Bolster . . . . None
Crash Avoidance:
  Collision Avoidance. . . . . . . Optional CIB & DBS
  Blind Spot Detection . . . . Optional
  Lane Keeping Assist. . . .Warning Only Optional
  Backup Camera . . . . Standard
  Pedestrian Crash Avoidance . . . . None
General:
  Auto. Crash Notification . . . . None
  Day Running Lamps . . . . None
Safety Belt/Restraint:
  Dynamic Head Restraints . . . . . .Standard Front
  Adjustable Belt . . . . Standard Front & Rear

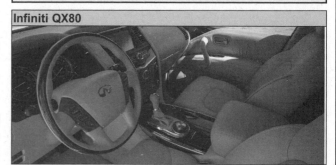
Infiniti QX80

Specifications

Drive. 4WD
Engine 5.6-liter V8
Transmission . . . . .7-sp. Automatic
Tow Rating (lbs.) . . . . .Very High-8500
Head/Leg Room (in.) . . . . .Very Cramped-39.9/39.6
Interior Space (cu. ft.). . . . . Very Roomy-151.3
Cargo Space (cu. ft.) Average-16.6
Wheelbase/Length (in.) 121.1/208.3

Ratings—10 Best, 1 Worst	
Combo Crash Tests	–
Safety Features	4
Rollover	8
Preventive Maintenance	2
Repair Costs	1
Warranty	4
Fuel Economy	3
Complaints	2
Insurance Costs	8
OVERALL RATING	**–**

Jaguar XF

Jaguar XF

At-a-Glance

Status/Year Series Started. Unchanged/2009
Twins . . . . –
Body Styles . . . . Sedan
Seating 5
Anti-Theft Device . . . . . . Std. Pass. Immobil. & Alarm
Parking Index Rating . . . . Hard
Where Made. . . . . Castle Bromwich, UK
Fuel Factor
  MPG Rating (city/hwy) Poor-17/28
  Driving Range (mi.) Short-380
  Fuel Type. . . . . Premium
  Annual Fuel Cost . . . . Very High-$2,709
  Gas Guzzler Tax . . . . No
  Greenhouse Gas Emissions (tons/yr.)Very High-10.2
  Barrels of Oil Used per year . . . . Very High-18.3

How the Competition Rates

Competitors	Rating	Pg.
BMW 7 Series	–	96
Mercedes-Benz S-Class	–	209
Volvo S80	–	268

Price Range	Retail	Markup
2.0L I4T	$46,975	9%
3.0L SC AWD	$53,000	9%
Supercharged	$68,100	9%
XFR-S	$99,000	9%

Safety Checklist

Crash Tests:
  Frontal. . . . .
  Side. . . . .
Airbags:
  Head . . . . Fr. & Rr. Roof Curtain
  Torso. . . . . .Front Pelvis/Torso from Seat
  Pelvis . . . . .Front Pelvis/Torso from Seat
  Roll Sensing . . . . No
  Knee Bolster . . . . None
Crash Avoidance:
  Collision Avoidance. . . . . . Optional CIB & DBS
  Blind Spot Detection . . . . Optional
  Lane Keeping Assist. . . . . None
  Backup Camera . . . . Optional
  Pedestrian Crash Avoidance . . . . None
General:
  Auto. Crash Notification . . . . None
  Day Running Lamps . . . . Standard
Safety Belt/Restraint:
  Dynamic Head Restraints . . . . . Standard Front
  Adjustable Belt . . . . Standard Front

Jaguar XF

Specifications

Drive. . . . . RWD
Engine 3.0-liter V6
Transmission . . . . .8-sp. Automatic
Tow Rating (lbs.) . . . .
Head/Leg Room (in.) . . . . .Very Cramped-37.3/41.5
Interior Space (cu. ft.). Cramped-95
Cargo Space (cu. ft.) Average-17.7
Wheelbase/Length (in.) 114.5/195.3

Ratings—10 Best, 1 Worst

Combo Crash Tests	–
Safety Features	9
Rollover	3
Preventive Maintenance	10
Repair Costs	–
Warranty	8
Fuel Economy	5
Complaints	–
Insurance Costs	5
OVERALL RATING	**–**

Jeep Cherokee

At-a-Glance

Status/Year Series Started	All New/2014
Twins	–
Body Styles	SUV
Seating	5
Anti-Theft Device	Std. Pass. Immobil. & Alarm
Parking Index Rating	Very Easy
Where Made	Toledo, OH
Fuel Factor	
MPG Rating (city/hwy)	Average-21/28
Driving Range (mi.)	Short-376
Fuel Type	Regular
Annual Fuel Cost	Average-$2,174
Gas Guzzler Tax	No
Greenhouse Gas Emissions (tons/yr.)	Average-8.3
Barrels of Oil Used per year	High-15

How the Competition Rates

Competitors	Rating	Pg.
Ford Escape	5	136
Mazda CX-5	6	196
Toyota RAV4	5	253

Price Range

	Retail	Markup
Sport FWD	$22,995	2%
Latitude 4WD	$26,495	3%
Trailhawk	$29,495	3%
Limited 4WD	$29,995	4%

Jeep Cherokee

Safety Checklist

Crash Tests:
Frontal . . . .
Side . . . .

Airbags:
Head . . . . Fr. & Rr. Roof Curtain
Torso . . . . Front Pelvis/Torso from Seat
Pelvis . . . . Fr. & Rr. Pelvis/Torso from Seat
Roll Sensing . . . . Yes
Knee Bolster . . . . Standard

Crash Avoidance:
Collision Avoidance . . . . . . Optional CIB & DBS
Blind Spot Detection . . . . Optional
Lane Keeping Assist . . . . Warning Only Optional
Backup Camera . . . . Optional
Pedestrian Crash Avoidance . . . . None

General:
Auto. Crash Notification . . . . None
Day Running Lamps . . . . Standard

Safety Belt/Restraint:
Dynamic Head Restraints . . . . . . Standard Front
Adjustable Belt . . . . Standard Front

Jeep Cherokee

Specifications

Drive	4WD
Engine	3.2-liter V6
Transmission	9-sp. Automatic
Tow Rating (lbs.)	Very Low-2000
Head/Leg Room (in.)	Cramped-39.4/41.1
Interior Space (cu. ft.)	Roomy-105.45
Cargo Space (cu. ft.)	Roomy-24.8
Wheelbase/Length (in.)	106.3/182

Jeep Compass Small SUV

Ratings—10 Best, 1 Worst

Combo Crash Tests	1
Safety Features	3
Rollover	3
Preventive Maintenance	9
Repair Costs	9
Warranty	8
Fuel Economy	5
Complaints	4
Insurance Costs	8
OVERALL RATING	**5**

Jeep Compass

Jeep Compass

At-a-Glance

Status/Year Series Started........ Unchanged/2007
Twins . . . . —
Body Styles . . . . SUV
Seating 5
Anti-Theft Device . . . . Std. Pass. Immobil.
Parking Index Rating . . . . Easy
Where Made. . . . . Belvidere, IL
Fuel Factor
  MPG Rating (city/hwy) Average-21/28
  Driving Range (mi.) . . . . Very Short-322
  Fuel Type. . . . . .Regular
  Annual Fuel Cost . . . . Average-$2,174
  Gas Guzzler Tax . . . . .No
  Greenhouse Gas Emissions (tons/yr.). . Average-7.7
  Barrels of Oil Used per year High-13.7

How the Competition Rates

Competitors	Rating	Pg.
Acura RDX	7	83
Honda CR-V	6	150
Subaru Forester	4	238

Price Range	Retail	Markup
Sport FWD	$18,495	1%
Latitude FWD	$22,195	3%
Latitude 4WD	$24,195	3%
Limited 4WD	$27,495	4%

Safety Checklist

Crash Tests:
  Frontal. . . . . .Very Poor
  Side. . . . . Poor
Airbags:
  Head . . . . Fr. & Rr. Roof Curtain
  Torso. . . . . Front Tosro from Seat
  Pelvis . . . . None
  Roll Sensing . . . . .Yes
  Knee Bolster . . . . None
Crash Avoidance:
  Collision Avoidance. . . . . None
  Blind Spot Detection . . . . None
  Lane Keeping Assist. . . . . None
  Backup Camera . . . . Optional
  Pedestrian Crash Avoidance . . . . None
General:
  Auto. Crash Notification . . . . None
  Day Running Lamps. . . . . Optional
Safety Belt/Restraint:
  Dynamic Head Restraints . . . . . .Standard Front
  Adjustable Belt . . . . .Standard Front

Jeep Compass

Specifications

Drive. . . . . FWD
Engine 2.4-liter I4
Transmission . . . . .6-sp. Automatic
Tow Rating (lbs.) . . . . Very Low-2000
Head/Leg Room (in.) Average-40.7/40.6
Interior Space (cu. ft.). Average-101.3
Cargo Space (cu. ft.) Average-22.7
Wheelbase/Length (in.) 103.7/175.1

Ratings—10 Best, 1 Worst

Combo Crash Tests	6
Safety Features	7
Rollover	2
Preventive Maintenance	8
Repair Costs	6
Warranty	8
Fuel Economy	3
Complaints	5
Insurance Costs	8
OVERALL RATING	**7**

Jeep Grand Cherokee

At-a-Glance

Status/Year Series Started Appearance Change/2011
Twins . . . . –
Body Styles . . . . SUV
Seating 5
Anti-Theft Device . . . . . . Std. Pass. Immobil. & Alarm
Parking Index Rating . . . . Average
Where Made. . . . . .Detroit, MI
Fuel Factor
  MPG Rating (city/hwy). Poor-17/25
  Driving Range (mi.) . . . . Very Long-489
  Fuel Type. . . . . .Regular
  Annual Fuel Cost . . . . High-$2,591
  Gas Guzzler Tax . . . . .No
  Greenhouse Gas Emissions (tons/yr.). High-9.7
  Barrels of Oil Used per year High-13.7

How the Competition Rates

Competitors	Rating	Pg.
Chevrolet Equinox	3	112
Ford Explorer	4	138
Toyota FJ Cruiser	–	248

Price Range	Retail	Markup
Laredo 4WD	$30,795	1%
Overland 4WD	$46,195	5%
Summit 4WD	$50,995	5%
SRT8 4WD	$63,195	5%

Jeep Grand Cherokee

Safety Checklist

Crash Tests:
  Frontal. . . . . Good
  Side. . . . . Poor
Airbags:
  Head . . . . Fr. & Rr. Roof Curtain
  Torso. . . . . .Front Pelvis/Torso from Seat
  Pelvis . . . . .Front Pelvis/Torso from Seat
  Roll Sensing . . . . .Yes
  Knee Bolster . . . . Standard
Crash Avoidance:
  Collision Avoidance. . . . . . Optional CIB & DBS
  Blind Spot Detection . . . . Optional
  Lane Keeping Assist. . . . . None
  Backup Camera . . . . Optional
  Pedestrian Crash Avoidance . . . . None
General:
  Auto. Crash Notification . . . . None
  Day Running Lamps . . . . Optional
Safety Belt/Restraint:
  Dynamic Head Restraints. . . . . .Standard Front
  Adjustable Belt . . . . .Standard Front

Jeep Grand Cherokee

Specifications

Drive. . . . . .RWD
Engine 3.6-liter V6
Transmission . . . . .8-sp. Automatic
Tow Rating (lbs.) Average-6200
Head/Leg Room (in.) Cramped-39.9/40.3
Interior Space (cu. ft.). Roomy-105.4
Cargo Space (cu. ft.) . . . . Very Roomy-36.3
Wheelbase/Length (in.) 114.8/189.8

Jeep Patriot

Ratings—10 Best, 1 Worst	
Combo Crash Tests	1
Safety Features	2
Rollover	2
Preventive Maintenance	9
Repair Costs	10
Warranty	8
Fuel Economy	5
Complaints	3
Insurance Costs	5
OVERALL RATING	**3**

Jeep Patriot

Jeep Patriot

At-a-Glance

Status/Year Series Started	Unchanged/2007
Twins	–
Body Styles	SUV
Seating	5
Anti-Theft Device	Std. Pass. Immobil.
Parking Index Rating	Easy
Where Made	Belvidere, IL
Fuel Factor	
MPG Rating (city/hwy)	Average-21/27
Driving Range (mi.)	Very Short-315
Fuel Type	Regular
Annual Fuel Cost	Average-$2,205
Gas Guzzler Tax	No
Greenhouse Gas Emissions (tons/yr.)	Average-8.0
Barrels of Oil Used per year	High-14.3

How the Competition Rates

Competitors	Rating	Pg.
Ford Escape	5	136
Mitsubishi Outlander Sport	6	215
Nissan Juke	4	219

Price Range	Retail	Markup
Sport 2WD	$15,995	1%
Sport 4WD	$18,295	1%
Latitude 4WD	$23,595	4%
Limited 4WD	$25,995	4%

Safety Checklist

Crash Tests:
Frontal	Very Poor
Side	Poor

Airbags:
Head	Fr. & Rr. Roof Curtain
Torso	Front Torso from Seat
Pelvis	None
Roll Sensing	Yes
Knee Bolster	None

Crash Avoidance:
Collision Avoidance	None
Blind Spot Detection	None
Lane Keeping Assist	None
Backup Camera	None
Pedestrian Crash Avoidance	None

General:
Auto. Crash Notification	None
Day Running Lamps	Optional

Safety Belt/Restraint:
Dynamic Head Restraints	Standard Front
Adjustable Belt	Standard Front

Jeep Patriot

Specifications

Drive	4WD
Engine	2.4-liter I4
Transmission	6-sp. Automatic
Tow Rating (lbs.)	Very Low-2000
Head/Leg Room (in.)	Average-41/40.6
Interior Space (cu. ft.)	Average-101.4
Cargo Space (cu. ft.)	Roomy-23
Wheelbase/Length (in.)	103.7/173.8

Ratings—10 Best, 1 Worst

Combo Crash Tests	–
Safety Features	1
Rollover	1
Preventive Maintenance	9
Repair Costs	10
Warranty	8
Fuel Economy	2
Complaints	1
Insurance Costs	5
OVERALL RATING	**–**

Jeep Wrangler

Jeep Wrangler Unlimited

At-a-Glance

Status/Year Series Started. Unchanged/2007
Twins . . . . –
Body Styles . . . . SUV
Seating 4
Anti-Theft Device . . . . Std. Pass. Immobil.
Parking Index Rating . . . . .Very Easy
Where Made. .Toledo, OH
Fuel Factor
  MPG Rating (city/hwy) . . . . .Very Poor-17/21
  Driving Range (mi.) . . . . .Very Short-346
  Fuel Type. . . . . .Regular
  Annual Fuel Cost . . . . Very High-$2,767
  Gas Guzzler Tax . . . . .No
  Greenhouse Gas Emissions (tons/yr.)Very High-10.2
  Barrels of Oil Used per year . . . . . . .Very High-18.3

How the Competition Rates

Competitors	Rating	Pg.
Nissan Xterra	–	229
Subaru Forester	4	238
Toyota FJ Cruiser	–	248

Price Range

Price Range	Retail	Markup
Sport	$22,395	3%
Sahara	$27,995	6%
Rubicon	$30,895	6%
Unlimited Rubicon	$34,495	6%

Safety Checklist

Crash Tests:
  Frontal. . . . .
  Side. . . . .
Airbags:
  Head . . . . None
  Torso. . . . . Front Head/Torso from Seat
  Pelvis . . . . None
  Roll Sensing . . . . No
  Knee Bolster . . . . None
Crash Avoidance:
  Collision Avoidance. . . . . None
  Blind Spot Detection . . . . None
  Lane Keeping Assist. . . . . None
  Backup Camera . . . . None
  Pedestrian Crash Avoidance . . . . None
General:
  Auto. Crash Notification . . . . None
  Day Running Lamps. . . . . Optional
Safety Belt/Restraint:
  Dynamic Head Restraints. . . . . None
  Adjustable Belt . . . . .Standard Front

Jeep Wrangler

Specifications

Drive. 4WD
Engine 3.6-liter V6
Transmission . . . . 5-sp. Auto w/Overdrive
Tow Rating (lbs.) . . . . Very Low-2000
Head/Leg Room (in.) Average-41.3/41
Interior Space (cu. ft.). . . . . .Very Cramped-88.4
Cargo Space (cu. ft.) Average-17.15
Wheelbase/Length (in.) 95.4/152.8

Ratings—10 Best, 1 Worst

Combo Crash Tests	–
Safety Features	3
Rollover	8
Preventive Maintenance	–
Repair Costs	–
Warranty	9
Fuel Economy	4
Complaints	–
Insurance Costs	5
OVERALL RATING	**–**

Kia Cadenza

Kia Cadenza

At-a-Glance

Status/Year Series Started	All New/2014
Twins	–
Body Styles	Sedan
Seating	5
Anti-Theft Device	Std. Pass. Immobil. & Alarm
Parking Index Rating	Average
Where Made	Hwasung, South Korea
Fuel Factor	
MPG Rating (city/hwy)	Poor-19/28
Driving Range (mi.)	Average-411
Fuel Type	Regular
Annual Fuel Cost	Average-$2,316
Gas Guzzler Tax	No
Greenhouse Gas Emissions (tons/yr.)	Average-8.3
Barrels of Oil Used per year	High-15.0

How the Competition Rates

Competitors	Rating	Pg.
Chrysler 300	4	123
Lexus ES	6	188
Lincoln MKS	3	194

Price Range

	Retail	Markup
Premium	$35,100	8%

Safety Checklist

Crash Tests:
- Frontal . . . .
- Side . . . .

Airbags:
- Head . . . . Fr. & Rr. Roof Curtain
- Torso . . . . Fr. & Rr. Torso from Seat
- Pelvis . . . . Front Pelvis/Torso from Seat
- Roll Sensing . . . . No
- Knee Bolster . . . . None

Crash Avoidance:
- Collision Avoidance . . . . None
- Blind Spot Detection . . . . Optional
- Lane Keeping Assist . . . . Warning Only Optional
- Backup Camera . . . . Standard
- Pedestrian Crash Avoidance . . . . None

General:
- Auto. Crash Notification . . . . . Dial Assist.-Free
- Day Running Lamps . . . . None

Safety Belt/Restraint:
- Dynamic Head Restraints . . . . None
- Adjustable Belt . . . . Standard Front

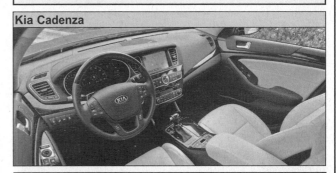
Kia Cadenza

Specifications

Drive	FWD
Engine	3.3-liter V6
Transmission	6-sp. Auto W/ Overdrive
Tow Rating (lbs.)	
Head/Leg Room (in.)	Very Roomy-40/45.5
Interior Space (cu. ft.)	Roomy-106.8
Cargo Space (cu. ft.)	Cramped-15.9
Wheelbase/Length (in.)	112/195.5

Kia Forte

Compact

Kia Forte

Ratings—10 Best, 1 Worst

Combo Crash Tests	1
Safety Features	1
Rollover	8
Preventive Maintenance	8
Repair Costs	10
Warranty	9
Fuel Economy	8
Complaints	–
Insurance Costs	1
OVERALL RATING	**5**

Kia Forte

Safety Checklist

Crash Tests:
Frontal . . . . Very Poor
Side . . . . Very Poor
Airbags:
Head . . . . Fr. & Rr. Roof Curtain
Torso . . . . Front Pelvis/Torso from Seat
Pelvis . . . . Front Pelvis/Torso from Seat
Roll Sensing . . . . No
Knee Bolster . . . . None
Crash Avoidance:
Collision Avoidance . . . . None
Blind Spot Detection . . . . None
Lane Keeping Assist . . . . None
Backup Camera . . . . Optional
Pedestrian Crash Avoidance . . . . None
General:
Auto. Crash Notification . . . . . Dial Assist.-Free
Day Running Lamps . . . . Optional
Safety Belt/Restraint:
Dynamic Head Restraints . . . . None
Adjustable Belt . . . . Standard Front

At-a-Glance

Status/Year Series Started . . . . All New/2014
Twins . . . . –
Body Styles . . . . Sedan, Coupe, Hatchback
Seating 5
Anti-Theft Device . Opt. Pass. Immobil. & Active Alarm
Parking Index Rating . . . . Very Easy
Where Made . . . . Hwasung, South Korea
Fuel Factor
  MPG Rating (city/hwy) Poor-24/36
  Driving Range (mi.) . . . . Very Long-522
  Fuel Type . . . . Regular
  Annual Fuel Cost . . . . Low-$1,822
  Gas Guzzler Tax . . . . No
  Greenhouse Gas Emissions (tons/yr.) Low-6.6
  Barrels of Oil Used per year Average-11.8

How the Competition Rates

Competitors	Rating	Pg.
Chevrolet Cruze	9	111
Honda Civic	6	148
Subaru Impreza	–	239

Price Range	Retail	Markup
LX AT	$17,400	4%
EX Coupe	$18,400	5%
EX	$19,400	5%
SX Coupe	$19,800	5%

Kia Forte

Specifications

Drive . . . . FWD
Engine 2.0-liter I-4
Transmission . . . . 6-sp. Automatic
Tow Rating (lbs.) . . . .
Head/Leg Room (in.) Average-39.1/42.2
Interior Space (cu. ft.) Average-98.2
Cargo Space (cu. ft.) Roomy-23.2
Wheelbase/Length (in.) 106.3/171.3

178

Kia Optima

Intermediate

Ratings—10 Best, 1 Worst	
Combo Crash Tests	5
Safety Features	2
Rollover	9
Preventive Maintenance	5
Repair Costs	6
Warranty	9
Fuel Economy	7
Complaints	4
Insurance Costs	1
OVERALL RATING	**5**

Kia Optima

Kia Optima

At-a-Glance

Status/Year Series Started Appearance Change/2011
Twins . . . . –
Body Styles . . . . Sedan
Seating 5
Anti-Theft Device . Std. Pass. Immobil. & Active Alarm
Parking Index Rating . . . . Easy
Where Made. . . . . West Point, GA
Fuel Factor
  MPG Rating (city/hwy) Good-24/34
  Driving Range (mi.) . . . . Very Long-512
  Fuel Type . . . . Regular
  Annual Fuel Cost . . . . Low-$1,860
  Gas Guzzler Tax . . . . No
  Greenhouse Gas Emissions (tons/yr.) Low-6.8
  Barrels of Oil Used per year Average-12.2

How the Competition Rates

Competitors	Rating	Pg.
Honda Accord	7	147
Nissan Altima	6	216
Toyota Camry	6	246

Price Range	Retail	Markup
LX	$21,500	5%
EX	$23,900	7%
SX	$25,250	7%
SXL Turbo	$36,300	7%

Safety Checklist

Crash Tests:
  Frontal. . . . . Good
  Side. . . . . .Very Poor
Airbags:
  Head . . . . Fr. & Rr. Roof Curtain
  Torso. . . . . .Front Pelvis/Torso from Seat
  Pelvis . . . . .Front Pelvis/Torso from Seat
  Roll Sensing . . . . No
  Knee Bolster . . . . None
Crash Avoidance:
  Collision Avoidance. . . . . None
  Blind Spot Detection . . . . Optional
  Lane Keeping Assist. . . . . None
  Backup Camera . . . . Optional
  Pedestrian Crash Avoidance . . . . None
General:
  Auto. Crash Notification . . . . . Dial Assist.-Free
  Day Running Lamps . . . . None
Safety Belt/Restraint:
  Dynamic Head Restraints . . . . None
  Adjustable Belt . . . . .Standard Front

Kia Optima

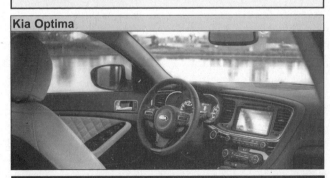

Specifications

Drive. . . . . FWD
Engine 2.4-liter I4
Transmission . . . . 6-sp. Auto w/Overdrive
Tow Rating (lbs.) . . . .
Head/Leg Room (in.) . . . . .Very Roomy-40/45.5
Interior Space (cu. ft.). Roomy-117.6
Cargo Space (cu. ft.) Cramped-15.4
Wheelbase/Length (in.) 110/190.7

Ratings—10 Best, 1 Worst

Combo Crash Tests	2
Safety Features	2
Rollover	7
Preventive Maintenance	6
Repair Costs	10
Warranty	9
Fuel Economy	9
Complaints	7
Insurance Costs	1
OVERALL RATING	**6**

Kia Rio

Kia Rio

Safety Checklist

Crash Tests:
Frontal . . . . Poor
Side . . . . Very Poor*
Airbags:
Head . . . . Fr. & Rr. Roof Curtain
Torso . . . . Front Pelvis/Torso from Seat
Pelvis . . . . Front Pelvis/Torso from Seat
Roll Sensing . . . . No
Knee Bolster . . . . None
Crash Avoidance:
Collision Avoidance. . . . . None
Blind Spot Detection . . . . Optional
Lane Keeping Assist. . . . . None
Backup Camera . . . . Optional
Pedestrian Crash Avoidance . . . . None
General:
Auto. Crash Notification . . . . . Dial Assist.-Free
Day Running Lamps . . . . None
Safety Belt/Restraint:
Dynamic Head Restraints. . . . . None
Adjustable Belt . . . . .Standard Front

At-a-Glance

Status/Year Series Started. Unchanged/2012
Twins . . . . Hyundai Accent
Body Styles . . . . Sedan, Hatchback
Seating 5
Anti-Theft Device .Opt. Pass. Immobil. & Active Alarm
Parking Index Rating . . . . .Very Easy
Where Made. . . . . Hwasung, South Korea
Fuel Factor
  MPG Rating (city/hwy) . . . . Very Good-27/37
  Driving Range (mi.) . . . . .Very Short-350
  Fuel Type. . . . . .Regular
  Annual Fuel Cost . . . . Very Low-$1,674
  Gas Guzzler Tax . . . . .No
  Greenhouse Gas Emissions (tons/yr.). Very Low-5.7
  Barrels of Oil Used per year Low-10.6

How the Competition Rates

Competitors	Rating	Pg.
Chevrolet Sonic	10	116
Hyundai Accent	6	155
Nissan Versa	2	228

Price Range

	Retail	Markup
LX Sedan	$14,700	4%
EX Sedan	$16,500	5%
EX Hatchback	$16,700	5%
SX Hatchback	$17,900	5%

Kia Rio

Specifications

Drive . . . . FWD
Engine 1.6-liter I4
Transmission . . . . .6-sp. Automatic
Tow Rating (lbs.) . . . .
Head/Leg Room (in.) Roomy-40/43.8
Interior Space (cu. ft.). . . . . . .Very Cramped-88.6
Cargo Space (cu. ft.) Cramped-13.7
Wheelbase/Length (in.) 101.2/171.9

*Additional injury potential in side test. See footnote on page 20.

Ratings—10 Best, 1 Worst	
Combo Crash Tests	8
Safety Features	4
Rollover	4
Preventive Maintenance	4
Repair Costs	7
Warranty	9
Fuel Economy	3
Complaints	1
Insurance Costs	3
OVERALL RATING	**5**

Kia Sorento

Kia Sorento

At-a-Glance

Status/Year Series Started Appearance Change/2011
Twins . . . . –
Body Styles . . . . SUV
Seating 5
Anti-Theft Device .Opt. Pass. Immobil. & Active Alarm
Parking Index Rating . . . . Easy
Where Made. . . . . West Point, GA
Fuel Factor
  MPG Rating (city/hwy) Poor-18/25
  Driving Range (mi.) . . . . .Very Short-359
  Fuel Type. . . . . .Regular
  Annual Fuel Cost . . . . High-$2,498
  Gas Guzzler Tax . . . . .No
  Greenhouse Gas Emissions (tons/yr.) High-8.8
  Barrels of Oil Used per year High-15.7

How the Competition Rates

Competitors	Rating	Pg.
Ford Edge	1	135
Nissan Rogue	–	225
Toyota Venza	4	258

Price Range	Retail	Markup
LX FWD	$24,100	4%
LX AWD V6	$27,500	4%
SX AWD	$36,800	6%
Limited AWD	$40,100	6%

Safety Checklist

Crash Tests:
  Frontal. . . . . Very Good
  Side. . . . . Average
Airbags:
  Head . . . . Fr. & Rr. Roof Curtain
  Torso. . . . . .Front Pelvis/Torso from Seat
  Pelvis . . . . .Front Pelvis/Torso from Seat
  Roll Sensing . . . . .Yes
  Knee Bolster . . . . None
Crash Avoidance:
  Collision Avoidance. . . . . None
  Blind Spot Detection . . . . Optional
  Lane Keeping Assist. . . . . None
  Backup Camera . . . . Optional
  Pedestrian Crash Avoidance . . . . None
General:
  Auto. Crash Notification . . . . . Dial Assist.-Free
  Day Running Lamps . . . . None
Safety Belt/Restraint:
  Dynamic Head Restraints . . . . . .Standard Front
  Adjustable Belt . . . . .Standard Front

Kia Sorento

Specifications

Drive. . . . . FWD
Engine 3.3-liter V6
Transmission . . . . .6-sp. Automatic
Tow Rating (lbs.) . . . . Very Low-3500
Head/Leg Room (in.) Cramped-39.2/41.3
Interior Space (cu. ft.). . . . . Very Roomy-142.2
Cargo Space (cu. ft.) . . . . .Very Cramped-9.1
Wheelbase/Length (in.) 106.3/184.4

Kia Soul

Ratings—10 Best, 1 Worst

Combo Crash Tests	9
Safety Features	4
Rollover	5
Preventive Maintenance	4
Repair Costs	8
Warranty	9
Fuel Economy	7
Complaints	–
Insurance Costs	1
OVERALL RATING	**7**

Kia Soul

Safety Checklist

Crash Tests:
- Frontal . . . . Good
- Side . . . . Very Good

Airbags:
- Head . . . . Fr. & Rr. Roof Curtain
- Torso . . . . Front Pelvis/Torso from Seat
- Pelvis . . . . Front Pelvis/Torso from Seat
- Roll Sensing . . . . .Yes
- Knee Bolster . . . . None

Crash Avoidance:
- Collision Avoidance . . . . None
- Blind Spot Detection . . . . None
- Lane Keeping Assist . . . . None
- Backup Camera . . . . Optional
- Pedestrian Crash Avoidance . . . . None

General:
- Auto. Crash Notification . . . . . Dial Assist.-Free
- Day Running Lamps . . . . None

Safety Belt/Restraint:
- Dynamic Head Restraints . . . . . .Standard Front
- Adjustable Belt . . . . .Standard Front

At-a-Glance

Status/Year Series Started . . . . All New/2014
Twins . . . . –
Body Styles . . . . Hatchback
Seating 5
Anti-Theft Device .Opt. Pass. Immobil. & Active Alarm
Parking Index Rating . . . . .Very Easy
Where Made . . . . Hwasung, South Korea
Fuel Factor
  MPG Rating (city/hwy) Good-24/30
  Driving Range (mi.) Short-375
  Fuel Type . . . . .Regular
  Annual Fuel Cost . . . . Low-$1,951
  Gas Guzzler Tax . . . . .No
  Greenhouse Gas Emissions (tons/yr.) Low-7.0
  Barrels of Oil Used per year Average-12.7

Kia Soul

How the Competition Rates

Competitors	Rating	Pg.
Mini Countryman	–	211
Scion xB	–	234
Toyota Yaris	6	259

Specifications

Drive . . . . FWD
Engine 1.6-liter I4
Transmission . . . . .6-sp. Automatic
Tow Rating (lbs.) . . . .
Head/Leg Room (in.) Cramped-39.6/40.9
Interior Space (cu. ft.) Average-101
Cargo Space (cu. ft.) Roomy-24.2
Wheelbase/Length (in.) 101.2/163

Price Range

	Retail	Markup
Base Manual	$14,700	2%
Base AT	$16,700	4%
+	$18,200	5%
!	$20,300	5%

Ratings—10 Best, 1 Worst

Combo Crash Tests	6
Safety Features	3
Rollover	3
Preventive Maintenance	4
Repair Costs	9
Warranty	9
Fuel Economy	5
Complaints	7
Insurance Costs	5
OVERALL RATING	**6**

Kia Sportage

Kia Sportage

At-a-Glance

Status/Year Series Started....... Unchanged/2011
Twins ....Hyundai Tucson
Body Styles .... SUV
Seating..................................... 5
Anti-Theft Device .Opt. Pass. Immobil. & Active Alarm
Parking Index Rating ....Very Easy
Where Made....................Zilina, Slovakia
Fuel Factor
  MPG Rating (city/hwy)........... Average-21/28
  Driving Range (mi.) Short-362
  Fuel Type.........................Regular
  Annual Fuel Cost .... Average-$2,174
  Gas Guzzler Tax ....No
  Greenhouse Gas Emissions (tons/yr.).. Average-7.7
  Barrels of Oil Used per year High-13.7

How the Competition Rates

Competitors	Rating	Pg.
Ford Escape	5	136
Honda CR-V	6	150
Jeep Compass	5	173

Price Range	Retail	Markup
Base FWD Manual	$19,000	2%
LX AWD	$22,700	5%
EX FWD	$24,200	6%
SW AWD	$28,400	7%

Safety Checklist

Crash Tests:
  Frontal............................. Good
  Side................................Poor
Airbags:
  Head .... Fr. & Rr. Roof Curtain
  Torso..........Front Pelvis/Torso from Seat
  Pelvis ....Front Pelvis/Torso from Seat
  Roll Sensing ....Yes
  Knee Bolster .... None
Crash Avoidance:
  Collision Avoidance.................. None
  Blind Spot Detection .... None
  Lane Keeping Assist................. None
  Backup Camera .... Optional
  Pedestrian Crash Avoidance .... None
General:
  Auto. Crash Notification ..... Dial Assist.-Free
  Day Running Lamps.............. Optional
Safety Belt/Restraint:
  Dynamic Head Restraints...... Optional Front
  Adjustable Belt ....Standard Front

Kia Sportage

Specifications

Drive................................... FWD
Engine 2.4-liter I4
Transmission ....6-sp. Automatic
Tow Rating (lbs.) .... Very Low-2000
Head/Leg Room (in.) ...Cramped-39.1/41.4
Interior Space (cu. ft.)............Average-100
Cargo Space (cu. ft.) Roomy-26.1
Wheelbase/Length (in.) 103.9/174.8

Ratings—10 Best, 1 Worst

Combo Crash Tests	–
Safety Features	5
Rollover	3
Preventive Maintenance	4
Repair Costs	1
Warranty	4
Fuel Economy	1
Complaints	7
Insurance Costs	8
OVERALL RATING	**–**

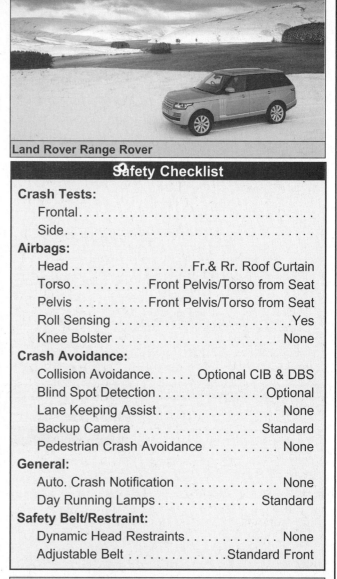

Land Rover Range Rover

Safety Checklist

Crash Tests:
Frontal..................................
Side....................................

Airbags:
Head ....Fr.& Rr. Roof Curtain
Torso...........Front Pelvis/Torso from Seat
Pelvis ....Front Pelvis/Torso from Seat
Roll Sensing ....Yes
Knee Bolster .... None

Crash Avoidance:
Collision Avoidance...... Optional CIB & DBS
Blind Spot Detection ....Optional
Lane Keeping Assist.............. None
Backup Camera .... Standard
Pedestrian Crash Avoidance .... None

General:
Auto. Crash Notification .... None
Day Running Lamps............. Standard

Safety Belt/Restraint:
Dynamic Head Restraints............ None
Adjustable Belt ....Standard Front

Land Rover Range Rover

At-a-Glance

Status/Year Series Started....... Unchanged/2013
Twins ....–
Body Styles .... SUV
Seating 5
Anti-Theft Device ...... Std. Pass. Immobil. & Alarm
Parking Index Rating ....Very Hard
Where Made................... Solihull, England
Fuel Factor
  MPG Rating (city/hwy) ....Very Poor-13/19
  Driving Range (mi.) Long-420
  Fuel Type.........................Premium
  Annual Fuel Cost ....Very High-$3,692
  Gas Guzzler Tax ....No
  Greenhouse Gas Emissions (tons/yr.)Very High-12.3
  Barrels of Oil Used per year ....Very High-22.0

How the Competition Rates

Competitors	Rating	Pg.
Audi Q7	–	91
Ford Explorer	4	138
Mercedes-Benz GL-Class	–	206

Price Range

	Retail	Markup
4D Utility	$83,545	10%
HSE	$88,545	10%
Supercharged	$99,995	10%
Autobiography	$135,995	10%

Land Rover Range Rover

Specifications

Drive.................................. 4WD
Engine 5.0-liter V8
Transmission ....8-sp. Automatic
Tow Rating (lbs.) High-7716
Head/Leg Room (in.) Average-42.5/39.1
Interior Space (cu. ft.)....................
Cargo Space (cu. ft.) Roomy-32.1
Wheelbase/Length (in.) 115/196.8

Ratings—10 Best, 1 Worst

Combo Crash Tests	–
Safety Features	7
Rollover	5
Preventive Maintenance	10
Repair Costs	6
Warranty	4
Fuel Economy	5
Complaints	4
Insurance Costs	5
OVERALL RATING	**–**

Land Rover Range Rover Evoque

Land Rover Range Rover Evoque

At-a-Glance

Status/Year Series Started	Unchanged/2013
Twins	–
Body Styles	SUV
Seating	5
Anti-Theft Device	Std. Pass. Immobil. & Alarm
Parking Index Rating	Easy
Where Made	Halewood, England
Fuel Factor	
MPG Rating (city/hwy)	Average-21/30
Driving Range (mi.)	Long-449
Fuel Type	Premium
Annual Fuel Cost	Average-$2,305
Gas Guzzler Tax	No
Greenhouse Gas Emissions (tons/yr.)	Average-7.6
Barrels of Oil Used per year	High-13.7

How the Competition Rates

Competitors	Rating	Pg.
Audi Q5	–	90
BMW X3	–	98
Volkswagen Tiguan	2	265

Price Range	Retail	Markup
Pure	$41,145	9%
Pure Premium	$47,145	9%
Dynamic Premium	$50,645	9%
Prestige Premium	$51,545	9%

Safety Checklist

Crash Tests:
Frontal . . . .
Side . . . .

Airbags:
Head . . . . Fr. & Rr. Roof Curtain
Torso . . . . Front Pelvis/Torso from Seat
Pelvis . . . . Front Pelvis/Torso from Seat
Roll Sensing . . . . Yes
Knee Bolster . . . . Standard

Crash Avoidance:
Collision Avoidance . . . . . . Optional CIB & DBS
Blind Spot Detection . . . . Optional
Lane Keeping Assist . . . . None
Backup Camera . . . . Standard
Pedestrian Crash Avoidance . . . . None

General:
Auto. Crash Notification . . . . None
Day Running Lamps . . . . Standard

Safety Belt/Restraint:
Dynamic Head Restraints . . . . None
Adjustable Belt . . . . Standard Front

Land Rover Range Rover Evoque

Specifications

Drive	AWD
Engine	2.0-liter I4
Transmission	9-sp. Automatic
Tow Rating (lbs.)	Very Low-3500
Head/Leg Room (in.)	Cramped-40.3/40.1
Interior Space (cu. ft.)	
Cargo Space (cu. ft.)	Average-20.3
Wheelbase/Length (in.)	104.8/171.5

Ratings—10 Best, 1 Worst

Combo Crash Tests	–
Safety Features	5
Rollover	4
Preventive Maintenance	4
Repair Costs	1
Warranty	4
Fuel Economy	1
Complaints	–
Insurance Costs	8
OVERALL RATING	**–**

Land Rover Range Rover Sport

Land Rover Range Rover Sport

At-a-Glance

Status/Year Series Started	All New/2014
Twins	–
Body Styles	SUV
Seating	5/7
Anti-Theft Device	Std. Pass. Immobil. & Alarm
Parking Index Rating	Very Hard
Where Made	Soliholl, England

Fuel Factor

MPG Rating (city/hwy)	Very Poor-14/19
Driving Range (mi.)	Long-440
Fuel Type	Premium
Annual Fuel Cost	Very High-$3,523
Gas Guzzler Tax	No
Greenhouse Gas Emissions (tons/yr.)	Very High-11.4
Barrels of Oil Used per year	Very High-20.6

How the Competition Rates

Competitors	Rating	Pg.
Chevrolet Tahoe	7	119
Mercedes-Benz GL-Class	–	206
Toyota Sequoia	–	254

Price Range

	Retail	Markup
SE	$63,495	10%
HSE	$68,495	10%
Supercharged	$79,995	10%
Autobiography	$93,295	10%

Safety Checklist

Crash Tests:
- Frontal . . . .
- Side . . . .

Airbags:
- Head . . . . Fr. & Rr. Roof Curtain
- Torso . . . . Front Pelvis/Torso from Seat
- Pelvis . . . . Front Pelvis/Torso from Seat
- Roll Sensing . . . . Yes
- Knee Bolster . . . . None

Crash Avoidance:
- Collision Avoidance . . . . . . Optional CIB & DBS
- Blind Spot Detection . . . . Optional
- Lane Keeping Assist . . . . None
- Backup Camera . . . . Standard
- Pedestrian Crash Avoidance . . . . None

General:
- Auto. Crash Notification . . . . None
- Day Running Lamps . . . . Standard

Safety Belt/Restraint:
- Dynamic Head Restraints . . . . None
- Adjustable Belt . . . . Standard Front

Land Rover Range Rover Sport

Specifications

Drive	4WD
Engine	5.0-liter V8
Transmission	8-sp. Automatic
Tow Rating (lbs.)	High-7716
Head/Leg Room (in.)	Average-39.4/42.2
Interior Space (cu. ft.)	
Cargo Space (cu. ft.)	Roomy-27.7
Wheelbase/Length (in.)	115.1/191

Ratings—10 Best, 1 Worst

Combo Crash Tests	–
Safety Features	4
Rollover	7
Preventive Maintenance	9
Repair Costs	3
Warranty	6
Fuel Economy	10
Complaints	3
Insurance Costs	3
OVERALL RATING	**–**

Lexus CT

Lexus CT

At-a-Glance

Status/Year Series Started Appearance Change/2011
Twins . . . . –
Body Styles . . . . Hatchback
Seating 5
Anti-Theft Device . . . . . . Std. Pass. Immobil. & Alarm
Parking Index Rating . . . . .Very Easy
Where Made. . . . . Kyushu, Japan
Fuel Factor
  MPG Rating (city/hwy) . . . . Very Good-43/40
  Driving Range (mi.) . . . . Very Long-495
  Fuel Type . . . . .Regular
  Annual Fuel Cost . . . . Very Low-$1,237
  Gas Guzzler Tax . . . . .No
  Greenhouse Gas Emissions (tons/yr.). Very Low-4.4
  Barrels of Oil Used per year . . . . Very Low-7.8

How the Competition Rates

Competitors	Rating	Pg.
Audi A4	6	87
Mercedes-Benz C-Class	4	203
Volkswagen Golf	–	262

Price Range

Price Range	Retail	Markup
Sedan	$32,050	5%
Premium Sedan	$33,175	5%

Safety Checklist

Crash Tests:
  Frontal. . . . .
  Side. . . . .
Airbags:
  Head . . . . Fr. & Rr. Roof Curtain
  Torso. . . . . .Front Pelvis/Torso from Seat
  Pelvis . . . . .Front Pelvis/Torso from Seat
  Roll Sensing . . . . No
  Knee Bolster . . . . Standard
Crash Avoidance:
  Collision Avoidance. . . . . . Optional CIB & DBS
  Blind Spot Detection . . . . None
  Lane Keeping Assist. . . . . None
  Backup Camera . . . . Optional
  Pedestrian Crash Avoidance . . . . None
General:
  Auto. Crash Notification . . Operator Assist.-Fee
  Day Running Lamps. . . . . Standard
Safety Belt/Restraint:
  Dynamic Head Restraints. . . . . None
  Adjustable Belt . . . . .Standard Front

Lexus CT

Specifications

Drive. . . . . FWD
Engine 1.8-liter I4
Transmission . . . . .eCVT
Tow Rating (lbs.) . . . .
Head/Leg Room (in.) Cramped-38.9/42.1
Interior Space (cu. ft.). . . . . .Very Cramped-86.1
Cargo Space (cu. ft.) Cramped-14.3
Wheelbase/Length (in.) 102.4/170.1

Lexus ES 350

Ratings—10 Best, 1 Worst

Combo Crash Tests	6
Safety Features	7
Rollover	7
Preventive Maintenance	4
Repair Costs	1
Warranty	6
Fuel Economy	5
Complaints	10
Insurance Costs	5
OVERALL RATING	**6**

Lexus ES 350

At-a-Glance

Status/Year Series Started........ Unchanged/2013
Twins .... –
Body Styles .... Sedan
Seating 5
Anti-Theft Device ...... Std. Pass. Immobil. & Alarm
Parking Index Rating .... Very Easy
Where Made.................... Kyushu, Japan
Fuel Factor
  MPG Rating (city/hwy) Average-21/31
  Driving Range (mi.) Long-423
  Fuel Type........................... Regular
  Annual Fuel Cost .... Average-$2,094
  Gas Guzzler Tax .... No
  Greenhouse Gas Emissions (tons/yr.).. Average-7.6
  Barrels of Oil Used per year High-13.7

How the Competition Rates

Competitors	Rating	Pg.
Acura TL	3	85
Hyundai Sonata	7	161
Volkswagen Passat	6	264

Price Range	Retail	Markup
350	$36,100	7%
300H	$38,850	7%

Safety Checklist

Crash Tests:
  Frontal............................. Good
  Side................................ Average
Airbags:
  Head .... Fr. & Rr. Roof Curtain
  Torso........ Fr. & Rr. Pelvis/Torso from Seat
  Pelvis .... Fr. & Rr. Pelvis/Torso from Seat
  Roll Sensing .... -
  Knee Bolster .... Standard
Crash Avoidance:
  Collision Avoidance...... Optional CIB & DBS
  Blind Spot Detection .... Optional
  Lane Keeping Assist....Warning Only Optional
  Backup Camera .... Optional
  Pedestrian Crash Avoidance .... None
General:
  Auto. Crash Notification .. Operator Assist.-Fee
  Day Running Lamps............. Standard
Safety Belt/Restraint:
  Dynamic Head Restraints............ None
  Adjustable Belt ....Standard Front

Lexus ES 350

Specifications

Drive.................................... FWD
Engine 3.5-liter V6
Transmission .... 6-sp. Automatic
Tow Rating (lbs.) ....
Head/Leg Room (in.) .....Very Cramped-37.5/41.9
Interior Space (cu. ft.)............ Average-100.1
Cargo Space (cu. ft.) Cramped-15.2
Wheelbase/Length (in.) 111/192.7

Ratings—10 Best, 1 Worst

Combo Crash Tests	–
Safety Features	8
Rollover	8
Preventive Maintenance	7
Repair Costs	1
Warranty	6
Fuel Economy	4
Complaints	4
Insurance Costs	3
OVERALL RATING	**–**

Lexus GS 350

Lexus GS 45h

At-a-Glance

Status/Year Series Started	Unchanged/2012
Twins	–
Body Styles	Sedan
Seating	5
Anti-Theft Device	Std. Pass. Immobil. & Alarm
Parking Index Rating	Very Easy
Where Made	Tahara, Japan
Fuel Factor	
MPG Rating (city/hwy)	Poor-19/29
Driving Range (mi.)	Short-391
Fuel Type	Premium
Annual Fuel Cost	High-$2,488
Gas Guzzler Tax	No
Greenhouse Gas Emissions (tons/yr.)	Average-8.0
Barrels of Oil Used per year	High-14.3

How the Competition Rates

Competitors	Rating	Pg.
BMW 5 Series	9	94
Hyundai Genesis	–	158
Mercedes-Benz E-Class	4	205

Price Range	Retail	Markup
350	$47,700	8%
350 AWD	$49,950	8%
450H	$59,600	8%

Safety Checklist

Crash Tests:
Frontal . . . .
Side . . . .

Airbags:
Head . . . . Fr. & Rr. Roof Curtain
Torso . . . . Fr. & Rr. Pelvis/Torso from Seat
Pelvis . . . . Fr. & Rr. Pelvis/Torso from Seat
Roll Sensing . . . . No
Knee Bolster . . . . Standard

Crash Avoidance:
Collision Avoidance . . . . . . Optional CIB & DBS
Blind Spot Detection . . . . Optional
Lane Keeping Assist . . . . Optional
Backup Camera . . . . Standard
Pedestrian Crash Avoidance . . . . None

General:
Auto. Crash Notification . . Operator Assist.-Fee
Day Running Lamps . . . . Standard

Safety Belt/Restraint:
Dynamic Head Restraints . . . . None
Adjustable Belt . . . . Standard Front

Lexus GS 450h

Specifications

Drive	RWD
Engine	3.5-liter V6
Transmission	8-sp. Automatic
Tow Rating (lbs.)	
Head/Leg Room (in.)	Cramped-38/42.3
Interior Space (cu. ft.)	Average-99
Cargo Space (cu. ft.)	Cramped-14.3
Wheelbase/Length (in.)	112.2/190.7

Ratings—10 Best, 1 Worst

Combo Crash Tests	–
Safety Features	9
Rollover	1
Preventive Maintenance	7
Repair Costs	2
Warranty	6
Fuel Economy	1
Complaints	8
Insurance Costs	8
OVERALL RATING	**–**

Lexus GX 460

Lexus GX 460

At-a-Glance

Status/Year Series Started Appearance Change/2003
Twins . . . . Toyota 4Runner
Body Styles . . . . SUV
Seating 7
Anti-Theft Device . . . . . . Std. Pass. Immobil. & Alarm
Parking Index Rating . . . . Very Hard
Where Made . . . . Tahara, Japan
Fuel Factor
  MPG Rating (city/hwy) . . . . Very Poor-15/20
  Driving Range (mi.) Short-389
  Fuel Type . . . . Premium
  Annual Fuel Cost . . . . Very High-$3,310
  Gas Guzzler Tax . . . . No
  Greenhouse Gas Emissions (tons/yr.)Very High-10.8
  Barrels of Oil Used per year . . . . Very High-19.4

How the Competition Rates

Competitors	Rating	Pg.
Chevrolet Suburban	6	118
Ford Expedition	2	137
Toyota Sequoia	–	254

Price Range	Retail	Markup
4WD	$49,085	8%
4WD Luxury	$60,715	9%
	–	

Safety Checklist

Crash Tests:
  Frontal . . . .
  Side . . . .
Airbags:
  Head . . . . Fr. & Rr. Roof Curtain
  Torso . . . . Fr. & Rr. Torso from Seat
  Pelvis . . . . .Front Pelvis/Torso from Seat
  Roll Sensing . . . . .Yes
  Knee Bolster . . . . Standard
Crash Avoidance:
  Collision Avoidance . . . . . . Optional CIB & DBS
  Blind Spot Detection . . . . Optional
  Lane Keeping Assist . . . .Warning Only Optional
  Backup Camera . . . . Standard
  Pedestrian Crash Avoidance . . . . None
General:
  Auto. Crash Notification . . Operator Assist.-Fee
  Day Running Lamps . . . . Standard
Safety Belt/Restraint:
  Dynamic Head Restraints . . . . . .Standard Front
  Adjustable Belt . . . . Standard Front & Rear

Lexus GX 460

Specifications

Drive 4WD
Engine 4.6-liter V8
Transmission . . . . .6-sp. Automatic
Tow Rating (lbs.) Average-6500
Head/Leg Room (in.) . . . . . . Very Cramped-38/41.7
Interior Space (cu. ft.) . . . . Very Roomy-129.7
Cargo Space (cu. ft.) . . . . . . Very Roomy-64.7
Wheelbase/Length (in.) 109.8/192.1

Ratings—10 Best, 1 Worst

Combo Crash Tests	6
Safety Features	8
Rollover	9
Preventive Maintenance	7
Repair Costs	1
Warranty	6
Fuel Economy	5
Complaints	–
Insurance Costs	5
OVERALL RATING	**7**

Lexus IS 250

Lexus IS 350

Safety Checklist

Crash Tests:
Frontal . . . . Poor
Side . . . . Very Good

Airbags:
Head . . . . Fr. & Rr. Roof Curtain
Torso . . . . Fr. & Rr. Pelvis/Torso from Seat
Pelvis . . . . Fr. & Rr. Pelvis/Torso from Seat
Roll Sensing . . . . No
Knee Bolster . . . . Standard

Crash Avoidance:
Collision Avoidance . . . . . . Optional CIB & DBS
Blind Spot Detection . . . . Optional
Lane Keeping Assist . . . Warning Only Optional
Backup Camera . . . . Standard
Pedestrian Crash Avoidance . . . . None

General:
Auto. Crash Notification . . Operator Assist.-Fee
Day Running Lamps . . . . Standard

Safety Belt/Restraint:
Dynamic Head Restraints . . . . None
Adjustable Belt . . . . Standard Front

At-a-Glance

Status/Year Series Started . . . . All New/2014
Twins . . . . –
Body Styles . . . . Sedan
Seating 5
Anti-Theft Device . . . . . . Std. Pass. Immobil. & Alarm
Parking Index Rating . . . . Easy
Where Made . . . . Tahara, Japan
Fuel Factor
  MPG Rating (city/hwy) Average-21/30
  Driving Range (mi.) Long-422
  Fuel Type . . . . Premium
  Annual Fuel Cost . . . . Average-$2,305
  Gas Guzzler Tax . . . . No
  Greenhouse Gas Emissions (tons/yr.) . . Average-8.3
  Barrels of Oil Used per year High-15.0

How the Competition Rates

Competitors	Rating	Pg.
Acura TSX	–	86
BMW 3 Series	10	92
Infiniti Q50	6	164

Price Range

Price Range	Retail	Markup
250	$35,950	8%
250 AWD	$38,485	8%
350	$39,465	8%
350 AWD	$41,700	8%

Lexus IS 350

Specifications

Drive . . . . RWD
Engine 2.5-liter V6
Transmission . . . . 6-sp. Automatic
Tow Rating (lbs.) . . . .
Head/Leg Room (in.) Roomy-38.2/44.8
Interior Space (cu. ft.) . . . . Very Cramped-90.2
Cargo Space (cu. ft.) Cramped-13.8
Wheelbase/Length (in.) 110.2/183.7

Ratings—10 Best, 1 Worst

Combo Crash Tests	–
Safety Features	8
Rollover	9
Preventive Maintenance	5
Repair Costs	1
Warranty	6
Fuel Economy	2
Complaints	9
Insurance Costs	8
OVERALL RATING	–

Lexus LS 460

Lexus LS 600h

At-a-Glance

Status/Year Series Started........ Unchanged/2007
Twins ....–
Body Styles ....Sedan
Seating 5
Anti-Theft Device ......Std. Pass. Immobil. & Alarm
Parking Index Rating .... Average
Where Made.................. Tahara, Japan
Fuel Factor
  MPG Rating (city/hwy)..........Very Poor-16/24
  Driving Range (mi.) Average-418
  Fuel Type.........................Premium
  Annual Fuel Cost ....Very High-$2,972
  Gas Guzzler Tax ....No
  Greenhouse Gas Emissions (tons/yr.).....High-9.6
  Barrels of Oil Used per year High-17.3

How the Competition Rates

Competitors	Rating	Pg.
BMW 7 Series	–	96
Jaguar XF	–	171
Mercedes-Benz S-Class	–	209

Price Range

Price Range	Retail	Markup
460 Base	$72,140	9%
460 L	$78,440	9%
460 L AWD	$81,925	9%
600H L	$120,060	9%

Safety Checklist

Crash Tests:
  Frontal. . . . .
  Side. . . . .
Airbags:
  Head . . . . Fr. & Rr. Roof Curtain
  Torso. . . . . Fr. & Rr. Torso from Seat
  Pelvis . . . . .Front Pelvis/Torso from Seat
  Roll Sensing . . . . No
  Knee Bolster . . . . Standard
Crash Avoidance:
  Collision Avoidance. . . . . . Optional CIB & DBS
  Blind Spot Detection . . . . Optional
  Lane Keeping Assist. . . . . None
  Backup Camera . . . . Standard
  Pedestrian Crash Avoidance . . . . Optional
General:
  Auto. Crash Notification . . Operator Assist.-Fee
  Day Running Lamps . . . . Standard
Safety Belt/Restraint:
  Dynamic Head Restraints . . . . . .Standard Front
  Adjustable Belt . . . . .Standard Front

Lexus LS 600h

Specifications

Drive. . . . . RWD
Engine 4.6-liter V8
Transmission . . . . .8-sp. Automatic
Tow Rating (lbs.) . . . .
Head/Leg Room (in.) Average-38/43.7
Interior Space (cu. ft.). Roomy-103
Cargo Space (cu. ft.) Average-18
Wheelbase/Length (in.) 116.9/200

Ratings—10 Best, 1 Worst

Combo Crash Tests	2
Safety Features	9
Rollover	4
Preventive Maintenance	7
Repair Costs	2
Warranty	6
Fuel Economy	3
Complaints	10
Insurance Costs	8
OVERALL RATING	**5**

Lexus RX 350

Lexus RX 350

At-a-Glance

Status/Year Series Started Unchanged/2010
Twins . . . . –
Body Styles . . . . SUV
Seating 5
Anti-Theft Device . . . . . . Std. Pass. Immobil. & Alarm
Parking Index Rating . . . . Hard
Where Made . . . . Cambridge, Ontario
Fuel Factor
  MPG Rating (city/hwy) Poor-18/25
  Driving Range (mi.) Average-395
  Fuel Type . . . . Regular
  Annual Fuel Cost . . . . High-$2,498
  Gas Guzzler Tax . . . . No
  Greenhouse Gas Emissions (tons/yr.) High-9.2
  Barrels of Oil Used per year High-16.5

How the Competition Rates

Competitors	Rating	Pg.
Audi Q5	–	90
Mercedes-Benz GLK-Class	–	207
Volvo XC90	–	270

Price Range	Retail	Markup
350 Base FWD	$39,760	7%
350 Base AWD	$41,160	7%
350 F-Sport	$47,450	7%
450H AWD	$47,810	6%

Safety Checklist

Crash Tests:
  Frontal . . . . Poor
  Side . . . . Very Poor
Airbags:
  Head . . . . Fr. & Rr. Roof Curtain
  Torso . . . . Fr. & Rr. Torso from Seat
  Pelvis . . . . Front Pelvis/Torso from Seat
  Roll Sensing . . . . Yes
  Knee Bolster . . . . Standard
Crash Avoidance:
  Collision Avoidance . . . . . . Optional CIB & DBS
  Blind Spot Detection . . . . Optional
  Lane Keeping Assist . . . . None
  Backup Camera . . . . Optional
  Pedestrian Crash Avoidance . . . . None
General:
  Auto. Crash Notification . . Operator Assist.-Fee
  Day Running Lamps . . . . Standard
Safety Belt/Restraint:
  Dynamic Head Restraints . . . . . . Standard Front
  Adjustable Belt . . . . Standard Front

Lexus RX 350

Specifications

Drive . . . . FWD
Engine 3.5-liter V6
Transmission . . . . .6-sp. Automatic
Tow Rating (lbs.) . . . . Very Low-3500
Head/Leg Room (in.) Average-39.1/43.1
Interior Space (cu. ft.) . . . . Very Roomy-139.7
Cargo Space (cu. ft.) . . . . .Very Roomy-40
Wheelbase/Length (in.) 107.9/187.8

Ratings—10 Best, 1 Worst

Combo Crash Tests	7
Safety Features	4
Rollover	7
Preventive Maintenance	6
Repair Costs	2
Warranty	3
Fuel Economy	4
Complaints	3
Insurance Costs	3
OVERALL RATING	**3**

Lincoln MKS

Lincoln MKS

At-a-Glance

Status/Year Series Started Unchanged/2009
Twins . . . . —
Body Styles . . . . Sedan
Seating 5
Anti-Theft Device . . . . . . Std. Pass. Immobil. & Alarm
Parking Index Rating . . . . .Very Hard
Where Made. .Chicago, IL
Fuel Factor
  MPG Rating (city/hwy) Poor-19/28
  Driving Range (mi.) Long-422
  Fuel Type. . . . . .Regular
  Annual Fuel Cost . . . . Average-$2,316
  Gas Guzzler Tax . . . . .No
  Greenhouse Gas Emissions (tons/yr.) . . Average-8.3
  Barrels of Oil Used per year High-15.0

How the Competition Rates

Competitors	Rating	Pg.
Chrysler 300	4	123
Infiniti Q50	6	164
Lexus ES	6	188

Price Range	Retail	Markup
FWD	$40,425	5%
AWD	$42,420	5%
Ecoboost AWD	$47,415	5%

Safety Checklist

Crash Tests:
  Frontal. . . . . Very Good
  Side. . . . . Poor
Airbags:
  Head . . . . Fr. & Rr. Roof Curtain
  Torso. . . . . Front Tosro from Seat
  Pelvis . . . . None
  Roll Sensing . . . . .Yes
  Knee Bolster . . . . None
Crash Avoidance:
  Collision Avoidance. . . . . .Warning Only Optional
  Blind Spot Detection . . . . Optional
  Lane Keeping Assist. . . . . Optional
  Backup Camera . . . . Optional
  Pedestrian Crash Avoidance . . . . None
General:
  Auto. Crash Notification . . . . . Dial Assist.-Free
  Day Running Lamps . . . . None
Safety Belt/Restraint:
  Dynamic Head Restraints . . . . None
  Adjustable Belt . . . . .Standard Front

Lincoln MKS

Specifications

Drive. . . . . FWD
Engine 3.7-liter V6
Transmission . . . . .6-sp. Automatic
Tow Rating (lbs.) . . . .
Head/Leg Room (in.) Average-39.7/41.9
Interior Space (cu. ft.). Roomy-105.8
Cargo Space (cu. ft.) Average-19.2
Wheelbase/Length (in.) 112.9/205.6

Lincoln MKZ — Intermediate

Lincoln MKZ

Ratings—10 Best, 1 Worst

Combo Crash Tests	5
Safety Features	4
Rollover	8
Preventive Maintenance	5
Repair Costs	3
Warranty	3
Fuel Economy	4
Complaints	8
Insurance Costs	5
OVERALL RATING	**4**

Lincoln MKZ

At-a-Glance

Status/Year Series Started Unchanged/2013
Twins . . . . Ford Fusion
Body Styles . . . . .Sedan
Seating 5
Anti-Theft Device . . . . . .Std. Pass. Immobil. & Alarm
Parking Index Rating . . . . Hard
Where Made. . . . . .Hermosillo, Mexico
Fuel Factor
  MPG Rating (city/hwy) Poor-19/28
  Driving Range (mi.) Short-389
  Fuel Type . . . . .Regular
  Annual Fuel Cost . . . . Average-$2,316
  Gas Guzzler Tax .No
  Greenhouse Gas Emissions (tons/yr.) . . Average-8.3
  Barrels of Oil Used per year High-15.0

How the Competition Rates

Competitors	Rating	Pg.
Buick LaCrosse	7	102
Cadillac CTS	–	106
Lexus ES	6	188

Price Range

	Retail	Markup
Hybrid	$35,925	5%
Base	$35,925	5%
Base AWD	$37,815	5%

Safety Checklist

Crash Tests:
  Frontal. . . . . Good
  Side. . . . . .Very Poor
Airbags:
  Head . . . . Fr. & Rr. Roof Curtain
  Torso. . . . . .Front Pelvis/Torso from Seat
  Pelvis . . . . .Front Pelvis/Torso from Seat
  Roll Sensing . . . . No
  Knee Bolster . . . . Standard
Crash Avoidance:
  Collision Avoidance. . . . .Warning Only Optional
  Blind Spot Detection . . . . Optional
  Lane Keeping Assist . . . . Optional
  Backup Camera . . . . Optional
  Pedestrian Crash Avoidance . . . . None
General:
  Auto. Crash Notification . . . . . Dial Assist.-Free
  Day Running Lamps . . . . Optional
Safety Belt/Restraint:
  Dynamic Head Restraints . . . . None
  Adjustable Belt . . . . .Standard Front

Lincoln MKZ

Specifications

Drive. . . . . FWD
Engine 3.7-liter V6
Transmission . . . . .6-sp. Automatic
Tow Rating (lbs.) . . . . Very Low-2000
Head/Leg Room (in.) Average-37.9/44.3
Interior Space (cu. ft.). Cramped-96.5
Cargo Space (cu. ft.) Cramped-15.4
Wheelbase/Length (in.) 112.2/194.1

Mazda CX-5

Ratings—10 Best, 1 Worst

Combo Crash Tests	9
Safety Features	5
Rollover	3
Preventive Maintenance	6
Repair Costs	7
Warranty	2
Fuel Economy	8
Complaints	2
Insurance Costs	5
OVERALL RATING	**6**

Mazda CX-5

At-a-Glance

Status/Year Series Started	Unchanged/2013
Twins	Std. Pass. Immobil.
Body Styles	SUV
Seating	5
Anti-Theft Device	–
Parking Index Rating	Easy
Where Made	Hiroshima, Japan
Fuel Factor	
MPG Rating (city/hwy)	Good-26/35
Driving Range (mi.)	Very Long-450
Fuel Type	Regular
Annual Fuel Cost	Very Low-$1,750
Gas Guzzler Tax	No
Greenhouse Gas Emissions (tons/yr.)	Very Low-6.3
Barrels of Oil Used per year	Low-11.4

How the Competition Rates

Competitors	Rating	Pg.
Buick Encore	9	101
Ford Escape	5	136
Honda CR-V	6	150

Price Range	Retail	Markup
Sport FWD	$22,595	3%
Touring FWD	$24,615	3%
Touring AWD	$25,865	3%
Grand Touring AWD	$28,870	3%

Safety Checklist

Crash Tests:
Frontal	Very Good
Side	Good

Airbags:
Head	Fr. & Rr. Roof Curtain
Torso	Front Pelvis/Torso from Seat
Pelvis	Front Pelvis/Torso from Seat
Roll Sensing	Yes
Knee Bolster	None

Crash Avoidance:
Collision Avoidance	Optional CIB & DBS
Blind Spot Detection	Optional
Lane Keeping Assist	None
Backup Camera	Optional
Pedestrian Crash Avoidance	None

General:
Auto. Crash Notification	Dial Assist.-Free
Day Running Lamps	Standard

Safety Belt/Restraint:
Dynamic Head Restraints	None
Adjustable Belt	Standard Front

Mazda CX-5

Specifications

Drive	FWD
Engine	2.0-liter I4
Transmission	6-sp. Manual
Tow Rating (lbs.)	Very Low-2000
Head/Leg Room (in.)	Cramped-40.1/41
Interior Space (cu. ft.)	Roomy-103.8
Cargo Space (cu. ft.)	Very Roomy-34.1
Wheelbase/Length (in.)	106.3/178.7

Ratings—10 Best, 1 Worst

Combo Crash Tests	1
Safety Features	3
Rollover	5
Preventive Maintenance	6
Repair Costs	4
Warranty	2
Fuel Economy	2
Complaints	6
Insurance Costs	5
OVERALL RATING	**1**

Mazda CX-9

Mazda CX-9

At-a-Glance

Status/Year Series Started. Unchanged/2007
Twins . . . . –
Body Styles . . . . SUV
Seating 7
Anti-Theft Device . . . . . .Std. Pass. Immobil. & Alarm
Parking Index Rating . . . . .Very Easy
Where Made. . . . . .Hiroshima, Japan
Fuel Factor
  MPG Rating (city/hwy) . . . . . .Very Poor-16/22
  Driving Range (mi.) Short-367
  Fuel Type. . . . . .Regular
  Annual Fuel Cost . . . . Very High-$2,821
  Gas Guzzler Tax . . . . .No
  Greenhouse Gas Emissions (tons/yr.). . . . High-10.1
  Barrels of Oil Used per year . . . . . . .Very High-18.3

How the Competition Rates

Competitors	Rating	Pg.
Acura MDX	8	82
Chevrolet Equinox	3	112
Nissan Murano	3	222

Price Range	Retail	Markup
Sport FWD	$29,785	6%
Touring FWD	$32,230	6%
Touring AWD	$33,820	6%
Grand Touring AWD	$36,375	6%

Safety Checklist

Crash Tests:
  Frontal. . . . . .Very Poor
  Side. . . . . .Very Poor
Airbags:
  Head . . . . Fr. & Rr. Roof Curtain
  Torso. . . . . Front Tosro from Seat
  Pelvis . . . . None
  Roll Sensing . . . . .Yes
  Knee Bolster . . . . None
Crash Avoidance:
  Collision Avoidance. . . . . None
  Blind Spot Detection . . . . Optional
  Lane Keeping Assist. . . . . None
  Backup Camera . . . . Optional
  Pedestrian Crash Avoidance . . . . None
General:
  Auto. Crash Notification . . . . . Dial Assist.-Free
  Day Running Lamps . . . . Optional
Safety Belt/Restraint:
  Dynamic Head Restraints. . . . . None
  Adjustable Belt . . . . .Standard Front

Mazda CX-9

Specifications

Drive. . . . . AWD
Engine 3.7-liter V6
Transmission . . . . .6-sp. Automatic
Tow Rating (lbs.) . . . . Very Low-3500
Head/Leg Room (in.) Cramped-39.6/40.9
Interior Space (cu. ft.). . . . . Very Roomy-139.4
Cargo Space (cu. ft.) Average-17.2
Wheelbase/Length (in.) 113.2/200.6

Ratings—10 Best, 1 Worst

Combo Crash Tests	–
Safety Features	1
Rollover	6
Preventive Maintenance	5
Repair Costs	9
Warranty	2
Fuel Economy	9
Complaints	10
Insurance Costs	1
OVERALL RATING	**–**

Mazda2

Mazda2

At-a-Glance

Status/Year Series Started. Unchanged/2011
Twins . . . . –
Body Styles . . . . Hatchback
Seating 5
Anti-Theft Device . . . . . . Std. Pass. Immobil. & Alarm
Parking Index Rating . . . . .Very Easy
Where Made. . . . . .Hiroshima, Japan
Fuel Factor
  MPG Rating (city/hwy) . . . . Very Good-28/34
  Driving Range (mi.) . . . . .Very Short-344
  Fuel Type. . . . . .Regular
  Annual Fuel Cost . . . . Very Low-$1,692
  Gas Guzzler Tax . . . . .No
  Greenhouse Gas Emissions (tons/yr.). Very Low-6.1
  Barrels of Oil Used per year Low-11.0

How the Competition Rates

Competitors	Rating	Pg.
Chevrolet Sonic	10	116
Nissan Versa	2	228
Toyota Yaris	6	259

Price Range	Retail	Markup
Sport Manual	$14,720	1%
Sport AT	$15,560	1%
Touring Manual	$16,210	1%
Touring AT	$17,050	1%

Safety Checklist

Crash Tests:
  Frontal. . . . .
  Side. . . . .
Airbags:
  Head . . . . Fr. & Rr. Roof Curtain
  Torso. . . . . .Front Tosro from Seat
  Pelvis . . . . None
  Roll Sensing . . . . No
  Knee Bolster . . . . None
Crash Avoidance:
  Collision Avoidance. . . . . None
  Blind Spot Detection . . . . None
  Lane Keeping Assist. . . . . None
  Backup Camera . . . . None
  Pedestrian Crash Avoidance . . . . None
General:
  Auto. Crash Notification . . . . None
  Day Running Lamps. . . . . None
Safety Belt/Restraint:
  Dynamic Head Restraints. . . . . None
  Adjustable Belt . . . . .Standard Front

Mazda2

Specifications

Drive. . . . . FWD
Engine 1.5-liter I4
Transmission . . . . .4-sp. Automatic
Tow Rating (lbs.) . . . .
Head/Leg Room (in.) Average-39.1/42.6
Interior Space (cu. ft.). . . . . .Very Cramped-87.1
Cargo Space (cu. ft.) Cramped-13.3
Wheelbase/Length (in.) 98/155.5

Ratings—10 Best, 1 Worst

Combo Crash Tests	–
Safety Features	6
Rollover	8
Preventive Maintenance	5
Repair Costs	9
Warranty	2
Fuel Economy	10
Complaints	–
Insurance Costs	1
OVERALL RATING	**–**

Mazda3

Mazda3

At-a-Glance

Status/Year Series Started	All New/2014
Twins	–
Body Styles	Sedan, Hatchback
Seating	5
Anti-Theft Device	Std. Pass. Immobil.
Parking Index Rating	Very Easy
Where Made	Hiroshima, Japan
Fuel Factor	
MPG Rating (city/hwy)	Very Good-30/41
Driving Range (mi.)	Very Long-450
Fuel Type	Regular
Annual Fuel Cost	Very Low-$1,508
Gas Guzzler Tax	No
Greenhouse Gas Emissions (tons/yr.)	Very Low-5.4
Barrels of Oil Used per year	Low-9.7

How the Competition Rates

Competitors	Rating	Pg.
Mitsubishi Lancer	5	212
Scion tC	6	233
Subaru Impreza	–	239

Price Range

	Retail	Markup
i	$17,995	3%
i Sport	$19,495	5%
s Touring	$24,595	5%
s Grand Touring	$25,995	5%

Safety Checklist

Crash Tests:
- Frontal . . . .
- Side . . . .

Airbags:
- Head . . . . Fr. & Rr. Roof Curtain
- Torso . . . . Front Pelvis/Torso from Seat
- Pelvis . . . . Front Pelvis/Torso from Seat
- Roll Sensing . . . . Yes
- Knee Bolster . . . . None

Crash Avoidance:
- Collision Avoidance . . . . . . Optional CIB & DBS
- Blind Spot Detection . . . . Optional
- Lane Keeping Assist . . . . Warning Only Optional
- Backup Camera . . . . Optional
- Pedestrian Crash Avoidance . . . . None

General:
- Auto. Crash Notification . . . . . Dial Assist.-Free
- Day Running Lamps . . . . Standard

Safety Belt/Restraint:
- Dynamic Head Restraints . . . . None
- Adjustable Belt . . . . Standard Front

Mazda3

Specifications

Drive	FWD
Engine	2.0-liter I4
Transmission	6-sp. Automatic
Tow Rating (lbs.)	
Head/Leg Room (in.)	Very Cramped-38.6/37.3
Interior Space (cu. ft.)	Cramped-96.3
Cargo Space (cu. ft.)	Very Cramped-12.4
Wheelbase/Length (in.)	106.3/180.3

Ratings—10 Best, 1 Worst

Combo Crash Tests	–
Safety Features	1
Rollover	3
Preventive Maintenance	4
Repair Costs	8
Warranty	2
Fuel Economy	5
Complaints	4
Insurance Costs	5
OVERALL RATING	**–**

Mazda5

Mazda5

At-a-Glance

Status/Year Series Started Unchanged/2006
Twins . . . . –
Body Styles . . . . Minivan
Seating 6
Anti-Theft Device . . . . . . Std. Pass. Immobil. & Alarm
Parking Index Rating . . . . Easy
Where Made . . . . Hiroshima, Japan
Fuel Factor
  MPG Rating (city/hwy) Average-22/28
  Driving Range (mi.) Short-387
  Fuel Type . . . . Regular
  Annual Fuel Cost . . . . Average-$2,113
  Gas Guzzler Tax . . . . No
  Greenhouse Gas Emissions (tons/yr.) . . Average-7.6
  Barrels of Oil Used per year High-13.7

How the Competition Rates

Competitors	Rating	Pg.
Honda Odyssey	–	152
Subaru Forester	4	238
Toyota Prius	5	250

Price Range

Price Range	Retail	Markup
Sport Manual	$19,940	5%
Sport AT	$20,940	5%
Touring	$22,070	5%
Grand Touring	$24,470	5%

Safety Checklist

Crash Tests:
  Frontal . . . .
  Side . . . .
Airbags:
  Head . . . . Fr. & Rr. Roof Curtain
  Torso . . . . Front Pelvis/Torso from Seat
  Pelvis . . . . Front Pelvis/Torso from Seat
  Roll Sensing . . . . No
  Knee Bolster . . . . None
Crash Avoidance:
  Collision Avoidance . . . . None
  Blind Spot Detection . . . . None
  Lane Keeping Assist . . . . None
  Backup Camera . . . . None
  Pedestrian Crash Avoidance . . . . None
General:
  Auto. Crash Notification . . . . None
  Day Running Lamps . . . . None
Safety Belt/Restraint:
  Dynamic Head Restraints . . . . None
  Adjustable Belt . . . . Standard Front

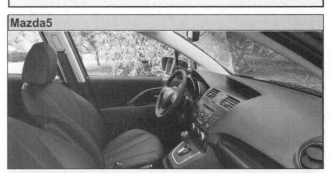
Mazda5

Specifications

Drive . . . . FWD
Engine 2.5-liter I4
Transmission . . . . 5-sp. Auto w/Overdrive
Tow Rating (lbs.) . . . .
Head/Leg Room (in.) Average-40.7/40.7
Interior Space (cu. ft.) Average-97.7
Cargo Space (cu. ft.) . . . . Very Roomy-44.4
Wheelbase/Length (in.) 108.3/180.5

Ratings—10 Best, 1 Worst	
Combo Crash Tests	–
Safety Features	4
Rollover	9
Preventive Maintenance	7
Repair Costs	10
Warranty	2
Fuel Economy	9
Complaints	–
Insurance Costs	3
OVERALL RATING	**–**

Mazda6

Mazda6

At-a-Glance

Status/Year Series Started	All New/2014
Twins	–
Body Styles	Sedan
Seating	5
Anti-Theft Device	Std. Pass. Immobil. & Alarm
Parking Index Rating	Average
Where Made	Flat Rock, MI
Fuel Factor	
MPG Rating (city/hwy)	Very Good-28/40
Driving Range (mi.)	Very Long-531
Fuel Type	Regular
Annual Fuel Cost	Very Low-$1,589
Gas Guzzler Tax	No
Greenhouse Gas Emissions (tons/yr.)	Very Low-6.1
Barrels of Oil Used per year	Low-11.0

How the Competition Rates

Competitors	Rating	Pg.
Dodge Avenger	3	125
Nissan Altima	6	216
Toyota Camry	6	246

Price Range	Retail	Markup
i Sport Manual	$20,880	5%
i Sport AT	$22,495	5%
i Touring	$24,495	6%
i Grand Touring	$29,495	6%

Safety Checklist

Crash Tests:
  Frontal . . . .
  Side . . . .
Airbags:
  Head . . . . Fr. & Rr. Roof Curtain
  Torso . . . . Front Pelvis/Torso from Seat
  Pelvis . . . . Front Pelvis/Torso from Seat
  Roll Sensing . . . . No
  Knee Bolster . . . . None
Crash Avoidance:
  Collision Avoidance . . . . . . Optional CIB & DBS
  Blind Spot Detection . . . . Optional
  Lane Keeping Assist . . . Warning Only Optional
  Backup Camera . . . . Optional
  Pedestrian Crash Avoidance . . . . None
General:
  Auto. Crash Notification . . . . . Dial Assist.-Free
  Day Running Lamps . . . . Standard
Safety Belt/Restraint:
  Dynamic Head Restraints . . . . None
  Adjustable Belt . . . . Standard Front

Mazda6

Specifications

Drive	FWD
Engine	2.5-liter I4
Transmission	6-sp. Automatic
Tow Rating (lbs.)	
Head/Leg Room (in.)	Cramped-38.4/42.2
Interior Space (cu. ft.)	Average-99.7
Cargo Space (cu. ft.)	Cramped-14.8
Wheelbase/Length (in.)	111.4/191.5

Ratings—10 Best, 1 Worst

Combo Crash Tests	–
Safety Features	1
Rollover	10
Preventive Maintenance	5
Repair Costs	7
Warranty	2
Fuel Economy	5
Complaints	10
Insurance Costs	8
OVERALL RATING	**–**

Mazda MX-5 Miata

At-a-Glance

Status/Year Series Started	Unchanged/2006
Twins	–
Body Styles	Coupe, Convertible
Seating	2
Anti-Theft Device	Std. Pass. Immobil. & Alarm
Parking Index Rating	Very Easy
Where Made	Hiroshima, Japan

Fuel Factor

MPG Rating (city/hwy)	Average-21/28
Driving Range (mi.)	Very Short-301
Fuel Type	Regular
Annual Fuel Cost	Average-$2,174
Gas Guzzler Tax	No
Greenhouse Gas Emissions (tons/yr.)	Average-8.0
Barrels of Oil Used per year	High-14.3

How the Competition Rates

Competitors	Rating	Pg.
Hyundai Veloster	–	163
Scion FR-S	–	232
Subaru BRZ	–	237

Price Range

	Retail	Markup
Sport Manual	$23,720	6%
Sport AT	$25,980	6%
Club	$27,305	6%
Grand Touring Hardtop	$30,350	6%

Mazda MX-5 Miata

Safety Checklist

Crash Tests:
Frontal	....
Side	....

Airbags:
Head	Front Head/Torso from Seat
Torso	Front Head/Torso from Seat
Pelvis	None
Roll Sensing	No
Knee Bolster	None

Crash Avoidance:
Collision Avoidance	None
Blind Spot Detection	None
Lane Keeping Assist	None
Backup Camera	None
Pedestrian Crash Avoidance	None

General:
Auto. Crash Notification	None
Day Running Lamps	None

Safety Belt/Restraint:
Dynamic Head Restraints	None
Adjustable Belt	None

Mazda MX-5 Miata

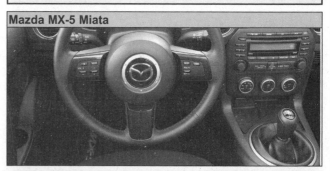

Specifications

Drive	RWD
Engine	2.0-liter I4
Transmission	6-sp. Automatic
Tow Rating (lbs.)	
Head/Leg Room (in.)	Cramped-37.4/43.1
Interior Space (cu. ft.)	
Cargo Space (cu. ft.)	Very Cramped-5.3
Wheelbase/Length (in.)	91.7/157.3

Mercedes-Benz C-Class Compact

Ratings—10 Best, 1 Worst

Combo Crash Tests	5
Safety Features	5
Rollover	8
Preventive Maintenance	1
Repair Costs	2
Warranty	2
Fuel Economy	5
Complaints	7
Insurance Costs	8
OVERALL RATING	**4**

Mercedes-Benz C250 Coupe

Mercedes-Benz C350 Sedan

At-a-Glance

Status/Year Series Started....... Unchanged/2008
Twins . . . .–
Body Styles . . . . Sedan, Coupe
Seating 5
Anti-Theft Device . . .Std. Act. Immobil. & Pass. Alarm
Parking Index Rating . . . . Easy
Where Made. . . . . Bremen, Germany
Fuel Factor
  MPG Rating (city/hwy) Average-20/29
  Driving Range (mi.) . . . . Very Long-453
  Fuel Type. . . . . Premium
  Annual Fuel Cost . . . . High-$2,407
  Gas Guzzler Tax . . . . .No
  Greenhouse Gas Emissions (tons/yr.). . Average-8.3
  Barrels of Oil Used per year High-15.0

How the Competition Rates

Competitors	Rating	Pg.
Audi A4	6	87
BMW 3 Series	10	92
Lexus IS	7	191

Price Range	Retail	Markup
C250 Sport	$35,800	8%
C300 Luxury 4Matic	$39,850	8%
C350 Coupe 4Matic	$45,850	8%
C63 AMG Coupe	$62,750	8%

Safety Checklist

Crash Tests:
  Frontal. . . . . .Poor
  Side. . . . . Good
Airbags:
  Head . . . . Fr. & Rr. Roof Curtain
  Torso. . . . . . .Std. Fr. & Opt. Rr. Torso from Seat
  Pelvis . . . . .Front Pelvis/Torso from Seat
  Roll Sensing . . . . No
  Knee Bolster . . . . Standard
Crash Avoidance:
  Collision Avoidance. . . . . . Optional CIB & DBS
  Blind Spot Detection . . . . Optional
  Lane Keeping Assist. . . . . Optional
  Backup Camera . . . . Optional
  Pedestrian Crash Avoidance . . . . None
General:
  Auto. Crash Notification . . Operator Assist.-Fee
  Day Running Lamps . . . . Standard
Safety Belt/Restraint:
  Dynamic Head Restraints. . . . . .Standard Front
  Adjustable Belt . . . . .Standard Front

Mercedes-Benz C350 Coupe

Specifications

Drive. . . . . AWD
Engine 3.5-liter V6
Transmission . . . . .7-sp. Automatic
Tow Rating (lbs.) . . . .
Head/Leg Room (in.) . . . . .Very Cramped-37.1/41.7
Interior Space (cu. ft.). . . . . .Very Cramped-88.2
Cargo Space (cu. ft.) . . . . .Very Cramped-12.4
Wheelbase/Length (in.) 108.7/180.8

Mercedes-Benz CLA-Class · Compact

Ratings—10 Best, 1 Worst

Combo Crash Tests	–
Safety Features	6
Rollover	8
Preventive Maintenance	1
Repair Costs	2
Warranty	2
Fuel Economy	8
Complaints	–
Insurance Costs	5
OVERALL RATING	**–**

Mercedes-Benz CLA250

At-a-Glance

```
Status/Year Series Started. . . . . . . . . . All New/2014
Twins . . . . . . . . . . . . . . . . . . . . . . . . . . . . . . . . –
Body Styles . . . . . . . . . . . . . . . . . . . . . . . . .Sedan
Seating . . . . . . . . . . . . . . . . . . . . . . . . . . . . . . . .5
Anti-Theft Device . . .Std. Act. Immobil. & Pass. Alarm
Parking Index Rating . . . . . . . . . . . . . . . . . . . .Easy
Where Made. . . . . . . . . . . . . Kecskemet, Hungary
Fuel Factor
  MPG Rating (city/hwy) . . . . . . . . . . . . . Good-26/38
  Driving Range (mi.) . . . . . . . . . . . . . . . Long-439
  Fuel Type. . . . . . . . . . . . . . . . . . . . .Premium
  Annual Fuel Cost . . . . . . . . . . . . . . . Low-$1,846
  Gas Guzzler Tax . . . . . . . . . . . . . . . . . . . . .No
  Greenhouse Gas Emissions (tons/yr.). Very Low-6.1
  Barrels of Oil Used per year . . . . . . . . . . . . Low-11
```

How the Competition Rates

Competitors	Rating	Pg.
Acura ILX	6	81
BMW 3 Series	10	92
Cadillac ATS	9	105

Price Range

	Retail	Markup
CLA250	$29,900	8%
CLA250 4Matic	$31,900	8%

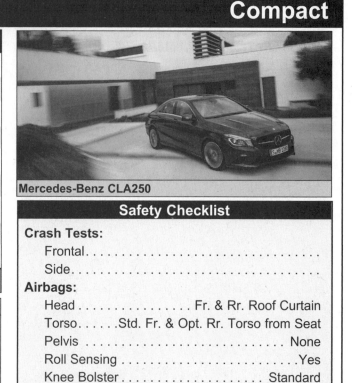

Mercedes-Benz CLA250

Safety Checklist

```
Crash Tests:
  Frontal. . . . . . . . . . . . . . . . . . . . . . . . . . . . . . .
  Side. . . . . . . . . . . . . . . . . . . . . . . . . . . . . . . . .
Airbags:
  Head . . . . . . . . . . . . . . . Fr. & Rr. Roof Curtain
  Torso. . . . . . .Std. Fr. & Opt. Rr. Torso from Seat
  Pelvis . . . . . . . . . . . . . . . . . . . . . . . . . . None
  Roll Sensing . . . . . . . . . . . . . . . . . . . . . . .Yes
  Knee Bolster . . . . . . . . . . . . . . . . . . . Standard
Crash Avoidance:
  Collision Avoidance. . . . . . Std. DBS & Opt. CIB
  Blind Spot Detection . . . . . . . . . . . . . . Optional
  Lane Keeping Assist . . . .Warning Only Optional
  Backup Camera . . . . . . . . . . . . . . . . . Optional
  Pedestrian Crash Avoidance . . . . . . . . . None
General:
  Auto. Crash Notification . . Operator Assist.-Fee
  Day Running Lamps . . . . . . . . . . . . . Standard
Safety Belt/Restraint:
  Dynamic Head Restraints. . . . . . . . . . . . None
  Adjustable Belt . . . . . . . . . . . . .Standard Front
```

Mercedes-Benz CLA250

Specifications

```
Drive. . . . . . . . . . . . . . . . . . . . . . . . . . . . . . . FWD
Engine . . . . . . . . . . . . . . . . . . . . . . . 2.0-liter I4
Transmission . . . . . . . . . . . . . . . .7-sp. Automatic
Tow Rating (lbs.) . . . . . . . . . . . . . . . . . . . . . . . .
Head/Leg Room (in.) . . . . . . . . . . . . . . . . . . . . .
Interior Space (cu. ft.). . . . . . . . . Very Cramped-88
Cargo Space (cu. ft.) . . . . . . . . . . . . . Cramped-13
Wheelbase/Length (in.) . . . . . . . . . . .106.3/182.3
```

Mercedes-Benz E-Class Intermediate

Ratings—10 Best, 1 Worst

Combo Crash Tests	3
Safety Features	9
Rollover	9
Preventive Maintenance	2
Repair Costs	2
Warranty	2
Fuel Economy	5
Complaints	10
Insurance Costs	3
OVERALL RATING	**4**

Mercedes-Benz E350 Coupe

Mercedes-Benz E350 Sedan

At-a-Glance

Status/Year Series Started Appearance Change/2010
Twins . . . . —
Body Styles . . . . Sedan, Coupe, Wagon, Convertible
Seating 5
Anti-Theft Device . . .Std. Act. Immobil. & Pass. Alarm
Parking Index Rating . . . . Average
Where Made. . . . . Bremen, Germany
Fuel Factor
  MPG Rating (city/hwy) Average-21/31
  Driving Range (mi.) . . . . Very Long-518
  Fuel Type. . . . . .Premium
  Annual Fuel Cost . . . . High-$2,364
  Gas Guzzler Tax . . . . .No
  Greenhouse Gas Emissions (tons/yr.). . Average-7.6
  Barrels of Oil Used per year High-13.7

How the Competition Rates

Competitors	Rating	Pg.
BMW 5 Series	9	94
Infiniti Q50	6	164
Lexus GS	–	189

Price Range	Retail	Markup
E250 Sport	$51,400	8%
E350 Luxury 4Matic	$54,400	8%
E550 Cabriolet	$67,300	8%
E63 AMG S	$102,370	8%

Safety Checklist

Crash Tests:
  Frontal. . . . . .Very Poor
  Side. . . . . Average
Airbags:
  Head . . . . Fr. & Rr. Roof Curtain
  Torso. . . . . . .Std. Fr. & Opt. Rr. Torso from Seat
  Pelvis . . . . .Front Pelvis/Torso from Seat
  Roll Sensing . . . . .Yes
  Knee Bolster . . . . Standard
Crash Avoidance:
  Collision Avoidance. . . . . . Std. DBS & Opt. CIB
  Blind Spot Detection . . . . Optional
  Lane Keeping Assist. . . . . Optional
  Backup Camera . . . . Optional
  Pedestrian Crash Avoidance . . . . Optional
General:
  Auto. Crash Notification . . Operator Assist.-Fee
  Day Running Lamps. . . . . Standard
Safety Belt/Restraint:
  Dynamic Head Restraints. . . . . .Standard Front
  Adjustable Belt . . . . Standard Front & Rear

Mercedes-Benz E350 Cabriolet

Specifications

Drive. . . . . RWD
Engine 3.5-liter V6
Transmission . . . . .7-sp. Automatic
Tow Rating (lbs.) . . . .
Head/Leg Room (in.) . . . . .Very Cramped-37.9/41.3
Interior Space (cu. ft.). . . . . .Very Roomy-125
Cargo Space (cu. ft.) Average-16.4
Wheelbase/Length (in.) 113.2/192.1

Ratings—10 Best, 1 Worst

Combo Crash Tests	–
Safety Features	8
Rollover	1
Preventive Maintenance	1
Repair Costs	2
Warranty	2
Fuel Economy	1
Complaints	7
Insurance Costs	8
OVERALL RATING	**–**

Mercedes-Benz GL450

At-a-Glance

Status/Year Series Started. Unchanged/2007
Twins . . . . –
Body Styles . . . . SUV
Seating 7
Anti-Theft Device . . .Std. Act. Immobil. & Pass. Alarm
Parking Index Rating . . . . .Very Hard
Where Made. . . . . Tuscaloosa, AL
Fuel Factor
  MPG Rating (city/hwy). . . . . . . .Very Poor-14/19
  Driving Range (mi.) Long-420
  Fuel Type. . . . . .Premium
  Annual Fuel Cost . . . . .Very High-$3,523
  Gas Guzzler Tax . . . . .No
  Greenhouse Gas Emissions (tons/yr.)Very High-11.4
  Barrels of Oil Used per year . . . . . . .Very High-20.6

How the Competition Rates

Competitors	Rating	Pg.
Audi Q7	–	91
Ford Expedition	2	137
Toyota Sequoia	–	254

Price Range	Retail	Markup
GL350 CDI	$63,000	8%
GL450	$64,550	8%
GL550	$88,600	8%
GL63 AMG	$118,160	8%

Mercedes-Benz GL350

Safety Checklist

Crash Tests:
  Frontal. . . . .
  Side. . . . .
Airbags:
  Head . . . . Fr. & Rr. Roof Curtain
  Torso. . . . . . .Std. Fr. & Opt. Rr. Torso from Seat
  Pelvis . . . . None
  Roll Sensing . . . . .Yes
  Knee Bolster . . . . Standard
Crash Avoidance:
  Collision Avoidance. . . . . . Std. DBS & Opt. CIB
  Blind Spot Detection . . . . Optional
  Lane Keeping Assist. . . . . Optional
  Backup Camera . . . . Optional
  Pedestrian Crash Avoidance . . . . None
General:
  Auto. Crash Notification . . Operator Assist.-Fee
  Day Running Lamps. . . . . Standard
Safety Belt/Restraint:
  Dynamic Head Restraints. . . . . .Standard Front
  Adjustable Belt . . . . .Standard Front

Mercedes-Benz GL550

Specifications

Drive. 4WD
Engine 4.7-liter V8
Transmission . . . . .7-sp. Automatic
Tow Rating (lbs.) . . . . Very Low-3500
Head/Leg Room (in.) Average-41.2/40.3
Interior Space (cu. ft.). . . . . Very Roomy-127.6
Cargo Space (cu. ft.) Cramped-16
Wheelbase/Length (in.) 121.1/201.6

Ratings—10 Best, 1 Worst

Combo Crash Tests	–
Safety Features	9
Rollover	2
Preventive Maintenance	1
Repair Costs	2
Warranty	2
Fuel Economy	3
Complaints	9
Insurance Costs	8
OVERALL RATING	**–**

Mercedes-Benz GLK250

Mercedes-Benz GLK350

Safety Checklist

Crash Tests:
Frontal . . . .
Side . . . .

Airbags:
Head . . . . Fr. & Rr. Roof Curtain
Torso . . . . Front Torso from Seat
Pelvis . . . . .Front Pelvis from Seat
Roll Sensing . . . . .Yes
Knee Bolster . . . . Standard

Crash Avoidance:
Collision Avoidance . . . . . . Optional CIB & DBS
Blind Spot Detection . . . . Optional
Lane Keeping Assist . . . . Optional
Backup Camera . . . . Optional
Pedestrian Crash Avoidance . . . . None

General:
Auto. Crash Notification . . Operator Assist.-Fee
Day Running Lamps . . . . Standard

Safety Belt/Restraint:
Dynamic Head Restraints . . . . . .Standard Front
Adjustable Belt . . . . .Standard Front

At-a-Glance

Status/Year Series Started Unchanged/2010
Twins . . . . –
Body Styles . . . . SUV
Seating 5
Anti-Theft Device . . .Std. Act. Immobil. & Pass. Alarm
Parking Index Rating . . . . Average
Where Made . . . . Bremen, Germany
Fuel Factor
  MPG Rating (city/hwy) Poor-19/24
  Driving Range (mi.) Average-409
  Fuel Type . . . . .Premium
  Annual Fuel Cost . . . . High-$2,669
  Gas Guzzler Tax . . . . .No
  Greenhouse Gas Emissions (tons/yr.) . . Average-7.7
  Barrels of Oil Used per year High-15.7

How the Competition Rates

Competitors	Rating	Pg.
Audi Q5	–	90
Cadillac SRX	8	107
Lexus RX	5	193

Price Range

Price Range	Retail	Markup
GLK350	$37,480	8%
GLK250 CDI 4Matic	$38,980	8%
GLK350 4Matic	$39,480	8%

Mercedes-Benz GLK350

Specifications

Drive . . . . AWD
Engine 3.5-liter V6
Transmission . . . . .7-sp. Automatic
Tow Rating (lbs.) . . . . Very Low-3500
Head/Leg Room (in.) Cramped-39/41.4
Interior Space (cu. ft.) . . . . .Very Cramped-79.6
Cargo Space (cu. ft.) Roomy-23.3
Wheelbase/Length (in.) 108.5/178.3

Ratings—10 Best, 1 Worst

Combo Crash Tests	10
Safety Features	6
Rollover	3
Preventive Maintenance	1
Repair Costs	1
Warranty	2
Fuel Economy	2
Complaints	9
Insurance Costs	8
OVERALL RATING	**5**

Mercedes-Benz ML350

At-a-Glance

Status/Year Series Started........ Unchanged/2012
Twins .... –
Body Styles .... SUV
Seating 5
Anti-Theft Device . . .Std. Act. Immobil. & Pass. Alarm
Parking Index Rating . . . . Hard
Where Made. . . . . Tuscaloosa, AL
Fuel Factor
  MPG Rating (city/hwy) . . . . .Very Poor-17/22
  Driving Range (mi.) . . . . Very Long-525
  Fuel Type. . . . . .Premium
  Annual Fuel Cost . . . . .Very High-$2,955
  Gas Guzzler Tax . . . . .No
  Greenhouse Gas Emissions (tons/yr.). High-9.6
  Barrels of Oil Used per year High-17.3

How the Competition Rates

Competitors	Rating	Pg.
BMW X5	–	99
Volkswagen Touareg	–	266
Volvo XC60	10	269

Price Range

Price Range	Retail	Markup
ML350	$47,790	8%
ML350 CDI 4Matic	$51,790	8%
ML550 4Matic	$59,450	8%
ML63 AMG 4Matic	$97,250	8%

Mercedes-Benz ML350

Safety Checklist

Crash Tests:
  Frontal. . . . . Very Good
  Side. . . . . Very Good
Airbags:
  Head . . . . Fr. & Rr. Roof Curtain
  Torso. . . . . . .Std. Fr. & Opt. Rr. Torso from Seat
  Pelvis . . . . .Front Pelvis/Torso from Seat
  Roll Sensing . . . . -
  Knee Bolster . . . . Standard
Crash Avoidance:
  Collision Avoidance. . . . . . Std. DBS & Opt. CIB
  Blind Spot Detection . . . . Optional
  Lane Keeping Assist. . . . . Optional
  Backup Camera . . . . Optional
  Pedestrian Crash Avoidance . . . . None
General:
  Auto. Crash Notification . . Operator Assist.-Fee
  Day Running Lamps. . . . . Standard
Safety Belt/Restraint:
  Dynamic Head Restraints. . . . . .Standard Front
  Adjustable Belt . . . . .Standard Front

Mercedes-Benz ML350

Specifications

Drive. 4WD
Engine 3.5-liter V6
Transmission . . . . .7-sp. Automatic
Tow Rating (lbs.) Average-7200
Head/Leg Room (in.) Cramped-40.4/40.3
Interior Space (cu. ft.). Roomy-123.2
Cargo Space (cu. ft.) . . . . Very Roomy-38.2
Wheelbase/Length (in.) 114.8/189.1

Ratings—10 Best, 1 Worst

Combo Crash Tests	–
Safety Features	9
Rollover	9
Preventive Maintenance	1
Repair Costs	1
Warranty	2
Fuel Economy	3
Complaints	–
Insurance Costs	3
OVERALL RATING	–

Mercedes-Benz S550

Mercedes-Benz S550

At-a-Glance

Status/Year Series Started	All New/2014
Twins	–
Body Styles	Sedan
Seating	5
Anti-Theft Device	Std. Act. Immobil. & Pass. Alarm
Parking Index Rating	Very Hard
Where Made	Sindelfingen, Germany
Fuel Factor	
MPG Rating (city/hwy)	Poor-17/26
Driving Range (mi.)	Long-425
Fuel Type	Premium
Annual Fuel Cost	Very High-$2,779
Gas Guzzler Tax	No
Greenhouse Gas Emissions (tons/yr.)	High-9.1
Barrels of Oil Used per year	High-16.5

How the Competition Rates

Competitors	Rating	Pg.
BMW 7 Series	–	96
Cadillac XTS	10	108
Jaguar XF	–	171

Price Range

	Retail	Markup
S350 CDI 4Matic	$93,000	8%
S550 4Matic	$98,000	8%
S600	$160,300	8%
S65 AMG	$212,000	8%

Safety Checklist

Crash Tests:
Frontal . . . .
Side . . . .
Airbags:
Head . . . . Fr. & Rr. Roof Curtain
Torso . . . . Fr. & Rr. Torso from Seat
Pelvis . . . . None
Roll Sensing . . . . Yes
Knee Bolster . . . . Standard
Crash Avoidance:
Collision Avoidance . . . . . . Std. DBS & Opt. CIB
Blind Spot Detection . . . . Optional
Lane Keeping Assist . . . . Optional
Backup Camera . . . . Optional
Pedestrian Crash Avoidance . . . . Optional
General:
Auto. Crash Notification . . Operator Assist.-Fee
Day Running Lamps . . . . Standard
Safety Belt/Restraint:
Dynamic Head Restraints . . . . None
Adjustable Belt . . . . Standard Front

Mercedes-Benz S550

Specifications

Drive	RWD
Engine	4.7-liter V8
Transmission	7-sp. Automatic
Tow Rating (lbs.)	
Head/Leg Room (in.)	Cramped-39.7/41.4
Interior Space (cu. ft.)	Roomy-112
Cargo Space (cu. ft.)	Average-16.3
Wheelbase/Length (in.)	124.6/206.5

Ratings—10 Best, 1 Worst

Combo Crash Tests	–
Safety Features	1
Rollover	8
Preventive Maintenance	8
Repair Costs	5
Warranty	8
Fuel Economy	9
Complaints	–
Insurance Costs	5
OVERALL RATING	**–**

Mini Cooper

Mini Cooper

At-a-Glance

Status/Year Series Started	All New/2014
Twins	–
Body Styles	Hatchback, Convertible
Seating	4
Anti-Theft Device	Std. Pass. Immobil.
Parking Index Rating	Very Easy
Where Made	Oxford, England
Fuel Factor	
MPG Rating (city/hwy)	Very Good-28/36
Driving Range (mi.)	Very Short-330
Fuel Type	Regular
Annual Fuel Cost	Very Low-$1,654
Gas Guzzler Tax	No
Greenhouse Gas Emissions (tons/yr.)	Very Low-6.1
Barrels of Oil Used per year	Low-11.0

How the Competition Rates

Competitors	Rating	Pg.
Kia Soul	7	182
Scion xB	–	234
Volkswagen Beetle	3	260

Price Range

Price Range	Retail	Markup
Base Hatchback	$19,700	11%
Base Roadster	$25,550	11%
S Roadster	$28,550	11%
John Cooper Convertible	$35,300	11%

Safety Checklist

Crash Tests:
Frontal . . . .
Side . . . .
Airbags:
Head . . . . Front Head/Torso from Seat
Torso . . . . Front Head/Torso from Seat
Pelvis . . . . None
Roll Sensing . . . . No
Knee Bolster . . . . None
Crash Avoidance:
Collision Avoidance . . . . None
Blind Spot Detection . . . . None
Lane Keeping Assist . . . . None
Backup Camera . . . . None
Pedestrian Crash Avoidance . . . . None
General:
Auto. Crash Notification . . . . None
Day Running Lamps . . . . Standard
Safety Belt/Restraint:
Dynamic Head Restraints . . . . None
Adjustable Belt . . . . None

Mini Cooper

Specifications

Drive	RWD
Engine	1.6-liter I4
Transmission	6-sp. Automatic
Tow Rating (lbs.)	. . . .
Head/Leg Room (in.)	Average-40.3/41.4
Interior Space (cu. ft.)	Very Cramped-78.7
Cargo Space (cu. ft.)	Very Cramped-8.7
Wheelbase/Length (in.)	98.2/151.1

Ratings—10 Best, 1 Worst	
Combo Crash Tests	–
Safety Features	1
Rollover	5
Preventive Maintenance	7
Repair Costs	6
Warranty	8
Fuel Economy	7
Complaints	6
Insurance Costs	3
OVERALL RATING	**–**

Mini Countryman

Mini Countryman

At-a-Glance

Status/Year Series Started Unchanged/2012
Twins . . . . –
Body Styles . . . . Hatchback
Seating 4
Anti-Theft Device . . . . Std. Pass. Immobil.
Parking Index Rating . . . . Easy
Where Made . . . . Graz, Austria
Fuel Factor
  MPG Rating (city/hwy) Good-25/30
  Driving Range (mi.) . . . . Very Short-335
  Fuel Type . . . . Premium
  Annual Fuel Cost . . . . Average-$2,070
  Gas Guzzler Tax . . . . No
  Greenhouse Gas Emissions (tons/yr.) Low-6.8
  Barrels of Oil Used per year Average-12.2

How the Competition Rates

Competitors	Rating	Pg.
Hyundai Veloster	–	163
Kia Soul	7	182
Nissan Juke	4	219

Price Range	Retail	Markup
Base	$22,000	11%
S	$25,600	11%
S ALL4	$27,300	11%
John Cooper ALL4	$34,850	11%

Safety Checklist

Crash Tests:
  Frontal . . . .
  Side . . . .
Airbags:
  Head . . . . Fr. & Rr. Roof Curtain
  Torso . . . . Front Tosro from Seat
  Pelvis . . . . None
  Roll Sensing . . . . No
  Knee Bolster . . . . Standard
Crash Avoidance:
  Collision Avoidance . . . . None
  Blind Spot Detection . . . . None
  Lane Keeping Assist . . . . None
  Backup Camera . . . . None
  Pedestrian Crash Avoidance . . . . None
General:
  Auto. Crash Notification . . . . None
  Day Running Lamps . . . . Standard
Safety Belt/Restraint:
  Dynamic Head Restraints . . . . None
  Adjustable Belt . . . . None

Mini Countryman

Specifications

Drive . . . . FWD
Engine 1.6-liter I4
Transmission . . . . 6-sp. Automatic
Tow Rating (lbs.) . . . .
Head/Leg Room (in.) Cramped-39.9/40.4
Interior Space (cu. ft.) . . . .
Cargo Space (cu. ft.) Average-16.5
Wheelbase/Length (in.) 102.2/161.7

Ratings—10 Best, 1 Worst

Combo Crash Tests	3
Safety Features	2
Rollover	6
Preventive Maintenance	9
Repair Costs	4
Warranty	10
Fuel Economy	8
Complaints	5
Insurance Costs	1
OVERALL RATING	**5**

Mitsubishi Lancer Evolution

Mitsubishi Lancer GT

At-a-Glance

Status/Year Series Started	Unchanged/2008
Twins	–
Body Styles	Sedan, Hatchback
Seating	5
Anti-Theft Device	Std. Pass. Immobil. & Alarm
Parking Index Rating	Very Easy
Where Made	Mizushima, Japan

Fuel Factor

MPG Rating (city/hwy)	Good-26/34
Driving Range (mi.)	Very Long-451
Fuel Type	Regular
Annual Fuel Cost	Low-$1,769
Gas Guzzler Tax	No
Greenhouse Gas Emissions (tons/yr.)	Very Low-6.3
Barrels of Oil Used per year	Low-11.4

How the Competition Rates

Competitors	Rating	Pg.
Honda Civic	6	148
Mazda Mazda3	–	199
Subaru Impreza	–	239

Price Range	Retail	Markup
ES	$18,095	4%
GT	$21,445	4%
Ralliart AWD	$28,395	4%
Evolution MR Touring AWD	$40,345	5%

Safety Checklist

Crash Tests:
Frontal	Poor
Side	Very Poor

Airbags:
Head	Fr. & Rr. Roof Curtain
Torso	Front Pelvis/Torso from Seat
Pelvis	Front Pelvis/Torso from Seat
Roll Sensing	No
Knee Bolster	Standard

Crash Avoidance:
Collision Avoidance	None
Blind Spot Detection	Optional
Lane Keeping Assist	None
Backup Camera	Optional
Pedestrian Crash Avoidance	None

General:
Auto. Crash Notification	None
Day Running Lamps	Optional

Safety Belt/Restraint:
Dynamic Head Restraints	None
Adjustable Belt	Standard Front

Mitsubishi Lancer Sportback

Specifications

Drive	FWD
Engine	2.0-liter I4
Transmission	SCVT
Tow Rating (lbs.)	
Head/Leg Room (in.)	Average-39.6/42.3
Interior Space (cu. ft.)	Cramped-93.5
Cargo Space (cu. ft.)	Very Cramped-12.3
Wheelbase/Length (in.)	103.7/180

Mitsubishi Mirage

Ratings—10 Best, 1 Worst	
Combo Crash Tests	–
Safety Features	2
Rollover	4
Preventive Maintenance	–
Repair Costs	–
Warranty	10
Fuel Economy	10
Complaints	–
Insurance Costs	5
OVERALL RATING	**–**

Mitsubishi Mirage ES

Mitsubishi Mirage ES

At-a-Glance

Status/Year Series Started	All New/2014
Twins	–
Body Styles	Hatchback
Seating	5
Anti-Theft Device	Std. Pass. Immobil. & Alarm
Parking Index Rating	Very Easy
Where Made	Laem Chabang, Thailand
Fuel Factor	
MPG Rating (city/hwy)	Very Good-34/42
Driving Range (mi.)	Very Short-342
Fuel Type	Regular
Annual Fuel Cost	Very Low-$1,384
Gas Guzzler Tax	No
Greenhouse Gas Emissions (tons/yr.)	Very Low-4.6
Barrels of Oil Used per year	Very Low-8.2

How the Competition Rates

Competitors	Rating	Pg.
Chevrolet Sonic	10	116
Fiat 500	4	132
Ford Fiesta	–	140

Price Range	Retail	Markup
DE Manual	$12,995	2%
DE AT	$13,995	2%
ES Manual	$14,195	2%
ES AT	$15,195	2%

Safety Checklist

Crash Tests:
Frontal . . . .
Side . . . .
Airbags:
Head . . . . Fr. & Rr. Roof Curtain
Torso . . . . Front Pelvis/Torso from Seat
Pelvis . . . . Front Pelvis/Torso from Seat
Roll Sensing . . . . No
Knee Bolster . . . . Standard
Crash Avoidance:
Collision Avoidance . . . . None
Blind Spot Detection . . . . None
Lane Keeping Assist . . . . None
Backup Camera . . . . Optional
Pedestrian Crash Avoidance . . . . None
General:
Auto. Crash Notification . . . . None
Day Running Lamps . . . . None
Safety Belt/Restraint:
Dynamic Head Restraints . . . . None
Adjustable Belt . . . . Standard Front

Mitsubishi Mirage ES

Specifications

Drive	FWD
Engine	1.2-liter I3
Transmission	5-sp. Manual
Tow Rating (lbs.)	
Head/Leg Room (in.)	Cramped-39.1/41.7
Interior Space (cu. ft.)	Very Cramped-86.1
Cargo Space (cu. ft.)	Average-17.2
Wheelbase/Length (in.)	96.5/148.8

Ratings—10 Best, 1 Worst

Combo Crash Tests	–
Safety Features	5
Rollover	3
Preventive Maintenance	4
Repair Costs	7
Warranty	10
Fuel Economy	6
Complaints	–
Insurance Costs	3
OVERALL RATING	**–**

Mitsubishi Outlander

Mitsubishi Outlander

At-a-Glance

Status/Year Series Started	All New/2014
Twins	–
Body Styles	SUV
Seating	7
Anti-Theft Device	Std. Pass. Immobil & Alarm
Parking Index Rating	Easy
Where Made	Okazaki, Japan / Mizushima, Japan

Fuel Factor

MPG Rating (city/hwy)	Average-24/29
Driving Range (mi.)	Long-432
Fuel Type	Regular
Annual Fuel Cost	Low-$1,977
Gas Guzzler Tax	No
Greenhouse Gas Emissions (tons/yr.)	Low-7.0
Barrels of Oil Used per year	Average-12.7

How the Competition Rates

Competitors	Rating	Pg.
Ford Explorer	4	138
Hyundai Santa Fe	–	159
Toyota Highlander	–	249

Price Range

	Retail	Markup
ES	$22,995	4%
SE 2WD	$23,795	4%
SE AWD	$25,795	4%
GT	$27,795	4%

Safety Checklist

Crash Tests:
Frontal . . . .
Side . . . .

Airbags:
Head . . . . Fr. & Rr. Roof Curtain
Torso . . . . Front Pelvis/Torso from Seat
Pelvis . . . . Front Pelvis/Torso from Seat
Roll Sensing . . . . Yes
Knee Bolster . . . . Standard

Crash Avoidance:
Collision Avoidance . . . . . . Optional CIB & DBS
Blind Spot Detection . . . . None
Lane Keeping Assist . . . . Warning Only Optional
Backup Camera . . . . Optional
Pedestrian Crash Avoidance . . . . None

General:
Auto. Crash Notification . . . . None
Day Running Lamps . . . . None

Safety Belt/Restraint:
Dynamic Head Restraints . . . . None
Adjustable Belt . . . . Standard Front

Mitsubishi Outlander

Specifications

Drive	4WD
Engine	2.4-liter I4
Transmission	SCVT
Tow Rating (lbs.)	Very Low-1500
Head/Leg Room (in.)	Average-40.6/40.9
Interior Space (cu. ft.)	Very Roomy-128.2
Cargo Space (cu. ft.)	Very Cramped-10.3
Wheelbase/Length (in.)	105.1/183.3

Ratings—10 Best, 1 Worst	
Combo Crash Tests	3
Safety Features	3
Rollover	3
Preventive Maintenance	9
Repair Costs	3
Warranty	10
Fuel Economy	7
Complaints	10
Insurance Costs	3
OVERALL RATING	**6**

Mitsubishi Outlander Sport

Mitsubishi Outlander Sport

At-a-Glance

Status/Year Series Started	Unchanged/2013
Twins	–
Body Styles	SUV
Seating	5
Anti-Theft Device	Std. Pass. Immobil & Alarm
Parking Index Rating	Very Easy
Where Made	Normal, IL
Fuel Factor	
MPG Rating (city/hwy)	Good-24/31
Driving Range (mi.)	Average-409
Fuel Type	Regular
Annual Fuel Cost	Low-$1,926
Gas Guzzler Tax	No
Greenhouse Gas Emissions (tons/yr.)	Low-6.8
Barrels of Oil Used per year	Average-12.2

How the Competition Rates

Competitors	Rating	Pg.
Acura RDX	7	83
Hyundai Tucson	4	162
Subaru XV Crosstrek	–	243

Price Range

	Retail	Markup
ES 2WD	$20,670	4%
ES 4WD	$22,070	4%
SE 2WD	$22,595	4%
SE 4WD	$23,995	4%

Safety Checklist

Crash Tests:
- Frontal . . . . Average
- Side . . . . Very Poor

Airbags:
- Head . . . . Fr. & Rr. Roof Curtain
- Torso . . . . Front Pelvis/Torso from Seat
- Pelvis . . . . Front Pelvis/Torso from Seat
- Roll Sensing . . . . Yes
- Knee Bolster . . . . Standard

Crash Avoidance:
- Collision Avoidance . . . . None
- Blind Spot Detection . . . . None
- Lane Keeping Assist . . . . None
- Backup Camera . . . . Optional
- Pedestrian Crash Avoidance . . . . None

General:
- Auto. Crash Notification . . . . None
- Day Running Lamps . . . . None

Safety Belt/Restraint:
- Dynamic Head Restraints . . . . None
- Adjustable Belt . . . . Standard Front

Mitsubishi Outlander Sport

Specifications

Drive	FWD
Engine	2.0-liter I4
Transmission	SCVT
Tow Rating (lbs.)	
Head/Leg Room (in.)	Cramped-39.4/41.6
Interior Space (cu. ft.)	Average-97.5
Cargo Space (cu. ft.)	Average-21.7
Wheelbase/Length (in.)	105.1/169.1

Ratings—10 Best, 1 Worst

Combo Crash Tests	8
Safety Features	2
Rollover	8
Preventive Maintenance	8
Repair Costs	8
Warranty	2
Fuel Economy	9
Complaints	1
Insurance Costs	1
OVERALL RATING	**6**

Nissan Altima

Nissan Altima

At-a-Glance

Status/Year Series Started Unchanged/2013
Twins . . . . –
Body Styles . . . . .Sedan
Seating 5
Anti-Theft Device . . . . . . Std. Pass. Immobil. & Alarm
Parking Index Rating . . . . Average
Where Made . . . . Smyrna, TN / Canton, MS
Fuel Factor
  MPG Rating (city/hwy) . . . . Very Good-27/38
  Driving Range (mi.) . . . . Very Long-559
  Fuel Type . . . . .Regular
  Annual Fuel Cost . . . . Very Low-$1,657
  Gas Guzzler Tax . . . . .No
  Greenhouse Gas Emissions (tons/yr.). Very Low-5.9
  Barrels of Oil Used per year Low-10.6

How the Competition Rates

Competitors	Rating	Pg.
Honda Accord	7	147
Kia Optima	5	179
Toyota Camry	6	246

Price Range

	Retail	Markup
Base	$22,010	7%
S 2.5L	$22,530	9%
SV 3.5L	$28,360	9%
SL 3.5L	$30,660	9%

Safety Checklist

Crash Tests:
  Frontal . . . . Very Good
  Side . . . . Average
Airbags:
  Head . . . . Fr. & Rr. Roof Curtain
  Torso . . . . .Front Pelvis/Torso from Seat
  Pelvis . . . . .Front Pelvis/Torso from Seat
  Roll Sensing . . . . No
  Knee Bolster . . . . None
Crash Avoidance:
  Collision Avoidance . . . . None
  Blind Spot Detection . . . . Optional
  Lane Keeping Assist . . . .Warning Only Optional
  Backup Camera . . . . Optional
  Pedestrian Crash Avoidance . . . . None
General:
  Auto. Crash Notification . . . . None
  Day Running Lamps . . . . None
Safety Belt/Restraint:
  Dynamic Head Restraints . . . . None
  Adjustable Belt . . . . .Standard Front

Nissan Altima

Specifications

Drive . . . . .FWD
Engine 2.5-liter I4
Transmission . . . . .CVT
Tow Rating (lbs.) . . . .
Head/Leg Room (in.) . . . . . . Very Roomy-40/45
Interior Space (cu. ft.) Average-101.9
Cargo Space (cu. ft.) Cramped-15.4
Wheelbase/Length (in.) 109.3/191.5

Ratings—10 Best, 1 Worst

Combo Crash Tests	–
Safety Features	4
Rollover	1
Preventive Maintenance	3
Repair Costs	3
Warranty	2
Fuel Economy	1
Complaints	3
Insurance Costs	8

OVERALL RATING — –

Nissan Armada

At-a-Glance

Status/Year Series Started	Unchanged/2004
Twins	–
Body Styles	SUV
Seating	8
Anti-Theft Device	Std. Pass. Immobil. & Alarm
Parking Index Rating	Very Hard
Where Made	Canton, MS
Fuel Factor	
MPG Rating (city/hwy)	Very Poor-13/19
Driving Range (mi.)	Long-424
Fuel Type	Regular
Annual Fuel Cost	Very High-$3,395
Gas Guzzler Tax	No
Greenhouse Gas Emissions (tons/yr.)	Very High-13.1
Barrels of Oil Used per year	Very High-23.5

How the Competition Rates

Competitors	Rating	Pg.
Chevrolet Suburban	6	118
Ford Expedition	2	137
Toyota Sequoia	–	254

Price Range	Retail	Markup
SV 2WD	$36,890	10%
SV 4WD	$42,390	10%
SL 4WD	$45,080	10%
Platinum 4WD	$52,360	10%

Nissan Armada

Safety Checklist

Crash Tests:
Frontal . . . .
Side . . . .
Airbags:
Head . . . . Fr. & Rr. Roof Curtain
Torso . . . . Front Pelvis/Torso from Seat
Pelvis . . . . Front Pelvis/Torso from Seat
Roll Sensing . . . . Yes
Knee Bolster . . . . None
Crash Avoidance:
Collision Avoidance . . . . None
Blind Spot Detection . . . . None
Lane Keeping Assist . . . . None
Backup Camera . . . . Optional
Pedestrian Crash Avoidance . . . . None
General:
Auto. Crash Notification . . . . None
Day Running Lamps . . . . None
Safety Belt/Restraint:
Dynamic Head Restraints . . . . . . Standard Front
Adjustable Belt . . . . Standard Front & Rear

Nissan Armada

Specifications

Drive	RWD
Engine	5.8-liter V8
Transmission	5-sp. Auto w/Overdrive
Tow Rating (lbs.)	High-8200
Head/Leg Room (in.)	Roomy-41/41.8
Interior Space (cu. ft.)	Very Roomy-127.3
Cargo Space (cu. ft.)	Average-20
Wheelbase/Length (in.)	123.2/207.7

Ratings—10 Best, 1 Worst

Combo Crash Tests	–
Safety Features	3
Rollover	2
Preventive Maintenance	3
Repair Costs	7
Warranty	2
Fuel Economy	1
Complaints	5
Insurance Costs	8

OVERALL RATING — –

Nissan Frontier

Nissan Frontier

At-a-Glance

Status/Year Series Started	Unchanged/2005
Twins	–
Body Styles	Pickup
Seating	5
Anti-Theft Device	Std. Pass. Immobil. & Alarm
Parking Index Rating	Very Hard
Where Made	Canton, MS

Fuel Factor
MPG Rating (city/hwy)	Very Poor-15/21
Driving Range (mi.)	Very Short-363
Fuel Type	Regular
Annual Fuel Cost	Very High-$2,989
Gas Guzzler Tax	No
Greenhouse Gas Emissions (tons/yr.)	Very High-10.7
Barrels of Oil Used per year	Very High-19.4

How the Competition Rates

Competitors	Rating	Pg.
Honda Ridgeline	–	154
Toyota Tacoma	1	256

Price Range

	Retail	Markup
S King Cab I4	$19,219	5%
SV Crew Cab 4WD SWB	$27,220	7%
PRO-4X King Cab	$31,040	8%
SL Crew Cab 4WD SWB	$33,620	8%

Safety Checklist

Crash Tests:
Frontal	
Side	

Airbags:
Head	Fr. & Rr. Roof Curtain
Torso	Front Pelvis/Torso from Seat
Pelvis	Front Pelvis/Torso from Seat
Roll Sensing	Yes
Knee Bolster	None

Crash Avoidance:
Collision Avoidance	None
Blind Spot Detection	None
Lane Keeping Assist	None
Backup Camera	Optional
Pedestrian Crash Avoidance	None

General:
Auto. Crash Notification	None
Day Running Lamps	None

Safety Belt/Restraint:
Dynamic Head Restraints	Standard Front
Adjustable Belt	Standard Front

Nissan Frontier

Specifications

Drive	4WD
Engine	4.0-liter V6
Transmission	5-sp. Automatic
Tow Rating (lbs.)	Average-6300
Head/Leg Room (in.)	Average-39.7/42.4
Interior Space (cu. ft.)	Very Cramped-87.7
Cargo Space (cu. ft.)	Roomy-33.5
Wheelbase/Length (in.)	125.9/205.5

Nissan Juke

Ratings—10 Best, 1 Worst

Combo Crash Tests	1
Safety Features	2
Rollover	5
Preventive Maintenance	8
Repair Costs	7
Warranty	2
Fuel Economy	7
Complaints	10
Insurance Costs	5
OVERALL RATING	**4**

Nissan Juke

Nissan Juke

At-a-Glance

Status/Year Series Started........ Unchanged/2011
Twins .... –
Body Styles .... SUV
Seating 5
Anti-Theft Device ...... Std. Pass. Immobil. & Alarm
Parking Index Rating .... Easy
Where Made.................... Oppama, Japan
Fuel Factor
  MPG Rating (city/hwy)............. Good-25/30
  Driving Range (mi.) .... Very Short-319
  Fuel Type............................. Regular
  Annual Fuel Cost .... Low-$1,904
  Gas Guzzler Tax .... No
  Greenhouse Gas Emissions (tons/yr.). Very Low-6.3
  Barrels of Oil Used per year Low-11.4

How the Competition Rates

Competitors	Rating	Pg.
Ford Escape	5	136
Kia Soul	7	182
Scion xB	–	234

Price Range	Retail	Markup
S	$18,990	5%
SV	$22,040	5%
SV AWD	$23,740	6%
SL AWD	$25,990	6%

Safety Checklist

Crash Tests:
  Frontal......................... Very Poor
  Side............................. Very Poor
Airbags:
  Head .... Fr.& Rr. Roof Curtain
  Torso.......... Front Pelvis/Torso from Seat
  Pelvis .... Front Pelvis/Torso from Seat
  Roll Sensing .... No
  Knee Bolster .... None
Crash Avoidance:
  Collision Avoidance................. None
  Blind Spot Detection .... None
  Lane Keeping Assist................ None
  Backup Camera .... Optional
  Pedestrian Crash Avoidance .... None
General:
  Auto. Crash Notification .... None
  Day Running Lamps................. None
Safety Belt/Restraint:
  Dynamic Head Restraints...... Standard Front
  Adjustable Belt .... Standard Front

Nissan Juke

Specifications

Drive................................... AWD
Engine 1.6-liter I4
Transmission .... CVT
Tow Rating (lbs.) ....
Head/Leg Room (in.) Average-39.6/42.1
Interior Space (cu. ft.)...... Very Cramped-87
Cargo Space (cu. ft.) .... Very Cramped-10.5
Wheelbase/Length (in.) 99.6/162.4

Nissan Leaf

Ratings—10 Best, 1 Worst

Combo Crash Tests	2
Safety Features	1
Rollover	8
Preventive Maintenance	7
Repair Costs	10
Warranty	2
Fuel Economy	10
Complaints	1
Insurance Costs	5
OVERALL RATING	**4**

Nissan Leaf

Nissan Leaf

At-a-Glance

Status/Year Series Started........ Unchanged/2011
Twins . . . . –
Body Styles . . . . Hatchback
Seating 5
Anti-Theft Device . . . . . . Std. Pass. Immobil. & Alarm
Parking Index Rating . . . . .Very Easy
Where Made. . . . . Oppama, Japan / Smyrna, TN
Fuel Factor
  MPG Rating (city/hwy) . . . . Very Good-126/101
  Driving Range (mi.) . . . . .Very Short-75
  Fuel Type. Electricity
  Annual Fuel Cost . . . . .Very Low-$370
  Gas Guzzler Tax .No
  Greenhouse Gas Emissions (tons/yr.). 0
  Barrels of Oil Used per year 0.0

How the Competition Rates

Competitors	Rating	Pg.
Chevrolet Volt	9	121
Honda Insight	–	151
Toyota Prius	5	250

Price Range	Retail	Markup
S	$28,800	7%
SV	$31,820	7%
SL	$34,840	7%

Safety Checklist

Crash Tests:
  Frontal. . . . . .Poor
  Side. . . . . .Very Poor
Airbags:
  Head . . . . Fr. & Rr. Roof Curtain
  Torso. . . . . .Front Pelvis/Torso from Seat
  Pelvis . . . . .Front Pelvis/Torso from Seat
  Roll Sensing . . . . No
  Knee Bolster . . . . None
Crash Avoidance:
  Collision Avoidance. . . . . None
  Blind Spot Detection . . . . None
  Lane Keeping Assist. . . . . None
  Backup Camera . . . . Standard
  Pedestrian Crash Avoidance . . . . None
General:
  Auto. Crash Notification . . . . None
  Day Running Lamps. . . . . None
Safety Belt/Restraint:
  Dynamic Head Restraints. . . . . None
  Adjustable Belt . . . . .Standard Front

Nissan Leaf

Specifications

Drive. . . . . FWD
Engine .80.0-liter Electric
Transmission . . . . Single Speed Reducer
Tow Rating (lbs.) . . . .
Head/Leg Room (in.) Roomy-41.2/42.1
Interior Space (cu. ft.). Cramped-92.5
Cargo Space (cu. ft.) Roomy-24
Wheelbase/Length (in.) 106.3/175

Nissan Maxima

Ratings—10 Best, 1 Worst

Combo Crash Tests	1
Safety Features	2
Rollover	9
Preventive Maintenance	6
Repair Costs	6
Warranty	2
Fuel Economy	4
Complaints	8
Insurance Costs	3
OVERALL RATING	**2**

Nissan Maxima

Nissan Maxima

At-a-Glance

Status/Year Series Started	Unchanged/2009
Twins	–
Body Styles	Sedan
Seating	5
Anti-Theft Device	Std. Pass. Immobil. & Alarm
Parking Index Rating	Average
Where Made	Smyrna, TN
Fuel Factor	
MPG Rating (city/hwy)	Poor-19/26
Driving Range (mi.)	Long-432
Fuel Type	Regular
Annual Fuel Cost	High-$2,380
Gas Guzzler Tax	No
Greenhouse Gas Emissions (tons/yr.)	Average-8.3
Barrels of Oil Used per year	High-15.0

How the Competition Rates

Competitors	Rating	Pg.
Chevrolet Impala	8	113
Honda Accord	7	147
Toyota Camry	6	246

Price Range

	Retail	Markup
S	$31,000	9%
SV	$34,090	9%

Safety Checklist

Crash Tests:

Frontal	Very Poor
Side	Very Poor

Airbags:

Head	Fr. & Rr. Roof Curtain
Torso	Front Pelvis/Torso from Seat
Pelvis	Front Pelvis/Torso from Seat
Roll Sensing	No
Knee Bolster	None

Crash Avoidance:

Collision Avoidance	None
Blind Spot Detection	None
Lane Keeping Assist	None
Backup Camera	Optional
Pedestrian Crash Avoidance	None

General:

Auto. Crash Notification	None
Day Running Lamps	None

Safety Belt/Restraint:

Dynamic Head Restraints	Standard Front
Adjustable Belt	Standard Front

Nissan Maxima

Specifications

Drive	FWD
Engine	3.5-liter V6
Transmission	SCVT
Tow Rating (lbs.)	Very Low-1000
Head/Leg Room (in.)	Average-38.5/43.8
Interior Space (cu. ft.)	Cramped-95.8
Cargo Space (cu. ft.)	Cramped-14.2
Wheelbase/Length (in.)	109.3/190.6

Ratings—10 Best, 1 Worst

Combo Crash Tests	2
Safety Features	5
Rollover	3
Preventive Maintenance	7
Repair Costs	3
Warranty	2
Fuel Economy	3
Complaints	9
Insurance Costs	10
OVERALL RATING	**3**

Nissan Murano

Nissan Murano

At-a-Glance

Status/Year Series Started........ Unchanged/2009
Twins . . . . –
Body Styles . . . . SUV
Seating 5
Anti-Theft Device . . . . . . Std. Pass. Immobil. & Alarm
Parking Index Rating . . . . Hard
Where Made. . . . . Kyushu, Japan
Fuel Factor
  MPG Rating (city/hwy) Poor-18/23
  Driving Range (mi.) Long-433
  Fuel Type. . . . . .Regular
  Annual Fuel Cost . . . . High-$2,579
  Gas Guzzler Tax . . . . .No
  Greenhouse Gas Emissions (tons/yr.) High-9.1
  Barrels of Oil Used per year High-16.5

How the Competition Rates

Competitors	Rating	Pg.
Acura MDX	8	82
Honda Pilot	2	153
Toyota Highlander	–	249

Price Range

Price Range	Retail	Markup
S 2WD	$28,440	9%
SV 2WD	$31,530	9%
SL AWD	$36,990	9%
LE AWD	$39,480	9%

Safety Checklist

Crash Tests:
  Frontal. . . . . .Very Poor
  Side. . . . . .Very Poor
Airbags:
  Head . . . . .Fr.& Rr. Roof Curtain
  Torso. . . . . .Front Pelvis/Torso from Seat
  Pelvis . . . . .Front Pelvis/Torso from Seat
  Roll Sensing . . . . .Yes
  Knee Bolster . . . . None
Crash Avoidance:
  Collision Avoidance. . . . . None
  Blind Spot Detection . . . . Optional
  Lane Keeping Assist . . . .Warning Only Optional
  Backup Camera . . . . Optional
  Pedestrian Crash Avoidance . . . . None
General:
  Auto. Crash Notification . . . . None
  Day Running Lamps . . . . None
Safety Belt/Restraint:
  Dynamic Head Restraints . . . . . .Standard Front
  Adjustable Belt . . . . Standard Front & Rear

Nissan Murano

Specifications

Drive. . . . . AWD
Engine 3.5-liter V6
Transmission . . . . .CVT
Tow Rating (lbs.) . . . . Very Low-3500
Head/Leg Room (in.) Roomy-40.1/43.6
Interior Space (cu. ft.). . . . . . . Very Roomy-140.4
Cargo Space (cu. ft.) Roomy-31.8
Wheelbase/Length (in.) 111.2/189.9

Nissan Pathfinder

Mid-Size SUV

Ratings—10 Best, 1 Worst	
Combo Crash Tests	6
Safety Features	3
Rollover	3
Preventive Maintenance	3
Repair Costs	8
Warranty	2
Fuel Economy	3
Complaints	1
Insurance Costs	10
OVERALL RATING	**3**

Nissan Pathfinder

Nissan Pathfinder

At-a-Glance

Status/Year Series Started	Unchanged/2013
Twins	Infiniti QX60
Body Styles	SUV
Seating	7
Anti-Theft Device	Std. Pass. Immobil. & Alarm
Parking Index Rating	Hard
Where Made	Smyrna, TN
Fuel Factor	
MPG Rating (city/hwy)	Poor-19/25
Driving Range (mi.)	Average-415
Fuel Type	Regular
Annual Fuel Cost	High-$2,415
Gas Guzzler Tax	No
Greenhouse Gas Emissions (tons/yr.)	High-8.7
Barrels of Oil Used per year	High-15.7

How the Competition Rates

Competitors	Rating	Pg.
Buick Enclave	7	100
Chevrolet Traverse	9	120
Toyota Highlander	–	249

Price Range	Retail	Markup
S 2WD	$28,700	10%
SV 2WD	$31,960	10%
SL 4WD	$36,500	10%
Platinum	$41,200	10%

Safety Checklist

Crash Tests:
Frontal	Average
Side	Good

Airbags:
Head	Fr. & Rr. Roof Curtain
Torso	Front Pelvis/Torso from Seat
Pelvis	Front Pelvis/Torso from Seat
Roll Sensing	Yes
Knee Bolster	None

Crash Avoidance:
Collision Avoidance	None
Blind Spot Detection	None
Lane Keeping Assist	None
Backup Camera	Optional
Pedestrian Crash Avoidance	None

General:
Auto. Crash Notification	None
Day Running Lamps	None

Safety Belt/Restraint:
Dynamic Head Restraints	None
Adjustable Belt	Standard Front & Rear

Nissan Pathfinder

Specifications

Drive	4WD
Engine	3.5-liter V6
Transmission	CVT
Tow Rating (lbs.)	Low-5000
Head/Leg Room (in.)	Roomy-41.1/42.3
Interior Space (cu. ft.)	Very Roomy-157.8
Cargo Space (cu. ft.)	Cramped-16
Wheelbase/Length (in.)	114.2/197.2

Ratings—10 Best, 1 Worst

Combo Crash Tests	–
Safety Features	3
Rollover	4
Preventive Maintenance	7
Repair Costs	4
Warranty	2
Fuel Economy	3
Complaints	2
Insurance Costs	5

OVERALL RATING — –

Nissan Quest

At-a-Glance

Status/Year Series Started	Unchanged/2011
Twins	–
Body Styles	Minivan
Seating	7
Anti-Theft Device	Std. Pass. Immobil. & Alarm
Parking Index Rating	Average
Where Made	Kyushu, Japan
Fuel Factor	
MPG Rating (city/hwy)	Poor-19/25
Driving Range (mi.)	Long-426
Fuel Type	Regular
Annual Fuel Cost	High-$2,415
Gas Guzzler Tax	No
Greenhouse Gas Emissions (tons/yr.)	High-8.7
Barrels of Oil Used per year	High-15.7

How the Competition Rates

Competitors	Rating	Pg.
Chrysler Town and Country	–	124
Honda Odyssey	–	152
Toyota Sienna	2	255

Price Range

	Retail	Markup
S	$25,990	7%
SV	$29,740	9%
SL	$33,520	9%
Le	$42,640	9%

Nissan Quest

Safety Checklist

Crash Tests:
Frontal . . . .
Side . . . .
Airbags:
Head . . . . .Fr.& Rr. Roof Curtain
Torso . . . . .Front Pelvis/Torso from Seat
Pelvis . . . . .Front Pelvis/Torso from Seat
Roll Sensing . . . . No
Knee Bolster . . . . None
Crash Avoidance:
Collision Avoidance . . . . None
Blind Spot Detection . . . . Optional
Lane Keeping Assist . . . .Warning Only Optional
Backup Camera . . . . Optional
Pedestrian Crash Avoidance . . . . None
General:
Auto. Crash Notification . . . . None
Day Running Lamps . . . . None
Safety Belt/Restraint:
Dynamic Head Restraints . . . . . .Standard Front
Adjustable Belt . . . . Standard Front & Rear

Nissan Quest

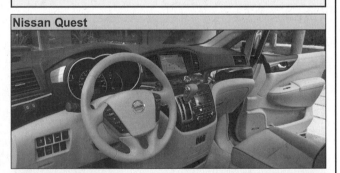

Specifications

Drive	FWD
Engine	3.5-liter V6
Transmission	CVT
Tow Rating (lbs.)	Very Low-3500
Head/Leg Room (in.)	Very Roomy-42.1/43.8
Interior Space (cu. ft.)	Very Roomy-177.8
Cargo Space (cu. ft.)	Very Roomy-37.1
Wheelbase/Length (in.)	118.1/200.8

Ratings—10 Best, 1 Worst

Combo Crash Tests	–
Safety Features	5
Rollover	3
Preventive Maintenance	7
Repair Costs	6
Warranty	2
Fuel Economy	7
Complaints	–
Insurance Costs	5
OVERALL RATING	**–**

Nissan Rogue

Nissan Rogue

At-a-Glance

Status/Year Series Started	All New/2014
Twins	–
Body Styles	SUV
Seating	7
Anti-Theft Device	Std. Pass. Immobil. & Alarm
Parking Index Rating	Average
Where Made	Smyrna, TN
Fuel Factor	
MPG Rating (city/hwy)	Good-25/32
Driving Range (mi.)	Average-402
Fuel Type	Regular
Annual Fuel Cost	Low-$1,855
Gas Guzzler Tax	No
Greenhouse Gas Emissions (tons/yr.)	Low-6.5
Barrels of Oil Used per year	Low-11.8

How the Competition Rates

Competitors	Rating	Pg.
Kia Sorento	5	181
Toyota Venza	4	258
Volvo XC60	10	269

Price Range

Price Range	Retail	Markup
S FWD	$22,490	5%
SV FWD	$24,230	5%
SV AWD	$25,580	5%
SL AWD	$29,420	5%

Safety Checklist

Crash Tests:
Frontal.....................................
Side..

Airbags:
Head................Fr. & Rr. Roof Curtain
Torso..........Front Pelvis/Torso from Seat
Pelvis.........Front Pelvis/Torso from Seat
Roll Sensing..........................Yes
Knee Bolster....................Standard

Crash Avoidance:
Collision Avoidance................None
Blind Spot Detection..............Optional
Lane Keeping Assist....Warning Only Optional
Backup Camera.................Standard
Pedestrian Crash Avoidance..........None

General:
Auto. Crash Notification.............None
Day Running Lamps.................None

Safety Belt/Restraint:
Dynamic Head Restraints............None
Adjustable Belt.............Standard Front

Nissan Rogue

Specifications

Drive	AWD
Engine	2.5-liter I4
Transmission	CVT
Tow Rating (lbs.)	Very Low-1000
Head/Leg Room (in.)	Very Roomy-41.6/43
Interior Space (cu. ft.)	Roomy-105.8
Cargo Space (cu. ft.)	Very Cramped-9.4
Wheelbase/Length (in.)	106.5/182.3

Nissan Sentra

Compact

Ratings—10 Best, 1 Worst	
Combo Crash Tests	3
Safety Features	1
Rollover	7
Preventive Maintenance	7
Repair Costs	9
Warranty	2
Fuel Economy	9
Complaints	3
Insurance Costs	3
OVERALL RATING	**3**

Nissan Sentra

Nissan Sentra

At-a-Glance

Status/Year Series Started........ Unchanged/2013
Twins .... –
Body Styles ....Sedan
Seating 5
Anti-Theft Device ...... Std. Pass. Immobil. & Alarm
Parking Index Rating ....Easy
Where Made.......................... Canton, MS
Fuel Factor
  MPG Rating (city/hwy)......... Very Good-30/39
  Driving Range (mi.) Long-442
  Fuel Type............................Regular
  Annual Fuel Cost .... Very Low-$1,537
  Gas Guzzler Tax ....No
  Greenhouse Gas Emissions (tons/yr.). Very Low-5.4
  Barrels of Oil Used per year Low-9.7

How the Competition Rates

Competitors	Rating	Pg.
Chevrolet Cruze	9	111
Honda Civic	6	148
Toyota Corolla	7	247

Price Range	Retail	Markup
S	$17,320	4%
SV	$18,030	7%
SR	$18,930	7%
SL	$19,820	7%

Safety Checklist

Crash Tests:
  Frontal........................Very Poor
  Side............................. Average
Airbags:
  Head................ Fr. & Rr. Roof Curtain
  Torso.........Front Pelvis/Torso from Seat
  Pelvis ....Front Pelvis/Torso from Seat
  Roll Sensing .... No
  Knee Bolster .... None
Crash Avoidance:
  Collision Avoidance.................. None
  Blind Spot Detection .... None
  Lane Keeping Assist................. None
  Backup Camera .... Optional
  Pedestrian Crash Avoidance .... None
General:
  Auto. Crash Notification .... None
  Day Running Lamps................. None
Safety Belt/Restraint:
  Dynamic Head Restraints............ None
  Adjustable Belt .... Standard Front

Nissan Sentra

Specifications

Drive...................................... FWD
Engine 1.8-liter I4
Transmission ....CVT
Tow Rating (lbs.) ....
Head/Leg Room (in.) Average-39.4/42.5
Interior Space (cu. ft.)............Cramped-95.9
Cargo Space (cu. ft.) Cramped-15.1
Wheelbase/Length (in.) 106.3/182.1

Ratings—10 Best, 1 Worst

Combo Crash Tests	–
Safety Features	3
Rollover	2
Preventive Maintenance	3
Repair Costs	4
Warranty	2
Fuel Economy	1
Complaints	3
Insurance Costs	5
OVERALL RATING	**–**

Nissan Titan

Nissan Titan

At-a-Glance

Status/Year Series Started	Unchanged/2004
Twins	–
Body Styles	Pickup
Seating	4
Anti-Theft Device	Std. Pass. Immobil. & Alarm
Parking Index Rating	Very Hard
Where Made	Canton, MS
Fuel Factor	
MPG Rating (city/hwy)	Very Poor-12/17
Driving Range (mi.)	Short-387
Fuel Type	Regular
Annual Fuel Cost	Very High-$3,720
Gas Guzzler Tax	No
Greenhouse Gas Emissions (tons/yr.)	Very High-13.1
Barrels of Oil Used per year	Very High-23.5

How the Competition Rates

Competitors	Rating	Pg.
Chevrolet Silverado	8	115
Ford F-150	1	139
Honda Ridgeline	–	154

Price Range

	Retail	Markup
S King Cab 2WD	$29,270	10%
SV Crew Cab 4WD SWB	$36,750	10%
PRO-4X Crew Cab 4WD	$39,690	10%
SL Crew Cab 4Wd	$43,190	10%

Safety Checklist

Crash Tests:
Frontal. . . . .
Side. . . . .
Airbags:
Head . . . . Fr. & Rr. Roof Curtain
Torso. . . . . Front Pelvis/Torso from Seat
Pelvis . . . . Front Pelvis/Torso from Seat
Roll Sensing . . . . .Yes
Knee Bolster . . . . None
Crash Avoidance:
Collision Avoidance. . . . . None
Blind Spot Detection . . . . None
Lane Keeping Assist. . . . . None
Backup Camera . . . . Optional
Pedestrian Crash Avoidance . . . . None
General:
Auto. Crash Notification . . . . None
Day Running Lamps . . . . None
Safety Belt/Restraint:
Dynamic Head Restraints . . . . . .Standard Front
Adjustable Belt . . . . .Standard Front

Nissan Titan

Specifications

Drive	4WD
Engine	5.6-liter V8
Transmission	5-sp. Auto w/Overdrive
Tow Rating (lbs.)	Average-7400
Head/Leg Room (in.)	Roomy-41/41.8
Interior Space (cu. ft.)	Roomy-112.8
Cargo Space (cu. ft.)	Very Roomy-58.1
Wheelbase/Length (in.)	139.8/224.6

Ratings—10 Best, 1 Worst	
Combo Crash Tests	1
Safety Features	1
Rollover	5
Preventive Maintenance	8
Repair Costs	10
Warranty	2
Fuel Economy	8
Complaints	7
Insurance Costs	1
OVERALL RATING	**2**

Nissan Versa

Nissan Versa

At-a-Glance

Status/Year Series Started	Unchanged/2006
Twins	–
Body Styles	Sedan, Hatchback
Seating	5
Anti-Theft Device	Opt. Pass. Immobil.
Parking Index Rating	Very Easy
Where Made	Aguascalientes, Mexico
Fuel Factor	
MPG Rating (city/hwy)	Good-26/35
Driving Range (mi.)	Very Short-318
Fuel Type	Regular
Annual Fuel Cost	Very Low-$1,750
Gas Guzzler Tax	No
Greenhouse Gas Emissions (tons/yr.)	Very Low-6.1
Barrels of Oil Used per year	Low-11.0

How the Competition Rates

Competitors	Rating	Pg.
Chevrolet Sonic	10	116
Hyundai Accent	6	155
Toyota Yaris	6	259

Price Range	Retail	Markup
S	$12,990	4%
S Plus	$13,790	4%
SV	$15,240	4%
SI	$16,890	4%

Nissan Versa

Safety Checklist

Crash Tests:
Frontal . . . . Very Poor
Side . . . . Very Poor

Airbags:
Head . . . . Fr. & Rr. Roof Curtain
Torso . . . . .Front Pelvis/Torso from Seat
Pelvis . . . . .Front Pelvis/Torso from Seat
Roll Sensing . . . . No
Knee Bolster . . . . None

Crash Avoidance:
Collision Avoidance . . . . None
Blind Spot Detection . . . . None
Lane Keeping Assist . . . . None
Backup Camera . . . . Optional
Pedestrian Crash Avoidance . . . . None

General:
Auto. Crash Notification . . . . None
Day Running Lamps . . . . None

Safety Belt/Restraint:
Dynamic Head Restraints . . . . None
Adjustable Belt . . . . Standard Front

Nissan Versa

Specifications

Drive	FWD
Engine	1.6-liter I4
Transmission	4-sp. Automatic
Tow Rating (lbs.)	
Head/Leg Room (in.)	Average-39.8/41.8
Interior Space (cu. ft.)	Very Cramped-90.2
Cargo Space (cu. ft.)	Cramped-14.9
Wheelbase/Length (in.)	102.4/175.4

Nissan Xterra

Ratings—10 Best, 1 Worst	
Combo Crash Tests	–
Safety Features	4
Rollover	1
Preventive Maintenance	3
Repair Costs	7
Warranty	2
Fuel Economy	1
Complaints	3
Insurance Costs	10
OVERALL RATING	**–**

Nissan Xterra

Nissan Xterra

At-a-Glance

Status/Year Series Started........ Unchanged/2005
Twins .... –
Body Styles .... SUV
Seating 5
Anti-Theft Device ...... Std. Pass. Immobil. & Alarm
Parking Index Rating .... Easy
Where Made....................... Canton, MS
Fuel Factor
  MPG Rating (city/hwy)........... Very Poor-15/20
  Driving Range (mi.) .... Very Short-357
  Fuel Type............................. Regular
  Annual Fuel Cost .... Very High-$3,044
  Gas Guzzler Tax ....No
  Greenhouse Gas Emissions (tons/yr.)Very High-10.8
  Barrels of Oil Used per year .... Very High-19.4

How the Competition Rates

Competitors	Rating	Pg.
Hyundai Santa Fe	–	159
Toyota FJ Cruiser	–	248
Volvo XC90	–	270

Price Range	Retail	Markup
X 2WD	$23,110	6%
S 2WD	$25,020	6%
S 4WD	$27,070	6%
PRO-4X	$31,090	7%

Safety Checklist

Crash Tests:
  Frontal...................................
  Side......................................
Airbags:
  Head .... Fr. & Rr. Roof Curtain
  Torso...........Front Pelvis/Torso from Seat
  Pelvis ....Front Pelvis/Torso from Seat
  Roll Sensing ....Yes
  Knee Bolster .... None
Crash Avoidance:
  Collision Avoidance.................. None
  Blind Spot Detection................. None
  Lane Keeping Assist................. None
  Backup Camera .... Optional
  Pedestrian Crash Avoidance .... None
General:
  Auto. Crash Notification .... None
  Day Running Lamps................. None
Safety Belt/Restraint:
  Dynamic Head Restraints......Standard Front
  Adjustable Belt .... Standard Front & Rear

Nissan Xterra

Specifications

Drive...................................... 4WD
Engine 4.0-liter V6
Transmission .... .5-sp. Automatic
Tow Rating (lbs.) ....
Head/Leg Room (in.) Average-39.9/42.4
Interior Space (cu. ft.)............. Average-99.8
Cargo Space (cu. ft.) .... Very Roomy-36.3
Wheelbase/Length (in.) 106.3/178.7

Ratings—10 Best, 1 Worst	
Combo Crash Tests	–
Safety Features	4
Rollover	4
Preventive Maintenance	3
Repair Costs	1
Warranty	6
Fuel Economy	2
Complaints	9
Insurance Costs	8
OVERALL RATING	**–**

Porsche Cayenne

Porsche Cayenne

At-a-Glance

Status/Year Series Started Unchanged/2011
Twins . . . . Volkswagen Touareg
Body Styles . . . . SUV
Seating 5
Anti-Theft Device . Std. Pass. Immobil. & Active Alarm
Parking Index Rating . . . . Hard
Where Made. . . . . Leipzig, Germany
Fuel Factor
  MPG Rating (city/hwy) . . . . Very Poor-17/23
  Driving Range (mi.) . . . . Very Short-358
  Fuel Type. . . . . Premium
  Annual Fuel Cost . . . . Very High-$2,905
  Gas Guzzler Tax . . . . No
  Greenhouse Gas Emissions (tons/yr.) High-9.1
  Barrels of Oil Used per year High-16.5

How the Competition Rates

Competitors	Rating	Pg.
Audi Q7	–	91
BMW X5	–	99
Land Rover Range Rover	–	184

Price Range	Retail	Markup
Base	$48,850	
S	$65,850	
GTS	$82,050	
Turbo	$108,750	

Safety Checklist

Crash Tests:
  Frontal. . . . .
  Side. . . . .
Airbags:
  Head . . . . Fr. & Rr. Roof Curtain
  Torso. . . . . Fr. & Rr. Torso from Seat
  Pelvis . . . . None
  Roll Sensing . . . . .Yes
  Knee Bolster . . . . Standard Front
Crash Avoidance:
  Collision Avoidance. . . . . DBS Standard
  Blind Spot Detection . . . . Optional
  Lane Keeping Assist. . . . . None
  Backup Camera . . . . None
  Pedestrian Crash Avoidance . . . . None
General:
  Auto. Crash Notification . . . . None
  Day Running Lamps . . . . Standard
Safety Belt/Restraint:
  Dynamic Head Restraints. . . . . None
  Adjustable Belt . . . . .Standard Front

Porsche Cayenne

Specifications

Drive. . . . . AWD
Engine 3.6-liter V6
Transmission . . . . .8-sp. Automatic
Tow Rating (lbs.) Average-5954
Head/Leg Room (in.) . . . . . Very Roomy-39.57/67.1
Interior Space (cu. ft.). . . . .
Cargo Space (cu. ft.) . . . . Very Roomy-62.9
Wheelbase/Length (in.) 114/190.8

Ratings—10 Best, 1 Worst

Combo Crash Tests	6
Safety Features	2
Rollover	2
Preventive Maintenance	8
Repair Costs	10
Warranty	8
Fuel Economy	1
Complaints	5
Insurance Costs	5
OVERALL RATING	**5**

Ram 1500

Ram 1500

Safety Checklist

Crash Tests:
Frontal . . . . Poor
Side . . . . Very Good

Airbags:
Head . . . . Fr. & Rr. Roof Curtain
Torso . . . . Front Torso from Seat
Pelvis . . . . None
Roll Sensing . . . . Yes
Knee Bolster . . . . None

Crash Avoidance:
Collision Avoidance . . . . None
Blind Spot Detection . . . . None
Lane Keeping Assist . . . . None
Backup Camera . . . . Optional
Pedestrian Crash Avoidance . . . . None

General:
Auto. Crash Notification . . . . None
Day Running Lamps . . . . Optional

Safety Belt/Restraint:
Dynamic Head Restraints . . . . None
Adjustable Belt . . . . Standard Front

At-a-Glance

Status/Year Series Started Unchanged/2009
Twins . . . . –
Body Styles . . . . Pickup
Seating 5/6
Anti-Theft Device . . . . . . Std. Pass. Immobil. & Alarm
Parking Index Rating . . . . Very Hard
Where Made . . . . Warren, MI / Saltillo, Mexico
Fuel Factor
  MPG Rating (city/hwy) . . . . Very Poor-13/19
  Driving Range (mi.) Short-394
  Fuel Type . . . . Regular
  Annual Fuel Cost . . . . Very High-$3,395
  Gas Guzzler Tax . . . . No
  Greenhouse Gas Emissions (tons/yr.) Very High-12.2
  Barrels of Oil Used per year . . . . Very High-22.0

How the Competition Rates

Competitors	Rating	Pg.
Chevrolet Silverado	8	115
Ford F-150	1	139
Toyota Tundra	–	257

Ram 1500

Specifications

Drive 4WD
Engine 5.7-liter V8
Transmission . . . . 6-sp. Automatic
Tow Rating (lbs.) . . . . Very High-8650
Head/Leg Room (in.) Average-41/41
Interior Space (cu. ft.) Roomy-116.6
Cargo Space (cu. ft.) . . . . Very Roomy-57.5
Wheelbase/Length (in.) 140.5/229

Price Range

Price Range	Retail	Markup
Tradesman Reg Cab LWB 2WD	$24,585	7%
SLT Quad Cab SWB 4WD	$35,420	7%
Sport Crew Cab LWB 4WD	$43,115	9%
Laramie Longhorn Crew Cab 4WD	$49,030	9%

Ratings—10 Best, 1 Worst

Combo Crash Tests	–
Safety Features	1
Rollover	10
Preventive Maintenance	1
Repair Costs	3
Warranty	2
Fuel Economy	6
Complaints	2
Insurance Costs	1
OVERALL RATING	**–**

Scion FR-S

At-a-Glance

Status/Year Series Started	Unchanged/2013
Twins	Subaru BRZ
Body Styles	Coupe
Seating	4
Anti-Theft Device	Std. Pass. Immobil.
Parking Index Rating	Very Easy
Where Made	Gunma, Japan
Fuel Factor	
MPG Rating (city/hwy)	Average-22/30
Driving Range (mi.)	Very Short-330
Fuel Type	Premium
Annual Fuel Cost	Average-$2,238
Gas Guzzler Tax	No
Greenhouse Gas Emissions (tons/yr.)	Low-7.3
Barrels of Oil Used per year	Average-13.2

How the Competition Rates

Competitors	Rating	Pg.
Hyundai Veloster	–	163
Mazda MX-5 Miata	–	202
Subaru BRZ	–	237

Price Range

	Retail	Markup
Base Manual	$24,500	5%
Base AT	$25,600	5%
10 Series Manual	$27,425	5%
10 Series AT	$28,675	5%

Scion FR-S

Safety Checklist

Crash Tests:
Frontal . . . .
Side . . . .

Airbags:
Head . . . . Fr. & Rr. Roof Curtain
Torso . . . . Front Pelvis/Torso from Seat
Pelvis . . . . Front Pelvis/Torso from Seat
Roll Sensing . . . . No
Knee Bolster . . . . None

Crash Avoidance:
Collision Avoidance . . . . None
Blind Spot Detection . . . . None
Lane Keeping Assist . . . . None
Backup Camera . . . . None
Pedestrian Crash Avoidance . . . . None

General:
Auto. Crash Notification . . . . None
Day Running Lamps . . . . Standard

Safety Belt/Restraint:
Dynamic Head Restraints . . . . None
Adjustable Belt . . . . None

Scion FR-S

Specifications

Drive	RWD
Engine	2.0-liter I4
Transmission	6-sp. Manual
Tow Rating (lbs.)	
Head/Leg Room (in.)	Very Cramped-37.1/41.9
Interior Space (cu. ft.)	Very Cramped-76.5
Cargo Space (cu. ft.)	Very Cramped-6.9
Wheelbase/Length (in.)	101.2/166.7

Ratings—10 Best, 1 Worst	
Combo Crash Tests	6
Safety Features	2
Rollover	8
Preventive Maintenance	10
Repair Costs	5
Warranty	2
Fuel Economy	6
Complaints	10
Insurance Costs	1
OVERALL RATING	**6**

Scion tC

Scion tC

Scion tC

Safety Checklist

Crash Tests:
Frontal . . . . Average
Side . . . . Good
Airbags:
Head . . . . Fr. & Rr. Roof Curtain
Torso . . . . Front Pelvis/Torso from Seat
Pelvis . . . . Front Pelvis/Torso from Seat
Roll Sensing . . . . No
Knee Bolster . . . . Standard
Crash Avoidance:
Collision Avoidance . . . . None
Blind Spot Detection . . . . None
Lane Keeping Assist . . . . None
Backup Camera . . . . None
Pedestrian Crash Avoidance . . . . None
General:
Auto. Crash Notification . . . . None
Day Running Lamps . . . . None
Safety Belt/Restraint:
Dynamic Head Restraints . . . . . . Standard Front
Adjustable Belt . . . . None

At-a-Glance

Status/Year Series Started Appearance Change/2011
Twins . . . . —
Body Styles . . . . Coupe
Seating 5
Anti-Theft Device . . . . Std. Pass. Immobil.
Parking Index Rating . . . . Easy
Where Made . . . . Toyota City, Japan
Fuel Factor
  MPG Rating (city/hwy) Average-23/31
  Driving Range (mi.) Short-377
  Fuel Type . . . . Regular
  Annual Fuel Cost . . . . Low-$1,977
  Gas Guzzler Tax . . . . No
  Greenhouse Gas Emissions (tons/yr.) Low-7.0
  Barrels of Oil Used per year Average-12.7

How the Competition Rates

Competitors	Rating	Pg.
Mazda Mazda3	—	199
Mitsubishi Lancer	5	212
Subaru Impreza	—	239

Price Range	Retail	Markup
Base Manual	$19,210	5%
Base AT	$20,210	5%
10 Series Manual	$21,440	5%
10 Series AT	$22,440	5%

Scion tC

Specifications

Drive . . . . FWD
Engine 2.5-liter I4
Transmission . . . . 6-sp. Automatic
Tow Rating (lbs.) . . . .
Head/Leg Room (in.) . . . . . Very Cramped-37.7/41.8
Interior Space (cu. ft.) . . . . Very Cramped-88.4
Cargo Space (cu. ft.) . . . . . . Very Roomy-34.5
Wheelbase/Length (in.) 106.3/174

Ratings—10 Best, 1 Worst

Combo Crash Tests	–
Safety Features	1
Rollover	4
Preventive Maintenance	7
Repair Costs	8
Warranty	2
Fuel Economy	5
Complaints	7
Insurance Costs	1
OVERALL RATING	**–**

Scion xB

Scion xB

Scion xB

At-a-Glance

Status/Year Series Started	Unchanged/2008
Twins	–
Body Styles	Hatchback
Seating	5
Anti-Theft Device	None
Parking Index Rating	Very Easy
Where Made	Iwata, Japan
Fuel Factor	
MPG Rating (city/hwy)	Average-22/28
Driving Range (mi.)	Very Short-341
Fuel Type	Regular
Annual Fuel Cost	Average-$2,113
Gas Guzzler Tax	No
Greenhouse Gas Emissions (tons/yr.)	Average-7.6
Barrels of Oil Used per year	High-13.7

How the Competition Rates

Competitors	Rating	Pg.
Kia Soul	7	182
Mini Cooper	–	210
Toyota Yaris	6	259

Price Range	Retail	Markup
Base Manual	$16,800	5%
Base AT	$17,750	5%
10 Series Manual	$19,210	5%
10 Series AT	$20,160	5%

Safety Checklist

Crash Tests:
Frontal . . . .
Side . . . .

Airbags:
Head . . . . Fr.& Rr. Roof Curtain
Torso . . . . Front Pelvis/Torso from Seat
Pelvis . . . . Front Pelvis/Torso from Seat
Roll Sensing . . . . No
Knee Bolster . . . . None

Crash Avoidance:
Collision Avoidance . . . . None
Blind Spot Detection . . . . None
Lane Keeping Assist . . . . None
Backup Camera . . . . None
Pedestrian Crash Avoidance . . . . None

General:
Auto. Crash Notification . . . . None
Day Running Lamps . . . . None

Safety Belt/Restraint:
Dynamic Head Restraints . . . . None
Adjustable Belt . . . . Standard Front

Scion xB

Specifications

Drive	FWD
Engine	2.4-liter I4
Transmission	4-sp. Automatic
Tow Rating (lbs.)	
Head/Leg Room (in.)	Cramped-40/40.8
Interior Space (cu. ft.)	Average-100.8
Cargo Space (cu. ft.)	Very Cramped-11.6
Wheelbase/Length (in.)	102.4/167.3

Scion xD

Ratings—10 Best, 1 Worst

Combo Crash Tests	–
Safety Features	1
Rollover	5
Preventive Maintenance	10
Repair Costs	8
Warranty	2
Fuel Economy	8
Complaints	10
Insurance Costs	1
OVERALL RATING	**–**

Scion xD

Scion xD

At-a-Glance

Status/Year Series Started	Unchanged/2008
Twins	–
Body Styles	Hatchback
Seating	5
Anti-Theft Device	None
Parking Index Rating	Easy
Where Made	Takaoka City, Japan
Fuel Factor	
MPG Rating (city/hwy)	Good-27/33
Driving Range (mi.)	Very Short-323
Fuel Type	Regular
Annual Fuel Cost	Very Low-$1,750
Gas Guzzler Tax	No
Greenhouse Gas Emissions (tons/yr.)	Very Low-6.3
Barrels of Oil Used per year	Low-11.4

How the Competition Rates

Competitors	Rating	Pg.
Chevrolet Sonic	10	116
Hyundai Accent	6	155
Kia Rio	6	180

Price Range	Retail	Markup
Manual	$15,745	5%
AT	$16,545	5%

Safety Checklist

Crash Tests:
Frontal . . . .
Side . . . .

Airbags:
Head . . . . Fr. & Rr. Roof Curtain
Torso . . . . Front Torso from Seat
Pelvis . . . . None
Roll Sensing . . . . No
Knee Bolster . . . . None

Crash Avoidance:
Collision Avoidance . . . . None
Blind Spot Detection . . . . None
Lane Keeping Assist . . . . None
Backup Camera . . . . None
Pedestrian Crash Avoidance . . . . None

General:
Auto. Crash Notification . . . . None
Day Running Lamps . . . . None

Safety Belt/Restraint:
Dynamic Head Restraints . . . . . . Standard Front
Adjustable Belt . . . . Standard Front

Scion xD

Specifications

Drive	FWD
Engine	1.8-liter I4
Transmission	4-sp. Automatic
Tow Rating (lbs.)	
Head/Leg Room (in.)	Very Cramped-38.9/40.3
Interior Space (cu. ft.)	Very Cramped-84.5
Cargo Space (cu. ft.)	Very Cramped-10.5
Wheelbase/Length (in.)	96.9/154.7

Ratings—10 Best, 1 Worst

Combo Crash Tests	–
Safety Features	1
Rollover	2
Preventive Maintenance	3
Repair Costs	3
Warranty	1
Fuel Economy	10
Complaints	3
Insurance Costs	3
OVERALL RATING	**–**

Smart ForTwo

Smart ForTwo

At-a-Glance

```
Status/Year Series Started. . . . . . . Unchanged/2008
Twins . . . . . . . . . . . . . . . . . . . . . . . . . . . . . . . . . . –
Body Styles . . . . . . . . . . . . . . . . . . . . . . Hatchback
Seating. . . . . . . . . . . . . . . . . . . . . . . . . . . . . . . . . 2
Anti-Theft Device . . .Std. Act. Immobil. & Pass. Alarm
Parking Index Rating . . . . . . . . . . . . . . . . .Very Easy
Where Made. . . . . . . . . . . . . . . . . .Hambach, France
Fuel Factor
  MPG Rating (city/hwy). . . . . . . . . Very Good-34/38
  Driving Range (mi.) . . . . . . . . . . . . .Very Short-311
  Fuel Type. . . . . . . . . . . . . . . . . . . . . . . . .Premium
  Annual Fuel Cost . . . . . . . . . . . . . Very Low-$1,568
  Gas Guzzler Tax . . . . . . . . . . . . . . . . . . . . . . .No
  Greenhouse Gas Emissions (tons/yr.). Very Low-5.1
  Barrels of Oil Used per year . . . . . . . . Very Low-9.1
```

How the Competition Rates

Competitors	Rating	Pg.
Fiat 500	4	132
Ford Fiesta	–	140
Mitsubishi Mirage	–	213

Price Range

	Retail	Markup
pure	$12,490	8%
passion Coupe	$14,890	8%
passion Cabriolet	$17,890	8%

Safety Checklist

```
Crash Tests:
  Frontal. . . . . . . . . . . . . . . . . . . . . . . . . . . . . .
  Side. . . . . . . . . . . . . . . . . . . . . . . . . . . . . . . .
Airbags:
  Head . . . . . . . . . . . . . . . .Front Roof Curtain
  Torso. . . . . . . . . . . . . . .Front Torso from Seat
  Pelvis . . . . . . . . . . . . . . . . . . . . . . . . . None
  Roll Sensing . . . . . . . . . . . . . . . . . . . . . . No
  Knee Bolster . . . . . . . . . . . . . . . . . . Standard
Crash Avoidance:
  Collision Avoidance. . . . . . . . . . . . . . . . None
  Blind Spot Detection . . . . . . . . . . . . . . . None
  Lane Keeping Assist. . . . . . . . . . . . . . . . None
  Backup Camera . . . . . . . . . . . . . . . . . . None
  Pedestrian Crash Avoidance . . . . . . . . . None
General:
  Auto. Crash Notification . . . . . . . . . . . . None
  Day Running Lamps . . . . . . . . . . . . . . Optional
Safety Belt/Restraint:
  Dynamic Head Restraints. . . . . . . . . . . None
  Adjustable Belt . . . . . . . . . . . . . . . . . . None
```

Specifications

```
Drive. . . . . . . . . . . . . . . . . . . . . . . . . . . . .RWD
Engine . . . . . . . . . . . . . . . . . . . . . . . . 1.0-liter I3
Transmission . . . . . . . . . . . . . . .5-sp. Automatic
Tow Rating (lbs.) . . . . . . . . . . . . . . . . . . . . . . .
Head/Leg Room (in.) . . . . . . . .Cramped-39.7/41.2
Interior Space (cu. ft.). . . . . . . .Very Cramped-45.4
Cargo Space (cu. ft.) . . . . . . . .Very Cramped-7.8
Wheelbase/Length (in.) . . . . . . . . . . .73.5/106.1
```

Ratings—10 Best, 1 Worst

Combo Crash Tests	–
Safety Features	1
Rollover	10
Preventive Maintenance	1
Repair Costs	3
Warranty	2
Fuel Economy	6
Complaints	1
Insurance Costs	1
OVERALL RATING	**–**

Subaru BRZ

Subaru BRZ

At-a-Glance

Status/Year Series Started Unchanged/2013
Twins . . . . .Scion FR-S
Body Styles . . . . .Coupe
Seating 4
Anti-Theft Device. . Std. Pass. Immobil. & Opt. Act. Alarm
Parking Index Rating . . . . .Very Easy
Where Made . . . . Gunma, Japan
Fuel Factor
  MPG Rating (city/hwy) Average-22/30
  Driving Range (mi.) . . . . .Very Short-330
  Fuel Type . . . . .Premium
  Annual Fuel Cost . . . . Average-$2,238
  Gas Guzzler Tax . . . . .No
  Greenhouse Gas Emissions (tons/yr.) Low-6.5
  Barrels of Oil Used per year Average-11.8

How the Competition Rates

Competitors	Rating	Pg.
Hyundai Veloster	–	163
Mazda MX-5 Miata	–	202
Scion FR-S	–	232

Price Range

	Retail	Markup
Premium Manual	$25,595	5%
Limited Manual	$27,595	5%
Limited AT	$28,695	5%

Safety Checklist

Crash Tests:
  Frontal . . . .
  Side . . . .
Airbags:
  Head . . . . .Fr.& Rr. Roof Curtain
  Torso . . . . .Front Pelvis/Torso from Seat
  Pelvis . . . . .Front Pelvis/Torso from Seat
  Roll Sensing . . . . No
  Knee Bolster . . . . None
Crash Avoidance:
  Collision Avoidance . . . . None
  Blind Spot Detection . . . . None
  Lane Keeping Assist . . . . None
  Backup Camera . . . . None
  Pedestrian Crash Avoidance . . . . None
General:
  Auto. Crash Notification . . . . None
  Day Running Lamps . . . . Standard
Safety Belt/Restraint:
  Dynamic Head Restraints . . . . None
  Adjustable Belt . . . . None

Subaru BRZ

Specifications

Drive . . . . .RWD
Engine 2.0-liter I4
Transmission . . . . .6-sp. Manual
Tow Rating (lbs.) . . . .
Head/Leg Room (in.) . . . . .Very Cramped-37.1/41.9
Interior Space (cu. ft.) . . . . .Very Cramped-76.5
Cargo Space (cu. ft.) . . . . .Very Cramped-6.9
Wheelbase/Length (in.) 101.2/166.7

Subaru Forester

Ratings—10 Best, 1 Worst	
Combo Crash Tests	7
Safety Features	7
Rollover	4
Preventive Maintenance	3
Repair Costs	7
Warranty	2
Fuel Economy	7
Complaints	–
Insurance Costs	1
OVERALL RATING	**4**

Subaru Forester

Subaru Forester

At-a-Glance

Status/Year Series Started	All New/2014
Twins	–
Body Styles	SUV
Seating	5
Anti-Theft Device	Std. Pass Immobil. & Act. Alarm
Parking Index Rating	Easy
Where Made	Gunma, Japan
Fuel Factor	
MPG Rating (city/hwy)	Good-24/32
Driving Range (mi.)	Long-430
Fuel Type	Regular
Annual Fuel Cost	Low-$1,903
Gas Guzzler Tax	No
Greenhouse Gas Emissions (tons/yr.)	Low-6.8
Barrels of Oil Used per year	Average-12.2

How the Competition Rates

Competitors	Rating	Pg.
Hyundai Tucson	4	162
Mazda CX-5	6	196
Toyota RAV4	5	253

Price Range	Retail	Markup
2.5i	$22,995	6%
2.5i Limited	$27,995	7%
2.5i Touring	$29,995	7%
2.0 XT Touring	$32,995	7%

Safety Checklist

Crash Tests:
Frontal	Average
Side	Very Good

Airbags:
Head	Fr.& Rr. Roof Curtain
Torso	Front Pelvis/Torso from Seat
Pelvis	Front Pelvis/Torso from Seat
Roll Sensing	Yes
Knee Bolster	Standard

Crash Avoidance:
Collision Avoidance	Optional CIB & DBS
Blind Spot Detection	None
Lane Keeping Assist	Warning Only Optional
Backup Camera	Optional
Pedestrian Crash Avoidance	Optional

General:
Auto. Crash Notification	None
Day Running Lamps	Standard

Safety Belt/Restraint:
Dynamic Head Restraints	None
Adjustable Belt	Standard Front

Subaru Forester

Specifications

Drive	AWD
Engine	2.5-liter I4
Transmission	CVT
Tow Rating (lbs.)	Very Low-1500
Head/Leg Room (in.)	Very Roomy-41.4/43
Interior Space (cu. ft.)	Very Cramped-78.7
Cargo Space (cu. ft.)	Very Roomy-34.4
Wheelbase/Length (in.)	103.9/180.9

Ratings—10 Best, 1 Worst

Combo Crash Tests	–
Safety Features	2
Rollover	7
Preventive Maintenance	3
Repair Costs	7
Warranty	2
Fuel Economy	9
Complaints	8
Insurance Costs	1

OVERALL RATING	–

Subaru Impreza

At-a-Glance

Status/Year Series Started	Unchanged/2012
Twins	–
Body Styles	Sedan, Wagon
Seating	5
Anti-Theft Device	Std. Pass. Immobil & Act. Alarm
Parking Index Rating	Easy
Where Made	Gunma, Japan
Fuel Factor	
MPG Rating (city/hwy)	Very Good-27/36
Driving Range (mi.)	Long-441
Fuel Type	Regular
Annual Fuel Cost	Very Low-$1,691
Gas Guzzler Tax	No
Greenhouse Gas Emissions (tons/yr.)	Very Low-6.1
Barrels of Oil Used per year	Low-11.0

How the Competition Rates

Competitors	Rating	Pg.
Dodge Dart	9	128
Honda Civic	6	148
Mitsubishi Lancer	5	212

Price Range

	Retail	Markup
Base	$18,895	5%
Premium Wagon	$20,795	5%
WRX	$25,995	6%
WRX Sti Limited	$37,845	6%

Subaru Impreza

Safety Checklist

Crash Tests:
Frontal. . . . .
Side. . . . .

Airbags:
Head . . . . Fr.& Rr. Roof Curtain
Torso. . . . . Front Pelvis/Torso from Seat
Pelvis . . . . Front Pelvis/Torso from Seat
Roll Sensing . . . . No
Knee Bolster . . . . Standard

Crash Avoidance:
Collision Avoidance. . . . . None
Blind Spot Detection . . . . None
Lane Keeping Assist. . . . . None
Backup Camera . . . . Optional
Pedestrian Crash Avoidance . . . . None

General:
Auto. Crash Notification . . . . None
Day Running Lamps . . . . Standard

Safety Belt/Restraint:
Dynamic Head Restraints. . . . . None
Adjustable Belt . . . . .Standard Front

Subaru Impreza

Specifications

Drive	AWD
Engine	2.0-liter I4
Transmission	CVT
Tow Rating (lbs.)	
Head/Leg Room (in.)	Roomy-39.8/43.5
Interior Space (cu. ft.)	Average-98.9
Cargo Space (cu. ft.)	Very Cramped-12
Wheelbase/Length (in.)	104.1/180.3

Subaru Legacy Intermediate

Ratings—10 Best, 1 Worst

Combo Crash Tests	7
Safety Features	3
Rollover	9
Preventive Maintenance	2
Repair Costs	9
Warranty	2
Fuel Economy	7
Complaints	6
Insurance Costs	1
OVERALL RATING	**5**

Subaru Legacy

At-a-Glance

Status/Year Series Started........ Unchanged/2010
Twins . . . . —
Body Styles . . . . .Sedan
Seating 5
Anti-Theft Device . . . Std. Pass. Immobil & Act. Alarm
Parking Index Rating . . . . Average
Where Made. . . . . .Lafayette, IN
Fuel Factor
  MPG Rating (city/hwy) Good-24/32
  Driving Range (mi.) . . . . Very Long-500
  Fuel Type. . . . . .Regular
  Annual Fuel Cost . . . . Low-$1,903
  Gas Guzzler Tax . . . . .No
  Greenhouse Gas Emissions (tons/yr.). Low-6.8
  Barrels of Oil Used per year Average-12.2

How the Competition Rates

Competitors	Rating	Pg.
Chevrolet Malibu	–	114
Ford Fusion	5	143
Mazda Mazda6	–	201

Price Range

Price Range	Retail	Markup
Base	$21,295	6%
Premium	$23,295	6%
Sport	$25,245	6%
3.6R Limited	$28,895	7%

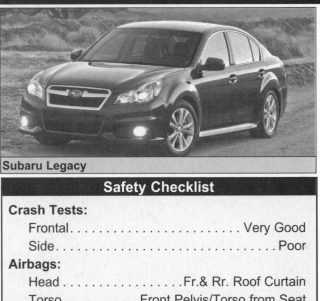

Subaru Legacy

Safety Checklist

Crash Tests:
  Frontal. . . . . Very Good
  Side. . . . . Poor
Airbags:
  Head . . . . .Fr.& Rr. Roof Curtain
  Torso. . . . . .Front Pelvis/Torso from Seat
  Pelvis . . . . .Front Pelvis/Torso from Seat
  Roll Sensing . . . . No
  Knee Bolster . . . . None
Crash Avoidance:
  Collision Avoidance. . . . . . Optional CIB & DBS
  Blind Spot Detection . . . . None
  Lane Keeping Assist . . . .Warning Only Optional
  Backup Camera . . . . Optional
  Pedestrian Crash Avoidance . . . . Optional
General:
  Auto. Crash Notification . . . . None
  Day Running Lamps . . . . Standard
Safety Belt/Restraint:
  Dynamic Head Restraints. . . . . None
  Adjustable Belt . . . . .Standard Front

Subaru Legacy

Check Surroundings Before Backing Up

Specifications

Drive. . . . . AWD
Engine 2.5-liter I4
Transmission . . . . .CVT
Tow Rating (lbs.) . . . .
Head/Leg Room (in.) Roomy-40.3/43
Interior Space (cu. ft.). Roomy-103
Cargo Space (cu. ft.) Cramped-14.7
Wheelbase/Length (in.) 108.3/187.2

Ratings—10 Best, 1 Worst

Combo Crash Tests	10
Safety Features	5
Rollover	3
Preventive Maintenance	2
Repair Costs	8
Warranty	2
Fuel Economy	7
Complaints	4
Insurance Costs	5
OVERALL RATING	**6**

Subaru Outback

Subaru Outback

At-a-Glance

Status/Year Series Started Unchanged/2010
Twins . . . . –
Body Styles . . . . Station Wagon
Seating 5
Anti-Theft Device . . . Std. Pass. Immobil & Act. Alarm
Parking Index Rating . . . . Average
Where Made. . . . . Lafayette, IN
Fuel Factor
  MPG Rating (city/hwy) Good-24/30
  Driving Range (mi.) . . . . Very Long-488
  Fuel Type . . . . Regular
  Annual Fuel Cost . . . . Low-$1,951
  Gas Guzzler Tax . . . . .No
  Greenhouse Gas Emissions (tons/yr.) Low-7.0
  Barrels of Oil Used per year Average-12.7

How the Competition Rates

Competitors	Rating	Pg.
BMW 3 Series	10	92
Toyota Venza	4	258
Volkswagen Jetta	6	263

Price Range

Price Range	Retail	Markup
Base	$24,495	6%
Premium	$26,795	6%
Limited	$29,095	7%
3.6R Limited	$32,095	7%

Safety Checklist

Crash Tests:
  Frontal. . . . . Very Good
  Side . . . . Very Good
Airbags:
  Head . . . . .Fr.& Rr. Roof Curtain
  Torso. . . . . .Front Pelvis/Torso from Seat
  Pelvis . . . . .Front Pelvis/Torso from Seat
  Roll Sensing . . . . .Yes
  Knee Bolster . . . . None
Crash Avoidance:
  Collision Avoidance. . . . . . Optional CIB & DBS
  Blind Spot Detection . . . . None
  Lane Keeping Assist. . . .Warning Only Optional
  Backup Camera . . . . Optional
  Pedestrian Crash Avoidance . . . . Optional
General:
  Auto. Crash Notification . . . . None
  Day Running Lamps . . . . Standard
Safety Belt/Restraint:
  Dynamic Head Restraints . . . . None
  Adjustable Belt . . . . .Standard Front

Subaru Outback

Specifications

Drive. . . . . AWD
Engine 2.5-liter I4
Transmission . . . . .CVT
Tow Rating (lbs.) . . . .
Head/Leg Room (in.) Roomy-40.8/43
Interior Space (cu. ft.). Roomy-105.4
Cargo Space (cu. ft.) . . . . Very Roomy-34.3
Wheelbase/Length (in.) 107.9/189

Ratings—10 Best, 1 Worst

Combo Crash Tests	–
Safety Features	5
Rollover	3
Preventive Maintenance	2
Repair Costs	8
Warranty	2
Fuel Economy	1
Complaints	7
Insurance Costs	8
OVERALL RATING	**–**

Subaru Tribeca

At-a-Glance

Status/Year Series Started	Unchanged/2006
Twins	–
Body Styles	SUV
Seating	7
Anti-Theft Device	Std. Pass. Immobil & Act. Alarm
Parking Index Rating	Average
Where Made	Lafayette, IN
Fuel Factor	
MPG Rating (city/hwy)	Very Poor-16/21
Driving Range (mi.)	Very Short-303
Fuel Type	Regular
Annual Fuel Cost	Very High-$2,871
Gas Guzzler Tax	No
Greenhouse Gas Emissions (tons/yr.)	Very High-10.2
Barrels of Oil Used per year	Very High-18.3

How the Competition Rates

Competitors	Rating	Pg.
Honda Pilot	2	153
Nissan Pathfinder	3	223
Toyota Highlander	–	249

Price Range

	Retail	Markup
Limited	$34,095	7%
Limited w/RES & Nav	$38,095	7%

Subaru Tribeca

Safety Checklist

Crash Tests:
Frontal . . . .
Side . . . .

Airbags:
Head . . . . .Fr.& Rr. Roof Curtain
Torso. . . . . .Front Pelvis/Torso from Seat
Pelvis . . . . .Front Pelvis/Torso from Seat
Roll Sensing . . . . .Yes
Knee Bolster . . . . None

Crash Avoidance:
Collision Avoidance. . . . . None
Blind Spot Detection . . . . None
Lane Keeping Assist. . . . . None
Backup Camera . . . . Standard
Pedestrian Crash Avoidance . . . . None

General:
Auto. Crash Notification . . . . None
Day Running Lamps . . . . Standard

Safety Belt/Restraint:
Dynamic Head Restraints . . . . . .Standard Front
Adjustable Belt . . . . Standard Front & Rear

Subaru Tribeca

Specifications

Drive	AWD
Engine	3.6-liter V6
Transmission	5-sp. Automatic
Tow Rating (lbs.)	Very Low-2000
Head/Leg Room (in.)	Cramped-38.9/42.3
Interior Space (cu. ft.)	Very Roomy-141.8
Cargo Space (cu. ft.)	Very Cramped-8.3
Wheelbase/Length (in.)	108.2/191.5

Subaru XV Crosstrek   Compact

Ratings—10 Best, 1 Worst

Combo Crash Tests	–
Safety Features	4
Rollover	4
Preventive Maintenance	3
Repair Costs	7
Warranty	2
Fuel Economy	8
Complaints	–
Insurance Costs	5
OVERALL RATING	**–**

Subaru XV Crosstrek

Subaru XV Crosstrek

At-a-Glance

Status/Year Series Started	Unchanged/2013
Twins	–
Body Styles	Station Wagon
Seating	5
Anti-Theft Device	Std. Pass. Immobil & Act. Alarm
Parking Index Rating	Easy
Where Made	Gunma, Japan
Fuel Factor	
MPG Rating (city/hwy)	Good-25/33
Driving Range (mi.)	Long-446
Fuel Type	Regular
Annual Fuel Cost	Low-$1,833
Gas Guzzler Tax	No
Greenhouse Gas Emissions (tons/yr.)	Low-6.5
Barrels of Oil Used per year	Average-11.8

How the Competition Rates

Competitors	Rating	Pg.
Hyundai Tucson	4	162
Jeep Compass	5	173
Toyota RAV4	5	253

Price Range

	Retail	Markup
Premium Manual	$21,995	5%
Premium AT	$22,995	6%
Limited	$24,495	6%
Limited w/Moon & Nav	$26,595	6%

Safety Checklist

Crash Tests:
- Frontal . . . .
- Side . . . .

Airbags:
- Head . . . . .Fr.& Rr. Roof Curtain
- Torso . . . . .Front Pelvis/Torso from Seat
- Pelvis . . . . .Front Pelvis/Torso from Seat
- Roll Sensing . . . . .Yes
- Knee Bolster . . . . Standard

Crash Avoidance:
- Collision Avoidance. . . . . None
- Blind Spot Detection . . . . None
- Lane Keeping Assist. . . . . None
- Backup Camera . . . . Optional
- Pedestrian Crash Avoidance . . . . None

General:
- Auto. Crash Notification . . . . None
- Day Running Lamps . . . . Standard

Safety Belt/Restraint:
- Dynamic Head Restraints. . . . . None
- Adjustable Belt . . . . .Standard Front

Subaru XV Crosstrek

Specifications

Drive	AWD
Engine	2.0-liter I4
Transmission	CVT
Tow Rating (lbs.)	
Head/Leg Room (in.)	Roomy-39.8/43.5
Interior Space (cu. ft.)	Average-97.5
Cargo Space (cu. ft.)	Average-22.3
Wheelbase/Length (in.)	103.7/175.2

Ratings—10 Best, 1 Worst

Combo Crash Tests	–
Safety Features	6
Rollover	1
Preventive Maintenance	9
Repair Costs	3
Warranty	2
Fuel Economy	2
Complaints	9
Insurance Costs	8

OVERALL RATING — –

Toyota 4Runner

Toyota 4Runner

At-a-Glance

Status/Year Series Started Appearance Change/2006
Twins . . . . Lexus GX
Body Styles . . . . SUV
Seating 5/7
Anti-Theft Device . . . Std. Pass. Immobil. & Opt. Pass. Alarm
Parking Index Rating . . . . Average
Where Made . . . . Tahara, Japan
Fuel Factor
  MPG Rating (city/hwy) . . . . Very Poor-17/21
  Driving Range (mi.) Long-428
  Fuel Type . . . . .Regular
  Annual Fuel Cost . . . . Very High-$2,767
  Gas Guzzler Tax . . . . .No
  Greenhouse Gas Emissions (tons/yr.)Very High-10.2
  Barrels of Oil Used per year . . . . Very High-18.3

How the Competition Rates

Competitors	Rating	Pg.
Chevrolet Tahoe	7	119
Ford Expedition	2	137
Nissan Armada	–	217

Price Range

Price Range	Retail	Markup
SR5 2WD	$32,820	9%
SR5 Premium 4WD	$37,615	9%
Trail Edition Premium	$38,645	9%
Limited 4WD	$43,400	9%

Safety Checklist

Crash Tests:
  Frontal . . . .
  Side . . . .
Airbags:
  Head . . . . Fr. & Rr. Roof Curtain
  Torso . . . . Front Pelvis/Torso from Seat
  Pelvis . . . . Front Pelvis/Torso from Seat
  Roll Sensing . . . . .Yes
  Knee Bolster . . . . Standard
Crash Avoidance:
  Collision Avoidance . . . . None
  Blind Spot Detection . . . . None
  Lane Keeping Assist . . . . None
  Backup Camera . . . . Standard
  Pedestrian Crash Avoidance . . . . None
General:
  Auto. Crash Notification . . Operator Assist.-Fee
  Day Running Lamps . . . . Standard
Safety Belt/Restraint:
  Dynamic Head Restraints . . . . . .Standard Front
  Adjustable Belt . . . . .Standard Front

Toyota 4Runner

Specifications

Drive 4WD
Engine 4.0-liter V6
Transmission . . . . .5-sp. Automatic
Tow Rating (lbs.) Low-4700
Head/Leg Room (in.) Cramped-39.3/41.7
Interior Space (cu. ft.) Cramped-97.3
Cargo Space (cu. ft.) . . . . . Very Roomy-47.2
Wheelbase/Length (in.) 109.8/190.2

Ratings—10 Best, 1 Worst

Combo Crash Tests	7
Safety Features	7
Rollover	8
Preventive Maintenance	10
Repair Costs	3
Warranty	2
Fuel Economy	5
Complaints	2
Insurance Costs	8
OVERALL RATING	**7**

Toyota Avalon

Toyota Avalon

At-a-Glance

Status/Year Series Started. Unchanged/2013
Twins . . . . –
Body Styles . . . . Sedan
Seating 5
Anti-Theft Device . . . . Std. Pass. Immobil.
Parking Index Rating . . . . Hard
Where Made. . . . . Georgetown, KY
Fuel Factor
  MPG Rating (city/hwy) Average-21/31
  Driving Range (mi.) Average-418
  Fuel Type . . . . Regular
  Annual Fuel Cost . . . . Average-$2,094
  Gas Guzzler Tax . . . . No
  Greenhouse Gas Emissions (tons/yr.) Low-7.3
  Barrels of Oil Used per year Average-13.2

How the Competition Rates

Competitors	Rating	Pg.
Cadillac XTS	10	108
Chevrolet Impala	8	113
Kia Cadenza	–	177

Price Range

	Retail	Markup
XLE	$31,340	11%
XLE Touring	$35,000	11%
Limited	$39,650	11%
Limited Hybrid	$41,400	11%

Safety Checklist

Crash Tests:
  Frontal. . . . . Average
  Side. . . . . Good
Airbags:
  Head . . . . .Fr.& Rr. Roof Curtain
  Torso. . . . . Fr. & Rr. Pelvis/Torso from Seat
  Pelvis . . . . Fr. & Rr. Pelvis/Torso from Seat
  Roll Sensing . . . . No
  Knee Bolster . . . . Standard
Crash Avoidance:
  Collision Avoidance. . . . . . Optional CIB & DBS
  Blind Spot Detection . . . . Optional
  Lane Keeping Assist. . . . . None
  Backup Camera . . . . Standard
  Pedestrian Crash Avoidance . . . . None
General:
  Auto. Crash Notification . . Operator Assist.-Fee
  Day Running Lamps . . . . Standard
Safety Belt/Restraint:
  Dynamic Head Restraints . . . . None
  Adjustable Belt . . . . .Standard Front

Toyota Avalon

Specifications

Drive. . . . . FWD
Engine 3.5-liter V6
Transmission . . . . .6-sp. Automatic
Tow Rating (lbs.) . . . . Very Low-1000
Head/Leg Room (in.) Cramped-38.5/42.1
Interior Space (cu. ft.). Roomy-103.6
Cargo Space (cu. ft.) Cramped-16
Wheelbase/Length (in.) 111/195.2

Toyota Camry   Intermediate

Ratings—10 Best, 1 Worst

Combo Crash Tests	5
Safety Features	5
Rollover	8
Preventive Maintenance	9
Repair Costs	4
Warranty	2
Fuel Economy	8
Complaints	7
Insurance Costs	3
OVERALL RATING	**6**

Toyota Camry

Toyota Camry

At-a-Glance

Status/Year Series Started. Unchanged/2012
Twins . . . . —
Body Styles . . . . Sedan
Seating 5
Anti-Theft Device . . . Std. Pass. Immobil. & Opt. Pass. Alarm
Parking Index Rating . . . . Average
Where Made. . . . . Georgetown, KY
Fuel Factor
  MPG Rating (city/hwy). Good-25/35
  Driving Range (mi.) . . . . Very Long-488
  Fuel Type. . . . . Regular
  Annual Fuel Cost . . . . Low-$1,793
  Gas Guzzler Tax . . . . No
  Greenhouse Gas Emissions (tons/yr.). Low-6.5
  Barrels of Oil Used per year Average-11.8

How the Competition Rates

Competitors	Rating	Pg.
Chevrolet Malibu	—	114
Ford Fusion	5	143
Honda Accord	7	147

Price Range

	Retail	Markup
L	$22,235	9%
SE Sport	$25,090	10%
Hybrid XLE	$27,670	9%
XLE V6	$30,465	10%

Safety Checklist

Crash Tests:
  Frontal. . . . . Average
  Side. . . . . Average
Airbags:
  Head . . . . Fr.& Rr. Roof Curtain
  Torso. . . . . Fr. & Rr. Pelvis/Torso from Seat
  Pelvis . . . . Fr. & Rr. Pelvis/Torso from Seat
  Roll Sensing . . . . No
  Knee Bolster . . . . Standard
Crash Avoidance:
  Collision Avoidance. . . . . None
  Blind Spot Detection . . . . Optional
  Lane Keeping Assist. . . . . None
  Backup Camera . . . . Standard
  Pedestrian Crash Avoidance . . . . None
General:
  Auto. Crash Notification . . Operator Assist.-Fee
  Day Running Lamps . . . . Standard
Safety Belt/Restraint:
  Dynamic Head Restraints. . . . . None
  Adjustable Belt . . . . Standard Front

Toyota Camry

Specifications

Drive. . . . . FWD
Engine 2.5-liter I4
Transmission . . . . 6-sp. Automatic
Tow Rating (lbs.) . . . .
Head/Leg Room (in.) Cramped-38.8/41.6
Interior Space (cu. ft.). Average-102.7
Cargo Space (cu. ft.) Cramped-15.4
Wheelbase/Length (in.) 109.3/189.2

Toyota Corolla | Compact

Ratings—10 Best, 1 Worst

Combo Crash Tests	8
Safety Features	2
Rollover	7
Preventive Maintenance	10
Repair Costs	8
Warranty	2
Fuel Economy	9
Complaints	–
Insurance Costs	1
OVERALL RATING	**7**

Toyota Corolla

Toyota Corolla

At-a-Glance

Status/Year Series Started	All New/2014
Twins	–
Body Styles	Sedan
Seating	5
Anti-Theft Device	Std. Pass. Immobil.
Parking Index Rating	Easy
Where Made	Blue Springs, MS
Fuel Factor	
MPG Rating (city/hwy)	Very Good-27/36
Driving Range (mi.)	Average-402
Fuel Type	Regular
Annual Fuel Cost	Very Low-$1,691
Gas Guzzler Tax	No
Greenhouse Gas Emissions (tons/yr.)	Very Low-5.9
Barrels of Oil Used per year	Low-10.6

How the Competition Rates

Competitors	Rating	Pg.
Honda Civic	6	148
Mazda Mazda3	–	199
Volkswagen Jetta	6	263

Price Range	Retail	Markup
L Manual	$16,800	6%
LE Plus	$18,700	8%
S Plus	$19,700	8%
S Premium	$20,400	8%

Safety Checklist

Crash Tests:
Frontal . . . . Good
Side . . . . Very Good

Airbags:
Head . . . . Fr.& Rr. Roof Curtain
Torso . . . . Front Pelvis/Torso from Seat
Pelvis . . . . Front Pelvis/Torso from Seat
Roll Sensing . . . . No
Knee Bolster . . . . Standard

Crash Avoidance:
Collision Avoidance . . . . None
Blind Spot Detection . . . . None
Lane Keeping Assist . . . . None
Backup Camera . . . . Optional
Pedestrian Crash Avoidance . . . . None

General:
Auto. Crash Notification . . . . None
Day Running Lamps . . . . Standard

Safety Belt/Restraint:
Dynamic Head Restraints . . . . None
Adjustable Belt . . . . Standard Front

Toyota Corolla

Specifications

Drive	FWD
Engine	1.8-liter I4
Transmission	4-sp. Automatic
Tow Rating (lbs.)	
Head/Leg Room (in.)	Cramped-38.3/42.3
Interior Space (cu. ft.)	Average-97.5
Cargo Space (cu. ft.)	Cramped-13
Wheelbase/Length (in.)	106.3/182.6

Toyota FJ Cruiser

Mid-Size SUV

Ratings—10 Best, 1 Worst

Combo Crash Tests	–
Safety Features	3
Rollover	1
Preventive Maintenance	9
Repair Costs	5
Warranty	2
Fuel Economy	2
Complaints	2
Insurance Costs	3
OVERALL RATING	**–**

Toyota FJ Cruiser

Toyota FJ Cruiser

At-a-Glance

Status/Year Series Started........ Unchanged/2007
Twins . . . . –
Body Styles . . . . SUV
Seating 5
Anti-Theft Device . . . . Std. Pass. Immobil
Parking Index Rating . . . . Hard
Where Made. . . . . Kyushu, Japan
Fuel Factor
  MPG Rating (city/hwy). . . . . .Very Poor-17/20
  Driving Range (mi.) . . . . .Very Short-346
  Fuel Type. . . . . .Regular
  Annual Fuel Cost . . . . Very High-$2,822
  Gas Guzzler Tax . . . . .No
  Greenhouse Gas Emissions (tons/yr.)Very High-10.2
  Barrels of Oil Used per year . . . . . . .Very High-18.3

How the Competition Rates

Competitors	Rating	Pg.
Jeep Wrangler	–	176
Nissan Xterra	–	229
Volkswagen Touareg	–	266

Price Range

Price Range	Retail	Markup
2WD AT	$27,130	8%
4WD Manual	$28,310	8%
4WD AT	$28,720	8%

Safety Checklist

Crash Tests:
  Frontal. . . . .
  Side. . . . .
Airbags:
  Head . . . . .Fr.& Rr. Roof Curtain
  Torso. . . . . Front Tosro from Seat
  Pelvis . . . . None
  Roll Sensing . . . . .Yes
  Knee Bolster . . . . None
Crash Avoidance:
  Collision Avoidance. . . . . None
  Blind Spot Detection . . . . None
  Lane Keeping Assist. . . . . None
  Backup Camera . . . . Standard
  Pedestrian Crash Avoidance . . . . None
General:
  Auto. Crash Notification . . . . None
  Day Running Lamps. . . . . Standard
Safety Belt/Restraint:
  Dynamic Head Restraints. . . . . .Standard Front
  Adjustable Belt . . . . .Standard Front

Specifications

Drive. 4WD
Engine 4.0-liter V6
Transmission . . . . .5-sp. Automatic
Tow Rating (lbs.) Low-4700
Head/Leg Room (in.) Roomy-41.3/41.9
Interior Space (cu. ft.). . . . .
Cargo Space (cu. ft.) Roomy-27.9
Wheelbase/Length (in.) 105.9/183.9

Ratings—10 Best, 1 Worst

Combo Crash Tests	–
Safety Features	8
Rollover	3
Preventive Maintenance	9
Repair Costs	2
Warranty	2
Fuel Economy	3
Complaints	–
Insurance Costs	8
OVERALL RATING	**–**

Toyota Highlander

Toyota Highlander

At-a-Glance

Status/Year Series Started	All New/2014
Twins	–
Body Styles	SUV
Seating	7/8
Anti-Theft Device	Std. Pass. Immobil. & Opt. Pass. Alarm
Parking Index Rating	Hard
Where Made	Princeton, IN
Fuel Factor	
MPG Rating (city/hwy)	Poor-18/24
Driving Range (mi.)	Short-389
Fuel Type	Regular
Annual Fuel Cost	High-$2,537
Gas Guzzler Tax	No
Greenhouse Gas Emissions (tons/yr.)	High-9.1
Barrels of Oil Used per year	High-16.5

How the Competition Rates

Competitors	Rating	Pg.
Buick Enclave	7	100
Chevrolet Traverse	9	120
Nissan Pathfinder	3	223

Price Range	Retail	Markup
Base 2WD I4	$28,870	10%
Plus 4WD	$33,150	10%
Limited 4WD	$39,250	10%
Limited Hybrid	$46,370	9%

Safety Checklist

Crash Tests:
Frontal . . . .
Side . . . .

Airbags:
Head . . . . Fr.& Rr. Roof Curtain
Torso . . . . Front Pelvis/Torso from Seat
Pelvis . . . . Front Pelvis/Torso from Seat
Roll Sensing . . . . .Yes
Knee Bolster . . . . Standard

Crash Avoidance:
Collision Avoidance . . . . . . Optional CIB & DBS
Blind Spot Detection . . . . Optional
Lane Keeping Assist . . . .Warning Only Optional
Backup Camera . . . . Standard
Pedestrian Crash Avoidance . . . . None

General:
Auto. Crash Notification . . Operator Assist.-Fee
Day Running Lamps . . . . Standard

Safety Belt/Restraint:
Dynamic Head Restraints . . . . None
Adjustable Belt . . . . .Standard Front

Toyota Highlander

Specifications

Drive	AWD
Engine	3.5-liter V6
Transmission	6-sp. Automatic
Tow Rating (lbs.)	Very Low-2000
Head/Leg Room (in.)	Very Roomy-40.7/44.2
Interior Space (cu. ft.)	Very Roomy-145
Cargo Space (cu. ft.)	Cramped-13.8
Wheelbase/Length (in.)	109.8/191.1

Ratings—10 Best, 1 Worst	
Combo Crash Tests	4
Safety Features	5
Rollover	6
Preventive Maintenance	10
Repair Costs	6
Warranty	2
Fuel Economy	10
Complaints	1
Insurance Costs	3
OVERALL RATING	**5**

Toyota Prius

Toyota Prius

At-a-Glance

Status/Year Series Started	Unchanged/2010
Twins	–
Body Styles	Hatchback
Seating	5
Anti-Theft Device	Std. Pass. Immobil.
Parking Index Rating	Very Easy
Where Made	Toyota City, Japan
Fuel Factor	
MPG Rating (city/hwy)	Very Good-51/48
Driving Range (mi.)	Very Long-590
Fuel Type	Regular
Annual Fuel Cost	Very Low-$1,037
Gas Guzzler Tax	No
Greenhouse Gas Emissions (tons/yr.)	Very Low-3.7
Barrels of Oil Used per year	Very Low-6.6

How the Competition Rates

Competitors	Rating	Pg.
Chevrolet Volt	9	121
Ford C-MAX	4	134
Honda Insight	–	151

Price Range	Retail	Markup
One	$23,215	5%
Three	$25,765	7%
Five	$30,005	7%
Plug-In Hybrid Adv	$39,525	4%

Safety Checklist

Crash Tests:
Frontal .... Poor
Side .... Good
Airbags:
Head .... Fr.& Rr. Roof Curtain
Torso .... Front Tosro from Seat
Pelvis .... None
Roll Sensing .... No
Knee Bolster .... Standard
Crash Avoidance:
Collision Avoidance ...... Optional CIB & DBS
Blind Spot Detection .... None
Lane Keeping Assist .... Optional
Backup Camera .... Optional
Pedestrian Crash Avoidance .... None
General:
Auto. Crash Notification .. Operator Assist.-Fee
Day Running Lamps .... Standard
Safety Belt/Restraint:
Dynamic Head Restraints ...... Standard Front
Adjustable Belt .... Standard Front

Toyota Prius

Specifications

Drive	FWD
Engine	1.7-liter I4
Transmission	eCVT
Tow Rating (lbs.)	
Head/Leg Room (in.)	Cramped-38.6/42.5
Interior Space (cu. ft.)	Cramped-93.7
Cargo Space (cu. ft.)	Average-21.6
Wheelbase/Length (in.)	106.3/176.4

Toyota Prius C

Ratings—10 Best, 1 Worst

Category	Rating
Combo Crash Tests	2
Safety Features	1
Rollover	7
Preventive Maintenance	9
Repair Costs	8
Warranty	2
Fuel Economy	10
Complaints	10
Insurance Costs	3
OVERALL RATING	**6**

Toyota Prius C

At-a-Glance

Status/Year Series Started. Unchanged/2013
Twins . . . . –
Body Styles . . . . Hatchback
Seating. 5
Anti-Theft Device . . . . Std. Pass. Immobil.
Parking Index Rating . . . . .Very Easy
Where Made. . . . . Toyota City, Japan
Fuel Factor
  MPG Rating (city/hwy) . . . . Very Good-53/46
  Driving Range (mi.) . . . . Very Long-471
  Fuel Type . . . . .Regular
  Annual Fuel Cost . . . . Very Low-$1,037
  Gas Guzzler Tax . . . . .No
  Greenhouse Gas Emissions (tons/yr.). Very Low-3.6
  Barrels of Oil Used per year . . . . Very Low-6.6

How the Competition Rates

Competitors	Rating	Pg.
Ford C-MAX	4	134
Honda Insight	–	151
Nissan Leaf	4	220

Price Range

Price Range	Retail	Markup
One	$19,080	5%
Two	$20,030	6%
Three	$21,765	7%
Four	$23,360	7%

Safety Checklist

Crash Tests:
  Frontal. . . . . .Poor
  Side. . . . . Very Poor*
Airbags:
  Head . . . . .Fr.& Rr. Roof Curtain
  Torso. . . . . .Front Pelvis/Torso from Seat
  Pelvis . . . . .Front Pelvis/Torso from Seat
  Roll Sensing . . . . No
  Knee Bolster . . . . Standard
Crash Avoidance:
  Collision Avoidance. . . . . None
  Blind Spot Detection . . . . None
  Lane Keeping Assist. . . . . None
  Backup Camera . . . . None
  Pedestrian Crash Avoidance . . . . None
General:
  Auto. Crash Notification . . . . None
  Day Running Lamps . . . . Standard
Safety Belt/Restraint:
  Dynamic Head Restraints. . . . . None
  Adjustable Belt . . . . None

Toyota Prius C

Specifications

Drive. . . . . FWD
Engine 1.5-liter I4
Transmission . . . . .CVT
Tow Rating (lbs.) . . . .
Head/Leg Room (in.) Cramped-38.6/41.7
Interior Space (cu. ft.). . . . . Very Cramped-87
Cargo Space (cu. ft.) Average-17
Wheelbase/Length (in.) 100.4/157.3

*Additional injury potential in side test. See footnote on page 20.

Ratings—10 Best, 1 Worst

Combo Crash Tests	7
Safety Features	4
Rollover	5
Preventive Maintenance	10
Repair Costs	5
Warranty	2
Fuel Economy	10
Complaints	–
Insurance Costs	5
OVERALL RATING	**7**

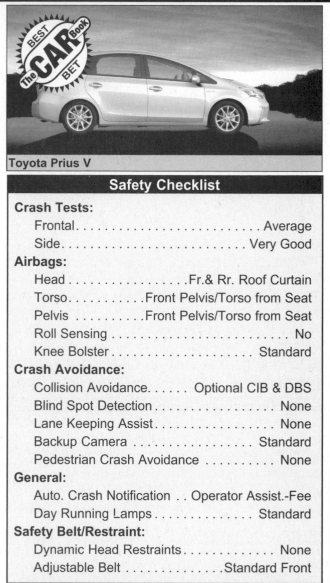

Toyota Prius V

At-a-Glance

Status/Year Series Started........ Unchanged/2013
Twins . . . .–
Body Styles . . . . Hatchback
Seating 5
Anti-Theft Device . . . . .Std. Pass. Immobil
Parking Index Rating . . . . Easy
Where Made. . . . . .Toyota City, Japan
Fuel Factor
  MPG Rating (city/hwy) . . . . Very Good-44/40
  Driving Range (mi.) . . . . .Very Long–501
  Fuel Type. . . . . .Regular
  Annual Fuel Cost . . . . Very Low-$1,222
  Gas Guzzler Tax . . . . .No
  Greenhouse Gas Emissions (tons/yr.). Very Low-4.4
  Barrels of Oil Used per year . . . . Very Low-7.8

How the Competition Rates

Competitors	Rating	Pg.
Ford C-MAX	4	134
Honda Insight	–	151
Mazda Mazda5	–	200

Price Range

	Retail	Markup
Two	$26,750	7%
Three	$27,515	7%
Five	$30,395	7%

Toyota Prius V

Safety Checklist

Crash Tests:
  Frontal. . . . . Average
  Side. . . . . Very Good
Airbags:
  Head . . . . .Fr.& Rr. Roof Curtain
  Torso. . . . . .Front Pelvis/Torso from Seat
  Pelvis . . . . .Front Pelvis/Torso from Seat
  Roll Sensing . . . . No
  Knee Bolster . . . . Standard
Crash Avoidance:
  Collision Avoidance. . . . . . Optional CIB & DBS
  Blind Spot Detection . . . . None
  Lane Keeping Assist. . . . . None
  Backup Camera . . . . Standard
  Pedestrian Crash Avoidance . . . . None
General:
  Auto. Crash Notification . . Operator Assist.-Fee
  Day Running Lamps . . . . Standard
Safety Belt/Restraint:
  Dynamic Head Restraints. . . . . None
  Adjustable Belt . . . . .Standard Front

Toyota Prius V

Specifications

Drive. . . . . FWD
Engine 1.8-liter I4
Transmission . . . . .CVT
Tow Rating (lbs.) . . . .
Head/Leg Room (in.) Average-40/41.3
Interior Space (cu. ft.). Cramped-97
Cargo Space (cu. ft.) . . . . .Very Roomy-34
Wheelbase/Length (in.) 109.4/181.7

Toyota RAV4 | Small SUV

Toyota RAV4

Ratings—10 Best, 1 Worst

Combo Crash Tests	4
Safety Features	5
Rollover	4
Preventive Maintenance	10
Repair Costs	4
Warranty	2
Fuel Economy	6
Complaints	6
Insurance Costs	8
OVERALL RATING	**5**

Toyota RAV4

Safety Checklist

Crash Tests:
Frontal.........................Very Poor
Side...............................Good
Airbags:
Head.................Fr.& Rr. Roof Curtain
Torso..........Front Pelvis/Torso from Seat
Pelvis..........Front Pelvis/Torso from Seat
Roll Sensing..........................Yes
Knee Bolster....................Standard
Crash Avoidance:
Collision Avoidance..................None
Blind Spot Detection...............Optional
Lane Keeping Assist.................None
Backup Camera....................Standard
Pedestrian Crash Avoidance..........None
General:
Auto. Crash Notification.............None
Day Running Lamps...............Standard
Safety Belt/Restraint:
Dynamic Head Restraints............None
Adjustable Belt...............Standard Front

At-a-Glance

Status/Year Series Started........Unchanged/2013
Twins.......................................–
Body Styles................................SUV
Seating......................................5
Anti-Theft Device.............Std. Pass. Immobil
Parking Index Rating.....................Easy
Where Made....Woodstock, Ontario / Tahara, Japan
Fuel Factor
  MPG Rating (city/hwy)............Average-22/29
  Driving Range (mi.).............Short-392
  Fuel Type.......................Regular
  Annual Fuel Cost............Average-$2,085
  Gas Guzzler Tax.......................No
  Greenhouse Gas Emissions (tons/yr.).......Low-7
  Barrels of Oil Used per year........Average-12.7

Toyota RAV4

How the Competition Rates

Competitors	Rating	Pg.
Ford Escape	5	136
Honda CR-V	6	150
Hyundai Tucson	4	162

Specifications

Drive...................................AWD
Engine............................2.5-liter I4
Transmission.................6-sp. Automatic
Tow Rating (lbs.)..............Very Low-1500
Head/Leg Room (in.)......Average-39.8/42.6
Interior Space (cu. ft.)......Average-101.9
Cargo Space (cu. ft.)......Very Roomy-38.4
Wheelbase/Length (in.)..........104.7/179.9

Price Range	Retail	Markup
LE 2WD	$23,300	7%
XLE 2WD	$24,290	7%
XLE AWD	$25,690	7%
Limited AWD	$28,410	7%

Ratings—10 Best, 1 Worst

Combo Crash Tests	–
Safety Features	4
Rollover	3
Preventive Maintenance	8
Repair Costs	3
Warranty	2
Fuel Economy	1
Complaints	8
Insurance Costs	10
OVERALL RATING	**–**

Toyota Sequoia

Toyota Sequoia

At-a-Glance

Status/Year Series Started........ Unchanged/2008
Twins . . . . –
Body Styles . . . . SUV
Seating 8
Anti-Theft Device . . . . . . Std. Pass. Immobil. & Alarm
Parking Index Rating . . . . Very Hard
Where Made. . . . . Princeton, IN
Fuel Factor
  MPG Rating (city/hwy) . . . . . .Very Poor-13/17
  Driving Range (mi.) Short-384
  Fuel Type. .Regular
  Annual Fuel Cost . . . . Very High-$3,539
  Gas Guzzler Tax . . . . .No
  Greenhouse Gas Emissions (tons/yr.)Very High-13.1
  Barrels of Oil Used per year . . . . . . .Very High-23.5

How the Competition Rates

Competitors	Rating	Pg.
Chevrolet Tahoe	7	119
Dodge Durango	7	129
Nissan Armada	–	217

Price Range

	Retail	Markup
SR5 2WD	$43,595	10%
SR5 4WD	$46,820	10%
Limited 4WD	$55,780	10%
Premium 4WD	$63,520	10%

Safety Checklist

Crash Tests:
  Frontal. . . . .
  Side. . . . .
Airbags:
  Head . . . . .Fr.& Rr. Roof Curtain
  Torso. . . . . Front Torso from Seat
  Pelvis . . . . None
  Roll Sensing .Yes
  Knee Bolster . . . . Standard
Crash Avoidance:
  Collision Avoidance. . . . . None
  Blind Spot Detection . . . . Optional
  Lane Keeping Assist. . . . . None
  Backup Camera . . . . Standard
  Pedestrian Crash Avoidance . . . . None
General:
  Auto. Crash Notification . . . . None
  Day Running Lamps . . . . Standard
Safety Belt/Restraint:
  Dynamic Head Restraints. . . . . None
  Adjustable Belt . . . . Standard Front & Rear

Toyota Sequoia

Specifications

Drive. 4WD
Engine 5.7-liter V8
Transmission . . . . .6-sp. Automatic
Tow Rating (lbs.) Average-7100
Head/Leg Room (in.) . . . . .Very Cramped-34.8/42.5
Interior Space (cu. ft.). . . . .
Cargo Space (cu. ft.) Average-18.9
Wheelbase/Length (in.) 122/205.1

Ratings—10 Best, 1 Worst

Combo Crash Tests	5
Safety Features	6
Rollover	5
Preventive Maintenance	7
Repair Costs	2
Warranty	2
Fuel Economy	3
Complaints	3
Insurance Costs	5
OVERALL RATING	**2**

Toyota Sienna

Toyota Sienna

At-a-Glance

Status/Year Series Started	Unchanged/2004
Twins	–
Body Styles	Minivan
Seating	7/8
Anti-Theft Device	Std. Pass. Immobil. & Alarm
Parking Index Rating	Hard
Where Made	Princeton, IN
Fuel Factor	
MPG Rating (city/hwy)	Poor-18/25
Driving Range (mi.)	Average-412
Fuel Type	Regular
Annual Fuel Cost	High-$2,498
Gas Guzzler Tax	No
Greenhouse Gas Emissions (tons/yr.)	Average-7.7
Barrels of Oil Used per year	High-15.7

How the Competition Rates

Competitors	Rating	Pg.
Dodge Grand Caravan	6	130
Honda Odyssey	–	152
Toyota Sienna	2	255

Price Range	Retail	Markup
L	$26,920	8%
LE AWD	$32,920	8%
XLE AWD	$36,185	9%
Limited FWD	$40,240	9%

Safety Checklist

Crash Tests:
Frontal	Poor
Side	Good

Airbags:
Head	Fr.& Rr. Roof Curtain
Torso	Front Pelvis/Torso from Seat
Pelvis	Front Pelvis/Torso from Seat
Roll Sensing	No
Knee Bolster	Standard

Crash Avoidance:
Collision Avoidance	Optional CIB & DBS
Blind Spot Detection	Optional
Lane Keeping Assist	None
Backup Camera	Optional
Pedestrian Crash Avoidance	None

General:
Auto. Crash Notification	Operator Assist.-Fee
Day Running Lamps	Standard

Safety Belt/Restraint:
Dynamic Head Restraints	Standard Front
Adjustable Belt	Standard Front & Rear

Specifications

Drive	FWD
Engine	3.5-liter V6
Transmission	6-sp. Automatic
Tow Rating (lbs.)	Very Low-3500
Head/Leg Room (in.)	Average-41/40.5
Interior Space (cu. ft.)	Very Roomy-164.4
Cargo Space (cu. ft.)	Very Roomy-39.1
Wheelbase/Length (in.)	119.3/200.2

Toyota Tacoma   Compact Pickup

Ratings—10 Best, 1 Worst

Combo Crash Tests	1
Safety Features	3
Rollover	3
Preventive Maintenance	9
Repair Costs	5
Warranty	2
Fuel Economy	1
Complaints	7
Insurance Costs	5
OVERALL RATING	**1**

Toyota Tacoma

Toyota Tacoma

At-a-Glance

Status/Year Series Started........ Unchanged/2009
Twins . . . . –
Body Styles . . . . Pickup
Seating 4
Anti-Theft Device . . . . Opt. Pass. Immobil.
Parking Index Rating . . . . .Very Hard
Where Made. . . . . .San Antonio, TX
Fuel Factor
  MPG Rating (city/hwy) . . . . .Very Poor-16/21
  Driving Range (mi.) Short-378
  Fuel Type. . . . . .Regular
  Annual Fuel Cost . . . . Very High-$2,871
  Gas Guzzler Tax . . . . .No
  Greenhouse Gas Emissions (tons/yr.)Very High-10.2
  Barrels of Oil Used per year . . . . . . .Very High-18.3

How the Competition Rates

Competitors	Rating	Pg.
Honda Ridgeline	–	154
Nissan Frontier	–	218

Price Range

Price Range	Retail	Markup
Base RegCab 2WD Manual	$17,875	6%
Prerunner Access Cab 2WD V6 AT	$23,560	7%
Base Access Cab 4WD AT	$25,250	7%
Base Dbl Cab 4WD V6 AT	$27,785	8%

Safety Checklist

Crash Tests:
  Frontal. . . . . .Very Poor
  Side. . . . . .Very Poor
Airbags:
  Head . . . . .Fr.& Rr. Roof Curtain
  Torso. . . . . Front Tosro from Seat
  Pelvis . . . . None
  Roll Sensing . . . . .Yes
  Knee Bolster . . . . None
Crash Avoidance:
  Collision Avoidance. . . . . None
  Blind Spot Detection . . . . None
  Lane Keeping Assist. . . . . None
  Backup Camera . . . . Optional
  Pedestrian Crash Avoidance . . . . None
General:
  Auto. Crash Notification . . . . None
  Day Running Lamps . . . . Standard
Safety Belt/Restraint:
  Dynamic Head Restraints . . . . . .Standard Front
  Adjustable Belt . . . . .Standard Front

Toyota Tacoma

Specifications

Drive. 4WD
Engine 4.0-liter V6
Transmission . . . . .5-sp. Automatic
Tow Rating (lbs.) . . . . Very Low-3500
Head/Leg Room (in.) Average-40/41.7
Interior Space (cu. ft.). . . . . . . .Very Cramped-88.7
Cargo Space (cu. ft.) . . . . Very Roomy-40.9
Wheelbase/Length (in.) 127.4/208.1

Toyota Tundra
Standard Pickup

Ratings—10 Best, 1 Worst	
Combo Crash Tests	–
Safety Features	5
Rollover	2
Preventive Maintenance	8
Repair Costs	4
Warranty	2
Fuel Economy	1
Complaints	9
Insurance Costs	5
OVERALL RATING	**–**

Toyota Tundra

Toyota Tundra

At-a-Glance

Status/Year Series Started Appearance Change/2007
Twins . . . . –
Body Styles . . . . Pickup
Seating 5/6
Anti-Theft Device . . . . . . Opt. Pass. Immobil. & Alarm
Parking Index Rating . . . . .Very Easy
Where Made. . . . . .San Antonio, TX
Fuel Factor
  MPG Rating (city/hwy) . . . . .Very Poor-13/17
  Driving Range (mi.) Short-384
  Fuel Type. Regular/E85
  Annual Fuel Cost . . . . .Very High-$3,539
  Gas Guzzler Tax . . . . .No
  Greenhouse Gas Emissions (tons/yr.)Very High-12.2
  Barrels of Oil Used per year . . . . . . .Very High-22.0

How the Competition Rates

Competitors	Rating	Pg.
Ford F-150	1	139
Nissan Titan	–	227
Ram 1500	5	231

Price Range	Retail	Markup
SR Reg Cab 2WD V6	$25,920	8%
SR5 Dbl Cab 4WD V8	$34,015	8%
Limited Crew Max 4WD V8	$41,895	8%
1794 Edition Crew Max 4WD V8	$47,320	8%

Safety Checklist

Crash Tests:
  Frontal. . . . .
  Side. . . . .
Airbags:
  Head . . . . .Fr.& Rr. Roof Curtain
  Torso. . . . . .Front Pelvis/Torso from Seat
  Pelvis . . . . .Front Pelvis/Torso from Seat
  Roll Sensing . . . . .Yes
  Knee Bolster . . . . Standard
Crash Avoidance:
  Collision Avoidance. . . . . None
  Blind Spot Detection . . . . Optional
  Lane Keeping Assist. . . . . None
  Backup Camera . . . . Standard
  Pedestrian Crash Avoidance . . . . None
General:
  Auto. Crash Notification . . . . None
  Day Running Lamps . . . . Standard
Safety Belt/Restraint:
  Dynamic Head Restraints. . . . . None
  Adjustable Belt . . . . Standard Front & Rear

Toyota Tundra

Specifications

Drive. 4WD
Engine 5.7-liter V8
Transmission . . . . 6-sp. Auto w/Overdrive
Tow Rating (lbs.) . . . . .Very High-9800
Head/Leg Room (in.) Average-39.7/42.5
Interior Space (cu. ft.). . . . . .Very Roomy-131
Cargo Space (cu. ft.) . . . . Very Roomy-67.1
Wheelbase/Length (in.) 145.7/228.9

Ratings—10 Best, 1 Worst

Combo Crash Tests	6
Safety Features	2
Rollover	4
Preventive Maintenance	6
Repair Costs	3
Warranty	2
Fuel Economy	4
Complaints	7
Insurance Costs	8
OVERALL RATING	**4**

Toyota Venza

Toyota Venza

Safety Checklist

Crash Tests:
Frontal . . . . Average
Side . . . . Good

Airbags:
Head . . . . Fr.& Rr. Roof Curtain
Torso . . . . Front Torso from Seat
Pelvis . . . . None
Roll Sensing . . . . No
Knee Bolster . . . . Standard

Crash Avoidance:
Collision Avoidance . . . . None
Blind Spot Detection . . . . None
Lane Keeping Assist . . . . None
Backup Camera . . . . Optional
Pedestrian Crash Avoidance . . . . None

General:
Auto. Crash Notification . . . . None
Day Running Lamps . . . . Standard

Safety Belt/Restraint:
Dynamic Head Restraints . . . . . . Standard Front
Adjustable Belt . . . . Standard Front

At-a-Glance

Status/Year Series Started Unchanged/2009
Twins . . . . –
Body Styles . . . . SUV
Seating 5
Anti-Theft Device . . . . . . Std. Pass. Immobil. & Alarm
Parking Index Rating . . . . Very Hard
Where Made . . . . Georgetown, KY
Fuel Factor
  MPG Rating (city/hwy) Poor-20/26
  Driving Range (mi.) Average-395
  Fuel Type . . . . Regular
  Annual Fuel Cost . . . . Average-$2,305
  Gas Guzzler Tax . . . . No
  Greenhouse Gas Emissions (tons/yr.) . . Average-8.0
  Barrels of Oil Used per year High-14.3

Toyota Venza

How the Competition Rates

Competitors	Rating	Pg.
Chevrolet Equinox	3	112
Honda Pilot	2	153
Nissan Murano	3	222

Price Range	Retail	Markup
LE FWD I4	$27,950	9%
XLE FWD I4	$31,810	10%
XLE AWD V6	$35,080	10%
Limited AWD V6	$39,570	10%

Specifications

Drive . . . . FWD
Engine 2.7-liter I4
Transmission . . . . .6-sp. Automatic
Tow Rating (lbs.) . . . . Very Low-1000
Head/Leg Room (in.) . . . . . Very Cramped-39.6/40.2
Interior Space (cu. ft.) Roomy-108
Cargo Space (cu. ft.) . . . . Very Roomy-36.2
Wheelbase/Length (in.) 109.3/189

Ratings—10 Best, 1 Worst

Combo Crash Tests	3
Safety Features	1
Rollover	5
Preventive Maintenance	10
Repair Costs	10
Warranty	2
Fuel Economy	9
Complaints	10
Insurance Costs	1
OVERALL RATING	**6**

Toyota Yaris

At-a-Glance

Status/Year Series Started	Unchanged/2012
Twins	–
Body Styles	Sedan, Hatchback
Seating	5
Anti-Theft Device	Std. Pass. Immobil.
Parking Index Rating	Very Easy
Where Made	–

Fuel Factor
MPG Rating (city/hwy)	Very Good-30/36
Driving Range (mi.)	Very Short-360
Fuel Type	Regular
Annual Fuel Cost	Very Low-$1,586
Gas Guzzler Tax	No
Greenhouse Gas Emissions (tons/yr.)	Very Low-5.7
Barrels of Oil Used per year	Low-10.3

How the Competition Rates

Competitors	Rating	Pg.
Chevrolet Sonic	10	116
Kia Rio	6	180
Nissan Versa	2	228

Price Range	Retail	Markup
L 2D Manual	$14,430	4%
L 4D AT	$15,455	4%
LE 4D	$16,490	4%
SE AT	$17,340	4%

Toyota Yaris

Safety Checklist

Crash Tests:
Frontal	Poor
Side	Poor

Airbags:
Head	Fr. & Rr. Roof Curtain
Torso	Front Pelvis/Torso from Seat
Pelvis	Front Pelvis/Torso from Seat
Roll Sensing	No
Knee Bolster	Standard

Crash Avoidance:
Collision Avoidance	None
Blind Spot Detection	None
Lane Keeping Assist	None
Backup Camera	None
Pedestrian Crash Avoidance	None

General:
Auto. Crash Notification	None
Day Running Lamps	None

Safety Belt/Restraint:
Dynamic Head Restraints	None
Adjustable Belt	None

Toyota Yaris

Specifications

Drive	FWD
Engine	1.5-liter I4
Transmission	4-sp. Automatic
Tow Rating (lbs.)	...
Head/Leg Room (in.)	Very Cramped-39.3/40.6
Interior Space (cu. ft.)	Very Cramped-85.1
Cargo Space (cu. ft.)	Cramped-15.6
Wheelbase/Length (in.)	98.9/153.5

Volkswagen Beetle

Ratings—10 Best, 1 Worst

Rating	
Combo Crash Tests	4
Safety Features	1
Rollover	8
Preventive Maintenance	8
Repair Costs	4
Warranty	5
Fuel Economy	6
Complaints	3
Insurance Costs	3
OVERALL RATING	**3**

Volkswagen Beetle

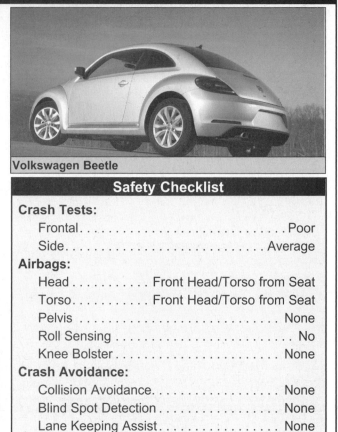

Volkswagen Beetle

At-a-Glance

Status/Year Series Started Unchanged/2012
Twins . . . . –
Body Styles . . . . Convertible, Hatchback
Seating 4
Anti-Theft Device . Std. Pass. Immobil. & Active Alarm
Parking Index Rating . . . . .Very Easy
Where Made. . . . . .Puebla, Mexico
Fuel Factor
  MPG Rating (city/hwy) Average-22/29
  Driving Range (mi.) . . . . .Very Short-358
  Fuel Type . . . . .Regular
  Annual Fuel Cost . . . . Average-$2,085
  Gas Guzzler Tax . . . . .No
  Greenhouse Gas Emissions (tons/yr.) Low-7.3
  Barrels of Oil Used per year Average-13.2

How the Competition Rates

Competitors	Rating	Pg.
Chevrolet Sonic	10	116
Hyundai Accent	6	155
Scion xD	–	235

Price Range

	Retail	Markup
2.5L Manual	$19,995	4%
TDI AT	$25,295	4%
2.0 T R-Line Convertible Manual	$28,995	4%
GSR AT	$31,095	4%

Safety Checklist

Crash Tests:
  Frontal. . . . . .Poor
  Side. . . . . Average
Airbags:
  Head . . . . Front Head/Torso from Seat
  Torso. . . . . Front Head/Torso from Seat
  Pelvis . . . . None
  Roll Sensing . . . . No
  Knee Bolster . . . . None
Crash Avoidance:
  Collision Avoidance. . . . . None
  Blind Spot Detection . . . . None
  Lane Keeping Assist. . . . . None
  Backup Camera . . . . Optional
  Pedestrian Crash Avoidance . . . . None
General:
  Auto. Crash Notification . . . . None
  Day Running Lamps . . . . Standard
Safety Belt/Restraint:
  Dynamic Head Restraints. . . . . None
  Adjustable Belt . . . . None

Volkswagen Beetle

Specifications

Drive. . . . . FWD
Engine 2.5-liter I5
Transmission . . . . .6-sp. Automatic
Tow Rating (lbs.) . . . .
Head/Leg Room (in.) Cramped-39.4/41.3
Interior Space (cu. ft.). . . . . .Very Cramped-85.1
Cargo Space (cu. ft.) Cramped-15.4
Wheelbase/Length (in.) 100/168.4

Ratings—10 Best, 1 Worst	
Combo Crash Tests	–
Safety Features	1
Rollover	9
Preventive Maintenance	7
Repair Costs	5
Warranty	5
Fuel Economy	6
Complaints	4
Insurance Costs	5
OVERALL RATING	**–**

Volkswagen CC

Volkswagen CC

At-a-Glance

Status/Year Series Started........ Unchanged/2009
Twins .... –
Body Styles ....Sedan
Seating 4
Anti-Theft Device . Std. Pass. Immobil. & Active Alarm
Parking Index Rating .... Average
Where Made................... Ewden, Germany
Fuel Factor
  MPG Rating (city/hwy).......... Average-22/31
  Driving Range (mi.) .... Very Long-468
  Fuel Type.............................Regular
  Annual Fuel Cost .... Low-$2,033
  Gas Guzzler Tax ....No
  Greenhouse Gas Emissions (tons/yr.).. Average-7.4
  Barrels of Oil Used per year Average-13.2

How the Competition Rates

Competitors	Rating	Pg.
Acura TL	3	85
Subaru Legacy	5	240
Toyota Camry	6	246

Price Range	Retail	Markup
Sport	$31,350	4%
Sport Plus	$32,850	4%
VR6 Luxury	$37,730	4%
VR6 4Motion	$41,420	4%

Safety Checklist

Crash Tests:
  Frontal.....................................
  Side.......................................
Airbags:
  Head .... Fr. & Rr. Roof Curtain
  Torso..........Front Pelvis/Torso from Seat
  Pelvis ....Front Pelvis/Torso from Seat
  Roll Sensing .... No
  Knee Bolster .... None
Crash Avoidance:
  Collision Avoidance................. None
  Blind Spot Detection .... None
  Lane Keeping Assist................ None
  Backup Camera .... Optional
  Pedestrian Crash Avoidance .... None
General:
  Auto. Crash Notification .... None
  Day Running Lamps............ Standard
Safety Belt/Restraint:
  Dynamic Head Restraints............ None
  Adjustable Belt ....Standard Front

Volkswagen CC

Specifications

Drive................................... FWD
Engine 2.0-liter I4
Transmission ....6-sp. Automatic
Tow Rating (lbs.) ....
Head/Leg Room (in.) .....Very Cramped-37.4/41.6
Interior Space (cu. ft.)............Cramped-93.6
Cargo Space (cu. ft.) Cramped-13.2
Wheelbase/Length (in.) 106.7/189.1

Ratings—10 Best, 1 Worst	
Combo Crash Tests	–
Safety Features	2
Rollover	7
Preventive Maintenance	8
Repair Costs	8
Warranty	5
Fuel Economy	6
Complaints	3
Insurance Costs	3
OVERALL RATING	**–**

Volkswagen Golf

Volkswagen Golf

At-a-Glance

Status/Year Series Started........ Unchanged/2010
Twins ....–
Body Styles .... Hatchback
Seating....................................5
Anti-Theft Device . Std. Pass. Immobil. & Active Alarm
Parking Index Rating .... Easy
Where Made................... Wolfgang, Germany
Fuel Factor
    MPG Rating (city/hwy) Average-23/30
    Driving Range (mi.) Short-373
    Fuel Type........................Regular
    Annual Fuel Cost .... Low-$2,002
    Gas Guzzler Tax ....No
    Greenhouse Gas Emissions (tons/yr.)..... Low-7.1
    Barrels of Oil Used per year Average-12.7

How the Competition Rates

Competitors	Rating	Pg.
Chevrolet Sonic	10	116
Mazda Mazda3	–	199
Subaru Impreza	–	239

Price Range	Retail	Markup
Base	$19,995	4%
Base w/Conv & Sun	$22,995	4%
TDI	$26,300	4%
TDI w/ Sun & Nav	$27,995	4%

Safety Checklist

Crash Tests:
    Frontal..
    Side..
Airbags:
    Head .... Fr. & Rr. Roof Curtain
    Torso...........Front Pelvis/Torso from Seat
    Pelvis ....Front Pelvis/Torso from Seat
    Roll Sensing .... No
    Knee Bolster .... Standard
Crash Avoidance:
    Collision Avoidance................. None
    Blind Spot Detection .... None
    Lane Keeping Assist................ None
    Backup Camera .... None
    Pedestrian Crash Avoidance .... None
General:
    Auto. Crash Notification .... None
    Day Running Lamps............. Standard
Safety Belt/Restraint:
    Dynamic Head Restraints............. None
    Adjustable Belt ....Standard Front

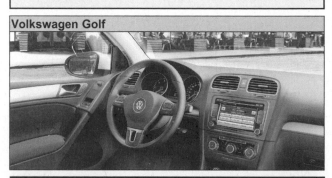

Volkswagen Golf

Specifications

Drive................................. FWD
Engine 2.5-liter I5
Transmission ....6-sp. Automatic
Tow Rating (lbs.) ....
Head/Leg Room (in.) Cramped-39.3/41.2
Interior Space (cu. ft.)............Cramped-92.9
Cargo Space (cu. ft.) Cramped-15.2
Wheelbase/Length (in.) 101.5/165.4

Volkswagen Jetta   Compact

Ratings—10 Best, 1 Worst	
Combo Crash Tests	8
Safety Features	1
Rollover	7
Preventive Maintenance	8
Repair Costs	5
Warranty	5
Fuel Economy	6
Complaints	5
Insurance Costs	3
OVERALL RATING	**6**

Volkswagen Jetta

Volkswagen Jetta SportWagon

At-a-Glance

Status/Year Series Started........ Unchanged/2011
Twins . . . . –
Body Styles . . . . Sedan, Wagon
Seating 5
Anti-Theft Device . Std. Pass. Immobil. & Active Alarm
Parking Index Rating . . . . Easy
Where Made. . . . . .Puebla, Mexico
Fuel Factor
  MPG Rating (city/hwy) Average-23/29
  Driving Range (mi.) Short-368
  Fuel Type. . . . . .Regular
  Annual Fuel Cost . . . . Low-$2,029
  Gas Guzzler Tax . . . . .No
  Greenhouse Gas Emissions (tons/yr.). Low-7.3
  Barrels of Oil Used per year Average-13.2

How the Competition Rates

Competitors	Rating	Pg.
Ford Focus	5	142
Honda Civic	6	148
Toyota Corolla	7	247

Price Range	Retail	Markup
Base Manual	$15,545	4%
S AT	$17,820	4%
TDI Wagon AT	$27,350	4%
Hybird SEL w/Prem	$31,445	4%

Safety Checklist

Crash Tests:
  Frontal. . . . . Average
  Side. . . . . Very Good
Airbags:
  Head . . . . Fr. & Rr. Roof Curtain
  Torso. . . . . .Front Pelvis/Torso from Seat
  Pelvis . . . . .Front Pelvis/Torso from Seat
  Roll Sensing . . . . No
  Knee Bolster . . . . None
Crash Avoidance:
  Collision Avoidance. . . . . None
  Blind Spot Detection . . . . None
  Lane Keeping Assist. . . . . None
  Backup Camera . . . . Optional
  Pedestrian Crash Avoidance . . . . None
General:
  Auto. Crash Notification . . . . None
  Day Running Lamps . . . . Standard
Safety Belt/Restraint:
  Dynamic Head Restraints. . . . . None
  Adjustable Belt . . . . .Standard Front

Volkswagen Jetta

Specifications

Drive. . . . . FWD
Engine 2.0-liter I4
Transmission . . . . .6-sp. Automatic
Tow Rating (lbs.) . . . .
Head/Leg Room (in.) . . . . .Very Cramped-38.2/41.2
Interior Space (cu. ft.). Cramped-94.1
Cargo Space (cu. ft.) Cramped-15.5
Wheelbase/Length (in.) 104.4/182.2

Ratings—10 Best, 1 Worst

Combo Crash Tests	8
Safety Features	1
Rollover	8
Preventive Maintenance	8
Repair Costs	4
Warranty	5
Fuel Economy	6
Complaints	6
Insurance Costs	3
OVERALL RATING	**6**

Volkswagen Passat

Volkswagen Passat

At-a-Glance

Status/Year Series Started Unchanged/2012
Twins . . . . –
Body Styles . . . . .Sedan
Seating 5
Anti-Theft Device . Std. Pass. Immobil. & Active Alarm
Parking Index Rating . . . . Average
Where Made. . . . . Chattanooga, TN
Fuel Factor
  MPG Rating (city/hwy) Average-22/31
  Driving Range (mi.) . . . . Very Long-468
  Fuel Type . . . . .Regular
  Annual Fuel Cost . . . . Low-$2,033
  Gas Guzzler Tax . . . . .No
  Greenhouse Gas Emissions (tons/yr.) Low-7.3
  Barrels of Oil Used per year Average-13.2

How the Competition Rates

Competitors	Rating	Pg.
Honda Accord	7	147
Hyundai Sonata	7	161
Nissan Altima	6	216

Price Range

	Retail	Markup
S 2.5L	$20,845	4%
SE 1.8T	$25,575	4%
SE TDI	$26,295	4%
SEL 3.6L	$33,895	4%

Safety Checklist

Crash Tests:
  Frontal. . . . . Very Good
  Side. . . . . Average
Airbags:
  Head . . . . Fr. & Rr. Roof Curtain
  Torso. . . . . .Front Pelvis/Torso from Seat
  Pelvis . . . . .Front Pelvis/Torso from Seat
  Roll Sensing . . . . No
  Knee Bolster . . . . None
Crash Avoidance:
  Collision Avoidance. . . . . None
  Blind Spot Detection . . . . None
  Lane Keeping Assist . . . . None
  Backup Camera . . . . Optional
  Pedestrian Crash Avoidance . . . . None
General:
  Auto. Crash Notification . . . . None
  Day Running Lamps . . . . Standard
Safety Belt/Restraint:
  Dynamic Head Restraints . . . . None
  Adjustable Belt . . . . .Standard Front

Volkswagen Passat

Specifications

Drive. . . . . FWD
Engine 2.5-liter I5
Transmission . . . . .6-sp. Automatic
Tow Rating (lbs.) . . . .
Head/Leg Room (in.) Cramped-38.3/42.4
Interior Space (cu. ft.). Average-102
Cargo Space (cu. ft.) Cramped-15.9
Wheelbase/Length (in.) 110.4/191.6

Volkswagen Tiguan

Small SUV

Ratings—10 Best, 1 Worst	
Combo Crash Tests	2
Safety Features	3
Rollover	3
Preventive Maintenance	7
Repair Costs	5
Warranty	5
Fuel Economy	5
Complaints	2
Insurance Costs	10
OVERALL RATING	**2**

Volkswagen Tiguan

Volkswagen Tiguan

At-a-Glance

Status/Year Series Started	Unchanged/2009
Twins	–
Body Styles	SUV
Seating	5
Anti-Theft Device	Std. Pass. Immobil. & Active Alarm
Parking Index Rating	Average
Where Made	Wolfgang, Germany
Fuel Factor	
MPG Rating (city/hwy)	Average-21/26
Driving Range (mi.)	Short-386
Fuel Type	Regular
Annual Fuel Cost	Average-$2,238
Gas Guzzler Tax	No
Greenhouse Gas Emissions (tons/yr.)	Average-8.0
Barrels of Oil Used per year	High-14.3

How the Competition Rates

Competitors	Rating	Pg.
Hyundai Tucson	4	162
Subaru Forester	4	238
Toyota RAV4	5	253

Price Range

Price Range	Retail	Markup
S	$25,020	4%
SE 4Motion	$28,950	4%
SEL	$32,670	4%
R-Line 4Motion	$38,490	4%

Safety Checklist

Crash Tests:
Frontal	Very Poor
Side	Poor

Airbags:
Head	Fr. & Rr. Roof Curtain
Torso	Front Pelvis/Torso from Seat
Pelvis	Front Pelvis/Torso from Seat
Roll Sensing	Yes
Knee Bolster	None

Crash Avoidance:
Collision Avoidance	None
Blind Spot Detection	None
Lane Keeping Assist	None
Backup Camera	Optional
Pedestrian Crash Avoidance	None

General:
Auto. Crash Notification	None
Day Running Lamps	Standard

Safety Belt/Restraint:
Dynamic Head Restraints	None
Adjustable Belt	Standard Front

Volkswagen Tiguan

Specifications

Drive	FWD
Engine	2.0-liter I4
Transmission	6-sp. Automatic
Tow Rating (lbs.)	Very Low-2200
Head/Leg Room (in.)	Very Cramped-39.1/40.1
Interior Space (cu. ft.)	Cramped-95.4
Cargo Space (cu. ft.)	Roomy-23.8
Wheelbase/Length (in.)	102.5/174.5

Volkswagen Touareg
Mid-Size SUV

Ratings—10 Best, 1 Worst	
Combo Crash Tests	
Safety Features	3
Rollover	4
Preventive Maintenance	8
Repair Costs	1
Warranty	5
Fuel Economy	2
Complaints	2
Insurance Costs	5
OVERALL RATING	**–**

Volkswagen Touareg

Volkswagen Touareg

At-a-Glance

Status/Year Series Started........ Unchanged/2011
Twins .... Porsche Cayenne
Body Styles .... SUV
Seating 5
Anti-Theft Device . Std. Pass. Immobil. & Active Alarm
Parking Index Rating .... Hard
Where Made................. Bratislava, Slovakia
Fuel Factor
  MPG Rating (city/hwy).......... Very Poor-17/23
  Driving Range (mi.) .... Very Long-508
  Fuel Type........................... Premium
  Annual Fuel Cost .... Very High-$2,905
  Gas Guzzler Tax .... No
  Greenhouse Gas Emissions (tons/yr.)..... High-9.6
  Barrels of Oil Used per year High-17.3

How the Competition Rates

Competitors	Rating	Pg.
Acura MDX	8	82
BMW X5	–	99
Volvo XC90	–	270

Price Range	Retail	Markup
Sport VR6	$43,995	5%
Lux VR6	$51,475	5%
R-Line TDI	$57,615	5%
Hybrid	$64,170	5%

Safety Checklist

Crash Tests:
  Frontal................................
  Side..................................
Airbags:
  Head .... Fr. & Rr. Roof Curtain
  Torso.......... Front Pelvis/Torso from Seat
  Pelvis .... Front Pelvis/Torso from Seat
  Roll Sensing .... Yes
  Knee Bolster .... None
Crash Avoidance:
  Collision Avoidance................. None
  Blind Spot Detection .... None
  Lane Keeping Assist................ None
  Backup Camera .... Optional
  Pedestrian Crash Avoidance .... None
General:
  Auto. Crash Notification .... None
  Day Running Lamps .... Standard
Safety Belt/Restraint:
  Dynamic Head Restraints .... None
  Adjustable Belt .... Standard Front

Volkswagen Touareg

Specifications

Drive................................... AWD
Engine 3.6-liter V6
Transmission .... 8-sp. Automatic
Tow Rating (lbs.) High-7716
Head/Leg Room (in.) Cramped-39.6/41.4
Interior Space (cu. ft.)............ Roomy-103.6
Cargo Space (cu. ft.) Roomy-32.1
Wheelbase/Length (in.) 113.9/188.8

Ratings—10 Best, 1 Worst	
Combo Crash Tests	9
Safety Features	8
Rollover	9
Preventive Maintenance	9
Repair Costs	7
Warranty	8
Fuel Economy	5
Complaints	6
Insurance Costs	5
OVERALL RATING	**10**

The CAR Book BEST BET

Volvo S60

Volvo S60

At-a-Glance

Status/Year Series Started Appearance Change/2011
Twins . . . . —
Body Styles . . . . Sedan
Seating 5
Anti-Theft Device . Std. Pass. Immobil. & Active Alarm
Parking Index Rating . . . . Average
Where Made . . . . Ghent, Belgium
Fuel Factor
  MPG Rating (city/hwy) Average-20/29
  Driving Range (mi.) Average-414
  Fuel Type . . . . Regular
  Annual Fuel Cost . . . . Average-$2,213
  Gas Guzzler Tax . . . . No
  Greenhouse Gas Emissions (tons/yr.) . . Average-8.0
  Barrels of Oil Used per year High-14.3

How the Competition Rates

Competitors	Rating	Pg.
Acura TL	3	85
Hyundai Sonata	7	161
Subaru Legacy	5	240

Price Range	Retail	Markup
T5 FWD	$32,400	6%
T5 AWD	$34,400	6%
T6	$39,250	6%
T6 R	$42,700	6%

Safety Checklist

Crash Tests:
  Frontal . . . . Very Good
  Side . . . . Average
Airbags:
  Head . . . . Fr. & Rr. Roof Curtain
  Torso . . . Front Pelvis/Torso/Shoulder from Seat
  Pelvis . . . . .Front Pelvis/Torso from Seat
  Roll Sensing . . . . .Yes
  Knee Bolster . . . . None
Crash Avoidance:
  Collision Avoidance . . . . . . Standard CIB & DBS
  Blind Spot Detection . . . . Optional
  Lane Keeping Assist . . . . Optional
  Backup Camera . . . . None
  Pedestrian Crash Avoidance . . . . Optional
General:
  Auto. Crash Notification . . . . None
  Day Running Lamps . . . . Standard
Safety Belt/Restraint:
  Dynamic Head Restraints . . . . None
  Adjustable Belt . . . . .Standard Front

Volvo S60

Specifications

Drive . . . . AWD
Engine 2.5-liter I5
Transmission . . . . 6-sp. Automatic
Tow Rating (lbs.) . . . .
Head/Leg Room (in.) Cramped-38.3/41.9
Interior Space (cu. ft.) Cramped-92
Cargo Space (cu. ft.) . . . . Very Cramped-12
Wheelbase/Length (in.) 109.3/182.5

Ratings—10 Best, 1 Worst

Combo Crash Tests	–
Safety Features	5
Rollover	7
Preventive Maintenance	9
Repair Costs	5
Warranty	8
Fuel Economy	5
Complaints	5
Insurance Costs	8

OVERALL RATING   –

Volvo S80

Volvo S80

At-a-Glance

Status/Year Series Started. Unchanged/2008
Twins . . . . –
Body Styles . . . . .Sedan
Seating 5
Anti-Theft Device . Std. Pass. Immobil. & Active Alarm
Parking Index Rating . . . . Average
Where Made. . . . . Torslanda, Sweden
Fuel Factor
  MPG Rating (city/hwy) Average-20/29
  Driving Range (mi.) Long-430
  Fuel Type . . . . .Regular
  Annual Fuel Cost . . . . Average-$2,213
  Gas Guzzler Tax . . . . .No
  Greenhouse Gas Emissions (tons/yr.). . Average-8.0
  Barrels of Oil Used per year High-14.3

How the Competition Rates

Competitors	Rating	Pg.
BMW 7 Series	–	96
Cadillac XTS	10	108
Jaguar XF	–	171

Price Range	Retail	Markup
FWD 3.2	$39,900	6%
AWD T6	$43,950	6%

Safety Checklist

Crash Tests:
  Frontal. . . . .
  Side. . . . .
Airbags:
  Head . . . . Fr. & Rr. Roof Curtain
  Torso. . . . . .Front Pelvis/Torso from Seat
  Pelvis . . . . .Front Pelvis/Torso from Seat
  Roll Sensing . . . . No
  Knee Bolster . . . . None
Crash Avoidance:
  Collision Avoidance. . . . . . Standard CIB & DBS
  Blind Spot Detection . . . . Optional
  Lane Keeping Assist. . . . . Optional
  Backup Camera . . . . None
  Pedestrian Crash Avoidance . . . . Optional
General:
  Auto. Crash Notification . . . . None
  Day Running Lamps . . . . Standard
Safety Belt/Restraint:
  Dynamic Head Restraints . . . . None
  Adjustable Belt . . . . .Standard Front

Volvo S80

Specifications

Drive . . . . FWD
Engine 3.2-liter I6
Transmission . . . . .6-sp. Automatic
Tow Rating (lbs.) . . . .
Head/Leg Room (in.) . . . . .Very Cramped-37.8/41.9
Interior Space (cu. ft.). Average-98
Cargo Space (cu. ft.) Cramped-14.9
Wheelbase/Length (in.) 111.6/191.1

Ratings—10 Best, 1 Worst

Combo Crash Tests	9
Safety Features	8
Rollover	3
Preventive Maintenance	9
Repair Costs	6
Warranty	8
Fuel Economy	3
Complaints	7
Insurance Costs	10
OVERALL RATING	**10**

Volvo XC60

Volvo XC60

Volvo XC60

At-a-Glance

Status/Year Series Started Appearance Change/2009
Twins . . . . –
Body Styles . . . . SUV
Seating 5
Anti-Theft Device . Std. Pass. Immobil. & Active Alarm
Parking Index Rating . . . . Average
Where Made. . . . . Ghent, Belgium
Fuel Factor
  MPG Rating (city/hwy) Poor-18/25
  Driving Range (mi.) Short-381
  Fuel Type . . . . .Regular
  Annual Fuel Cost . . . . High-$2,498
  Gas Guzzler Tax . . . . .No
  Greenhouse Gas Emissions (tons/yr.) High-9.2
  Barrels of Oil Used per year High-16.5

How the Competition Rates

Competitors	Rating	Pg.
Acura MDX	8	82
BMW X5	–	99
Mercedes-Benz M-Class	5	208

Price Range

	Retail	Markup
3.2 FWD	$34,850	6%
3.2 AWD	$36,850	6%
T6	$41,550	6%
T6 R	$45,800	6%

Safety Checklist

Crash Tests:
Frontal. . . . . Very Good
Side. . . . . Good
Airbags:
Head . . . . Fr. & Rr. Roof Curtain
Torso. . . Front Pelvis/Torso/Shoulder from Seat
Pelvis . . . . .Front Pelvis/Torso from Seat
Roll Sensing . . . . .Yes
Knee Bolster . . . . None
Crash Avoidance:
Collision Avoidance. . . . . . Standard CIB & DBS
Blind Spot Detection . . . . Optional
Lane Keeping Assist. . . . . Optional
Backup Camera . . . . None
Pedestrian Crash Avoidance . . . . Optional
General:
Auto. Crash Notification . . . . None
Day Running Lamps . . . . Standard
Safety Belt/Restraint:
Dynamic Head Restraints. . . . . None
Adjustable Belt . . . . .Standard Front

Volvo XC60

NXP 746

Specifications

Drive. . . . . AWD
Engine 3.2-liter I6
Transmission . . . . .6-sp. Automatic
Tow Rating (lbs.) . . . .
Head/Leg Room (in.) . . . . .Very Cramped-38.1/41.2
Interior Space (cu. ft.). Average-99
Cargo Space (cu. ft.) Roomy-30.8
Wheelbase/Length (in.) 109.2/182.8

Ratings—10 Best, 1 Worst

Combo Crash Tests	–
Safety Features	2
Rollover	2
Preventive Maintenance	8
Repair Costs	6
Warranty	8
Fuel Economy	2
Complaints	4
Insurance Costs	10

OVERALL RATING — –

Volvo XC90

At-a-Glance

Status/Year Series Started. Unchanged/2003
Twins . . . . –
Body Styles . . . . SUV
Seating 7
Anti-Theft Device . Std. Pass. Immobil. & Active Alarm
Parking Index Rating . . . . .Very Hard
Where Made. . . . . Torslanda, Sweden
Fuel Factor
  MPG Rating (city/hwy) . . . . .Very Poor-16/25
  Driving Range (mi.) Average-403
  Fuel Type . . . . .Regular
  Annual Fuel Cost . . . . High-$2,695
  Gas Guzzler Tax . . . . .No
  Greenhouse Gas Emissions (tons/yr.)Very High-10.2
  Barrels of Oil Used per year . . . . . . .Very High-18.3

How the Competition Rates

Competitors	Rating	Pg.
BMW X5	–	99
Mercedes-Benz M-Class	5	208
Volkswagen Touareg	–	266

Price Range

Price Range	Retail	Markup
3.2 FWD	$39,700	6%
3.2 AWD	$41,700	6%
3.2 R FWD	$42,700	6%
3.2 R AWD	$44,700	6%

Volvo XC90

Safety Checklist

Crash Tests:
  Frontal . . . .
  Side . . . .
Airbags:
  Head . . . . Fr. & Rr. Roof Curtain
  Torso. . . . . Front Tosro from Seat
  Pelvis . . . . None
  Roll Sensing . . . . .Yes
  Knee Bolster . . . . None
Crash Avoidance:
  Collision Avoidance. . . . . None
  Blind Spot Detection . . . . .Optional
  Lane Keeping Assist . . . . None
  Backup Camera . . . . None
  Pedestrian Crash Avoidance . . . . None
General:
  Auto. Crash Notification . . . . None
  Day Running Lamps . . . . Standard
Safety Belt/Restraint:
  Dynamic Head Restraints. . . . . None
  Adjustable Belt . . . . Standard Front & Rear

Volvo XC90

Specifications

Drive . . . . FWD
Engine 3.2-liter I6
Transmission . . . . .6-sp. Automatic
Tow Rating (lbs.) . . . .
Head/Leg Room (in.) Cramped-39.7/41
Interior Space (cu. ft.). Average-100.9
Cargo Space (cu. ft.) . . . . .Very Cramped-8.8
Wheelbase/Length (in.) 112.6/189.3

Use this page to keep some notes on the choices you are considering. Include any comments your friends make, statements made by the dealer that may be important later, and your own personal reactions to the car and the test drive. After you've looked at 4 or 5 cars, it's easy to mix up the details.

MAKE/MODEL: **PRICE RANGE:** **PAGE:**

PROS: CONS:

NOTES:

MAKE/MODEL: **PRICE RANGE:** **PAGE:**

PROS: CONS:

NOTES:

MAKE/MODEL: **PRICE RANGE:** **PAGE:**

PROS: CONS:

NOTES: